SH CK

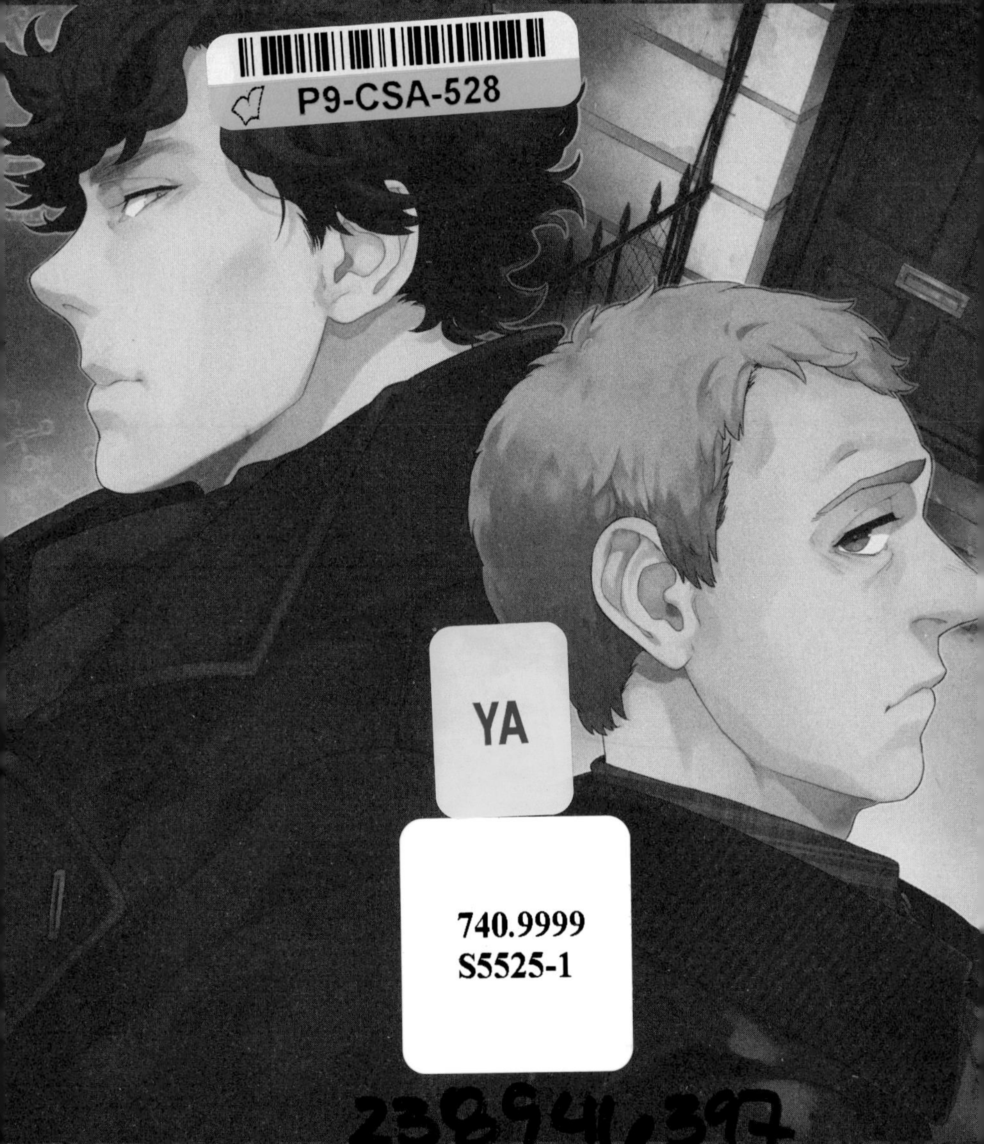

A STUDY IN PINK

SHERLOCK

A STUDY IN PINK

SCRIPT
STEVEN MOFFAT

ADAPTATION
JAY.

LETTERING
AMOONA SAOHIN

Originally published in Japanese by Kadokawa.
This manga is presented in its original right-to-left
reading format.

Based on the TV series **SHERLOCK**
co-created by **STEVEN MOFFAT** & **MARK GATISS**
and adapting Episode One: A Study In Pink.

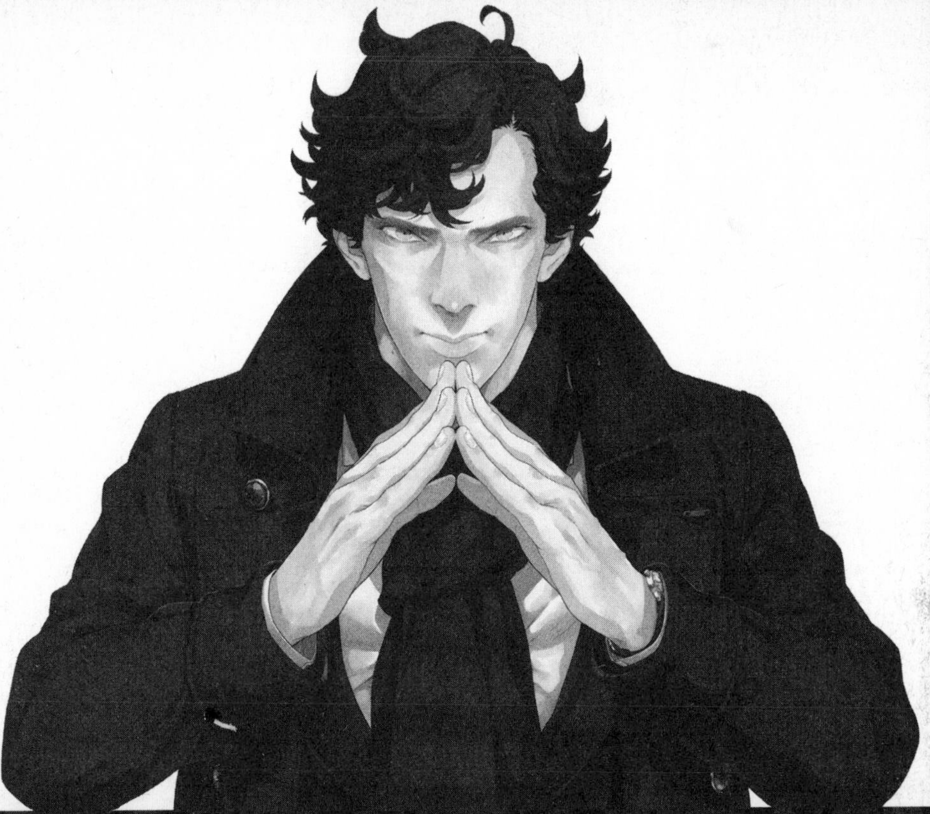

TITAN COMICS

SENIOR EDITORS
ANDREW JAMES
MARTIN EDEN

ASSISTANT EDITORS
JESSICA BURTON &
AMOONA SAOHIN

DESIGNER Dan Bura
PRODUCTION ASSISTANT Peter James
PRODUCTION SUPERVISORS Jackie Flook, Maria Pearson
PRODUCTION MANAGER Obi Onuora
ART DIRECTOR Oz Browne
SENIOR SALES MANAGER Steve Tothill
PRESS OFFICER Will O'Mullane
COMICS BRAND MANAGER Lucy Ripper

DIRECT SALES & MARKETING MANAGER Ricky Claydon
COMMERCIAL MANAGER Michelle Fairlamb
PUBLISHING MANAGER Darryl Tothill
PUBLISHING DIRECTOR Chris Teather
OPERATIONS DIRECTOR Leigh Baulch
EXECUTIVE DIRECTOR Vivian Cheung
PUBLISHER Nick Landau

SPECIAL THANKS TO: Steven Moffat, Mark Gatiss, Sue Vertue, Rachel Stone, and all at Hartswood, and Yuki Miyoshi and all at Kadokawa.

Sherlock: A Study in Pink
Published by Titan Comics, a division of Titan Publishing Group, Ltd. 144 Southwark Street, London SE1 0UP, UK.

10 9 8 7 6 5 4
First printed in USA in February 2017.
A CIP catalogue record for this title is available from the British Library.
www.titan-comics.com

TITAN COMICS

HARTSWOOD FILMS

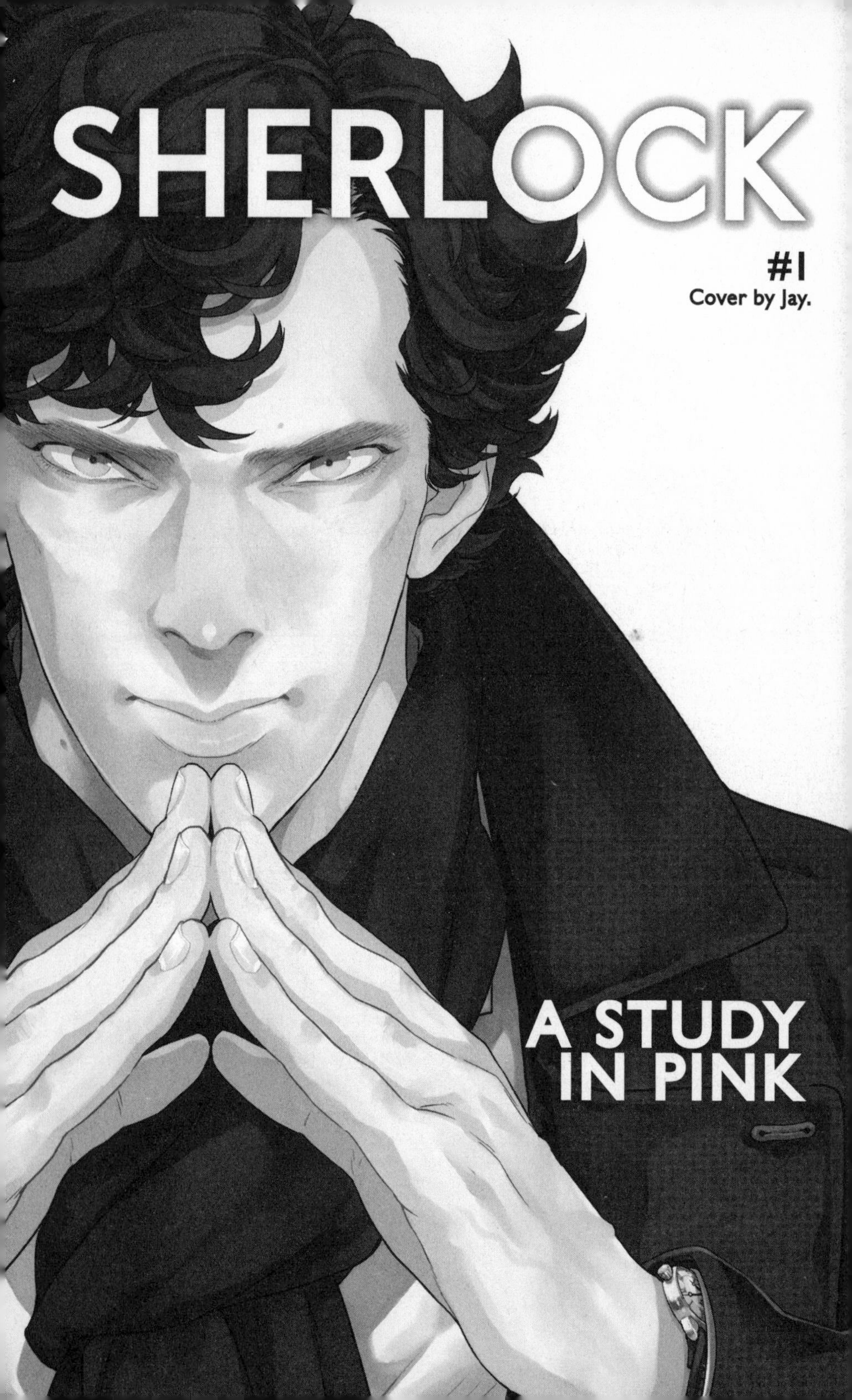
SHERLOCK
#1
Cover by Jay.
A STUDY
IN PINK

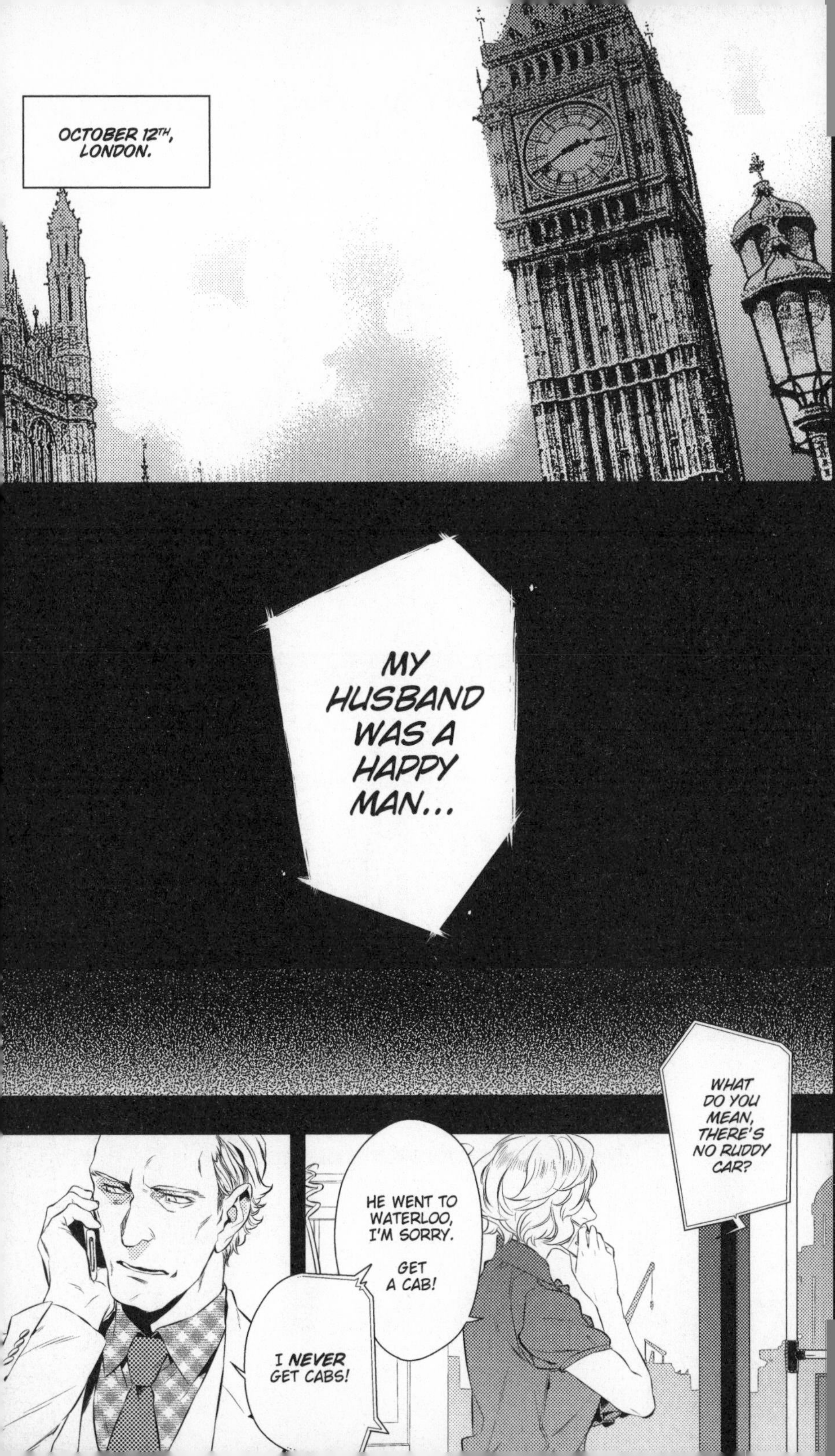
OCTOBER 12TH, LONDON.
MY HUSBAND WAS A HAPPY MAN...
WHAT DO YOU MEAN, THERE'S NO RUDDY CAR?
HE WENT TO WATERLOO, I'M SORRY.
GET A CAB!
I NEVER GET CABS!

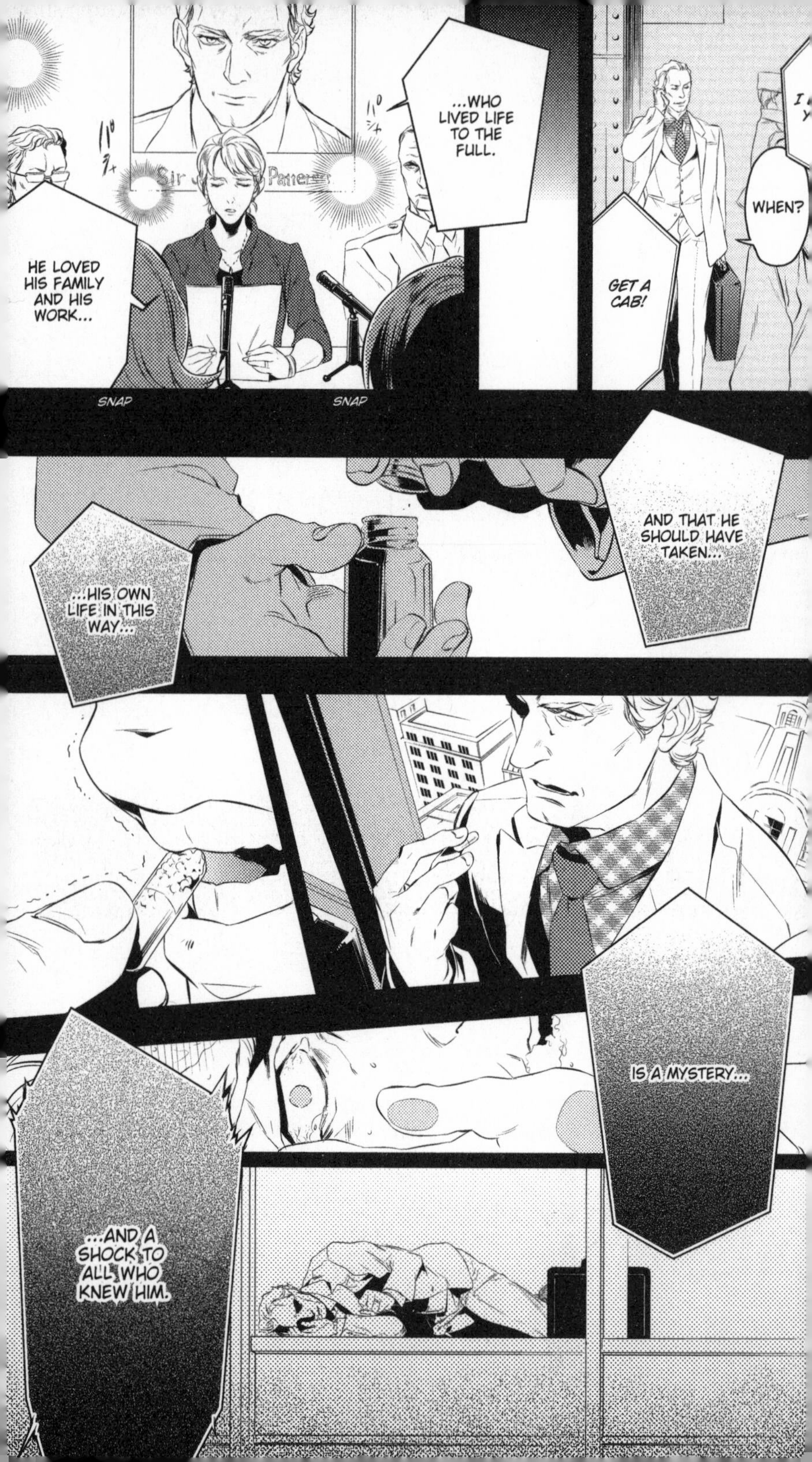
WHEN?
GET A CAB!
...WHO LIVED LIFE TO THE FULL.
HE LOVED HIS FAMILY AND HIS WORK...
SNAP
SNAP
AND THAT HE SHOULD HAVE TAKEN...
...HIS OWN LIFE IN THIS WAY...
IS A MYSTERY...
...AND A SHOCK TO ALL WHO KNEW HIM.

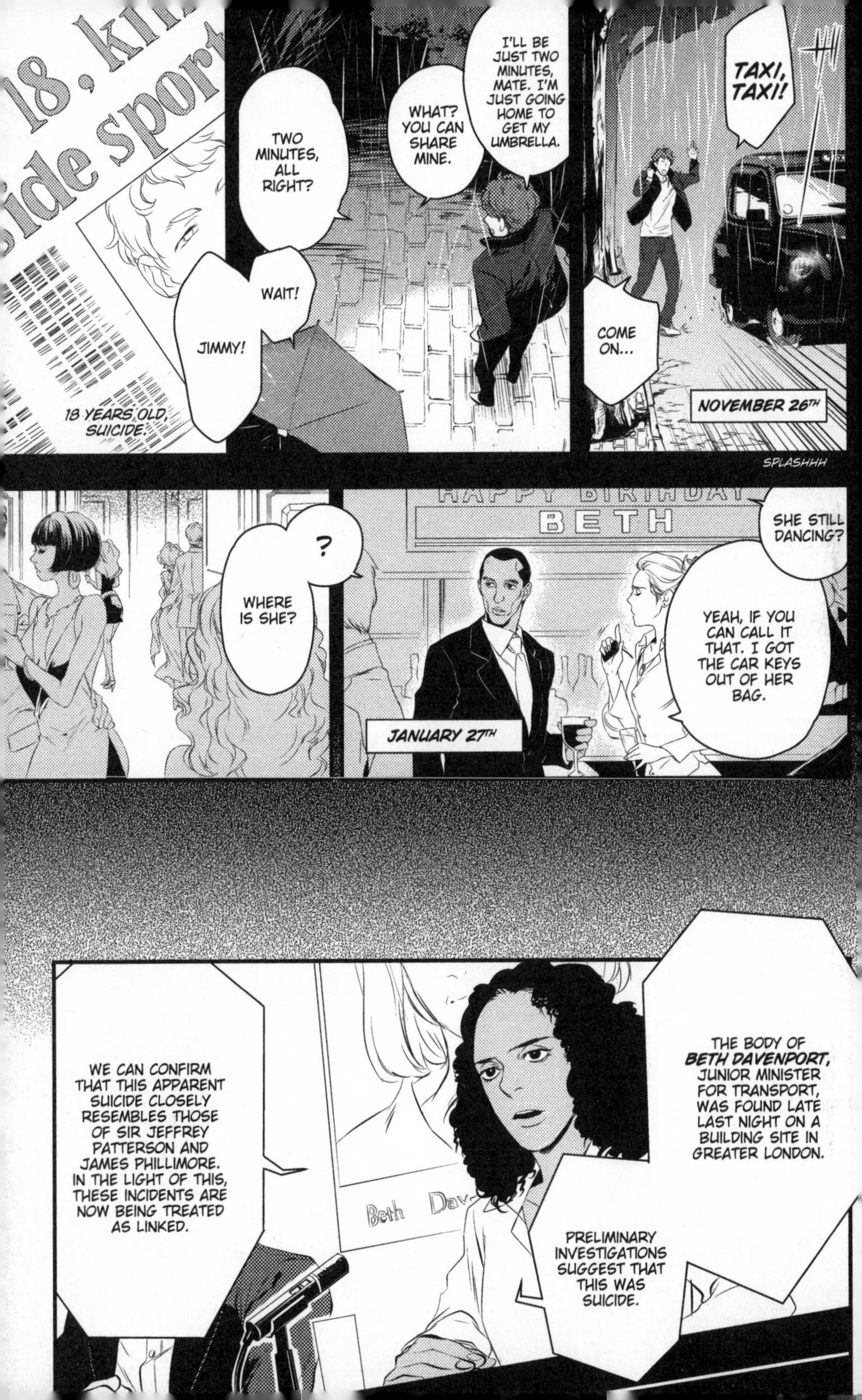
TAXI, TAXI!
COME ON...
NOVEMBER 26TH
SPLASHHH
I'LL BE JUST TWO MINUTES, MATE. I'M JUST GOING HOME TO GET MY UMBRELLA.
WHAT? YOU CAN SHARE MINE.
TWO MINUTES, ALL RIGHT?
WAIT!
JIMMY!
18 YEARS OLD, SUICIDE.
HAPPY BIRTHDAY
BETH
SHE STILL DANCING?
YEAH, IF YOU CAN CALL IT THAT. I GOT THE CAR KEYS OUT OF HER BAG.
JANUARY 27TH
?
WHERE IS SHE?
THE BODY OF BETH DAVENPORT, JUNIOR MINISTER FOR TRANSPORT, WAS FOUND LATE LAST NIGHT ON A BUILDING SITE IN GREATER LONDON.
PRELIMINARY INVESTIGATIONS SUGGEST THAT THIS WAS SUICIDE.
WE CAN CONFIRM THAT THIS APPARENT SUICIDE CLOSELY RESEMBLES THOSE OF SIR JEFFREY PATTERSON AND JAMES PHILLIMORE. IN THE LIGHT OF THIS, THESE INCIDENTS ARE NOW BEING TREATED AS LINKED.

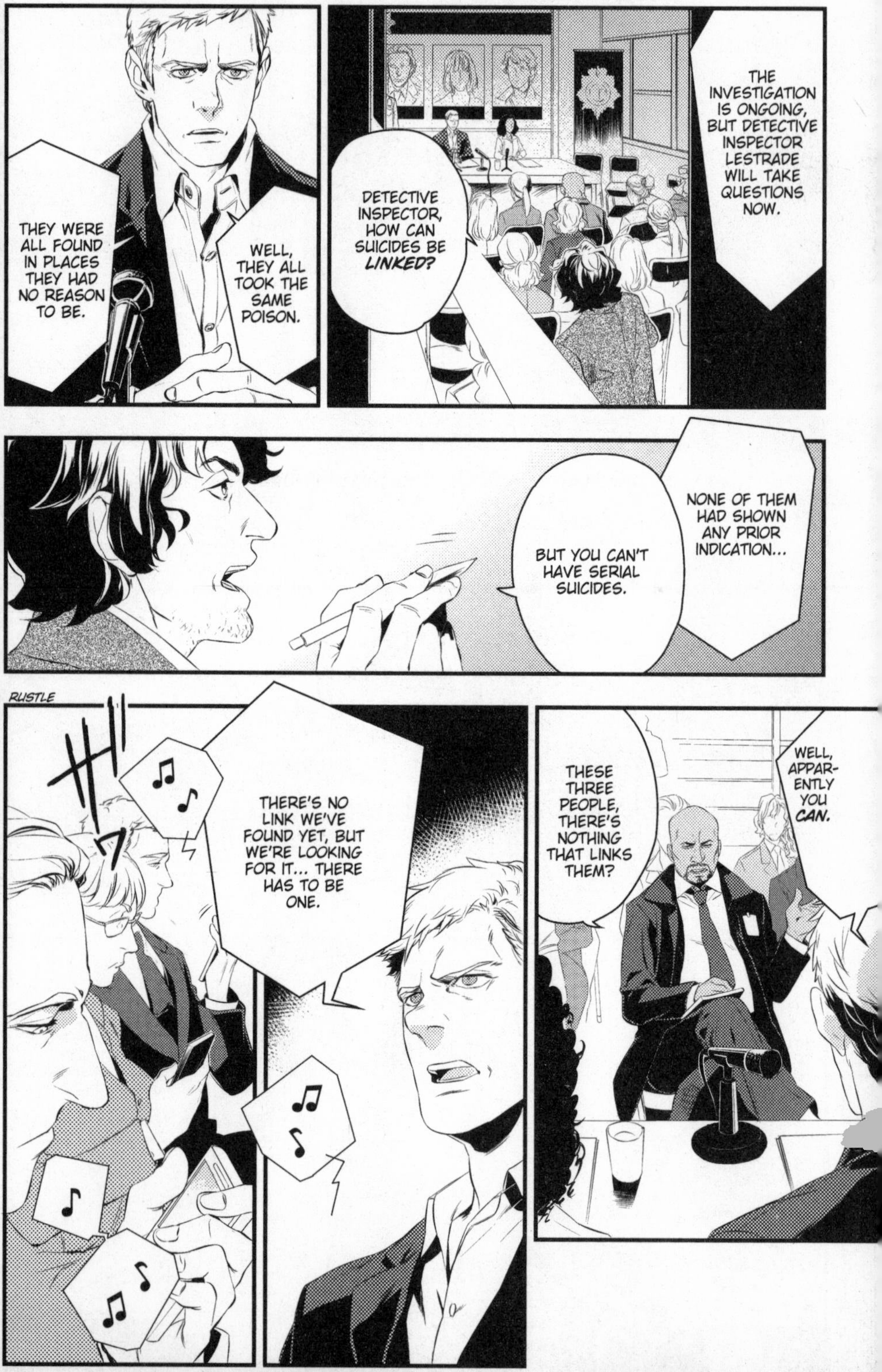
THE INVESTIGATION IS ONGOING, BUT DETECTIVE INSPECTOR LESTRADE WILL TAKE QUESTIONS NOW.
DETECTIVE INSPECTOR, HOW CAN SUICIDES BE ***LINKED?***
WELL, THEY ALL TOOK THE SAME POISON.
THEY WERE ALL FOUND IN PLACES THEY HAD NO REASON TO BE.
NONE OF THEM HAD SHOWN ANY PRIOR INDICATION…
BUT YOU CAN'T HAVE SERIAL SUICIDES.
WELL, APPARENTLY YOU ***CAN.***
THESE THREE PEOPLE, THERE'S NOTHING THAT LINKS THEM?
THERE'S NO LINK WE'VE FOUND YET, BUT WE'RE LOOKING FOR IT… THERE HAS TO BE ONE.
RUSTLE

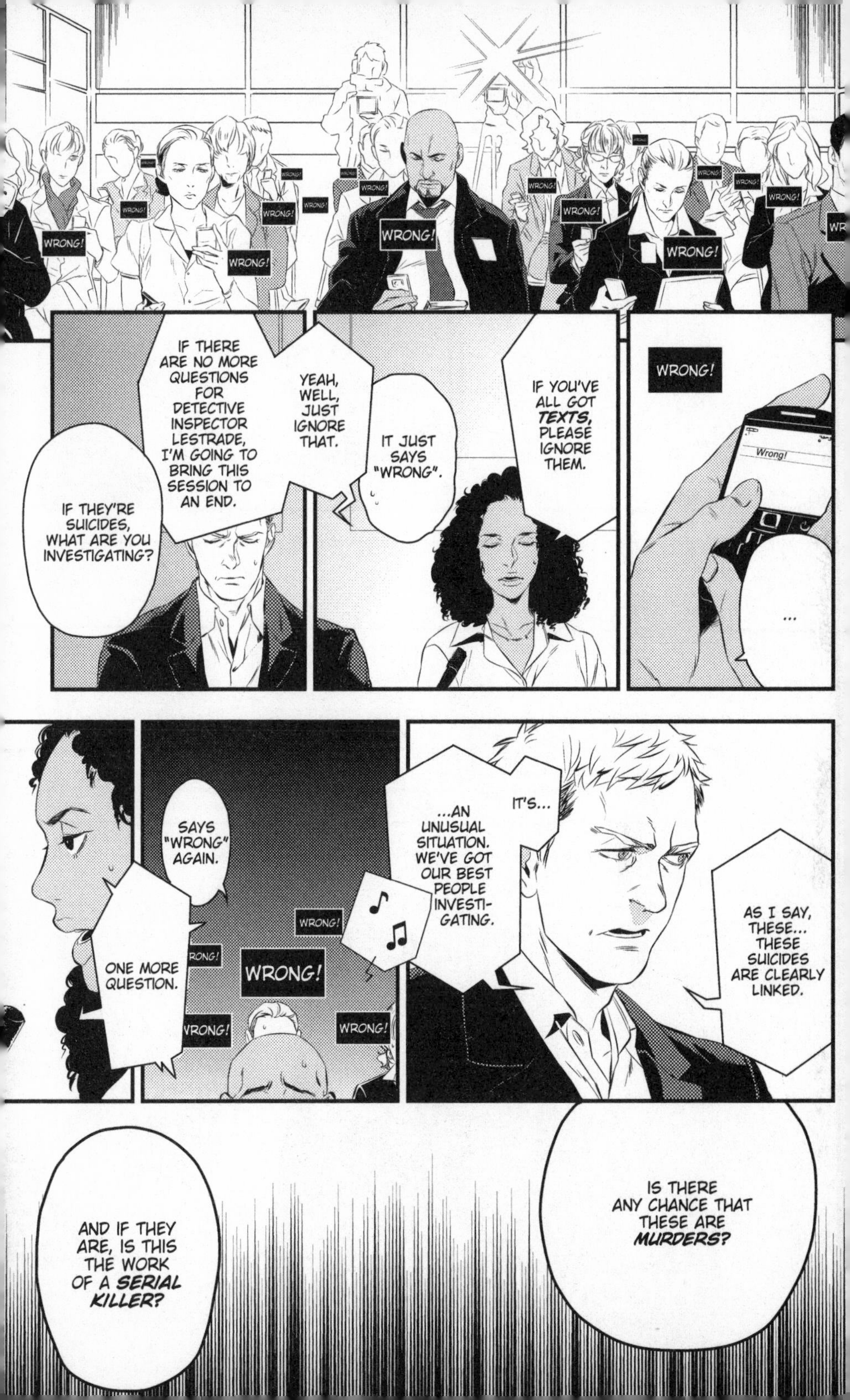
WRONG!
WRONG!
WRONG!
WRONG!
WRONG!
WRONG!
WRONG!
WRONG!
Wrong!
...
IF YOU'VE ALL GOT ***TEXTS,*** PLEASE IGNORE THEM.
IT JUST SAYS "WRONG".
YEAH, WELL, JUST IGNORE THAT.
IF THERE ARE NO MORE QUESTIONS FOR DETECTIVE INSPECTOR LESTRADE, I'M GOING TO BRING THIS SESSION TO AN END.
IF THEY'RE SUICIDES, WHAT ARE YOU INVESTIGATING?
AS I SAY, THESE... THESE SUICIDES ARE CLEARLY LINKED.
IT'S...
...AN UNUSUAL SITUATION. WE'VE GOT OUR BEST PEOPLE INVESTI-GATING.
SAYS "WRONG" AGAIN.
WRONG!
WRONG!
WRONG!
ONE MORE QUESTION.
IS THERE ANY CHANCE THAT THESE ARE ***MURDERS?***
AND IF THEY ARE, IS THIS THE WORK OF A ***SERIAL KILLER?***

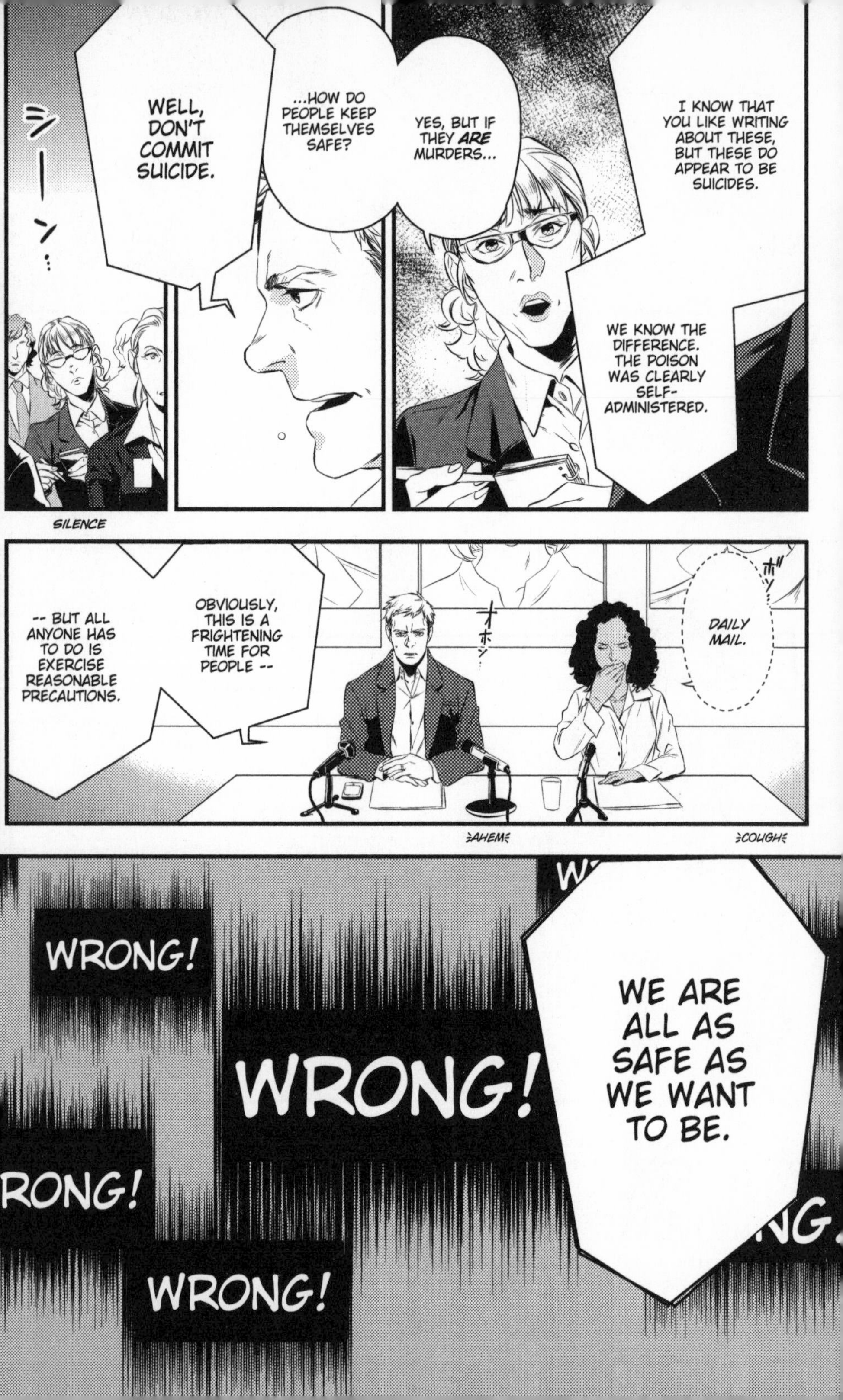
I KNOW THAT YOU LIKE WRITING ABOUT THESE, BUT THESE DO APPEAR TO BE SUICIDES.
WE KNOW THE DIFFERENCE. THE POISON WAS CLEARLY SELF-ADMINISTERED.
YES, BUT IF THEY *ARE* MURDERS...
...HOW DO PEOPLE KEEP THEMSELVES SAFE?
WELL, DON'T COMMIT SUICIDE.
SILENCE
DAILY MAIL.
COUGH
AHEM
OBVIOUSLY, THIS IS A FRIGHTENING TIME FOR PEOPLE --
-- BUT ALL ANYONE HAS TO DO IS EXERCISE REASONABLE PRECAUTIONS.
WE ARE ALL AS SAFE AS WE WANT TO BE.
WRONG!
WRONG!
RONG!
WRONG!

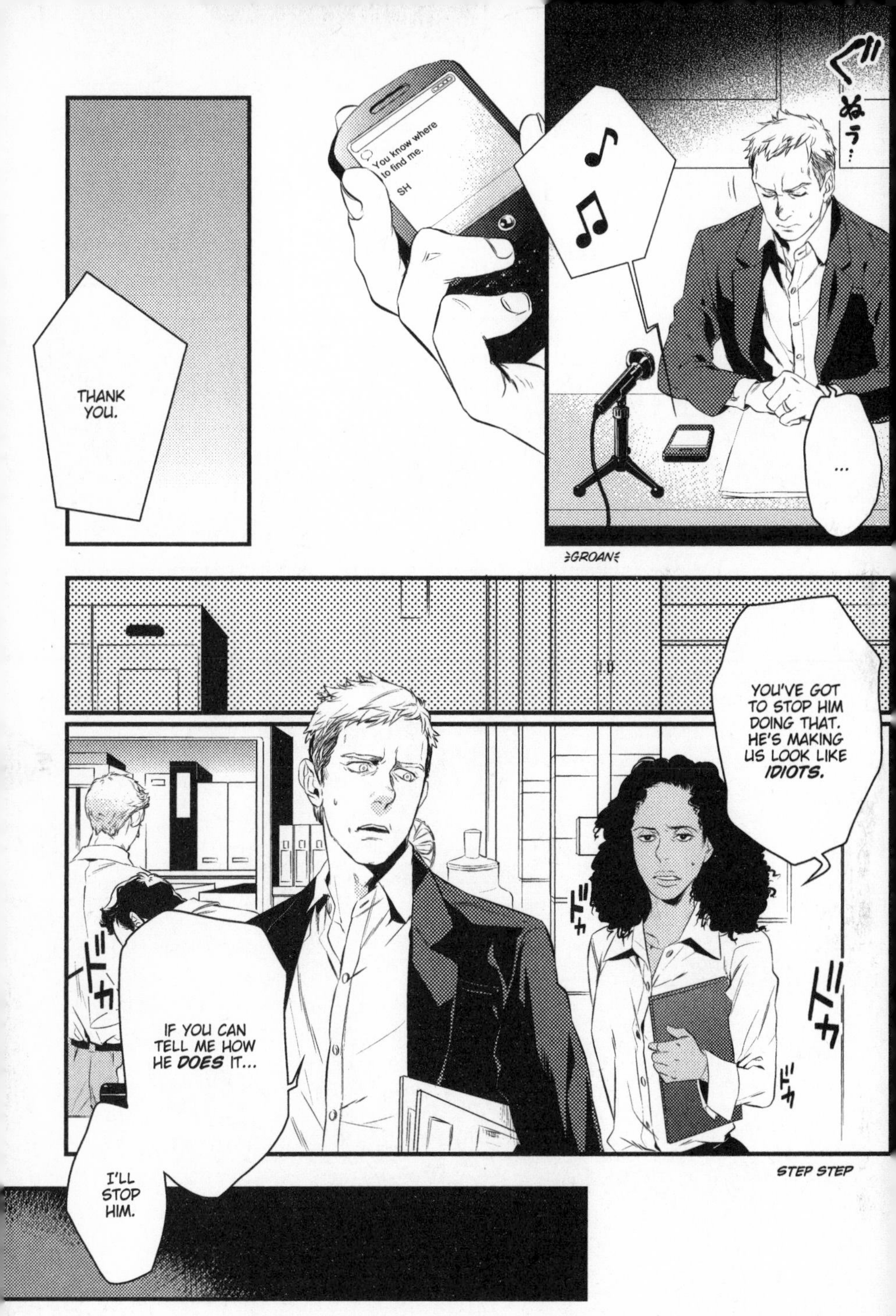

ぐぬぅ…
♪ ♫
…
GROAN
You know where to find me.
SH
THANK YOU.
YOU'VE GOT TO STOP HIM DOING THAT. HE'S MAKING US LOOK LIKE IDIOTS.
STEP STEP
IF YOU CAN TELL ME HOW HE DOES IT…
I'LL STOP HIM.

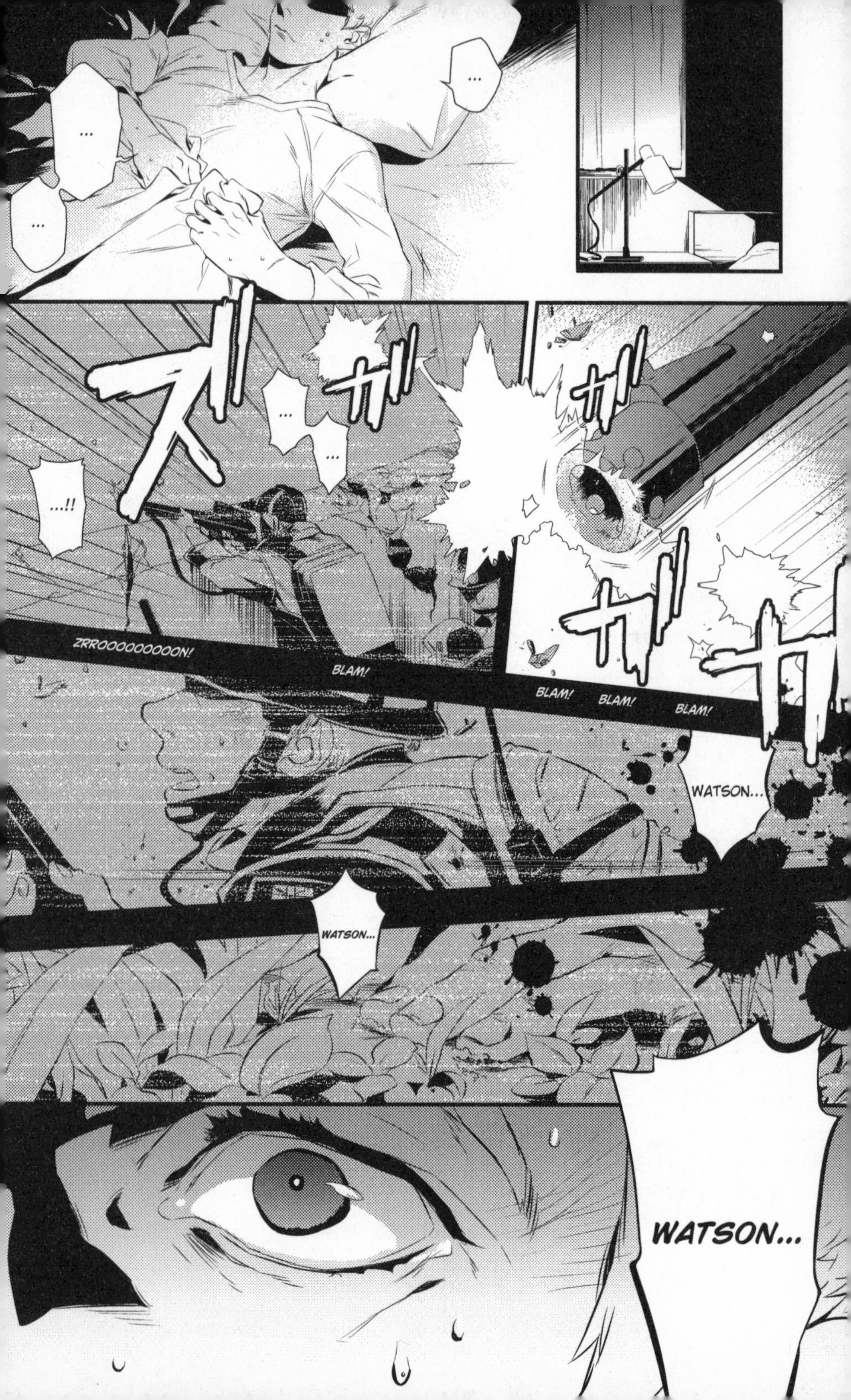
...
...
...
...
...
...!!
BLAM!
BLAM!
BLAM!
BLAM!
ZRROOOOOOOOON!
WATSON...
WATSON...
WATSON...

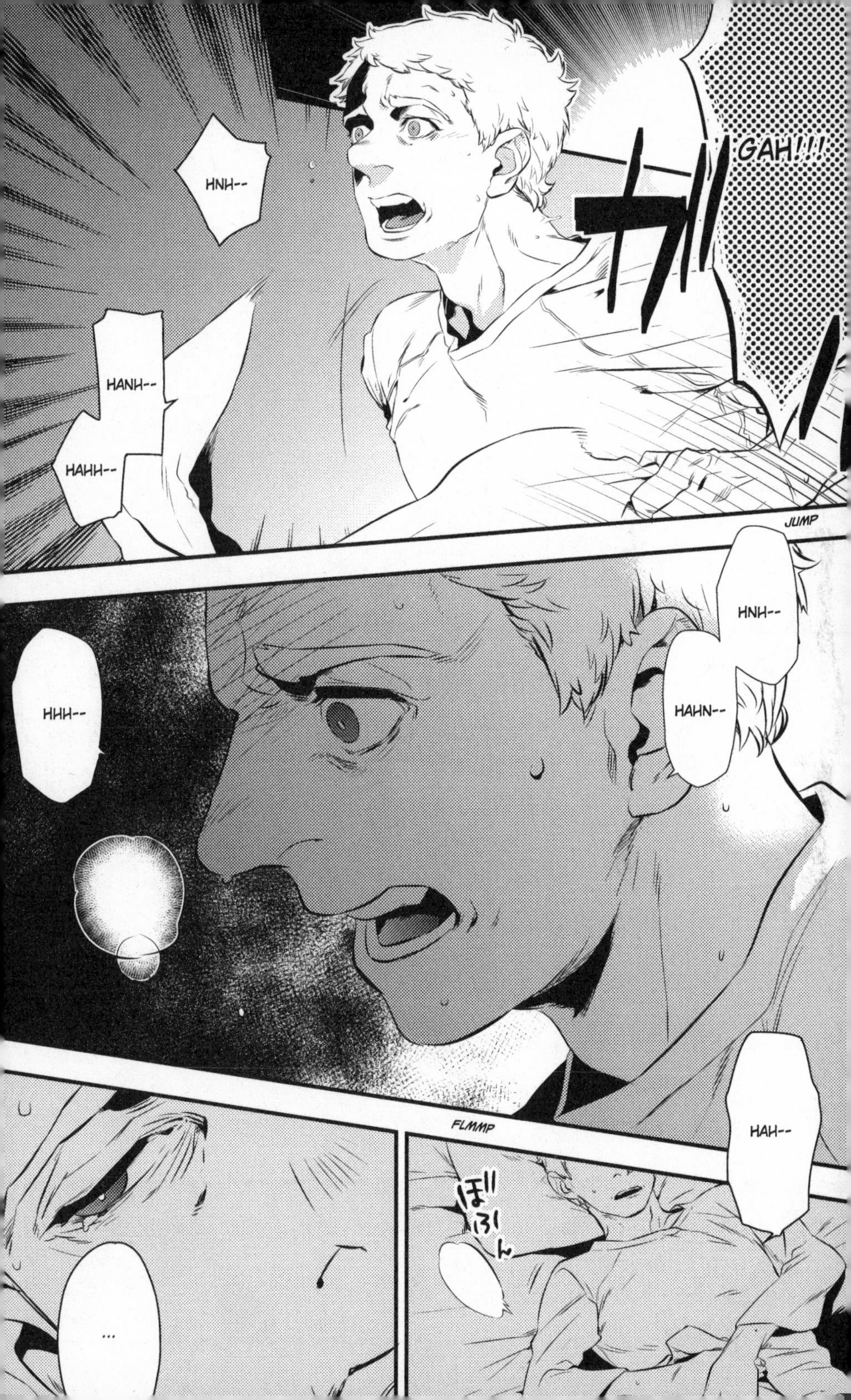
GAH!!!
HNH--
HANH--
HAHH--
JUMP
HNH--
HAHN--
HHH--
FLMMP
HAH--
ぼふん
...

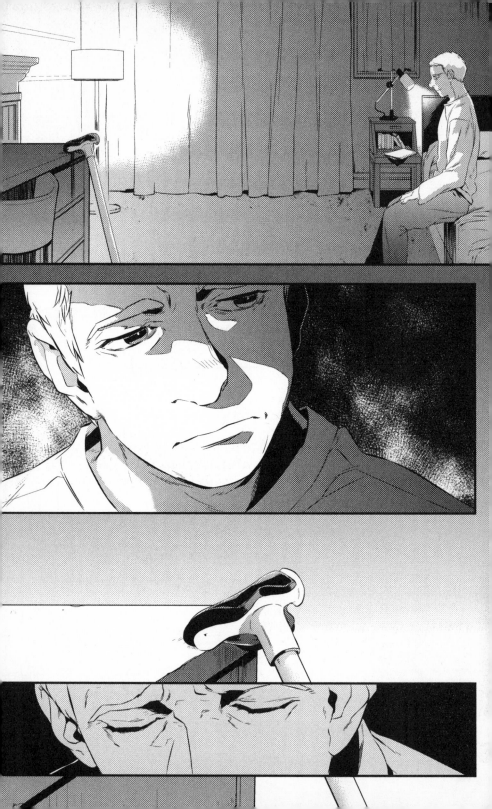

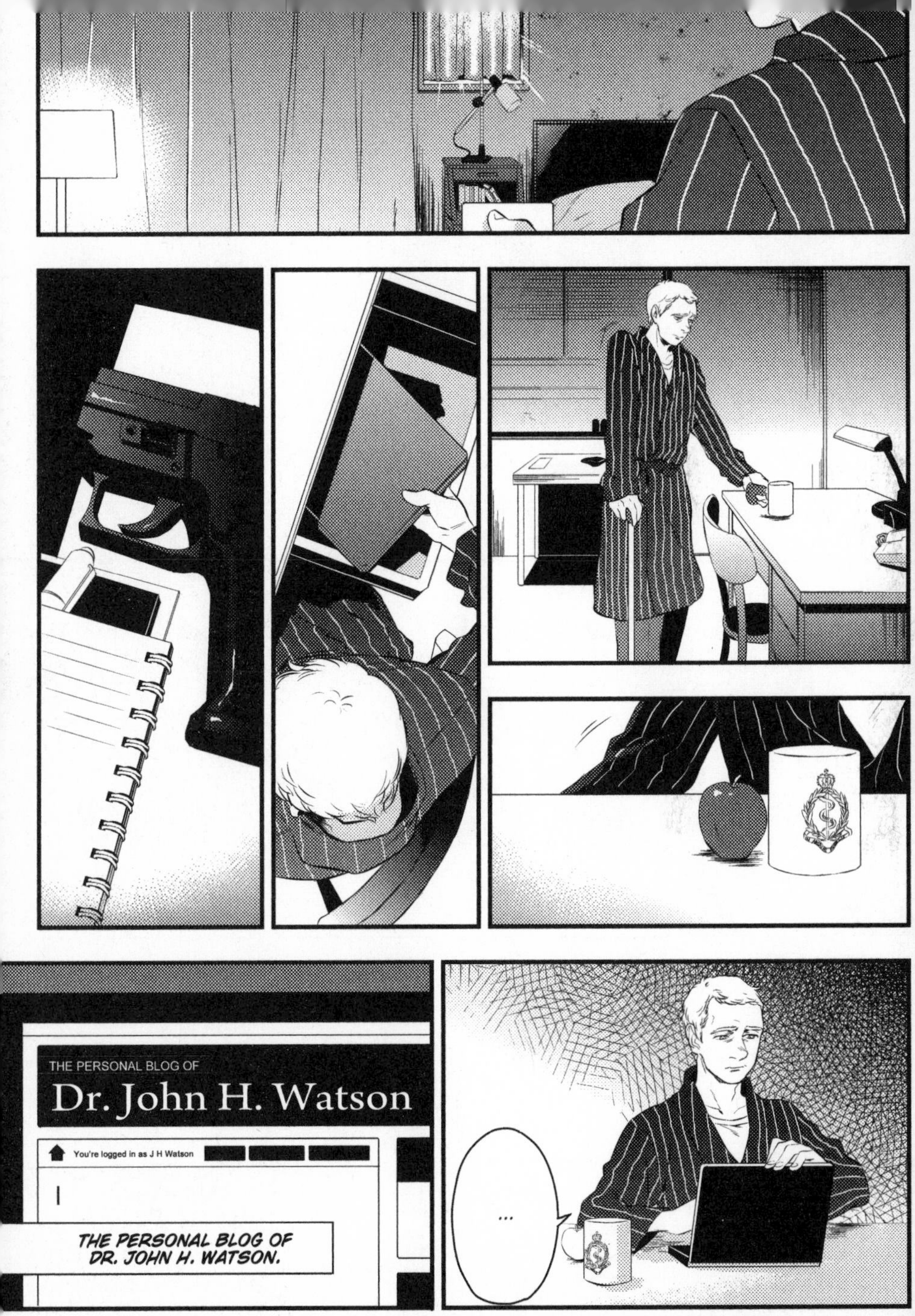
...
THE PERSONAL BLOG OF
Dr. John H. Watson
You're logged in as J H Watson
THE PERSONAL BLOG OF DR. JOHN H. WATSON.

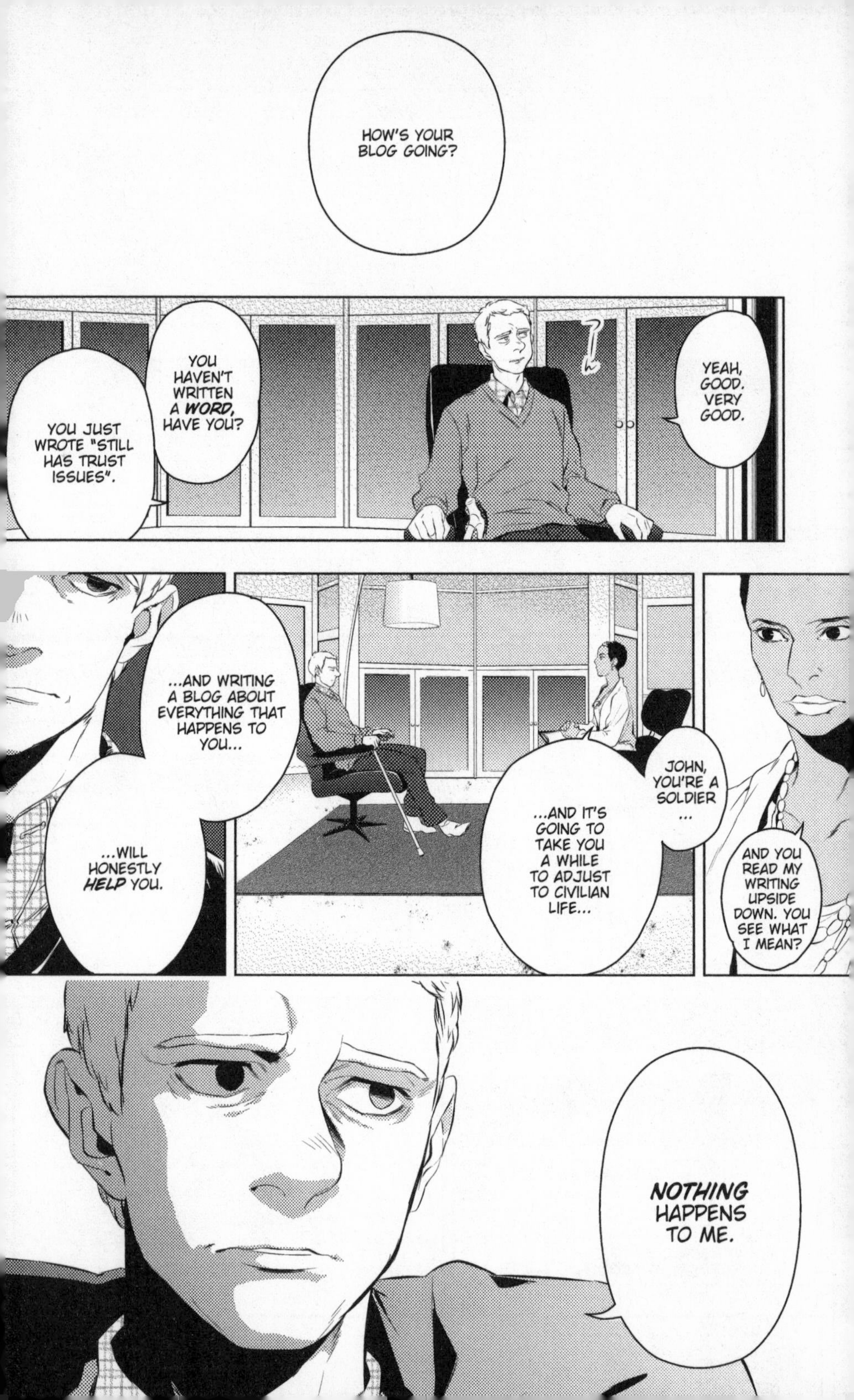
HOW'S YOUR BLOG GOING?
YEAH, GOOD. VERY GOOD.
YOU HAVEN'T WRITTEN A *WORD,* HAVE YOU?
YOU JUST WROTE "STILL HAS TRUST ISSUES".
AND YOU READ MY WRITING UPSIDE DOWN. YOU SEE WHAT I MEAN?
JOHN, YOU'RE A SOLDIER ...
...AND IT'S GOING TO TAKE YOU A WHILE TO ADJUST TO CIVILIAN LIFE...
...AND WRITING A BLOG ABOUT EVERYTHING THAT HAPPENS TO YOU...
...WILL HONESTLY *HELP* YOU.
NOTHING HAPPENS TO ME.

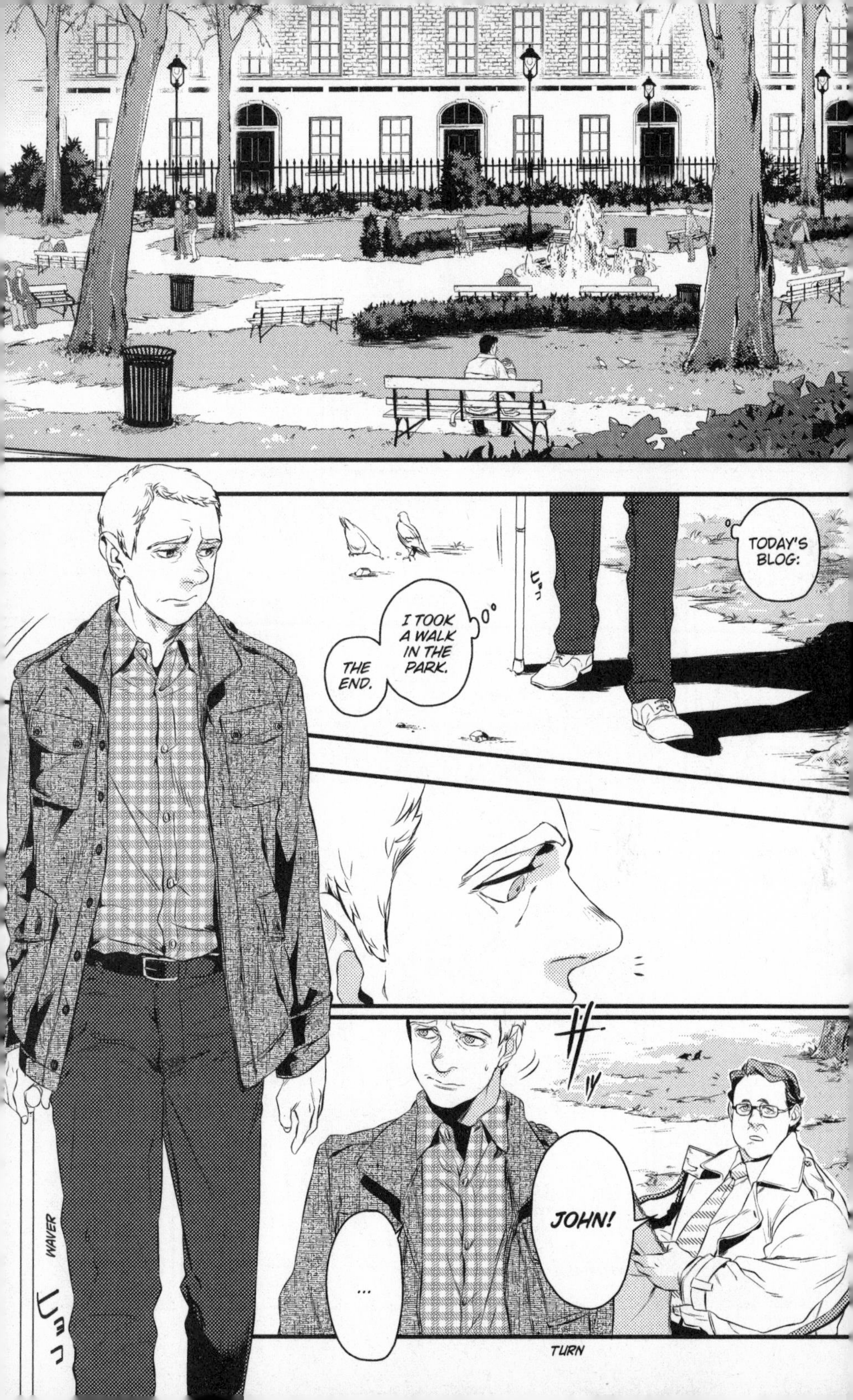

TODAY'S BLOG:
I TOOK A WALK IN THE PARK.
THE END.
JOHN!
...
TURN
WAVER

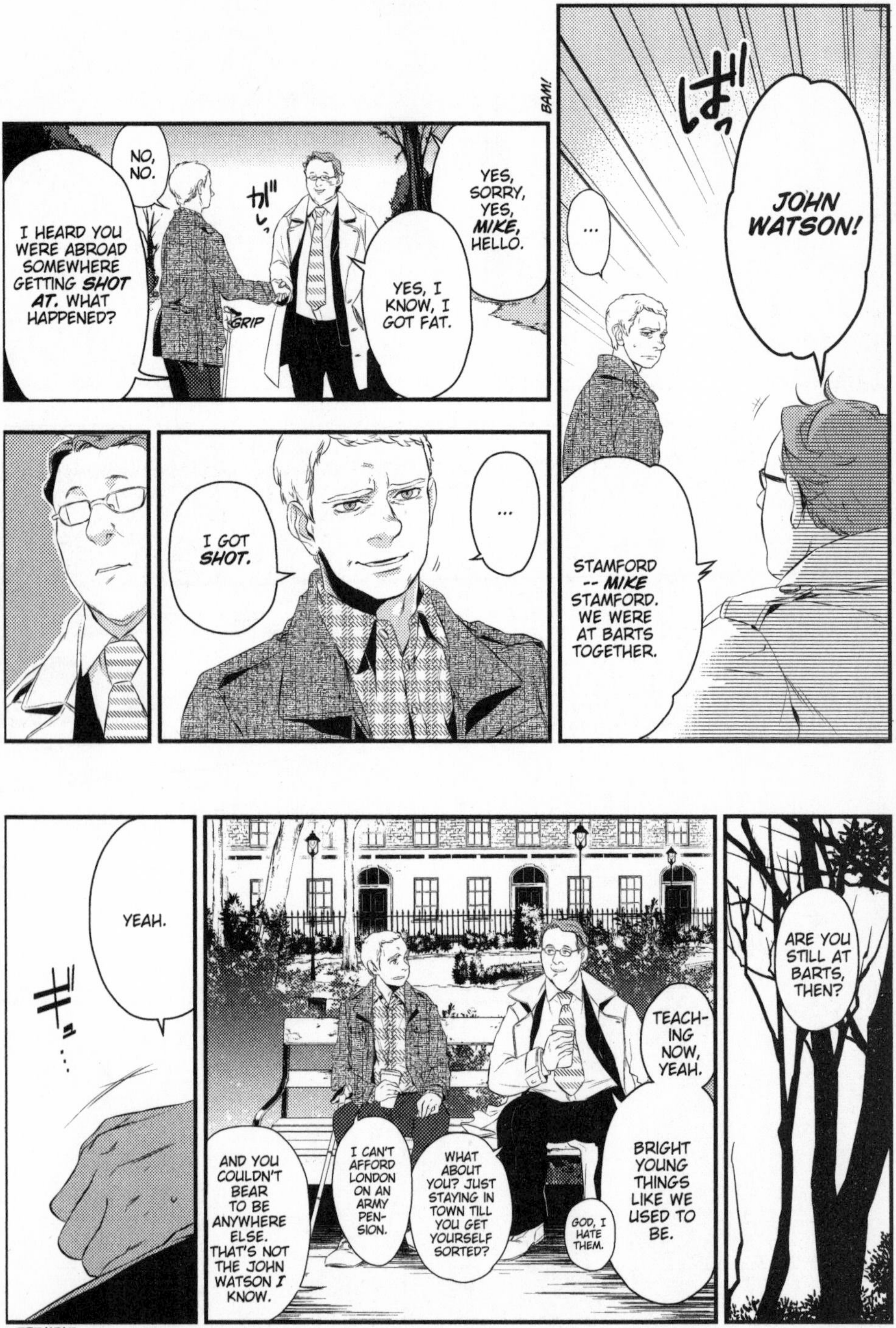
BAM!
ばっ
JOHN WATSON!
...
STAMFORD -- ***MIKE*** STAMFORD. WE WERE AT BARTS TOGETHER.
YES, SORRY, YES, ***MIKE,*** HELLO.
YES, I KNOW, I GOT FAT.
ガしっ
GRIP
NO, NO.
I HEARD YOU WERE ABROAD SOMEWHERE GETTING ***SHOT AT.*** WHAT HAPPENED?
...
I GOT ***SHOT.***
ARE YOU STILL AT BARTS, THEN?
TEACHING NOW, YEAH.
BRIGHT YOUNG THINGS LIKE WE USED TO BE.
GOD, I HATE THEM.
WHAT ABOUT YOU? JUST STAYING IN TOWN TILL YOU GET YOURSELF SORTED?
I CAN'T AFFORD LONDON ON AN ARMY PEN-SION.
AND YOU COULDN'T BEAR TO BE ANYWHERE ELSE. THAT'S NOT THE JOHN WATSON ***I*** KNOW.
YEAH.
ギュ…
TREMBLE

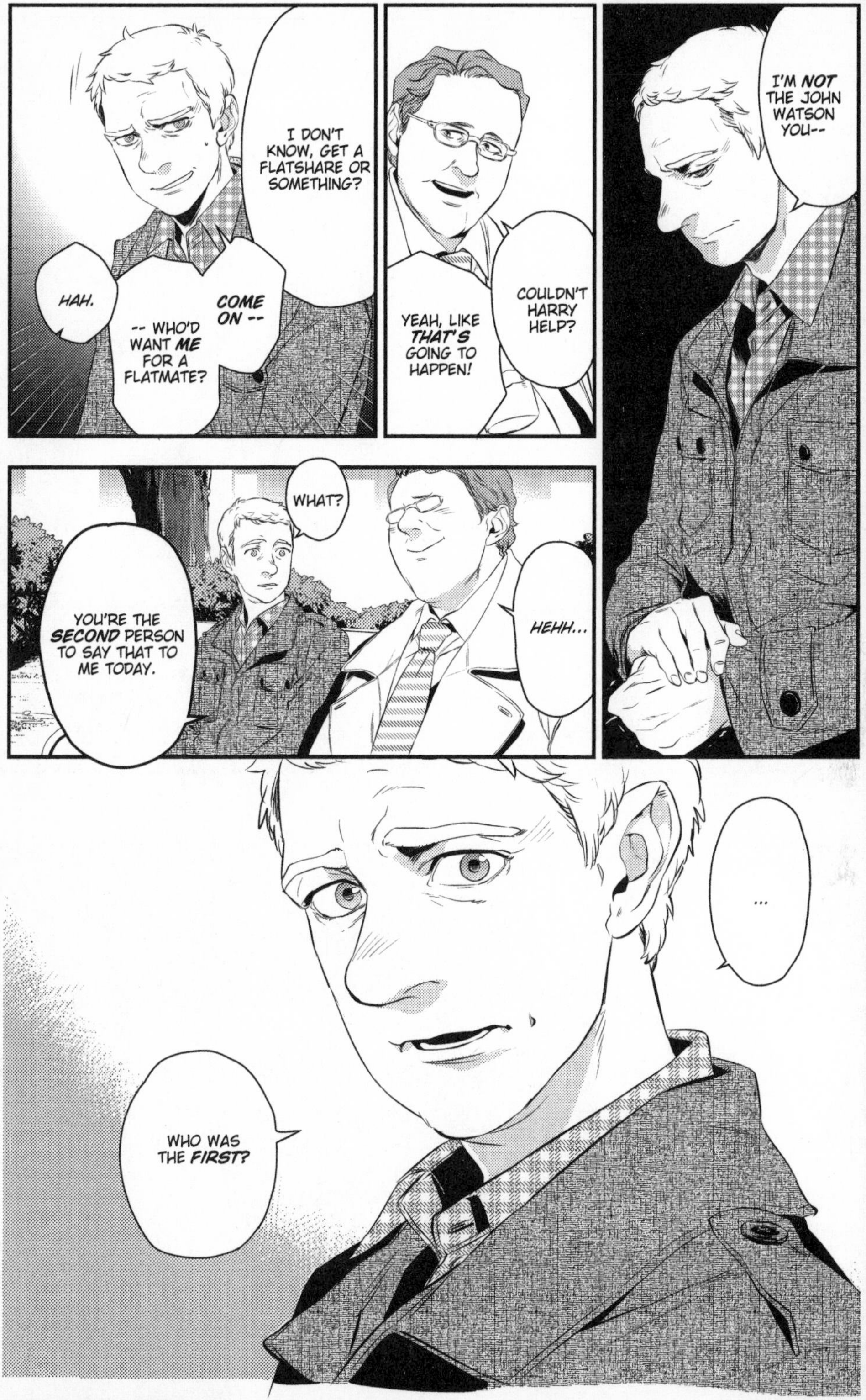
I'M **NOT** THE JOHN WATSON YOU--
COULDN'T HARRY HELP?
YEAH, LIKE **THAT'S** GOING TO HAPPEN!
I DON'T KNOW, GET A FLATSHARE OR SOMETHING?
COME ON --
-- WHO'D WANT **ME** FOR A FLATMATE?
HAH.
HEHH...
WHAT?
YOU'RE THE **SECOND** PERSON TO SAY THAT TO ME TODAY.
...
WHO WAS THE **FIRST?**

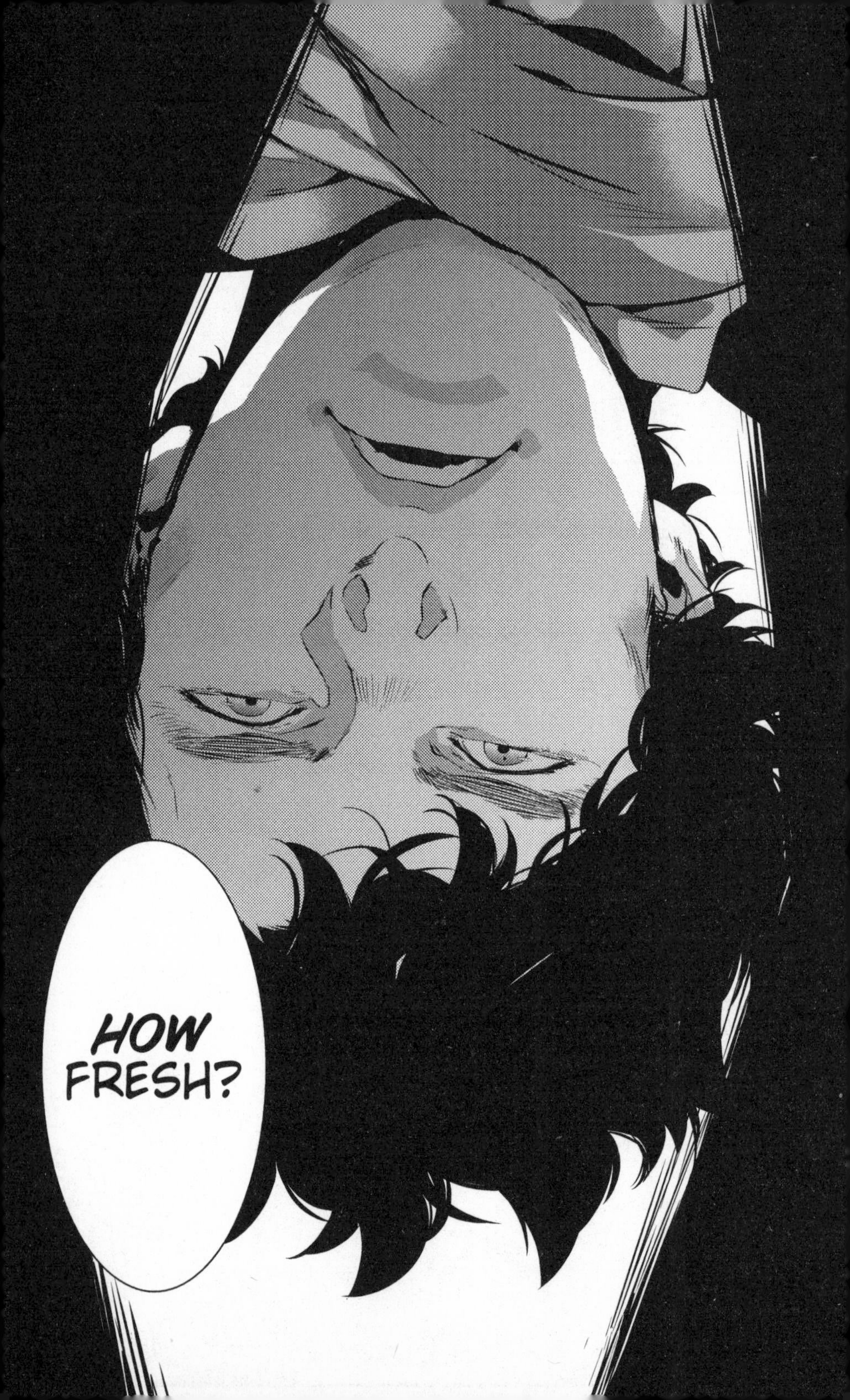
HOW FRESH?

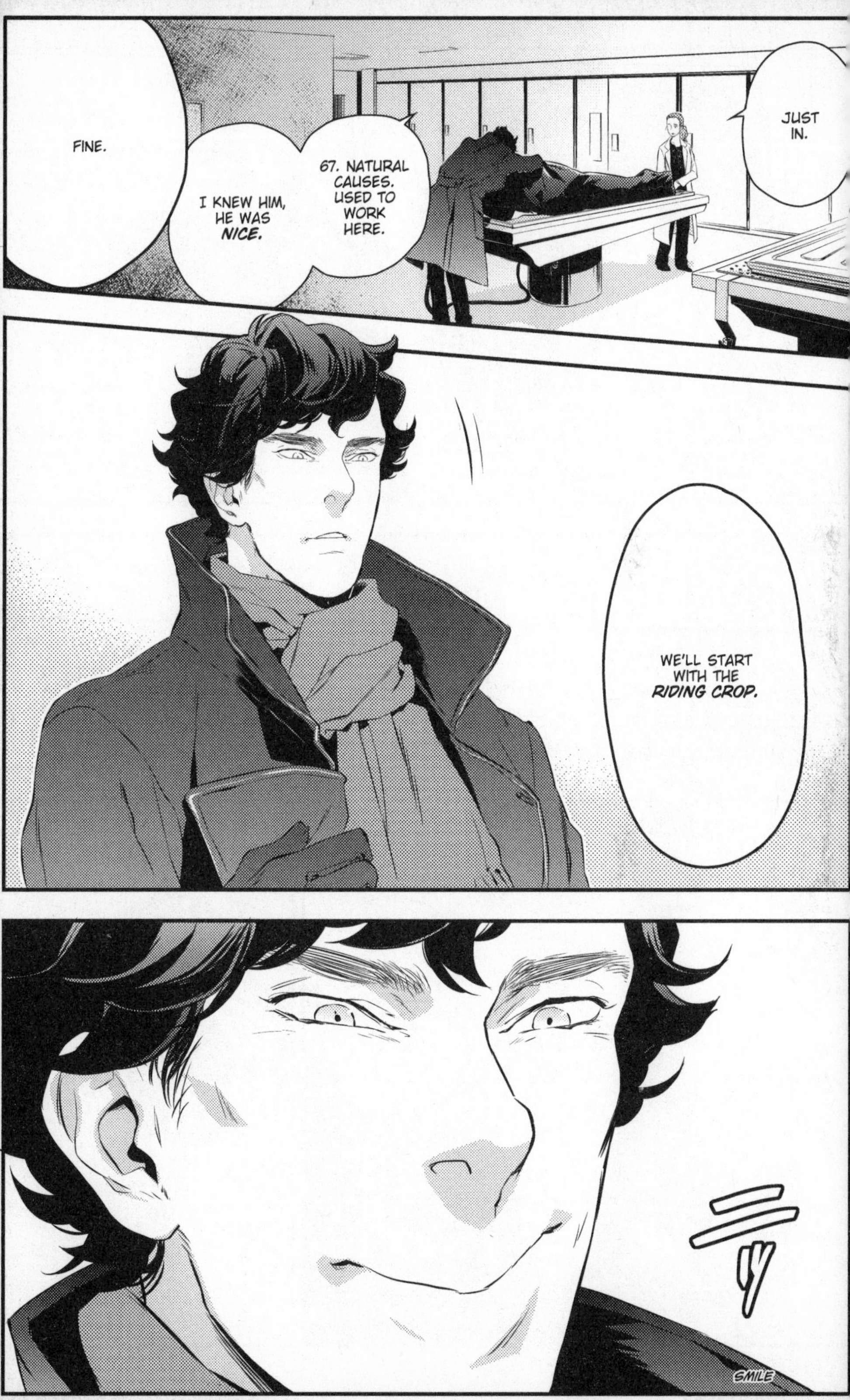
JUST IN.
67. NATURAL CAUSES. USED TO WORK HERE.
I KNEW HIM, HE WAS *NICE.*
FINE.
WE'LL START WITH THE *RIDING CROP.*
SMILE

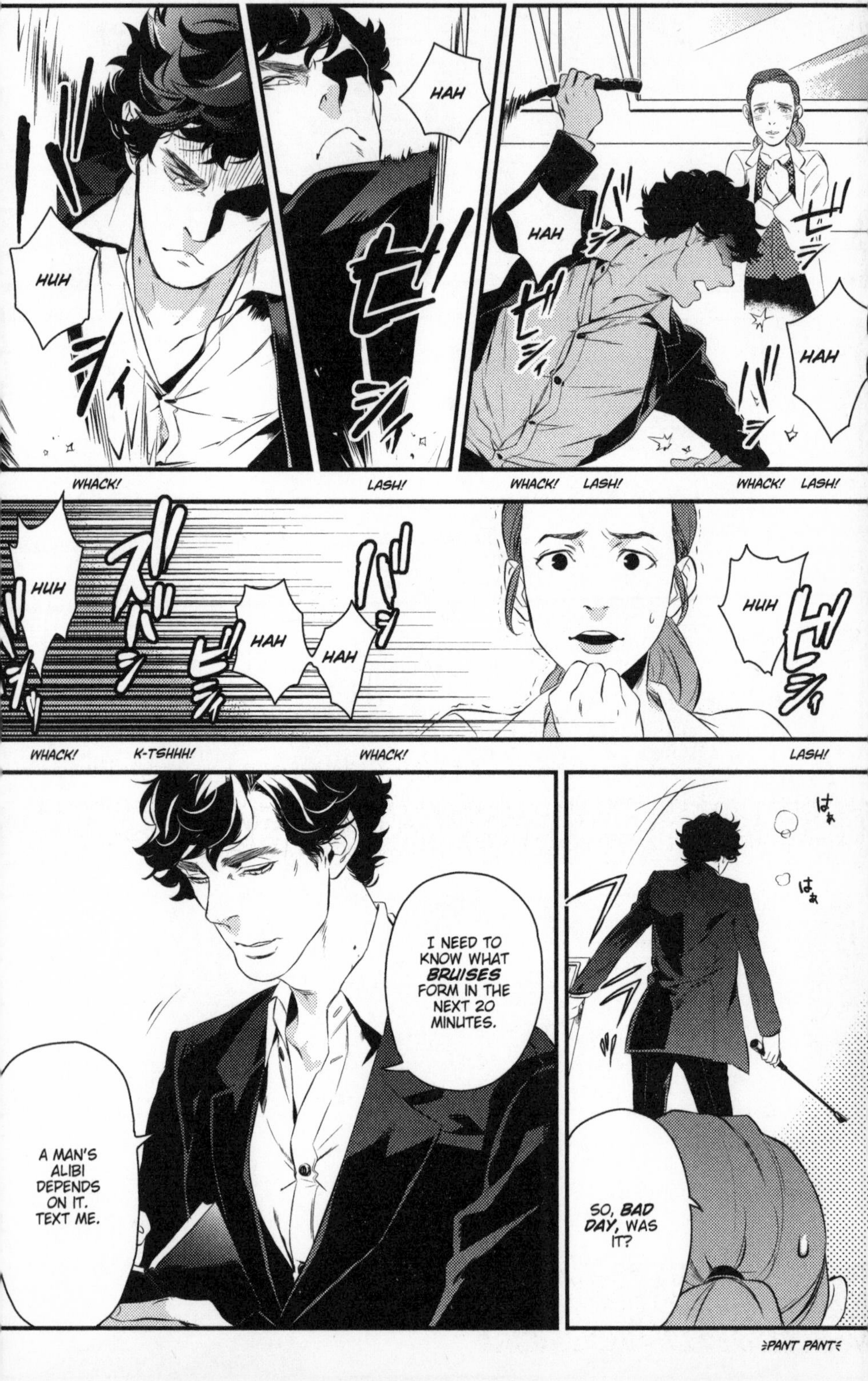
HAH
HAH
WHACK! LASH!
HAH
WHACK! LASH!
LASH!
HUH
WHACK!
HUH
LASH!
HAH
HAH
WHACK!
HUH
K-TSHHH!
WHACK!
はぁ
はぁ
SO, **BAD DAY,** WAS IT?
PANT PANT
I NEED TO KNOW WHAT **BRUISES** FORM IN THE NEXT 20 MINUTES.
A MAN'S ALIBI DEPENDS ON IT. TEXT ME.

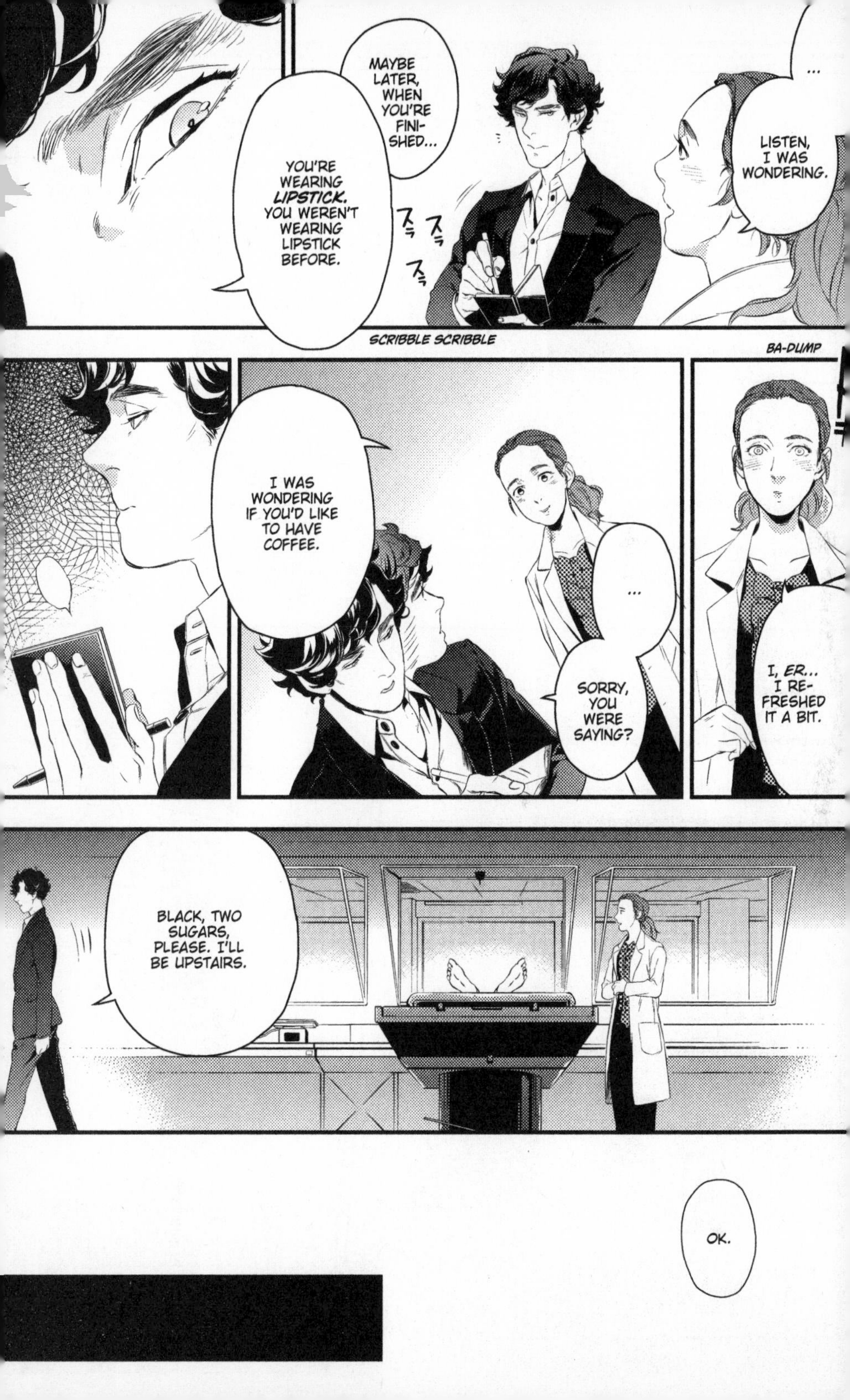
...
LISTEN, I WAS WONDERING.
BA-DUMP
MAYBE LATER, WHEN YOU'RE FINI-SHED...
YOU'RE WEARING LIPSTICK. YOU WEREN'T WEARING LIPSTICK BEFORE.
SCRIBBLE SCRIBBLE
I, ER... I RE-FRESHED IT A BIT.
...
SORRY, YOU WERE SAYING?
I WAS WONDERING IF YOU'D LIKE TO HAVE COFFEE.
BLACK, TWO SUGARS, PLEASE. I'LL BE UPSTAIRS.
OK.

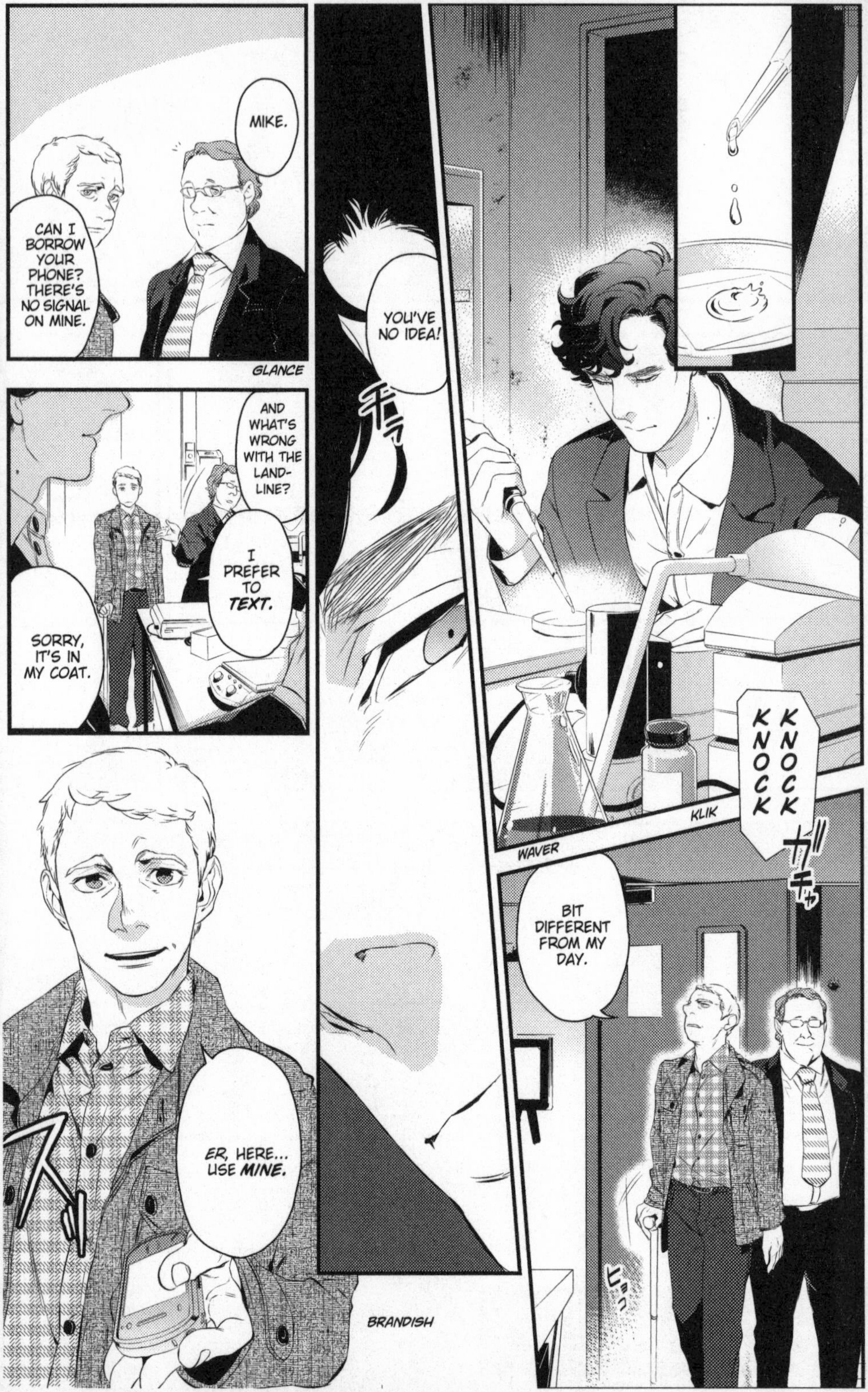
WAVER
KLIK
KNOCK KNOCK
BIT DIFFERENT FROM MY DAY.
YOU'VE NO IDEA!
BRANDISH
MIKE.
CAN I BORROW YOUR PHONE? THERE'S NO SIGNAL ON MINE.
GLANCE
AND WHAT'S WRONG WITH THE LAND-LINE?
I PREFER TO *TEXT.*
SORRY, IT'S IN MY COAT.
ER, HERE... USE *MINE.*

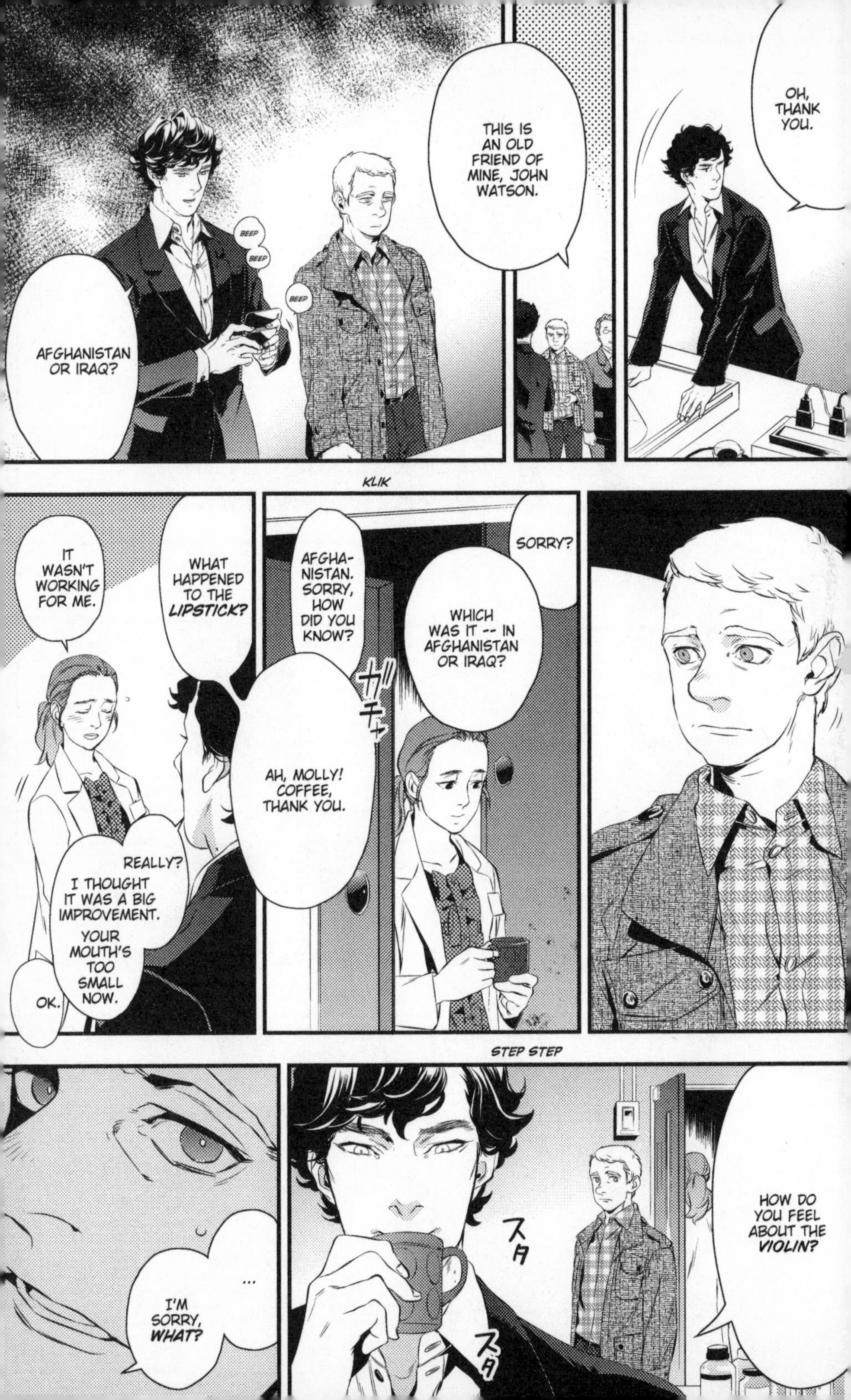
OH, THANK YOU.
THIS IS AN OLD FRIEND OF MINE, JOHN WATSON.
BEEP
BEEP
BEEP
AFGHANISTAN OR IRAQ?
KLIK
SORRY?
WHICH WAS IT -- IN AFGHANISTAN OR IRAQ?
AFGHA-NISTAN. SORRY, HOW DID YOU KNOW?
ガチャ
AH, MOLLY! COFFEE, THANK YOU.
WHAT HAPPENED TO THE **LIPSTICK?**
IT WASN'T WORKING FOR ME.
REALLY? I THOUGHT IT WAS A BIG IMPROVEMENT.
YOUR MOUTH'S TOO SMALL NOW.
OK.
STEP STEP
HOW DO YOU FEEL ABOUT THE **VIOLIN?**
スタ
スタ
...
I'M SORRY, **WHAT?**

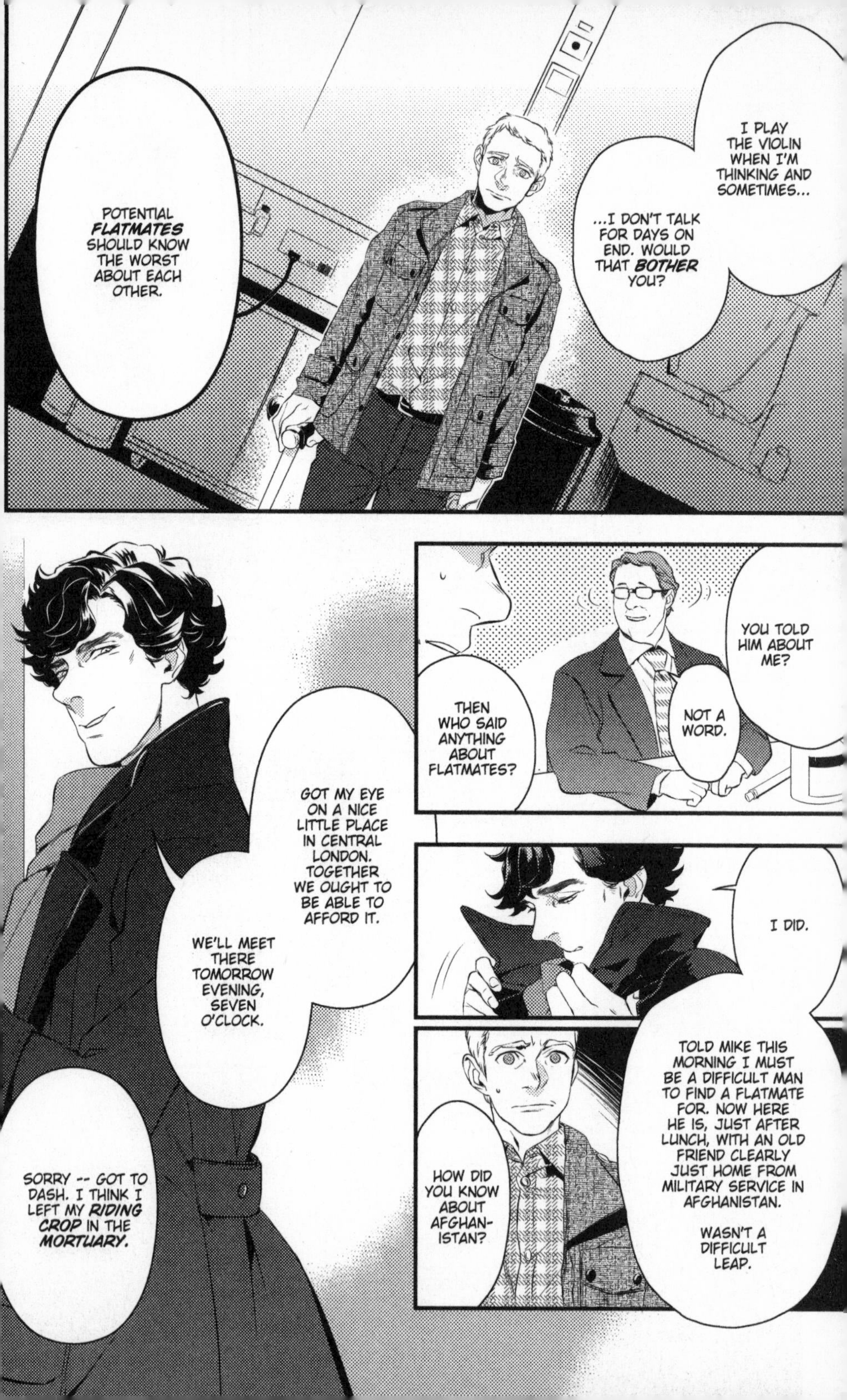
I PLAY THE VIOLIN WHEN I'M THINKING AND SOMETIMES...
...I DON'T TALK FOR DAYS ON END. WOULD THAT **BOTHER** YOU?
POTENTIAL **FLATMATES** SHOULD KNOW THE WORST ABOUT EACH OTHER.
YOU TOLD HIM ABOUT ME?
NOT A WORD.
THEN WHO SAID ANYTHING ABOUT FLATMATES?
I DID.
TOLD MIKE THIS MORNING I MUST BE A DIFFICULT MAN TO FIND A FLATMATE FOR. NOW HERE HE IS, JUST AFTER LUNCH, WITH AN OLD FRIEND CLEARLY JUST HOME FROM MILITARY SERVICE IN AFGHANISTAN.
WASN'T A DIFFICULT LEAP.
HOW DID YOU KNOW ABOUT AFGHAN-ISTAN?
GOT MY EYE ON A NICE LITTLE PLACE IN CENTRAL LONDON. TOGETHER WE OUGHT TO BE ABLE TO AFFORD IT.
WE'LL MEET THERE TOMORROW EVENING, SEVEN O'CLOCK.
SORRY -- GOT TO DASH. I THINK I LEFT MY **RIDING CROP** IN THE **MORTUARY.**

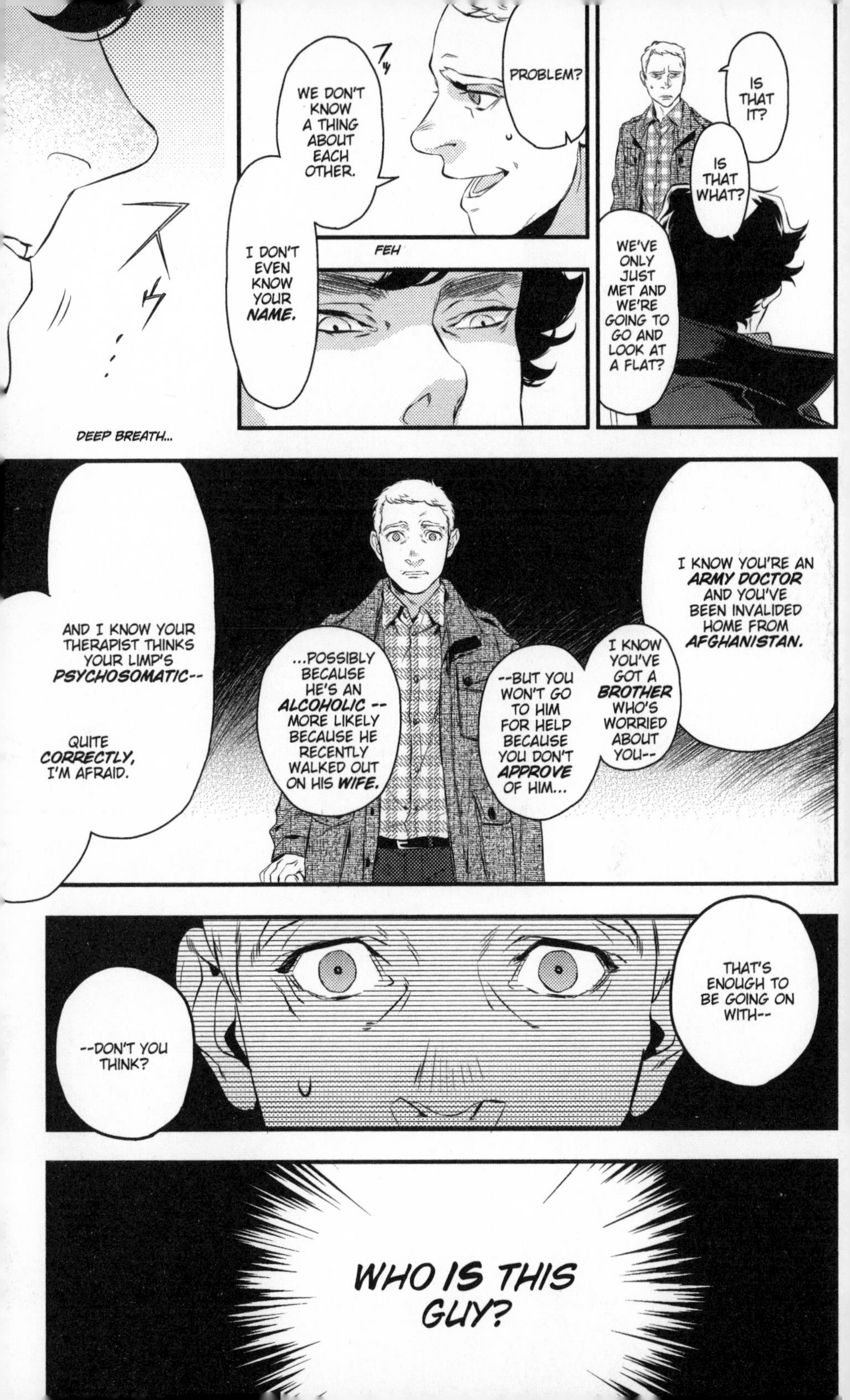
IS THAT IT?
IS THAT WHAT?
WE'VE ONLY JUST MET AND WE'RE GOING TO GO AND LOOK AT A FLAT?
PROBLEM?
WE DON'T KNOW A THING ABOUT EACH OTHER.
FEH
I DON'T EVEN KNOW YOUR NAME.
DEEP BREATH...
I KNOW YOU'RE AN ARMY DOCTOR AND YOU'VE BEEN INVALIDED HOME FROM AFGHANISTAN.
I KNOW YOU'VE GOT A BROTHER WHO'S WORRIED ABOUT YOU--
--BUT YOU WON'T GO TO HIM FOR HELP BECAUSE YOU DON'T APPROVE OF HIM...
...POSSIBLY BECAUSE HE'S AN ALCOHOLIC -- MORE LIKELY BECAUSE HE RECENTLY WALKED OUT ON HIS WIFE.
AND I KNOW YOUR THERAPIST THINKS YOUR LIMP'S PSYCHOSOMATIC--
QUITE CORRECTLY, I'M AFRAID.
THAT'S ENOUGH TO BE GOING ON WITH--
--DON'T YOU THINK?
WHO IS THIS GUY?

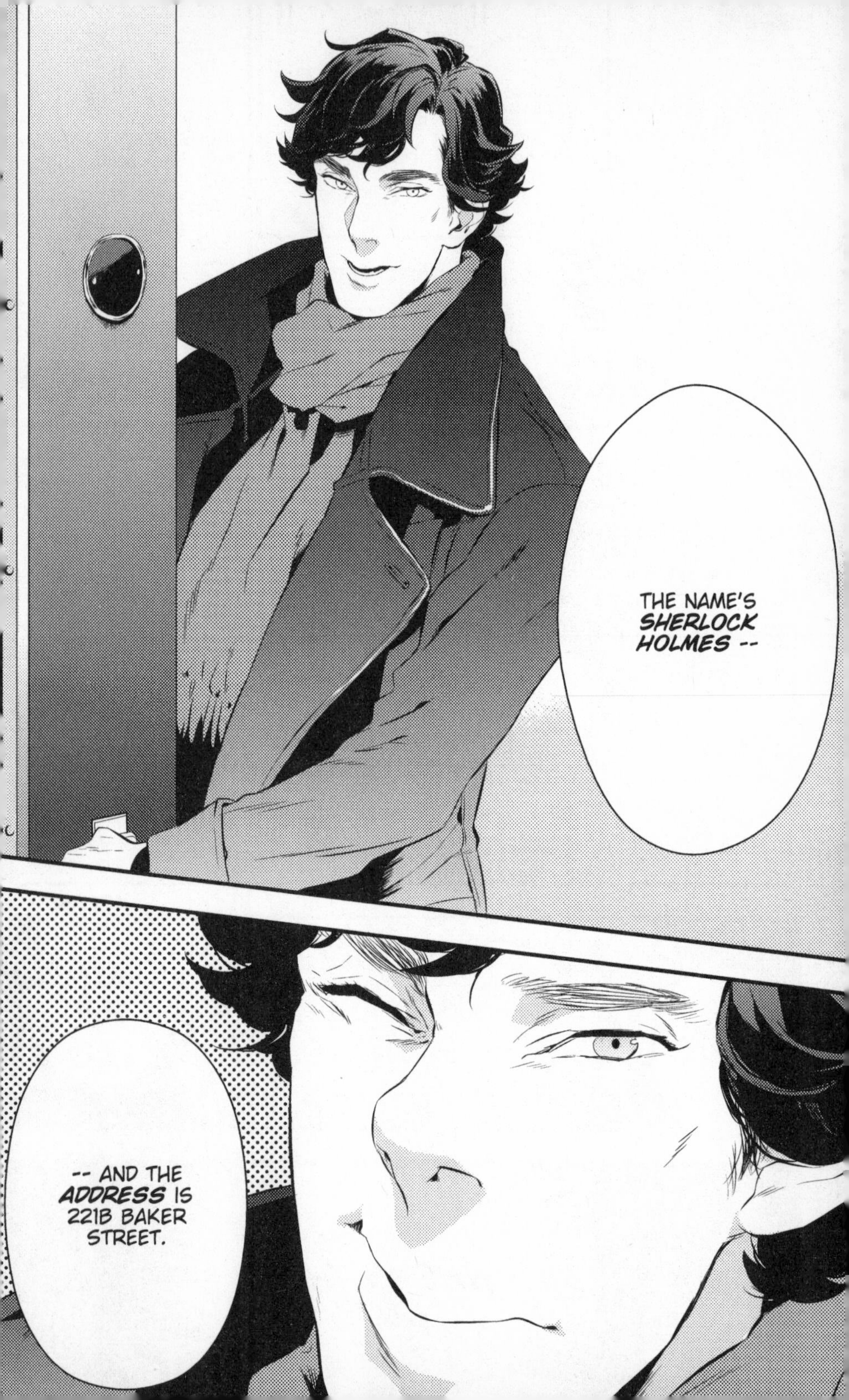
THE NAME'S SHERLOCK HOLMES --
-- AND THE ADDRESS IS 221B BAKER STREET.

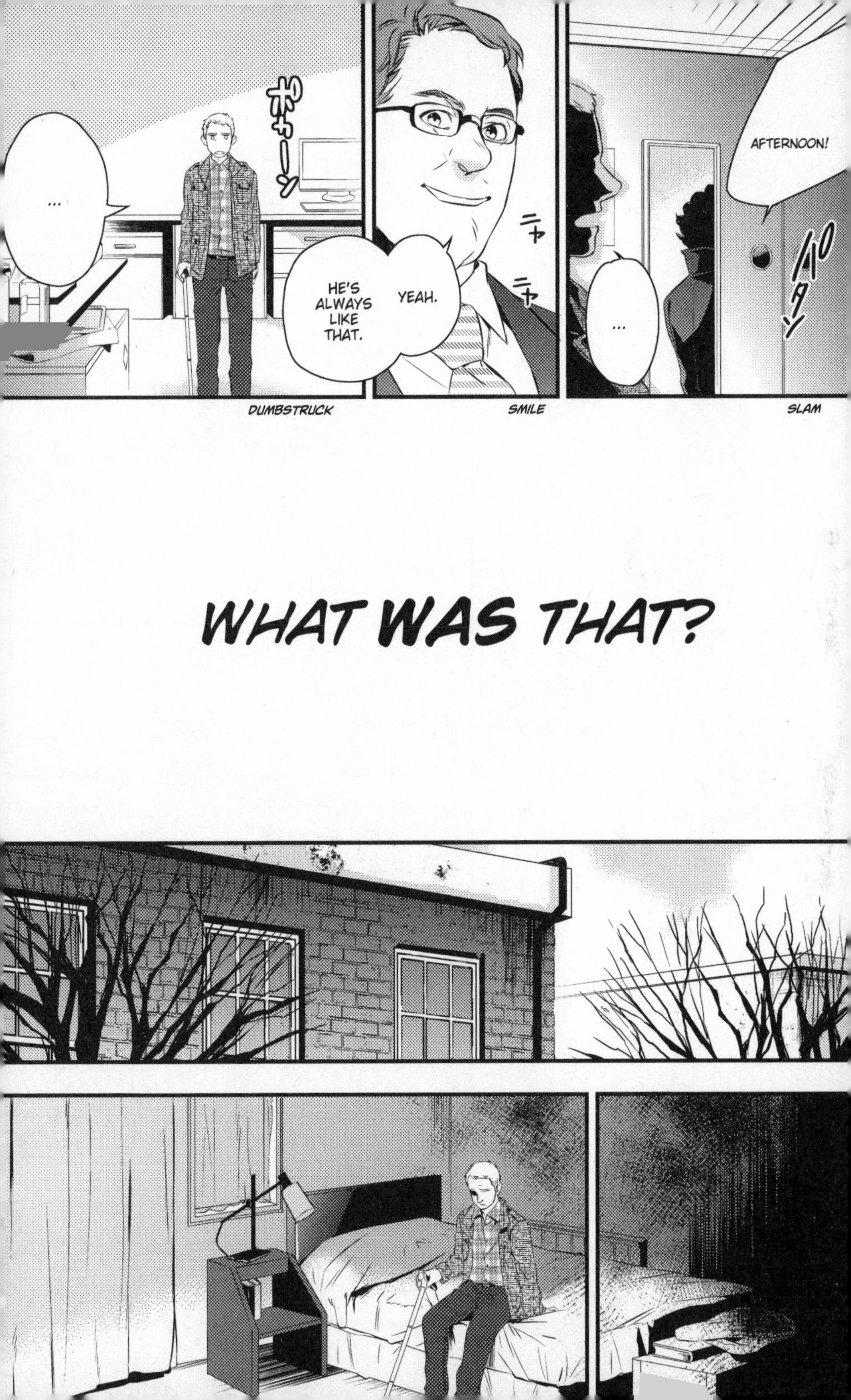
AFTERNOON!
パタン
...
SLAM
YEAH.
HE'S ALWAYS LIKE THAT.
ニヤ
ニヤ
SMILE
ポカーン
...
DUMBSTRUCK
WHAT WAS THAT?

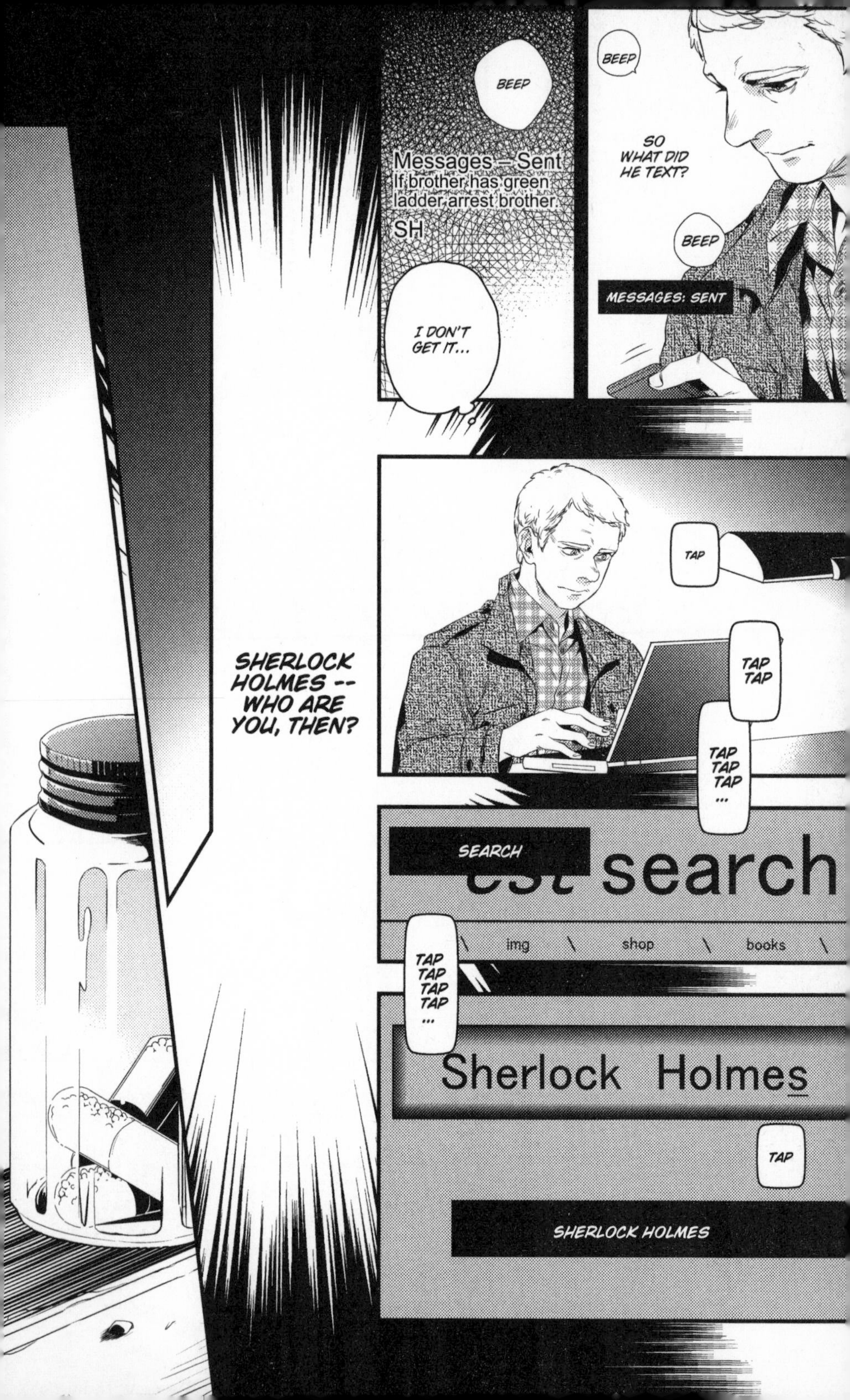
BEEP
SO WHAT DID HE TEXT?
BEEP
MESSAGES: SENT
BEEP
Messages – Sent
If brother has green ladder arrest brother.
SH
I DON'T GET IT...
TAP
TAP TAP
TAP TAP TAP ...
SEARCH
search
img \ shop \ books
TAP TAP TAP TAP ...
Sherlock Holmes
TAP
SHERLOCK HOLMES
SHERLOCK HOLMES -- WHO ARE YOU, THEN?

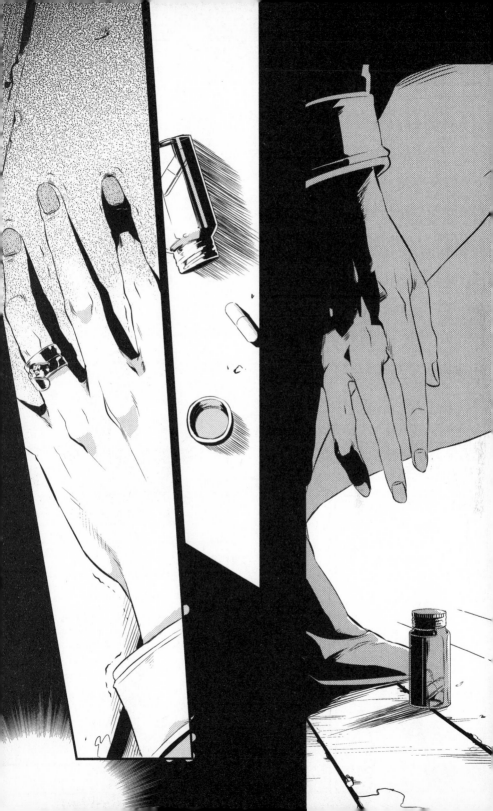

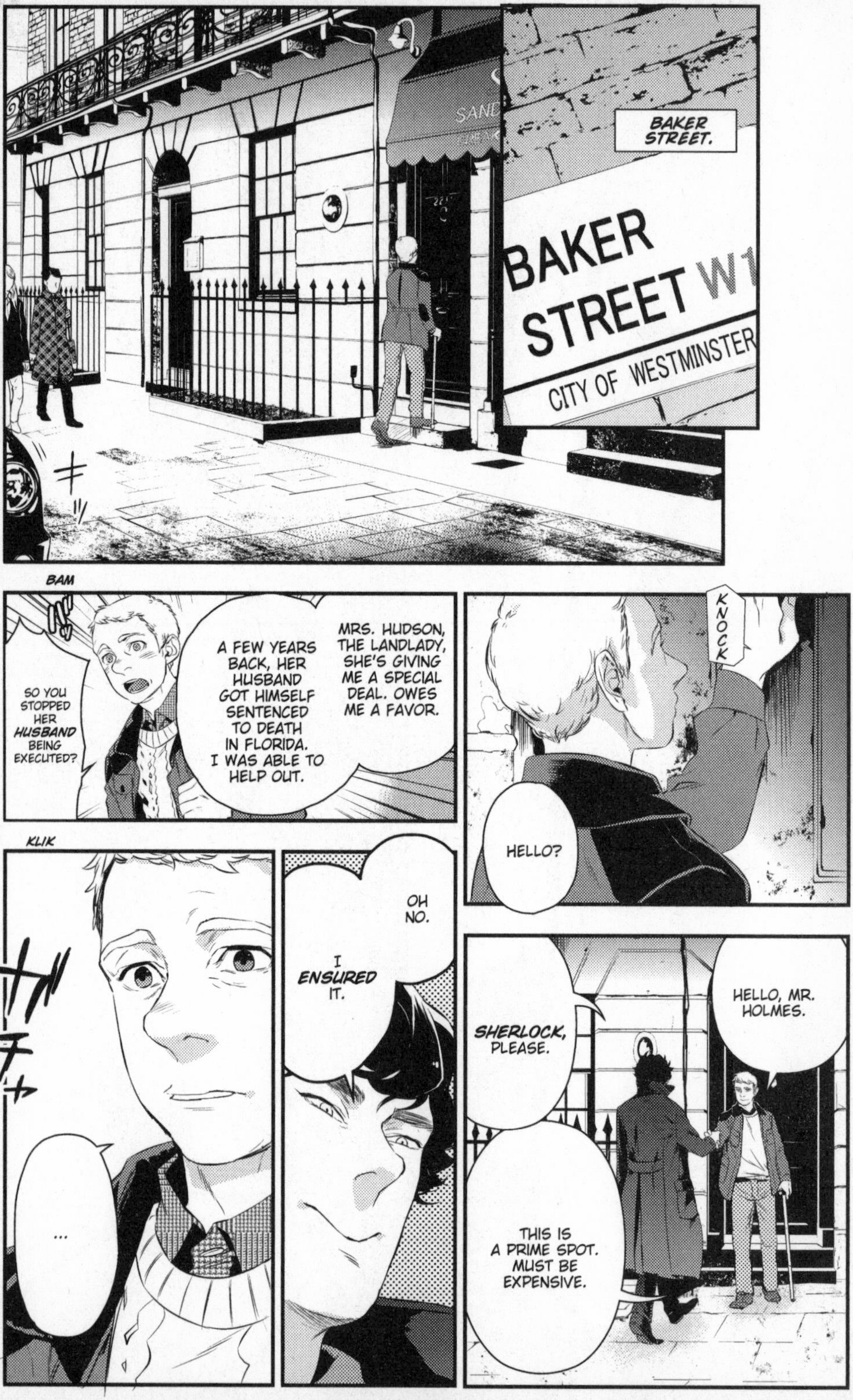
BAKER STREET.
BAKER STREET W1
CITY OF WESTMINSTER
KNOCK
HELLO?
BAM
MRS. HUDSON, THE LANDLADY, SHE'S GIVING ME A SPECIAL DEAL. OWES ME A FAVOR.
A FEW YEARS BACK, HER HUSBAND GOT HIMSELF SENTENCED TO DEATH IN FLORIDA. I WAS ABLE TO HELP OUT.
SO YOU STOPPED HER HUSBAND BEING EXECUTED?
HELLO, MR. HOLMES.
SHERLOCK, PLEASE.
THIS IS A PRIME SPOT. MUST BE EXPENSIVE.
OH NO.
I ENSURED IT.
KLIK
...

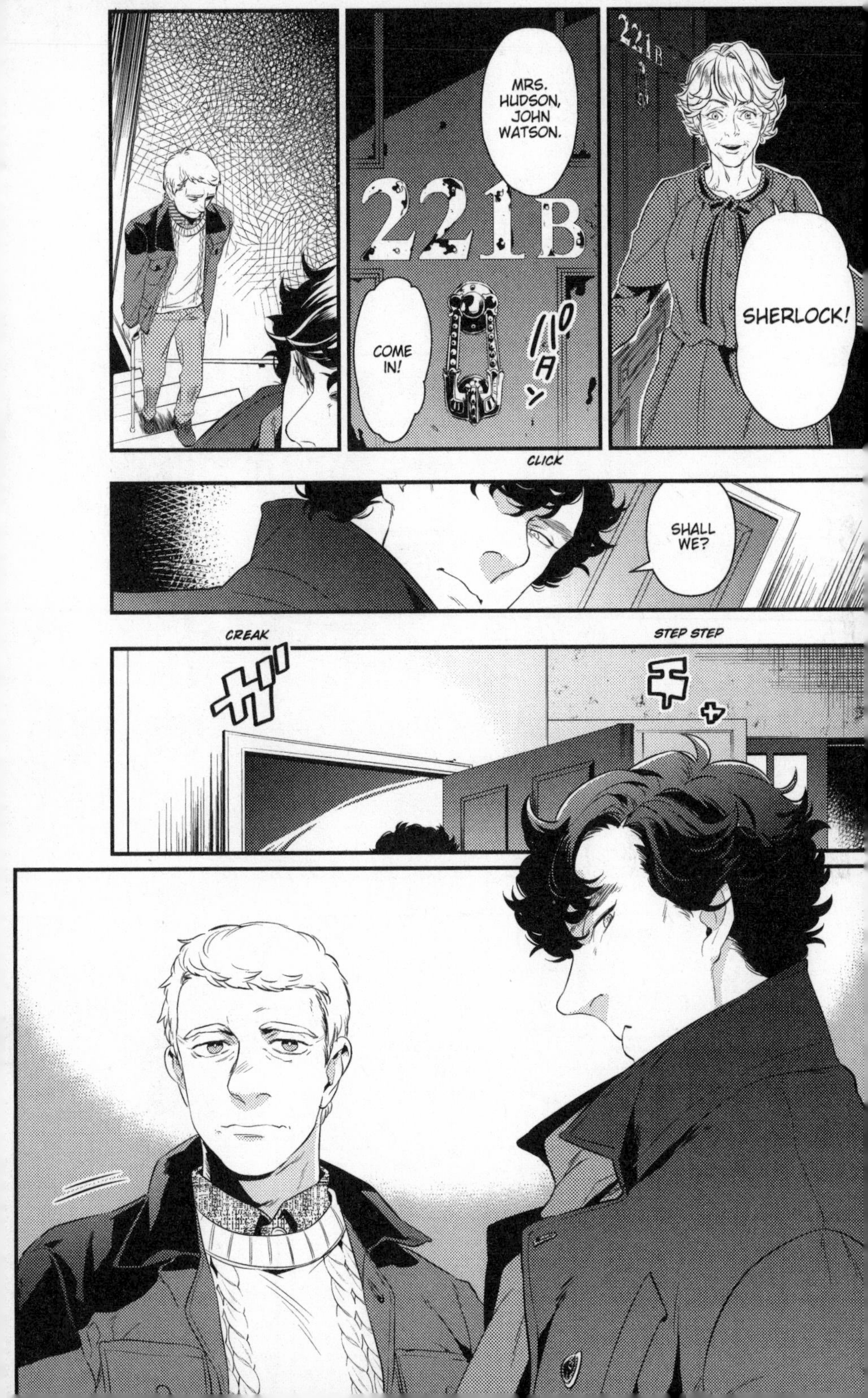
SHERLOCK!
MRS. HUDSON, JOHN WATSON.
COME IN!
パタン
CLICK
SHALL WE?
STEP STEP
CREAK

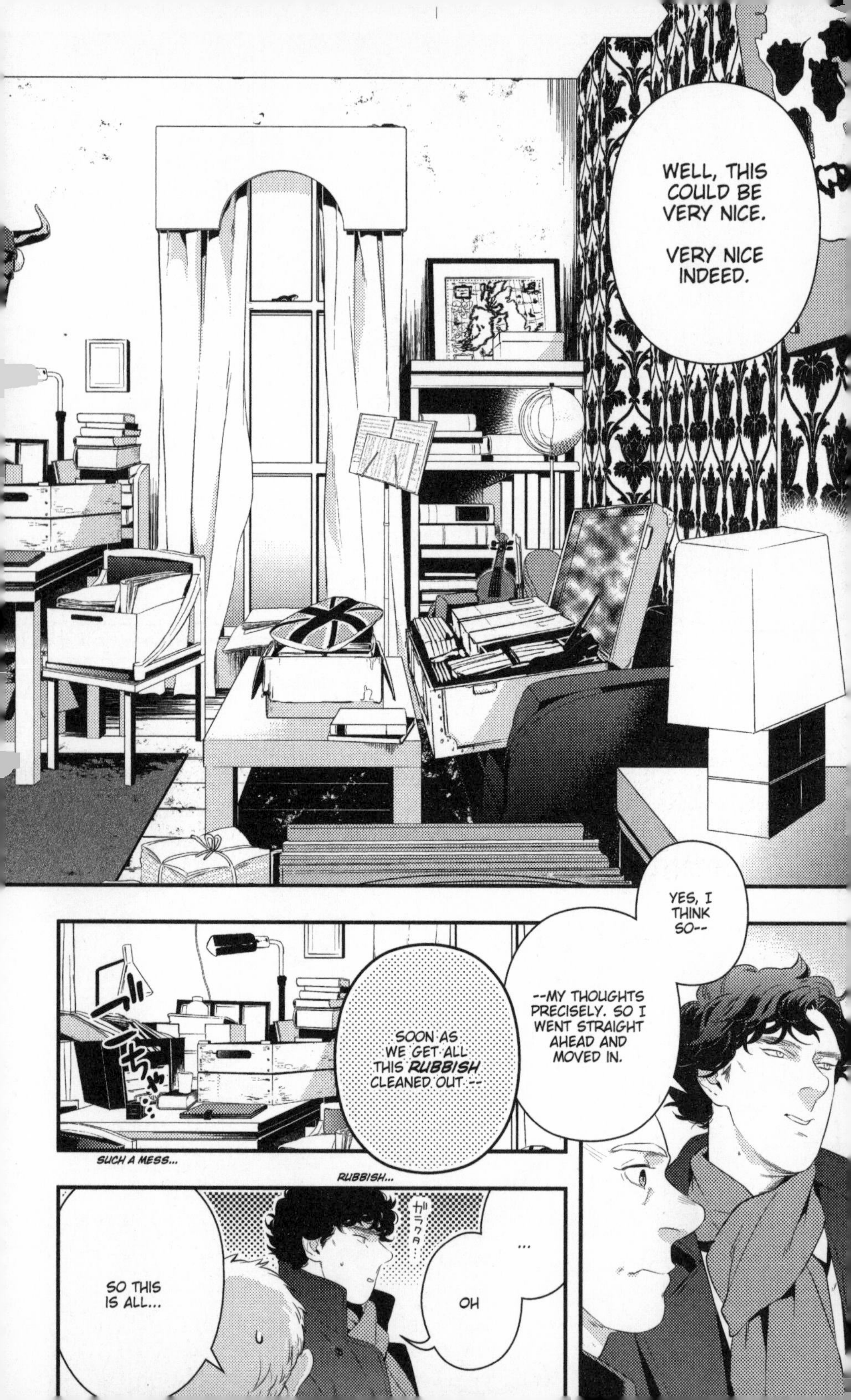
WELL, THIS COULD BE VERY NICE.
VERY NICE INDEED.
YES, I THINK SO--
--MY THOUGHTS PRECISELY. SO I WENT STRAIGHT AHEAD AND MOVED IN.
SOON AS WE GET ALL THIS **RUBBISH** CLEANED OUT--
SUCH A MESS...
RUBBISH...
ガラクタ…
...
OH
SO THIS IS ALL...

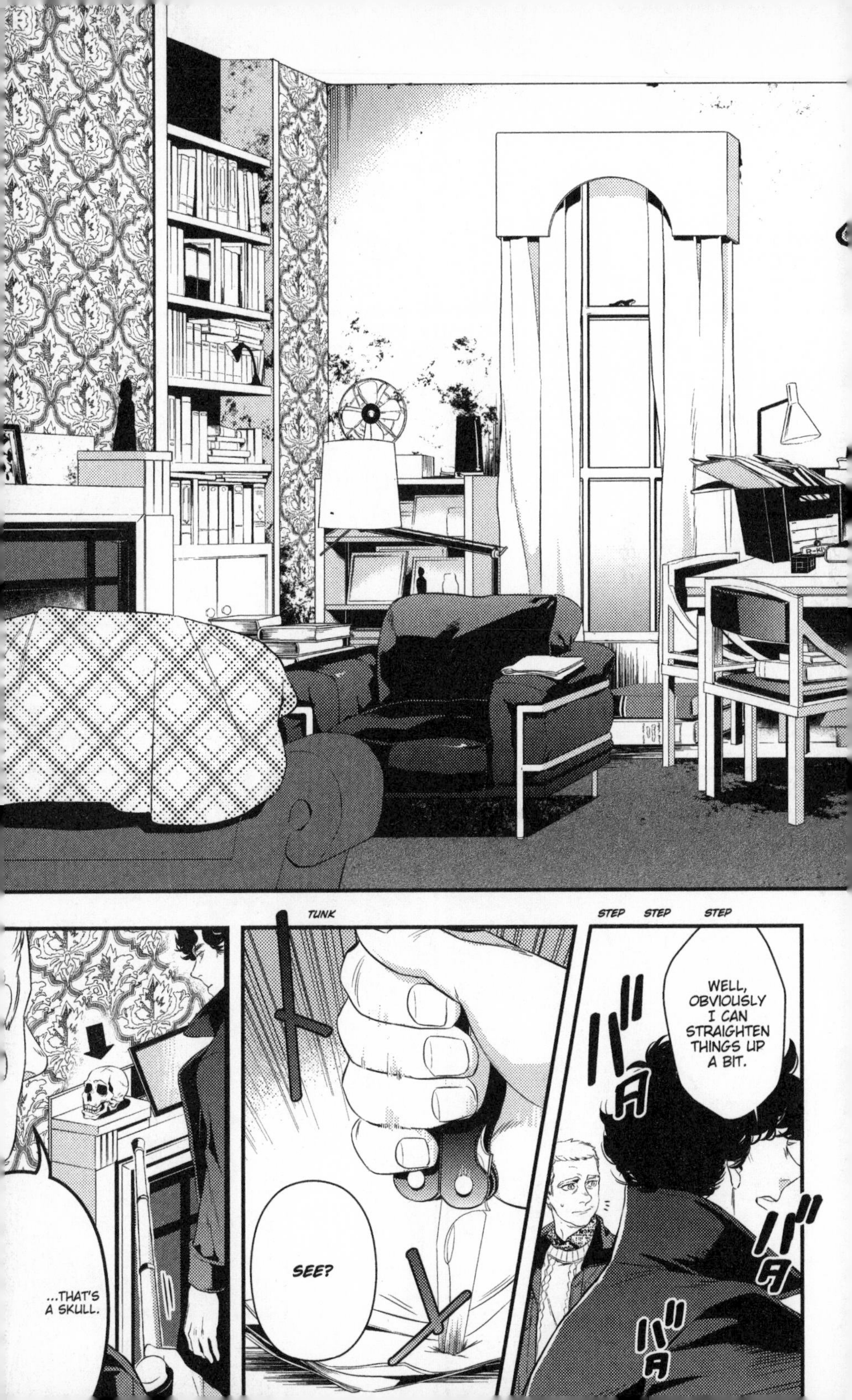
STEP STEP STEP
WELL, OBVIOUSLY I CAN STRAIGHTEN THINGS UP A BIT.
TUNK
SEE?
...THAT'S A SKULL.

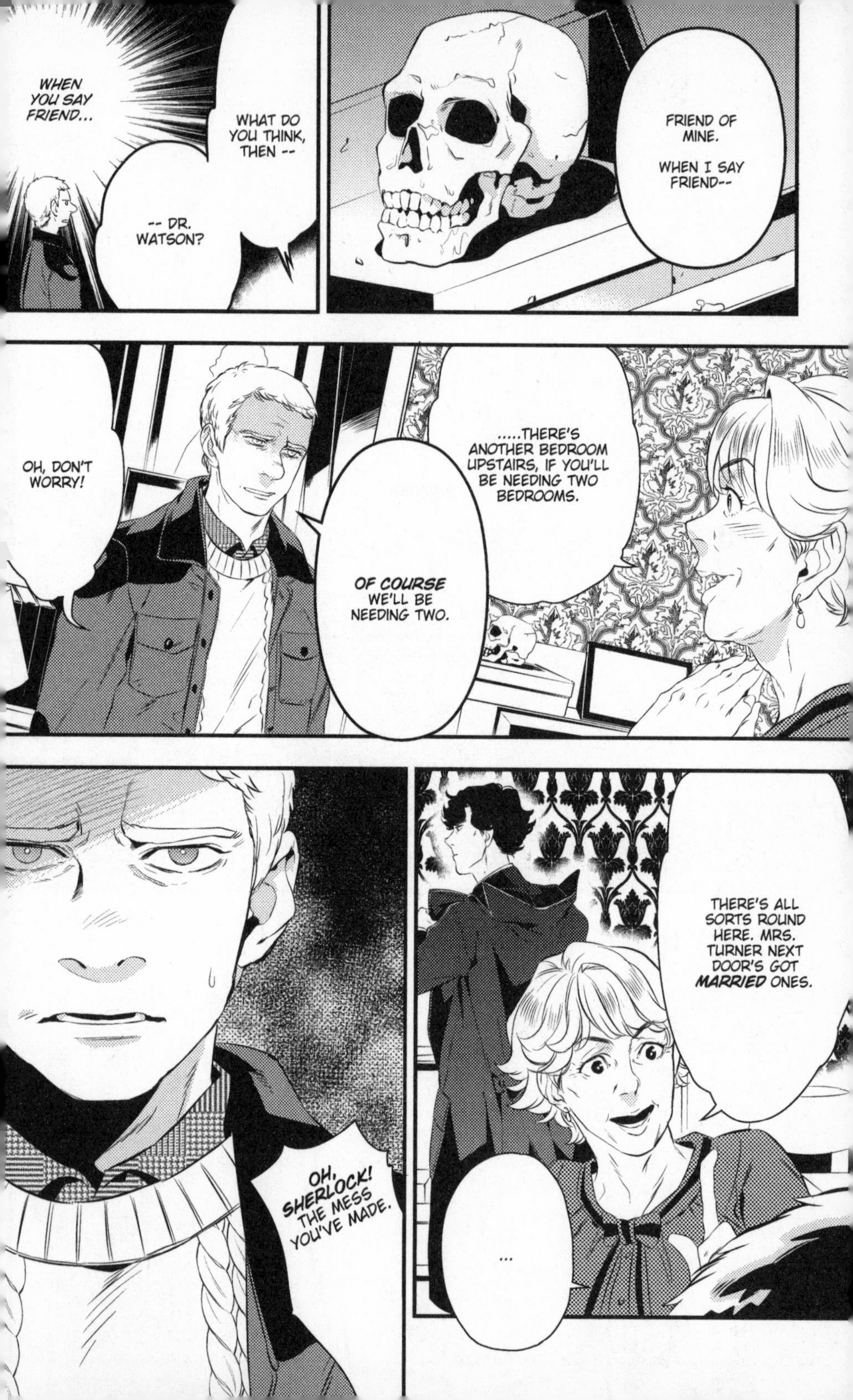
FRIEND OF MINE.
WHEN I SAY FRIEND--
WHAT DO YOU THINK, THEN --
-- DR. WATSON?
WHEN YOU SAY FRIEND...
.....THERE'S ANOTHER BEDROOM UPSTAIRS, IF YOU'LL BE NEEDING TWO BEDROOMS.
OF COURSE WE'LL BE NEEDING TWO.
OH, DON'T WORRY!
THERE'S ALL SORTS ROUND HERE. MRS. TURNER NEXT DOOR'S GOT MARRIED ONES.
...
OH, SHERLOCK! THE MESS YOU'VE MADE.

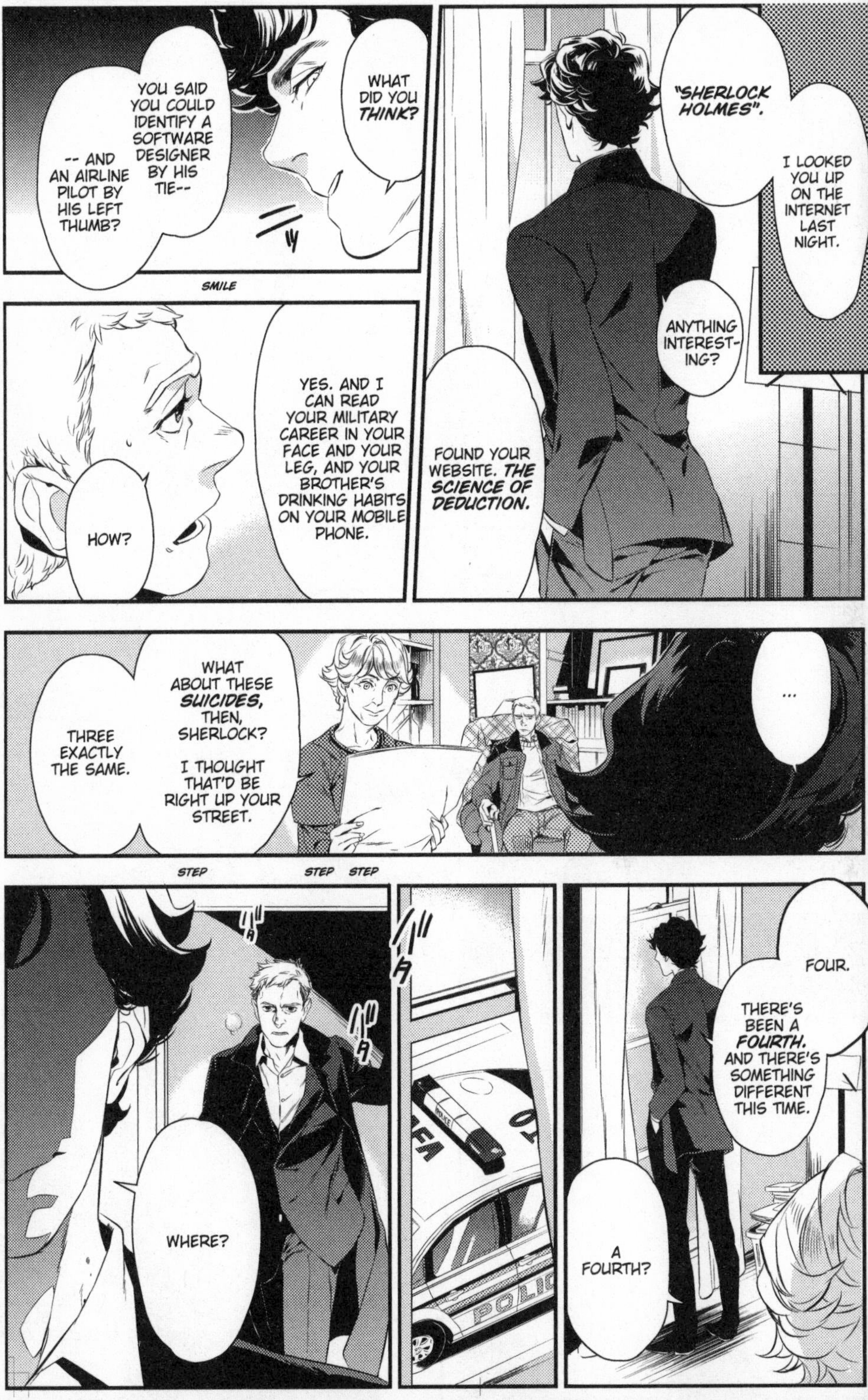
"SHERLOCK HOLMES".
I LOOKED YOU UP ON THE INTERNET LAST NIGHT.
ANYTHING INTERESTING?
FOUND YOUR WEBSITE. THE SCIENCE OF DEDUCTION.
WHAT DID YOU THINK?
YOU SAID YOU COULD IDENTIFY A SOFTWARE DESIGNER BY HIS TIE--
-- AND AN AIRLINE PILOT BY HIS LEFT THUMB?
SMILE
YES. AND I CAN READ YOUR MILITARY CAREER IN YOUR FACE AND YOUR LEG, AND YOUR BROTHER'S DRINKING HABITS ON YOUR MOBILE PHONE.
HOW?
...
WHAT ABOUT THESE SUICIDES, THEN, SHERLOCK?
I THOUGHT THAT'D BE RIGHT UP YOUR STREET.
THREE EXACTLY THE SAME.
STEP
STEP STEP
FOUR.
THERE'S BEEN A FOURTH. AND THERE'S SOMETHING DIFFERENT THIS TIME.
A FOURTH?
POLICE
WHERE?

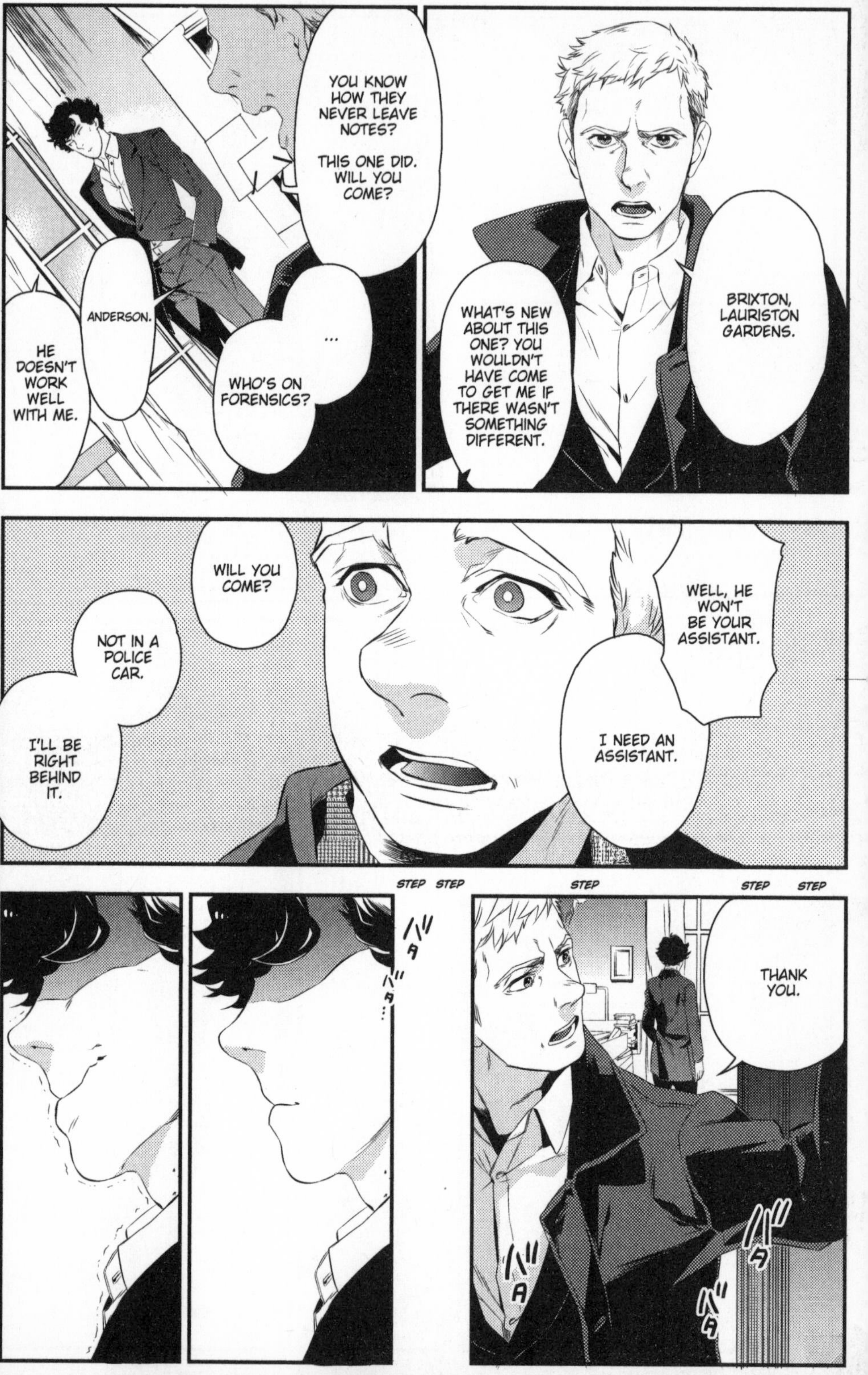
BRIXTON, LAURISTON GARDENS.
WHAT'S NEW ABOUT THIS ONE? YOU WOULDN'T HAVE COME TO GET ME IF THERE WASN'T SOMETHING DIFFERENT.
YOU KNOW HOW THEY NEVER LEAVE NOTES?
THIS ONE DID. WILL YOU COME?
...
WHO'S ON FORENSICS?
ANDERSON.
HE DOESN'T WORK WELL WITH ME.
WELL, HE WON'T BE YOUR ASSISTANT.
I NEED AN ASSISTANT.
WILL YOU COME?
NOT IN A POLICE CAR.
I'LL BE RIGHT BEHIND IT.
STEP STEP
STEP
THANK YOU.
STEP STEP

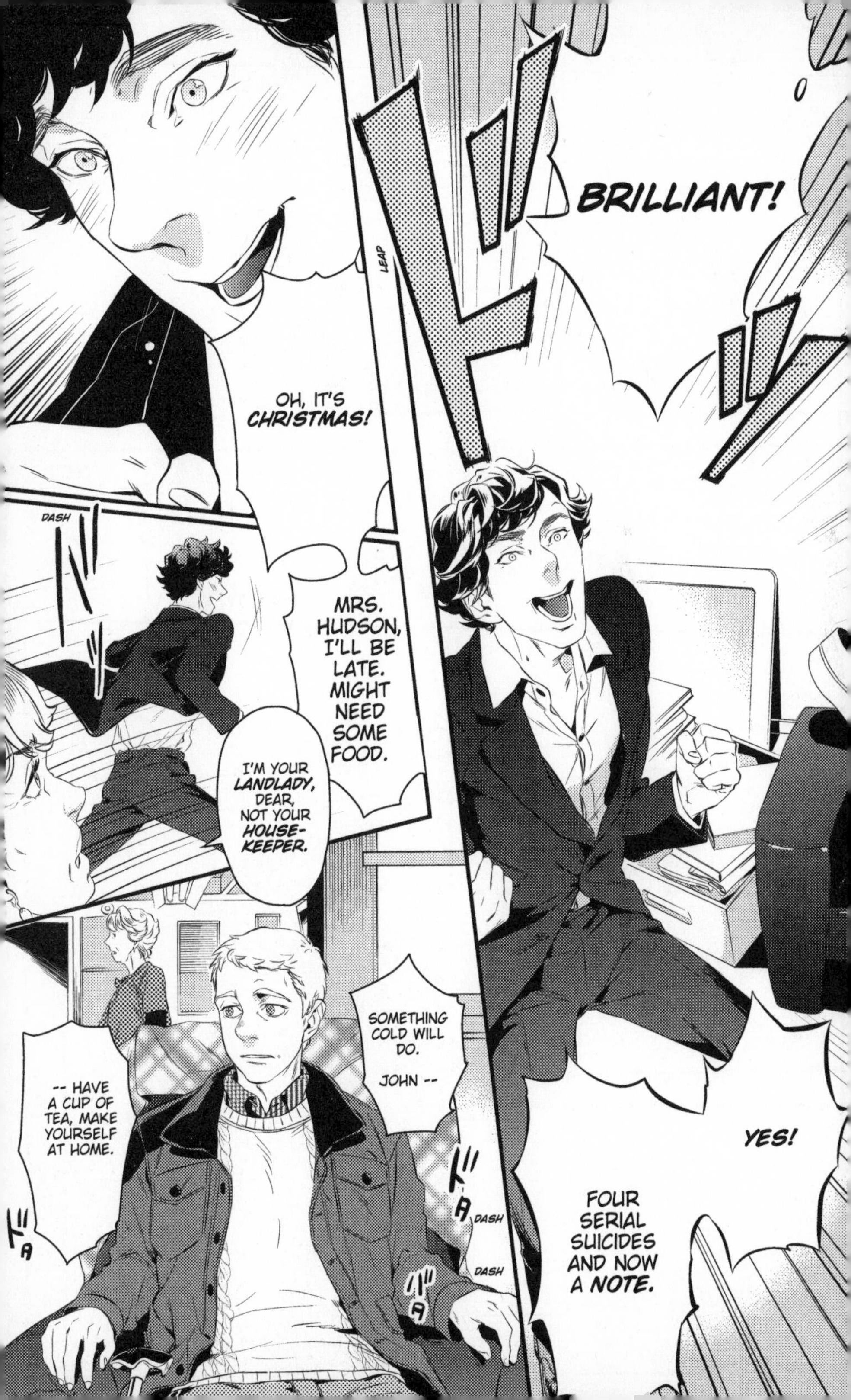
BRILLIANT!
LEAP
YES!
FOUR SERIAL SUICIDES AND NOW A NOTE.
OH, IT'S CHRISTMAS!
DASH
MRS. HUDSON, I'LL BE LATE. MIGHT NEED SOME FOOD.
I'M YOUR LANDLADY, DEAR, NOT YOUR HOUSE-KEEPER.
SOMETHING COLD WILL DO.
JOHN --
DASH
DASH
-- HAVE A CUP OF TEA, MAKE YOURSELF AT HOME.

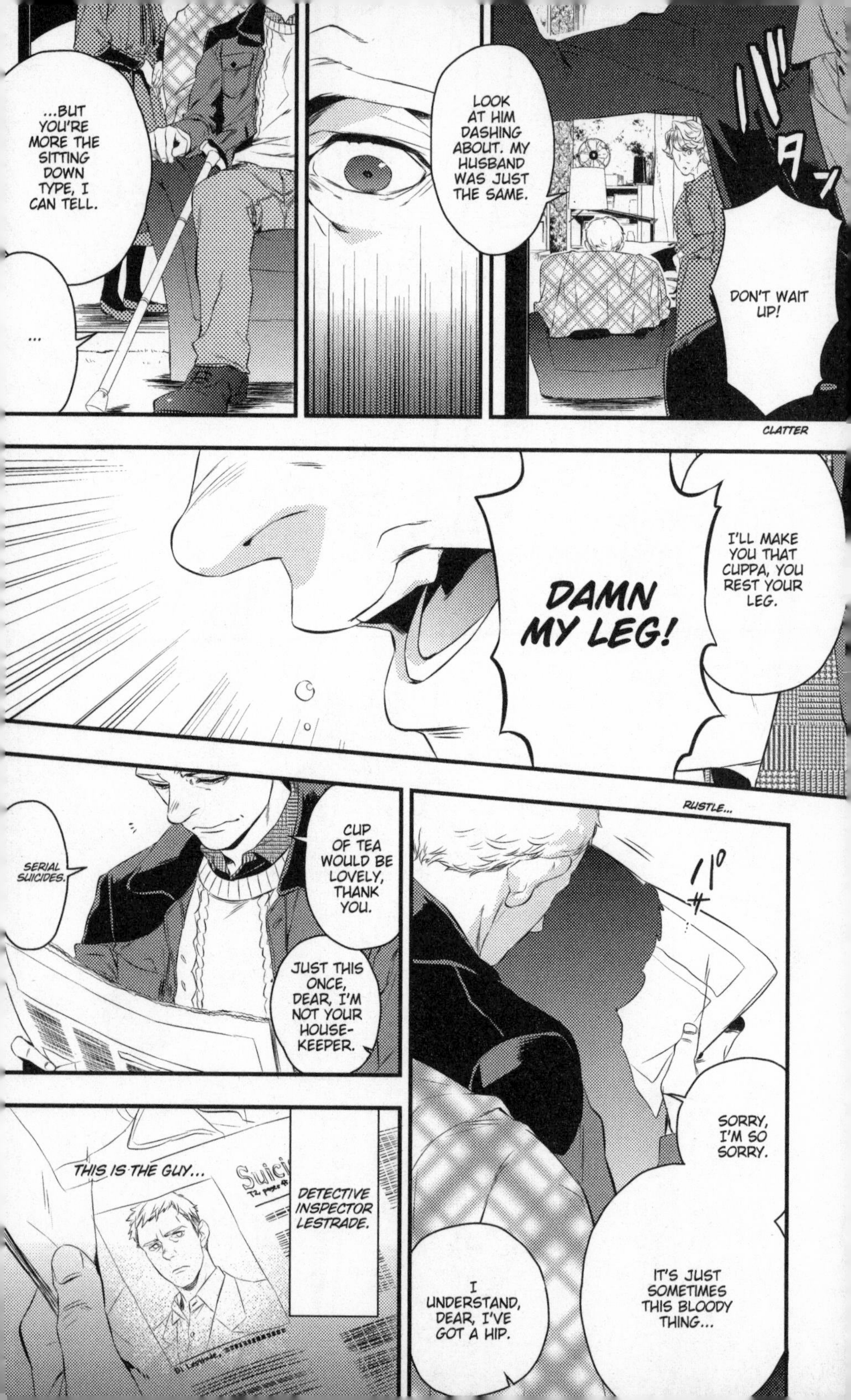
バタン
DON'T WAIT UP!
CLATTER
LOOK AT HIM DASHING ABOUT. MY HUSBAND WAS JUST THE SAME.
...BUT YOU'RE MORE THE SITTING DOWN TYPE, I CAN TELL.
...
I'LL MAKE YOU THAT CUPPA, YOU REST YOUR LEG.
DAMN MY LEG!
RUSTLE...
SORRY, I'M SO SORRY.
IT'S JUST SOMETIMES THIS BLOODY THING...
I UNDERSTAND, DEAR, I'VE GOT A HIP.
CUP OF TEA WOULD BE LOVELY, THANK YOU.
JUST THIS ONCE, DEAR, I'M NOT YOUR HOUSE-KEEPER.
SERIAL SUICIDES.
THIS IS THE GUY...
DETECTIVE INSPECTOR LESTRADE.

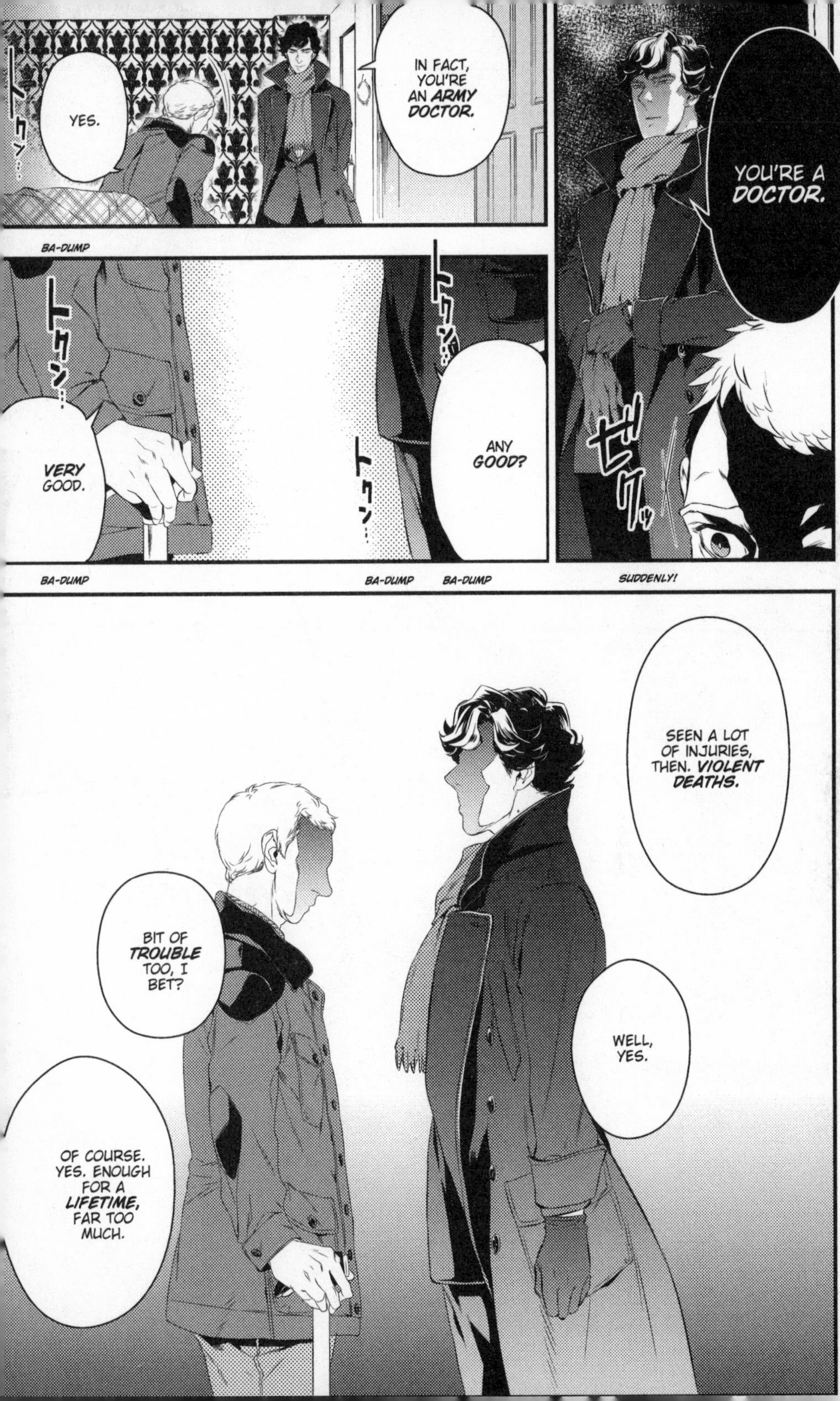
YOU'RE A DOCTOR.
ゼクッ
SUDDENLY!
IN FACT, YOU'RE AN ARMY DOCTOR.
YES.
トクン…
BA-DUMP
ANY GOOD?
トクン…
トクン…
BA-DUMP
BA-DUMP
VERY GOOD.
トクン…
BA-DUMP
SEEN A LOT OF INJURIES, THEN. VIOLENT DEATHS.
WELL, YES.
BIT OF TROUBLE TOO, I BET?
OF COURSE. YES. ENOUGH FOR A LIFETIME, FAR TOO MUCH.

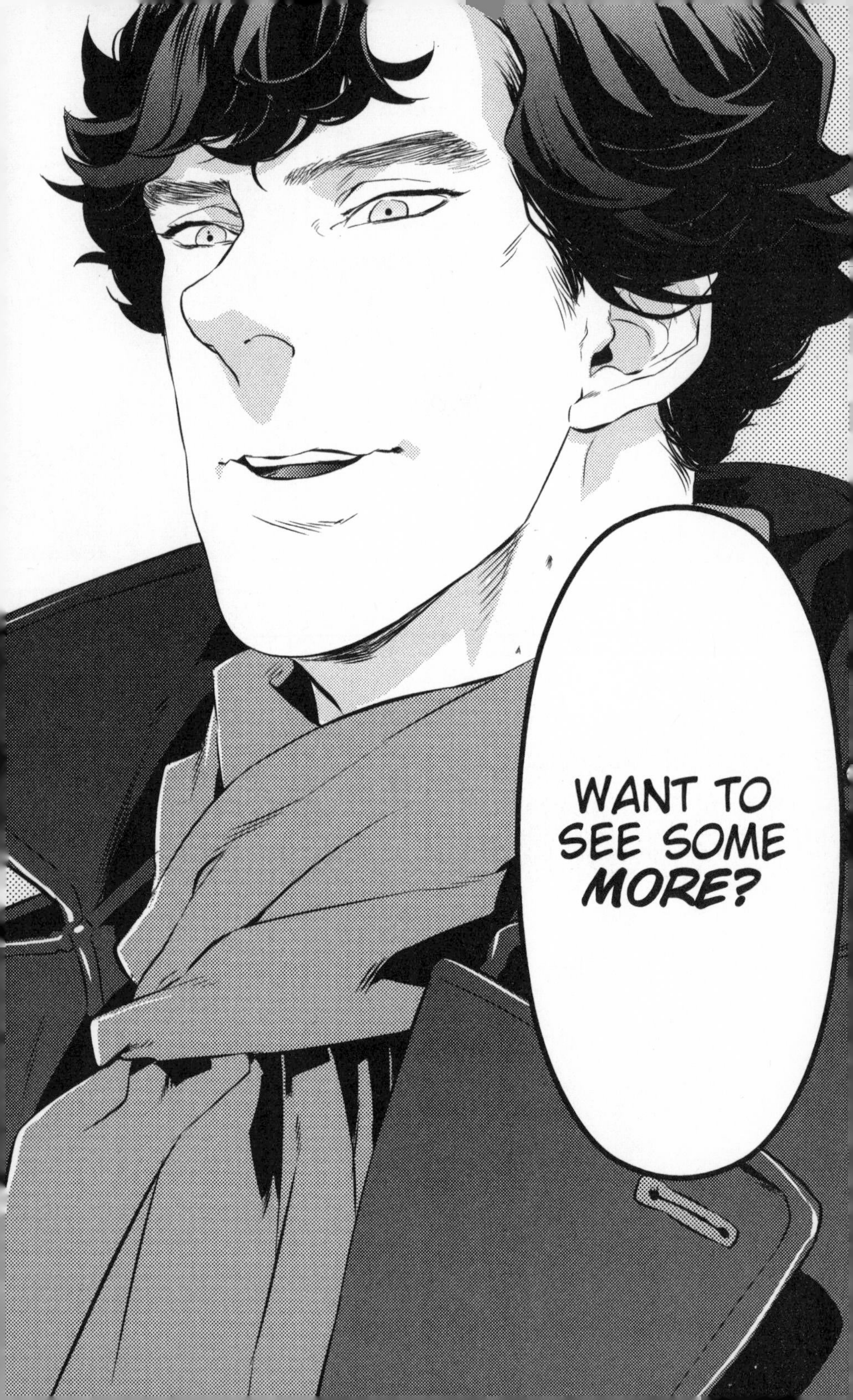
WANT TO SEE SOME *MORE?*

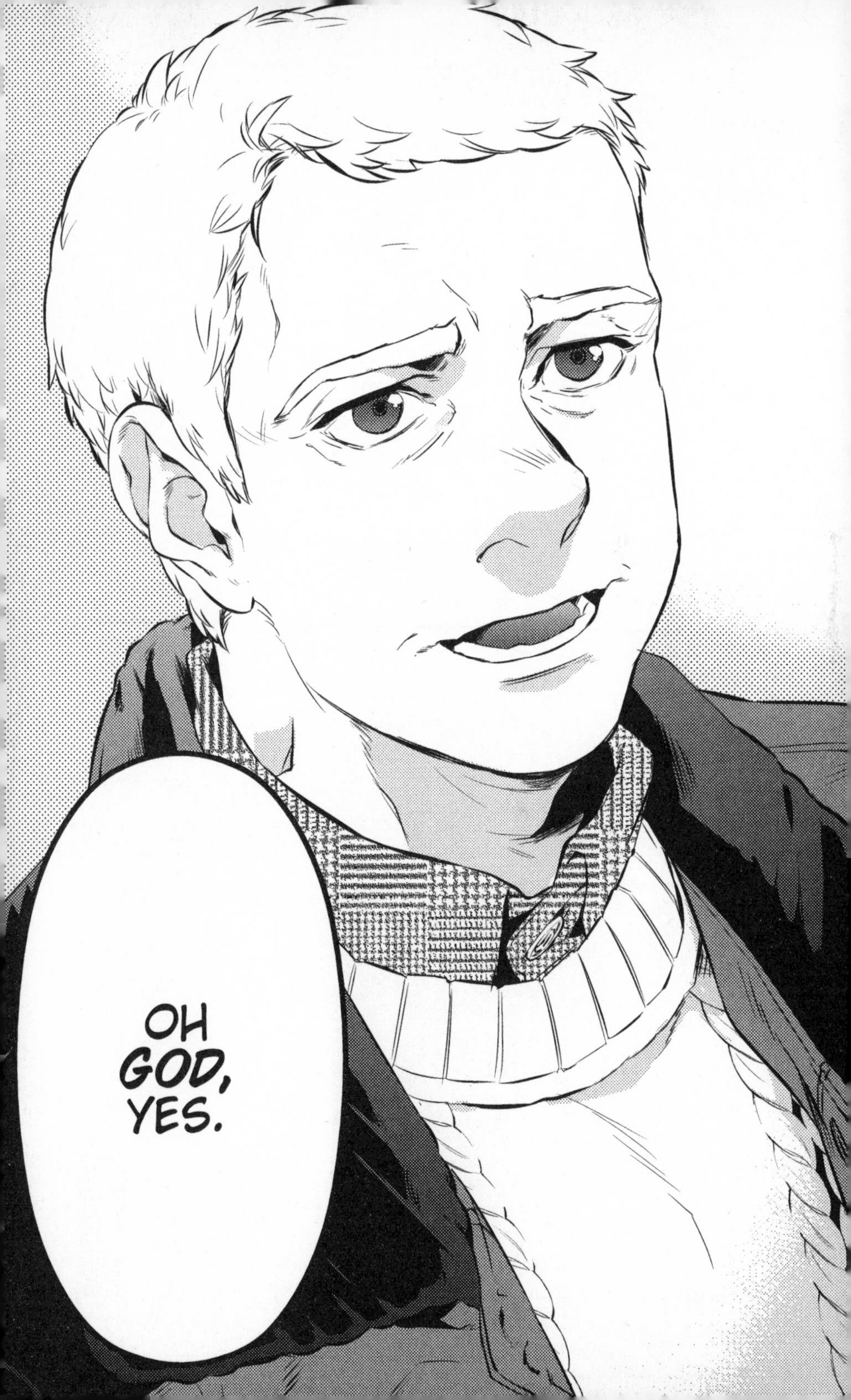
OH GOD, YES.

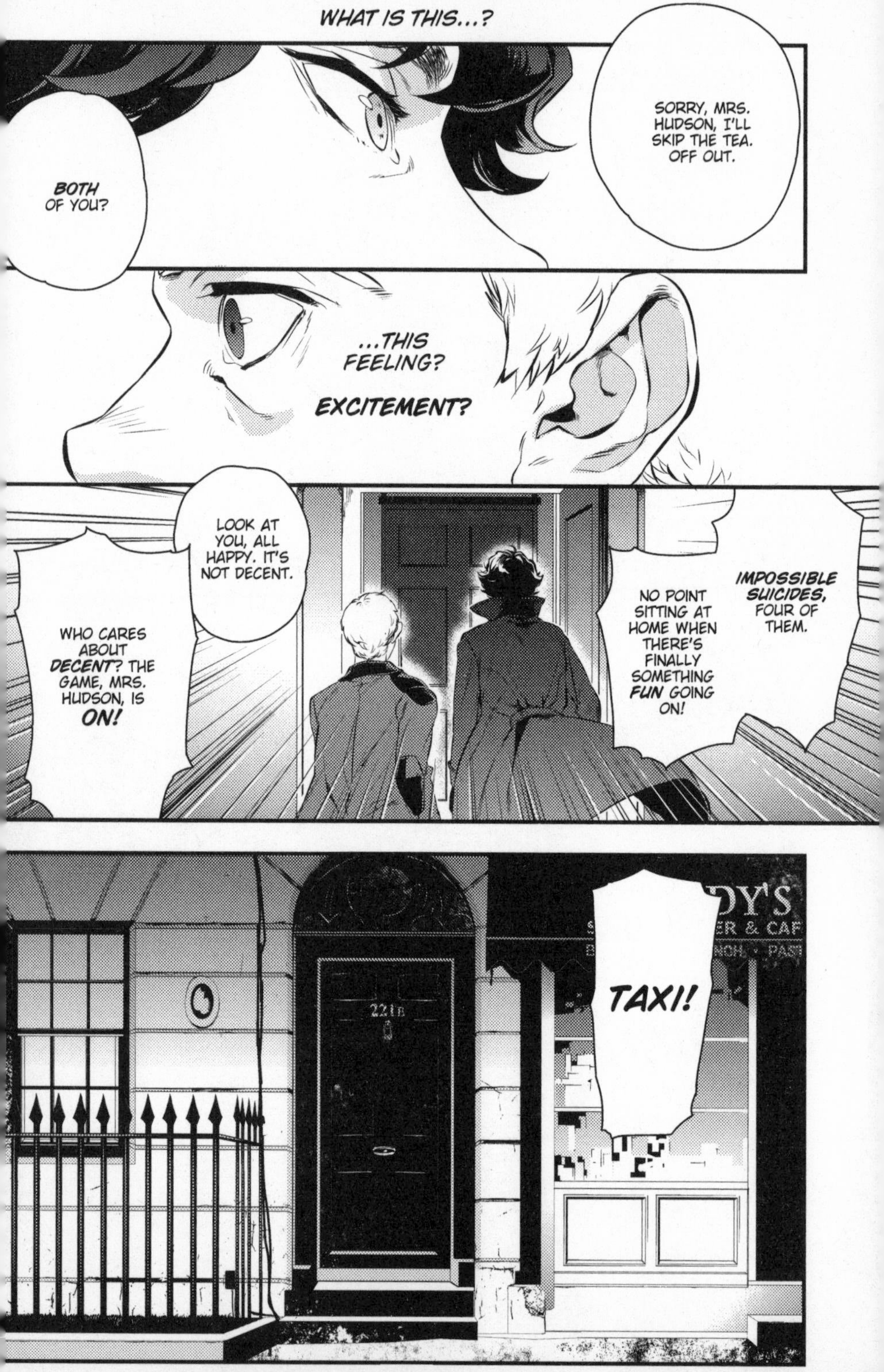
WHAT IS THIS...?
SORRY, MRS. HUDSON, I'LL SKIP THE TEA. OFF OUT.
BOTH OF YOU?
...THIS FEELING?
EXCITEMENT?
IMPOSSIBLE SUICIDES, FOUR OF THEM.
NO POINT SITTING AT HOME WHEN THERE'S FINALLY SOMETHING FUN GOING ON!
LOOK AT YOU, ALL HAPPY. IT'S NOT DECENT.
WHO CARES ABOUT DECENT? THE GAME, MRS. HUDSON, IS ON!
TAXI!
221B

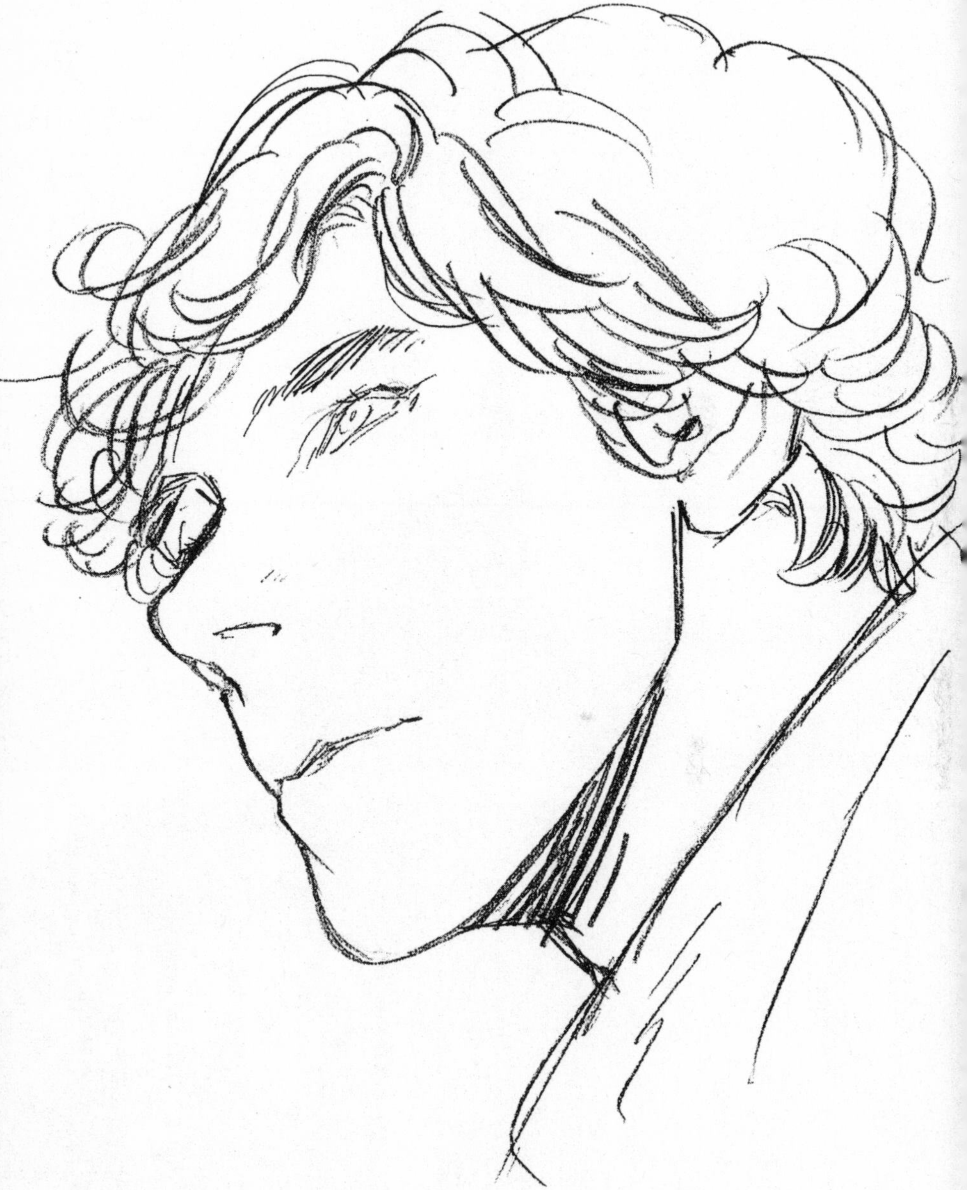

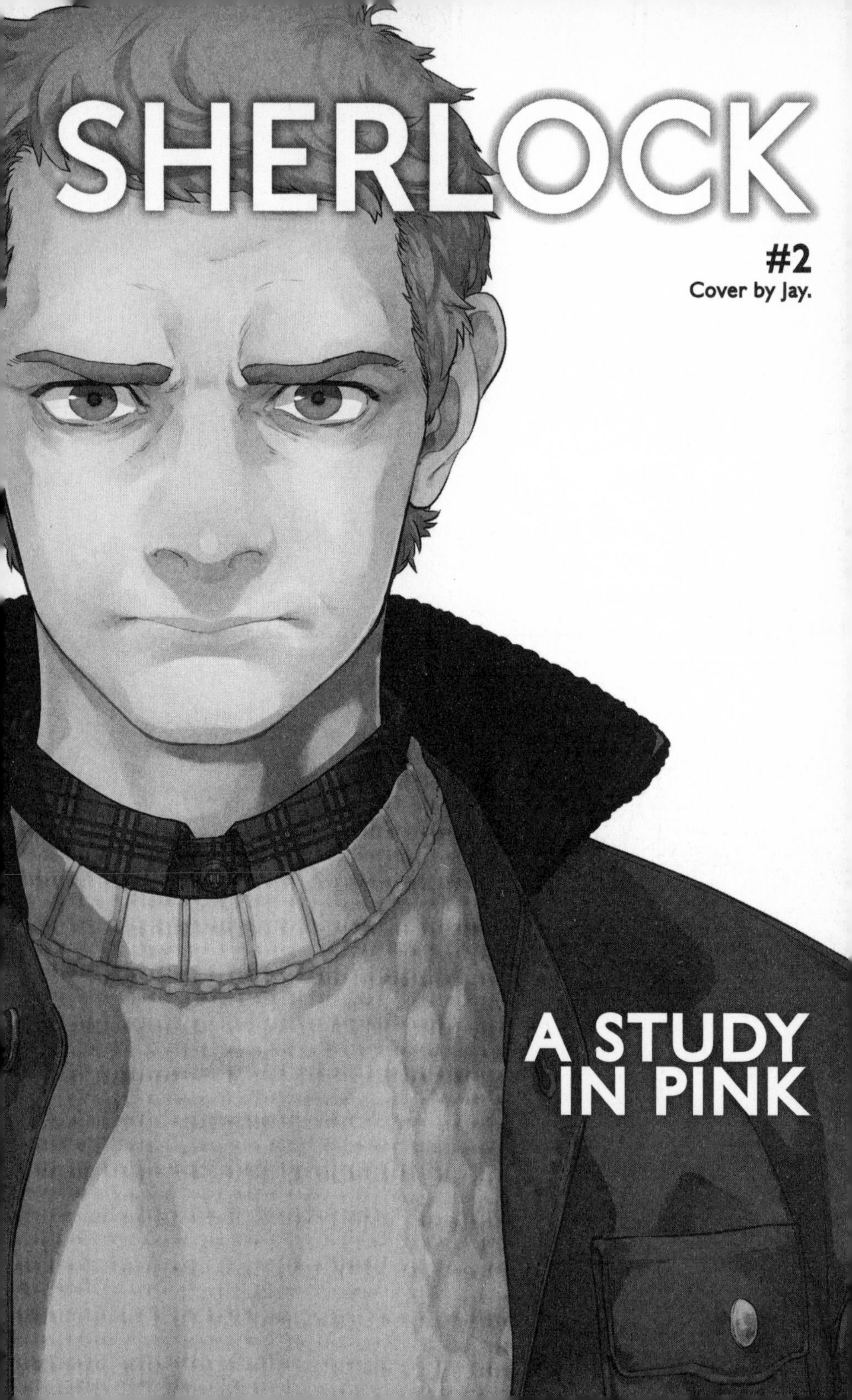
SHERLOCK
#2
Cover by Jay.
A STUDY IN PINK

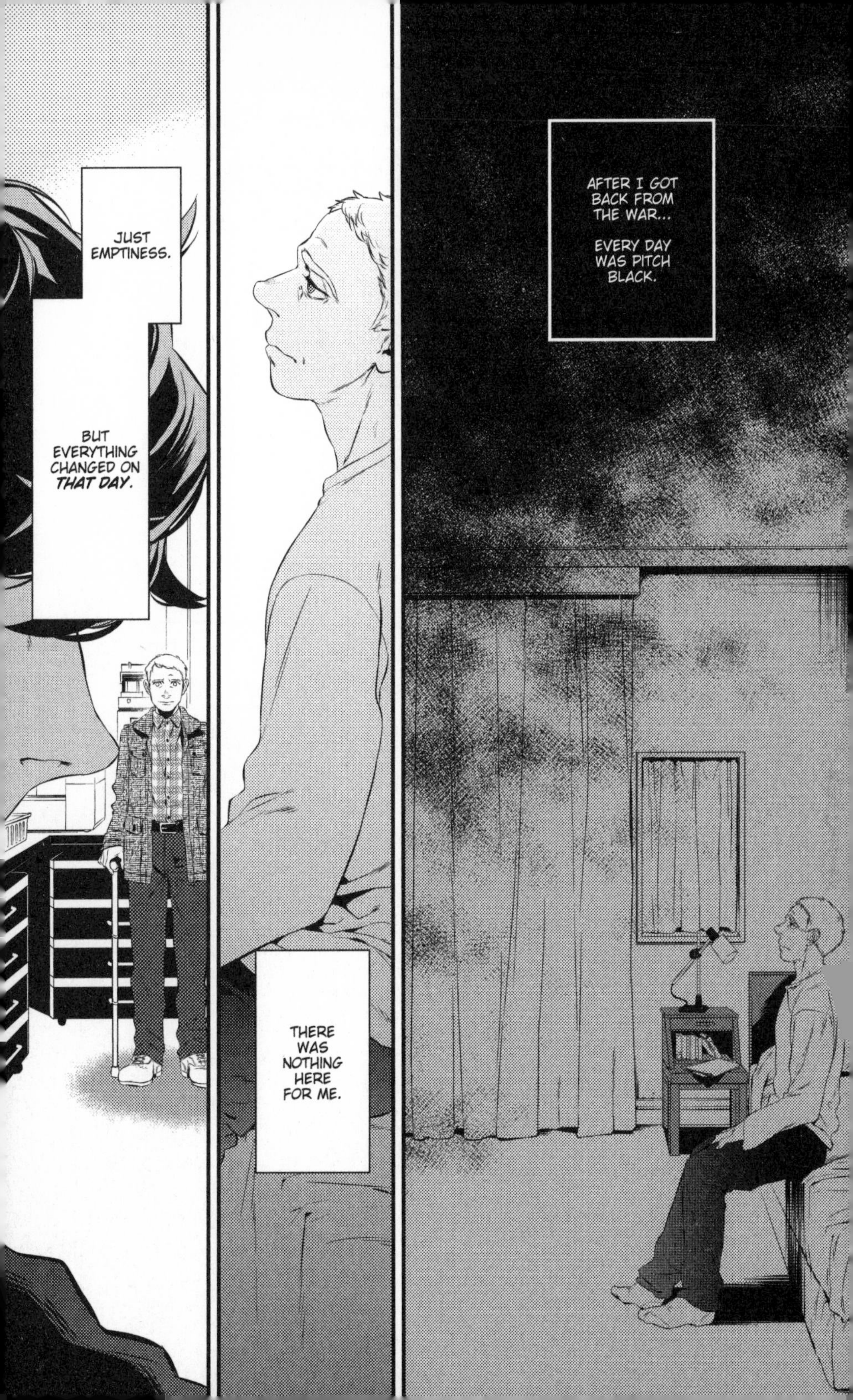
AFTER I GOT BACK FROM THE WAR...
EVERY DAY WAS PITCH BLACK.
THERE WAS NOTHING HERE FOR ME.
JUST EMPTINESS.
BUT EVERYTHING CHANGED ON *THAT DAY*.

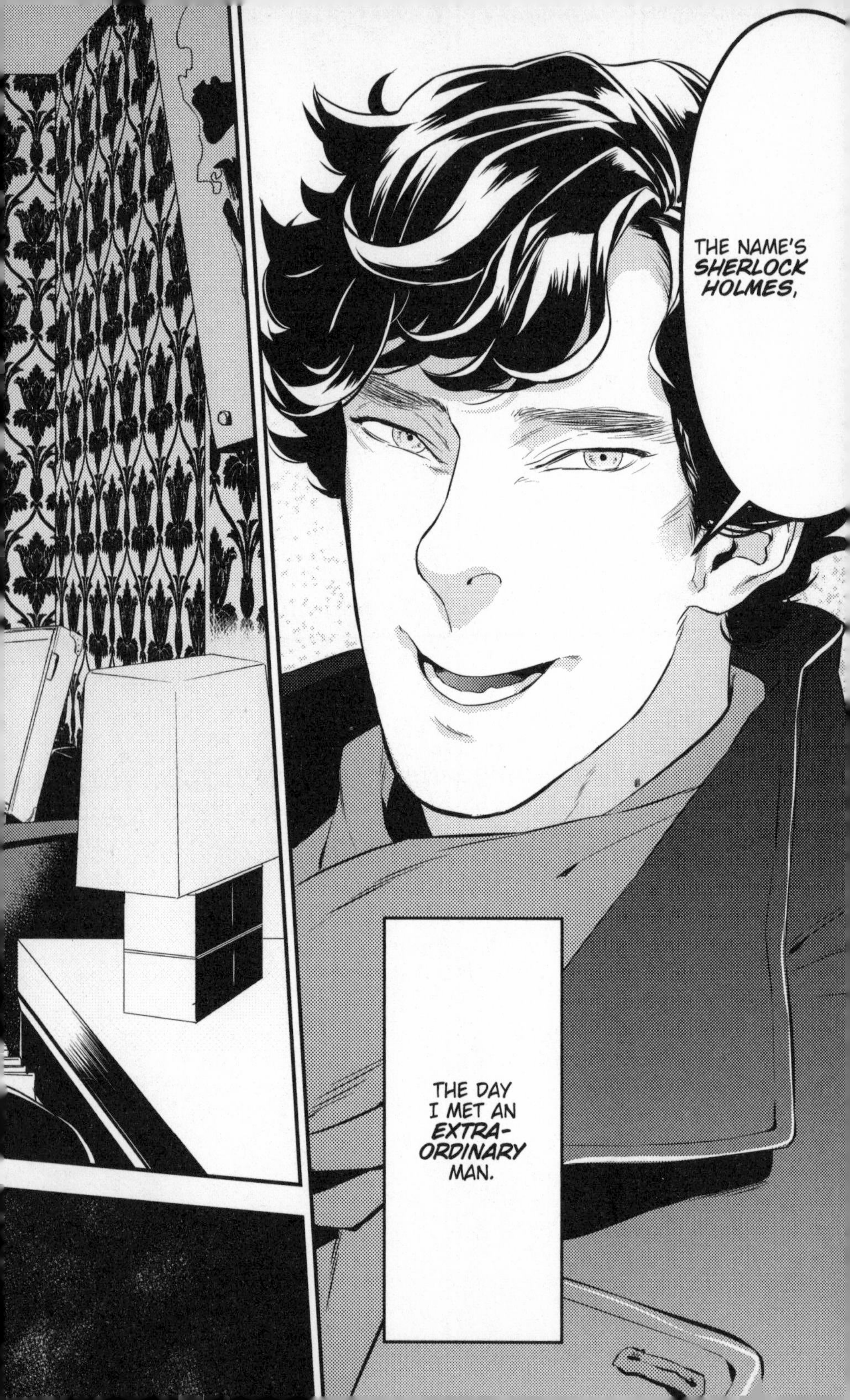
THE NAME'S *SHERLOCK HOLMES.*
THE DAY I MET AN *EXTRA-ORDINARY* MAN.

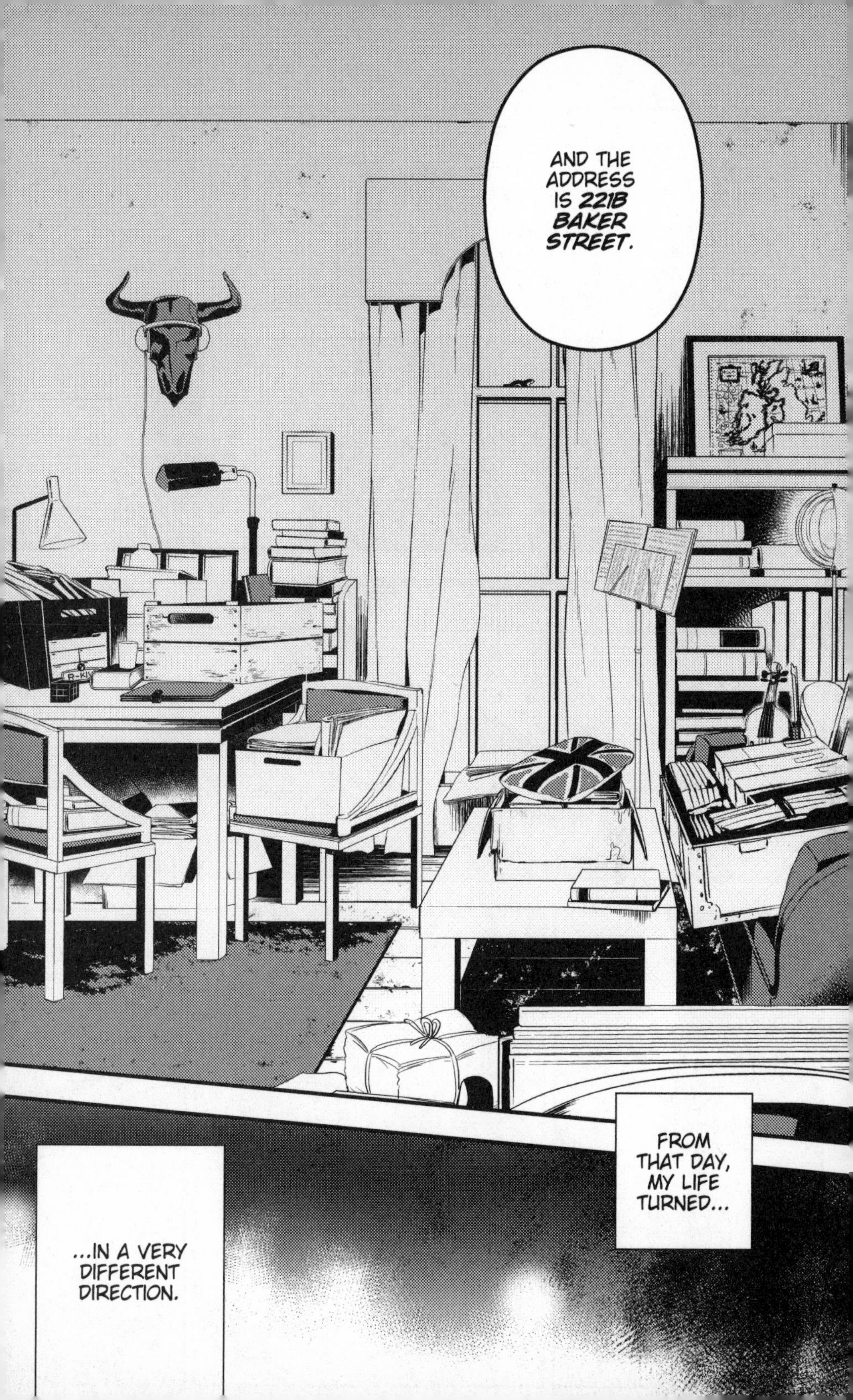
AND THE ADDRESS IS 221B BAKER STREET.
FROM THAT DAY, MY LIFE TURNED...
...IN A VERY DIFFERENT DIRECTION.

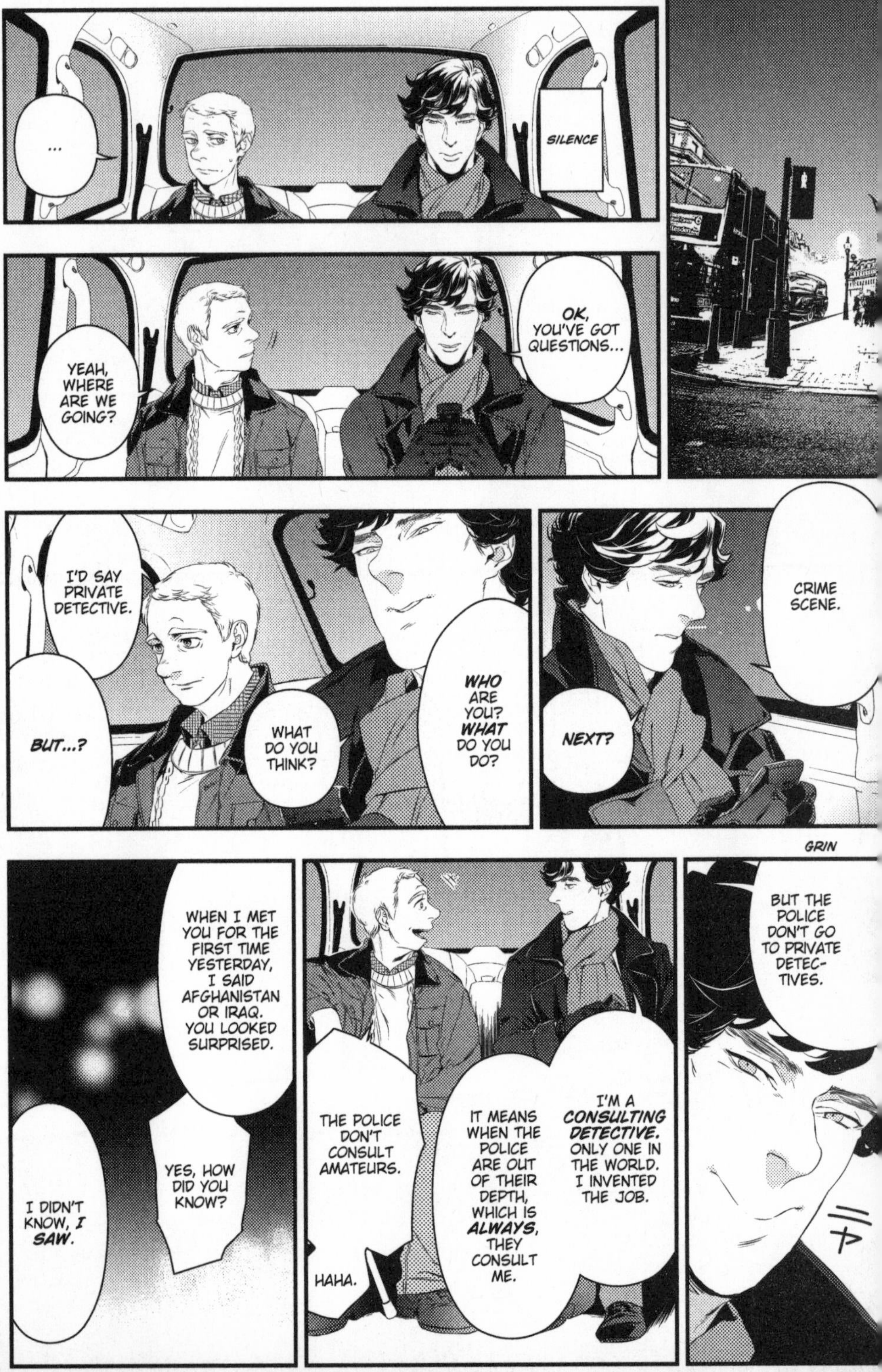
SILENCE
...
OK, YOU'VE GOT QUESTIONS...
YEAH, WHERE ARE WE GOING?
CRIME SCENE.
NEXT?
WHO ARE YOU? WHAT DO YOU DO?
WHAT DO YOU THINK?
I'D SAY PRIVATE DETECTIVE.
BUT...?
GRIN
BUT THE POLICE DON'T GO TO PRIVATE DETEC-TIVES.
ニヤ
I'M A CONSULTING DETECTIVE. ONLY ONE IN THE WORLD. I INVENTED THE JOB.
IT MEANS WHEN THE POLICE ARE OUT OF THEIR DEPTH, WHICH IS ALWAYS, THEY CONSULT ME.
THE POLICE DON'T CONSULT AMATEURS.
HAHA.
WHEN I MET YOU FOR THE FIRST TIME YESTERDAY, I SAID AFGHANISTAN OR IRAQ. YOU LOOKED SURPRISED.
YES, HOW DID YOU KNOW?
I DIDN'T KNOW, I SAW.

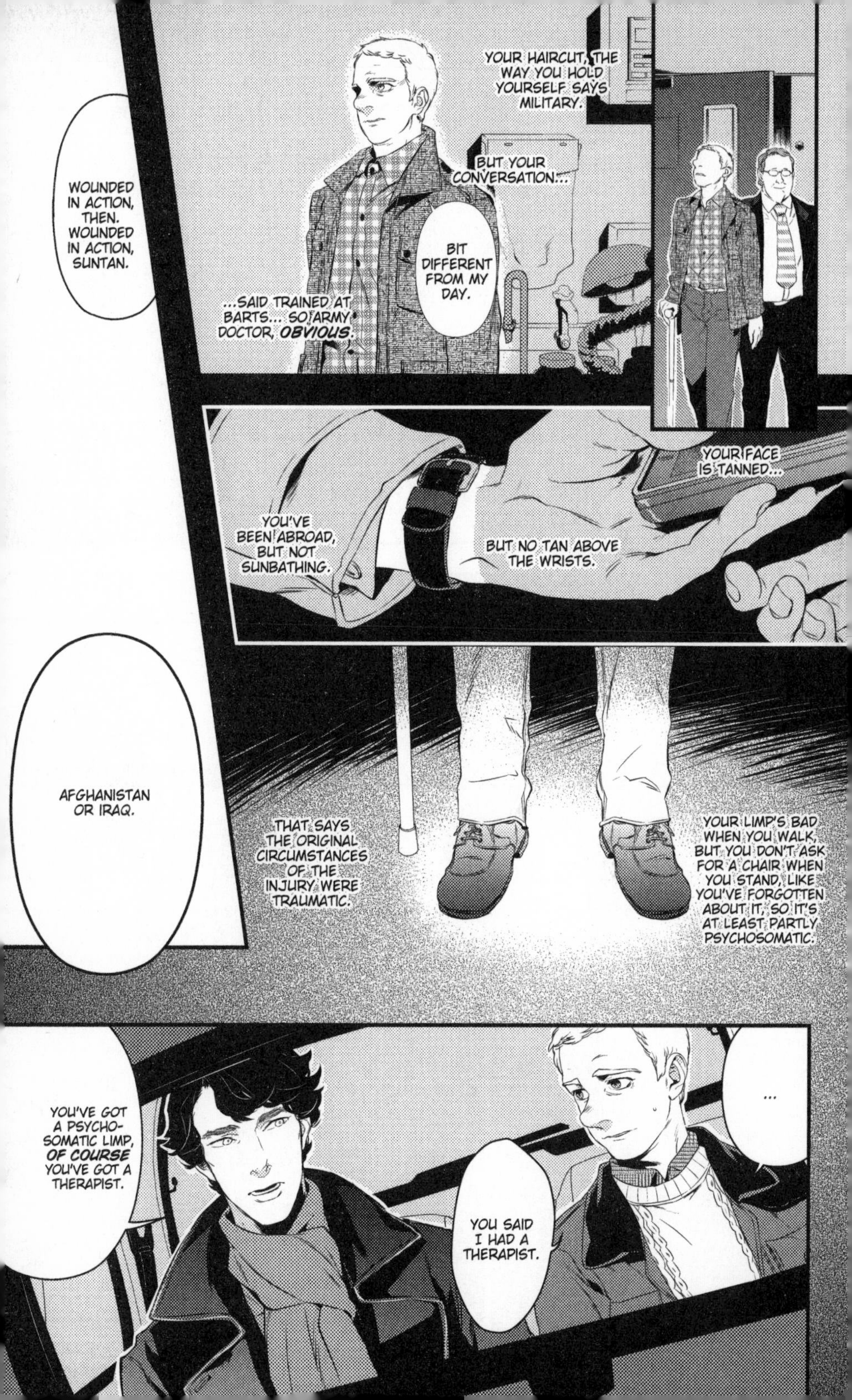
YOUR HAIRCUT, THE WAY YOU HOLD YOURSELF SAYS MILITARY.
BUT YOUR CONVERSATION...
BIT DIFFERENT FROM MY DAY.
...SAID TRAINED AT BARTS... SO ARMY DOCTOR, **OBVIOUS**.
WOUNDED IN ACTION, THEN. WOUNDED IN ACTION, SUNTAN.
YOUR FACE IS TANNED...
BUT NO TAN ABOVE THE WRISTS.
YOU'VE BEEN ABROAD, BUT NOT SUNBATHING.
YOUR LIMP'S BAD WHEN YOU WALK, BUT YOU DON'T ASK FOR A CHAIR WHEN YOU STAND, LIKE YOU'VE FORGOTTEN ABOUT IT, SO IT'S AT LEAST PARTLY PSYCHOSOMATIC.
THAT SAYS THE ORIGINAL CIRCUMSTANCES OF THE INJURY WERE TRAUMATIC.
AFGHANISTAN OR IRAQ.
...
YOU SAID I HAD A THERAPIST.
YOU'VE GOT A PSYCHO-SOMATIC LIMP, **OF COURSE** YOU'VE GOT A THERAPIST.

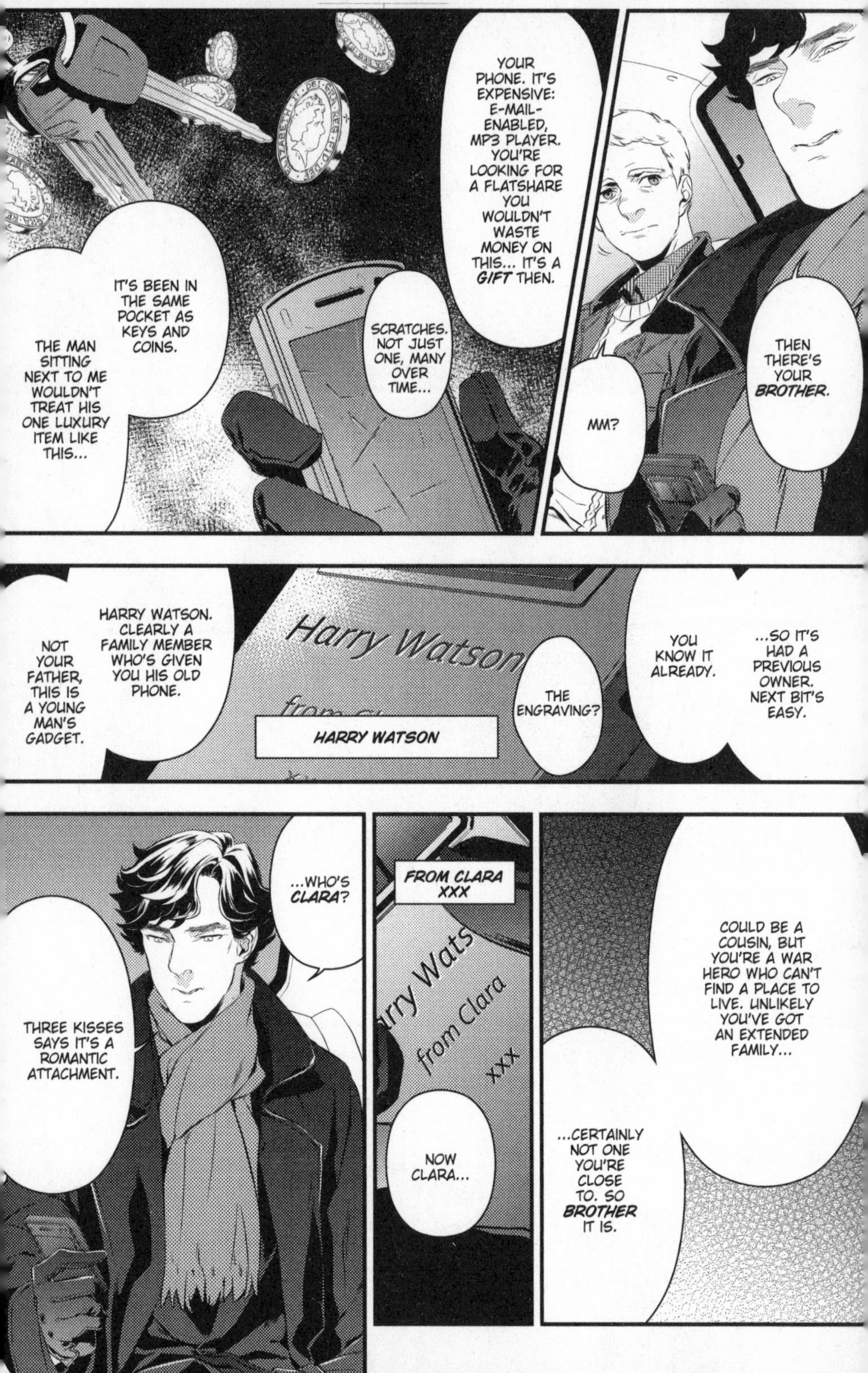
YOUR PHONE. IT'S EXPENSIVE: E-MAIL-ENABLED, MP3 PLAYER. YOU'RE LOOKING FOR A FLATSHARE YOU WOULDN'T WASTE MONEY ON THIS... IT'S A *GIFT* THEN.
SCRATCHES. NOT JUST ONE, MANY OVER TIME...
IT'S BEEN IN THE SAME POCKET AS KEYS AND COINS.
THE MAN SITTING NEXT TO ME WOULDN'T TREAT HIS ONE LUXURY ITEM LIKE THIS...
THEN THERE'S YOUR *BROTHER*.
MM?
...SO IT'S HAD A PREVIOUS OWNER. NEXT BIT'S EASY.
YOU KNOW IT ALREADY.
THE ENGRAVING?
Harry Watson
HARRY WATSON
HARRY WATSON. CLEARLY A FAMILY MEMBER WHO'S GIVEN YOU HIS OLD PHONE.
NOT YOUR FATHER, THIS IS A YOUNG MAN'S GADGET.
COULD BE A COUSIN, BUT YOU'RE A WAR HERO WHO CAN'T FIND A PLACE TO LIVE. UNLIKELY YOU'VE GOT AN EXTENDED FAMILY...
...CERTAINLY NOT ONE YOU'RE CLOSE TO. SO *BROTHER* IT IS.
FROM CLARA XXX
from Clara
xxx
NOW CLARA...
...WHO'S *CLARA*?
THREE KISSES SAYS IT'S A ROMANTIC ATTACHMENT.

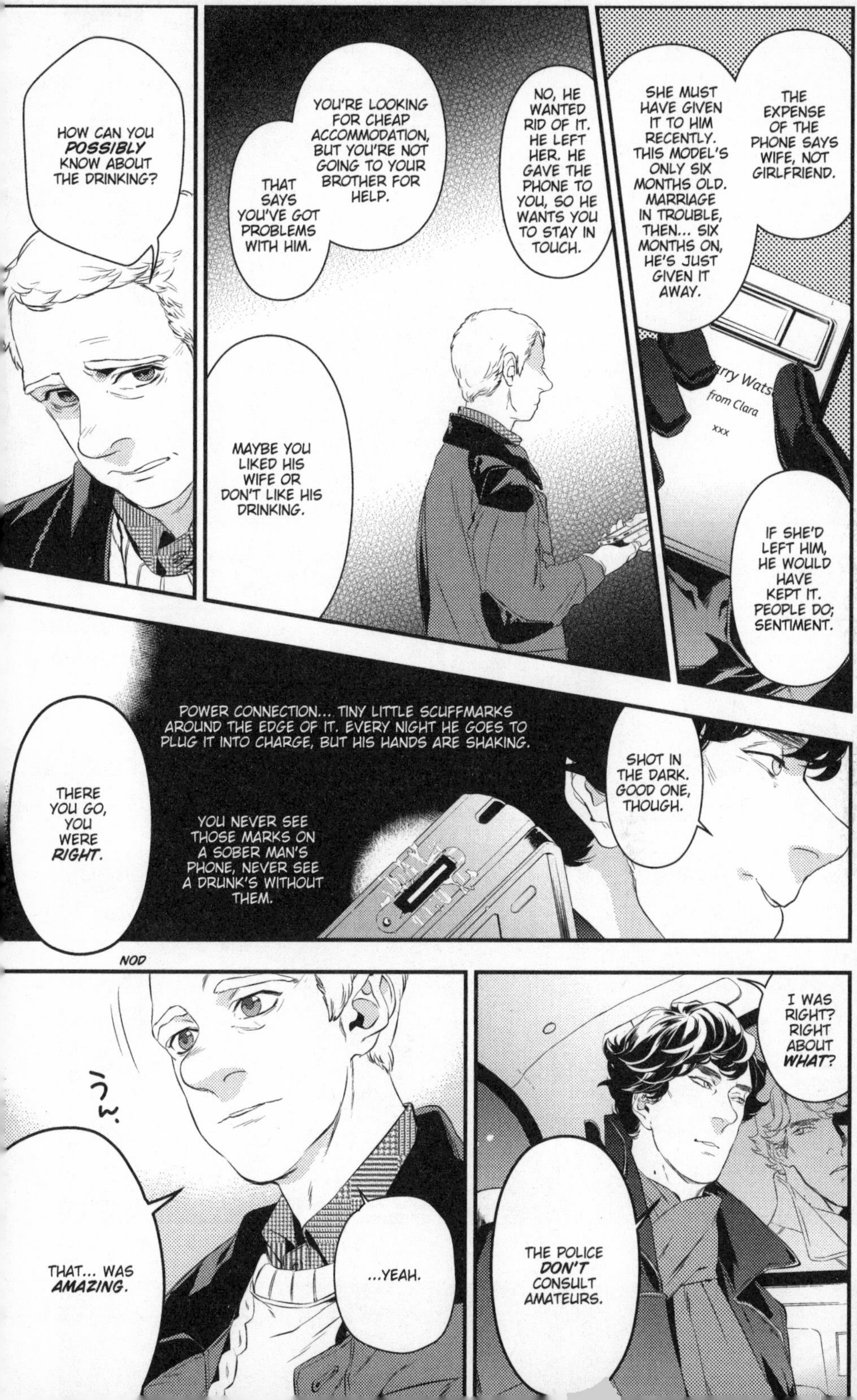
THE EXPENSE OF THE PHONE SAYS WIFE, NOT GIRLFRIEND.
SHE MUST HAVE GIVEN IT TO HIM RECENTLY. THIS MODEL'S ONLY SIX MONTHS OLD. MARRIAGE IN TROUBLE, THEN... SIX MONTHS ON, HE'S JUST GIVEN IT AWAY.
arry Wats
from Clara
xxx
IF SHE'D LEFT HIM, HE WOULD HAVE KEPT IT. PEOPLE DO; SENTIMENT.
NO, HE WANTED RID OF IT. HE LEFT HER. HE GAVE THE PHONE TO YOU, SO HE WANTS YOU TO STAY IN TOUCH.
YOU'RE LOOKING FOR CHEAP ACCOMMODATION, BUT YOU'RE NOT GOING TO YOUR BROTHER FOR HELP.
THAT SAYS YOU'VE GOT PROBLEMS WITH HIM.
MAYBE YOU LIKED HIS WIFE OR DON'T LIKE HIS DRINKING.
HOW CAN YOU ***POSSIBLY*** KNOW ABOUT THE DRINKING?
SHOT IN THE DARK. GOOD ONE, THOUGH.
POWER CONNECTION... TINY LITTLE SCUFFMARKS AROUND THE EDGE OF IT. EVERY NIGHT HE GOES TO PLUG IT INTO CHARGE, BUT HIS HANDS ARE SHAKING.
YOU NEVER SEE THOSE MARKS ON A SOBER MAN'S PHONE, NEVER SEE A DRUNK'S WITHOUT THEM.
THERE YOU GO, YOU WERE ***RIGHT***.
I WAS RIGHT? RIGHT ABOUT ***WHAT***?
THE POLICE ***DON'T*** CONSULT AMATEURS.
NOD
うん
...YEAH.
THAT... WAS ***AMAZING***.

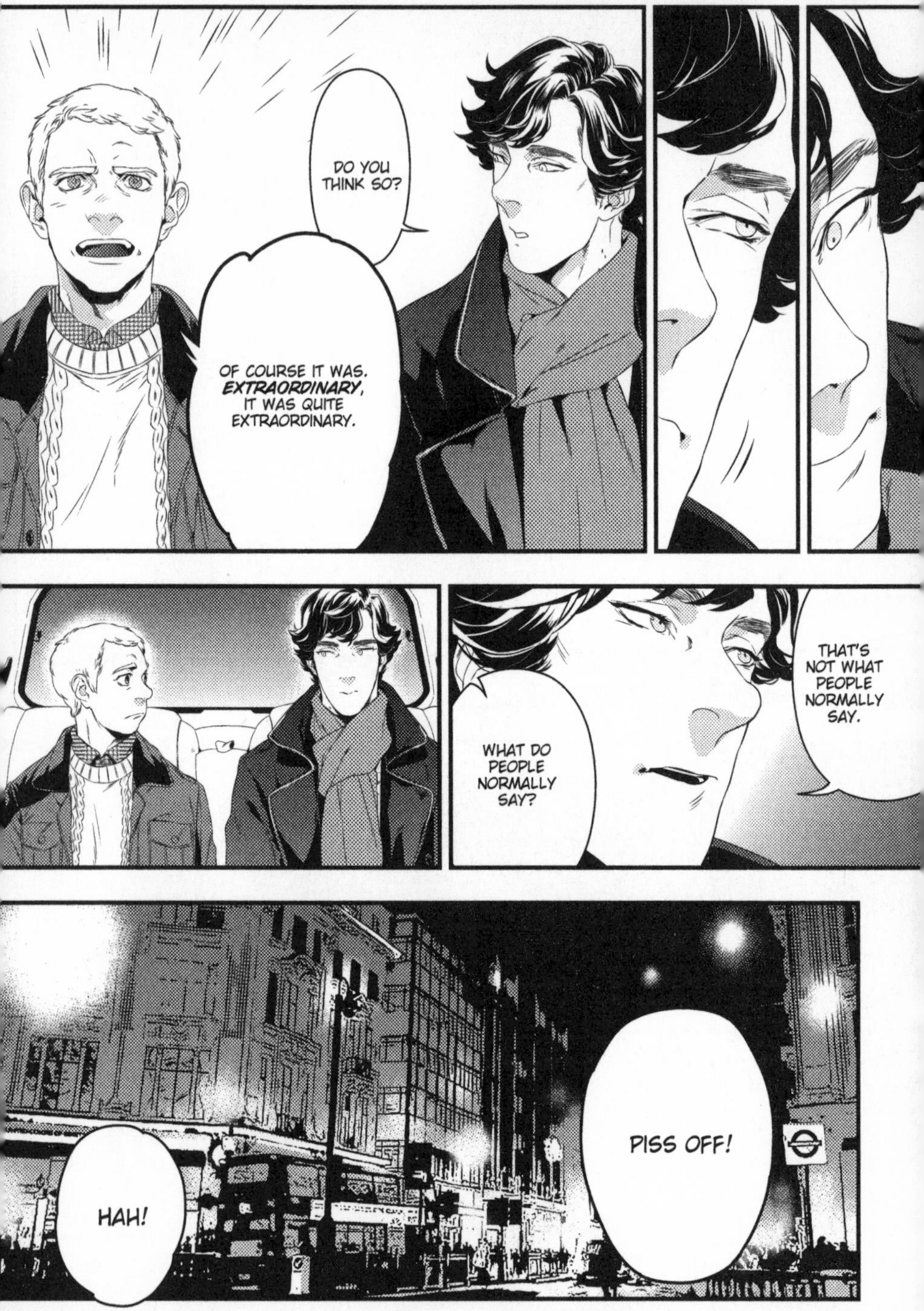
DO YOU THINK SO?
OF COURSE IT WAS. EXTRAORDINARY, IT WAS QUITE EXTRAORDINARY.
THAT'S NOT WHAT PEOPLE NORMALLY SAY.
WHAT DO PEOPLE NORMALLY SAY?
PISS OFF!
HAH!

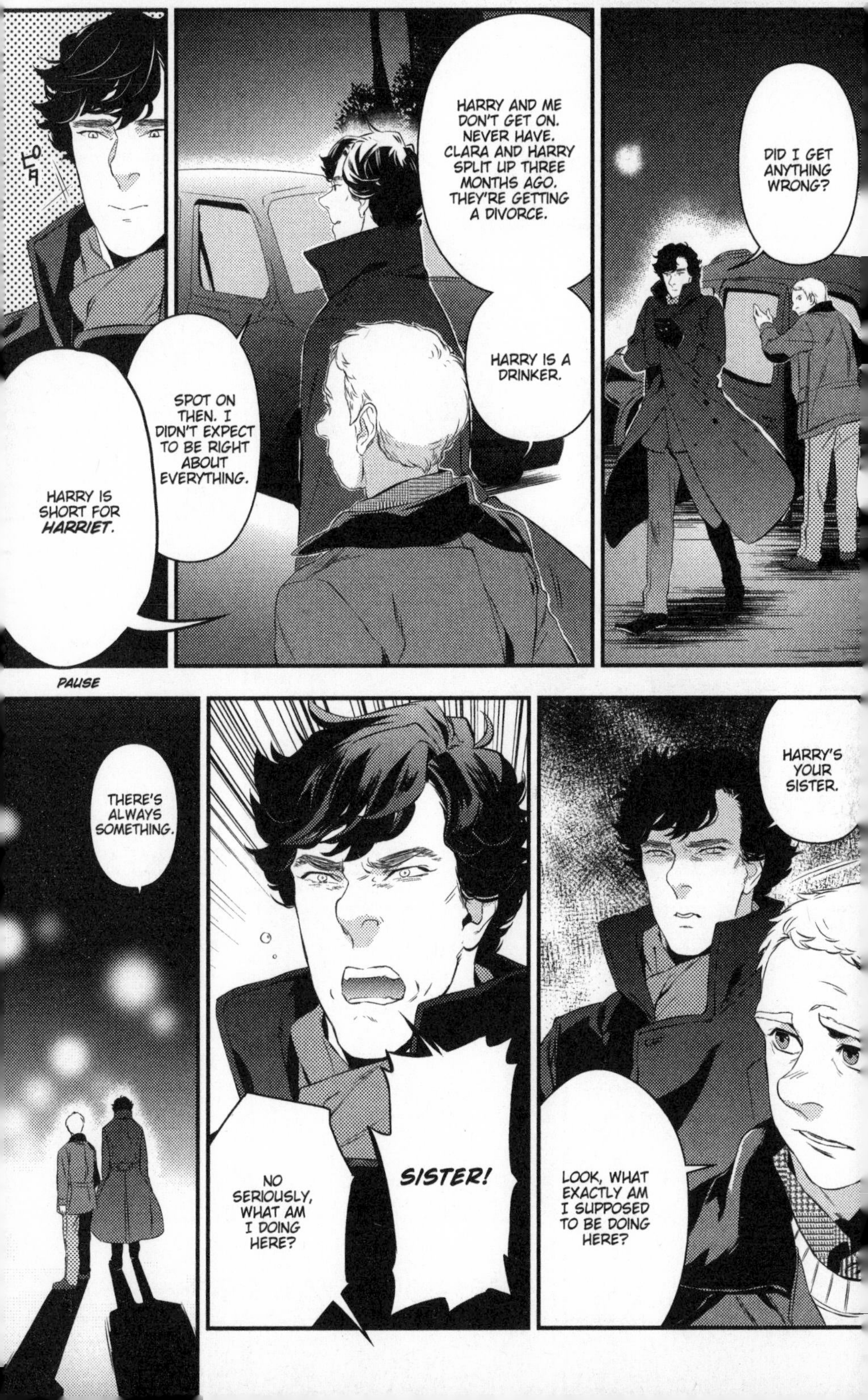
DID I GET ANYTHING WRONG?
HARRY AND ME DON'T GET ON. NEVER HAVE. CLARA AND HARRY SPLIT UP THREE MONTHS AGO. THEY'RE GETTING A DIVORCE.
HARRY IS A DRINKER.
ピク
SPOT ON THEN. I DIDN'T EXPECT TO BE RIGHT ABOUT EVERYTHING.
HARRY IS SHORT FOR *HARRIET*.
PAUSE
HARRY'S YOUR SISTER.
LOOK, WHAT EXACTLY AM I SUPPOSED TO BE DOING HERE?
SISTER!
NO SERIOUSLY, WHAT AM I DOING HERE?
THERE'S ALWAYS SOMETHING.

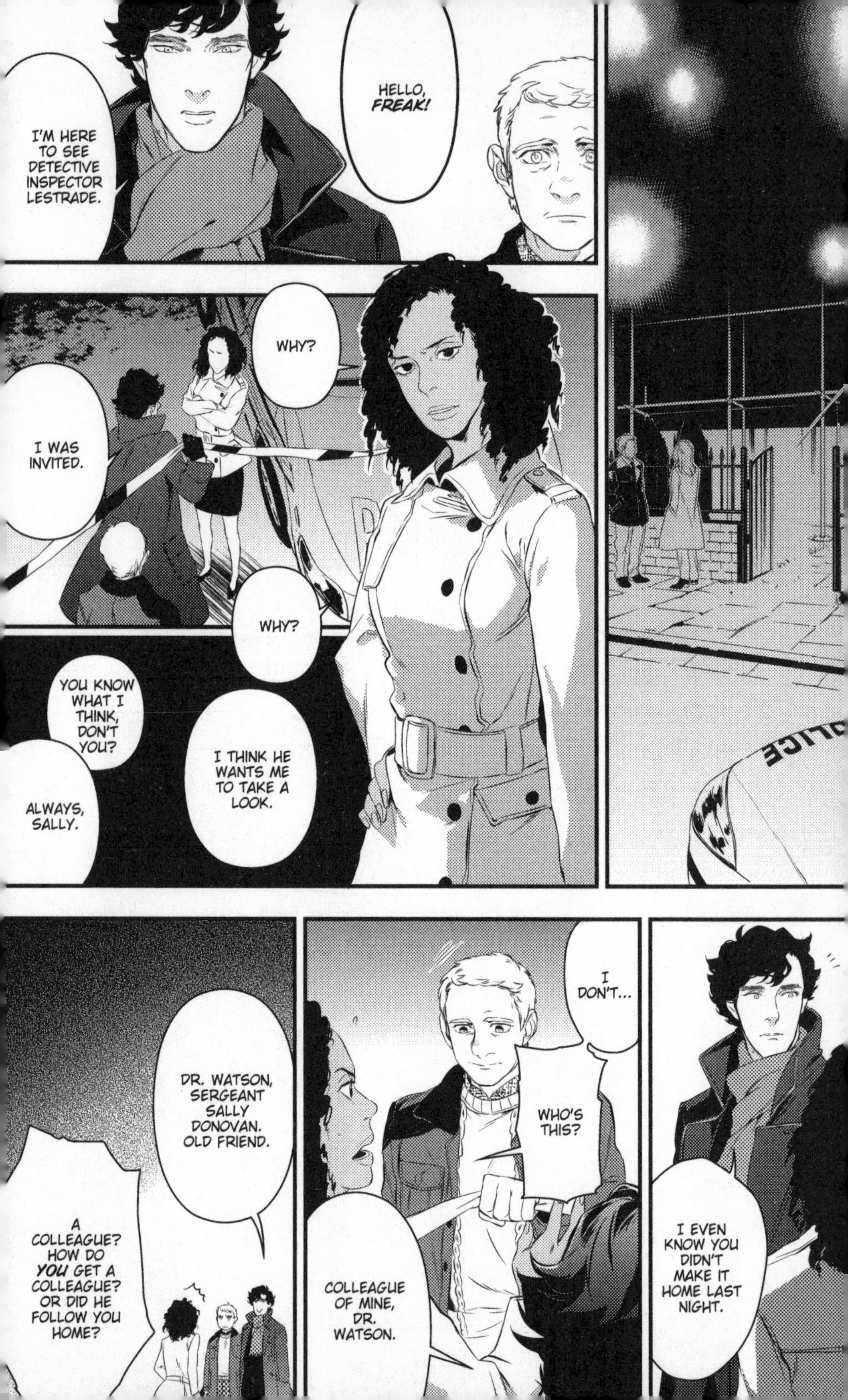
HELLO, *FREAK!*
I'M HERE TO SEE DETECTIVE INSPECTOR LESTRADE.
WHY?
I WAS INVITED.
WHY?
I THINK HE WANTS ME TO TAKE A LOOK.
YOU KNOW WHAT I THINK, DON'T YOU?
ALWAYS, SALLY.
I EVEN KNOW YOU DIDN'T MAKE IT HOME LAST NIGHT.
I DON'T...
WHO'S THIS?
COLLEAGUE OF MINE, DR. WATSON.
DR. WATSON, SERGEANT SALLY DONOVAN. OLD FRIEND.
A COLLEAGUE? HOW DO *YOU* GET A COLLEAGUE? OR DID HE FOLLOW YOU HOME?

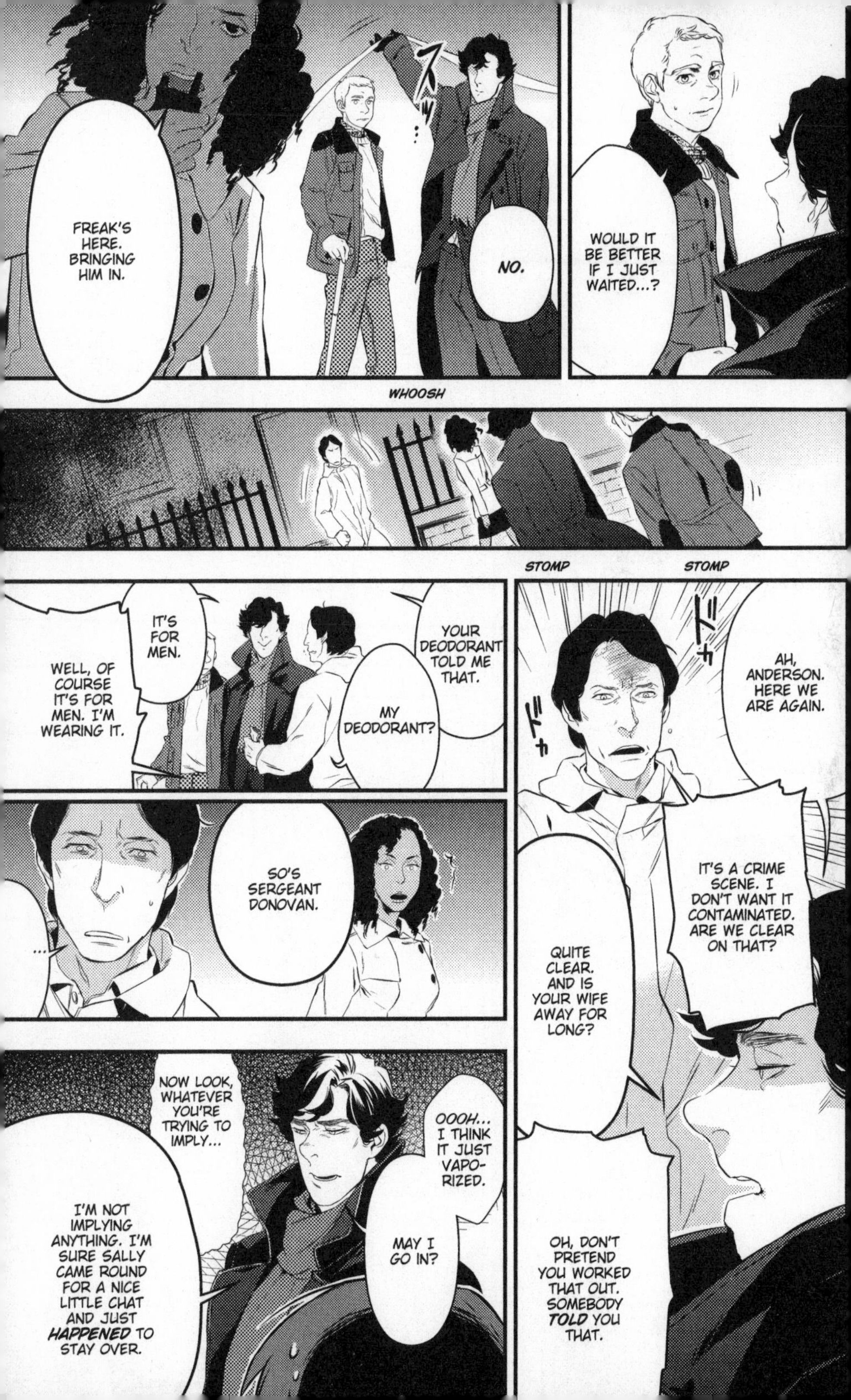
WOULD IT BE BETTER IF I JUST WAITED...?
NO.
FREAK'S HERE. BRINGING HIM IN.
WHOOSH
STOMP
STOMP
AH, ANDERSON. HERE WE ARE AGAIN.
IT'S A CRIME SCENE. I DON'T WANT IT CONTAMINATED. ARE WE CLEAR ON THAT?
QUITE CLEAR. AND IS YOUR WIFE AWAY FOR LONG?
OH, DON'T PRETEND YOU WORKED THAT OUT. SOMEBODY *TOLD* YOU THAT.
YOUR DEODORANT TOLD ME THAT.
MY DEODORANT?
IT'S FOR MEN.
WELL, OF COURSE IT'S FOR MEN. I'M WEARING IT.
SO'S SERGEANT DONOVAN.
...
NOW LOOK, WHATEVER YOU'RE TRYING TO IMPLY...
I'M NOT IMPLYING ANYTHING. I'M SURE SALLY CAME ROUND FOR A NICE LITTLE CHAT AND JUST *HAPPENED* TO STAY OVER.
OOOH... I THINK IT JUST VAPORIZED.
MAY I GO IN?

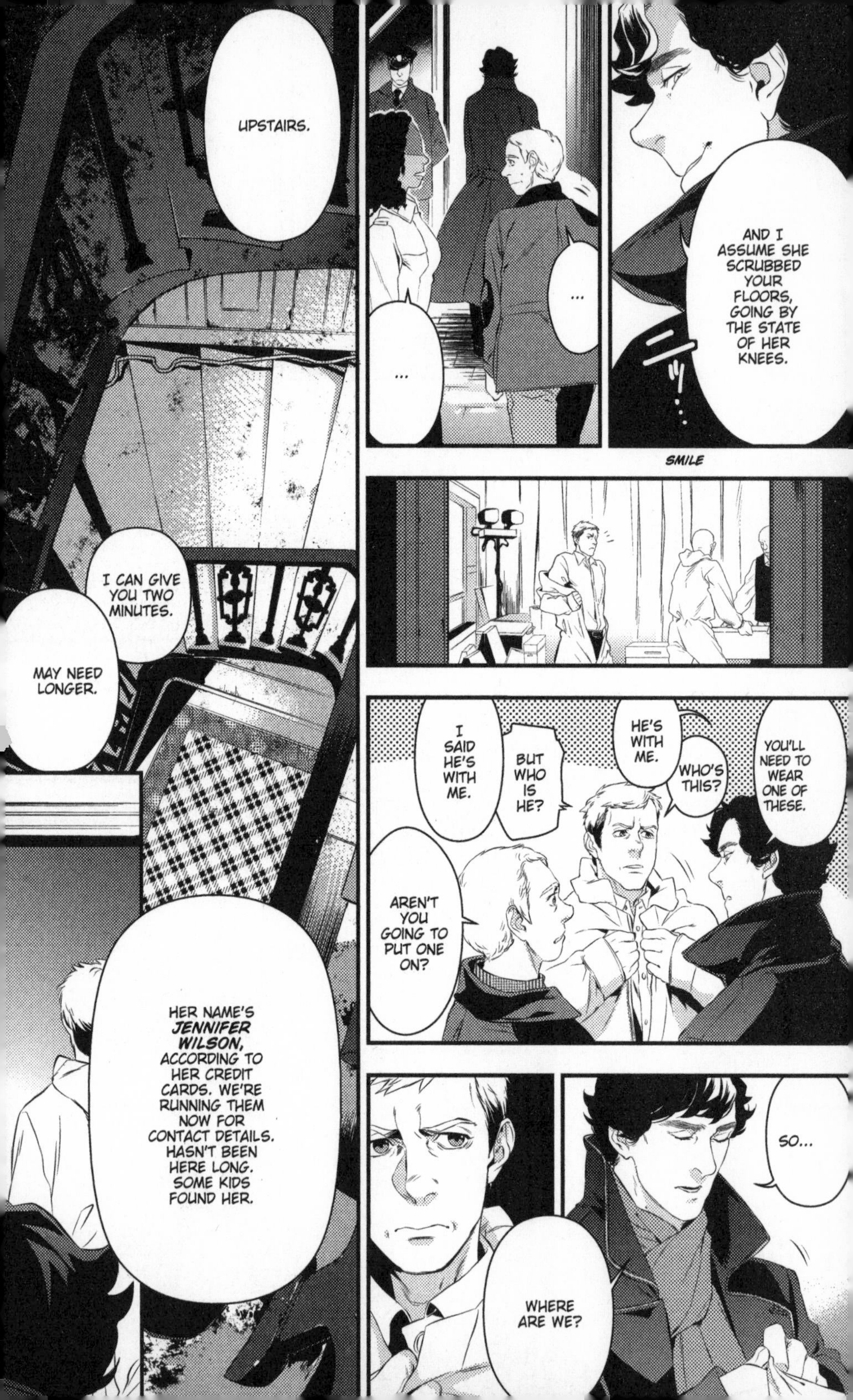
AND I ASSUME SHE SCRUBBED YOUR FLOORS, GOING BY THE STATE OF HER KNEES.
SMILE
...
...
YOU'LL NEED TO WEAR ONE OF THESE.
WHO'S THIS?
HE'S WITH ME.
BUT WHO IS HE?
I SAID HE'S WITH ME.
AREN'T YOU GOING TO PUT ONE ON?
SO...
WHERE ARE WE?
UPSTAIRS.
I CAN GIVE YOU TWO MINUTES.
MAY NEED LONGER.
HER NAME'S ***JENNIFER WILSON,*** ACCORDING TO HER CREDIT CARDS. WE'RE RUNNING THEM NOW FOR CONTACT DETAILS. HASN'T BEEN HERE LONG. SOME KIDS FOUND HER.

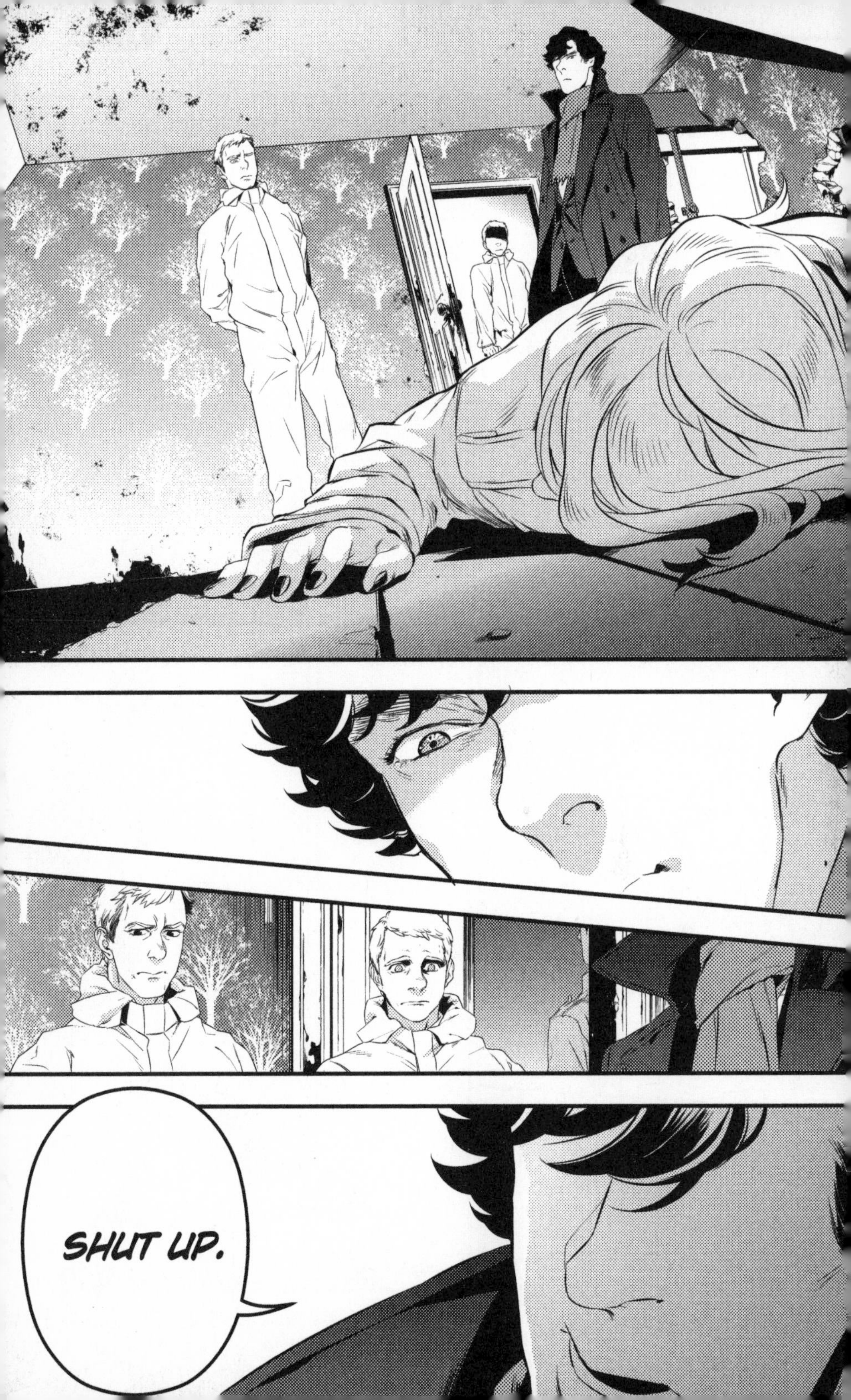
SHUT UP.

LEFT HANDED.

I DIDN'T SAY ANYTHING.

YOU WERE *THINKING.* IT'S ANNOYIING.

Rache

Rachel

Rache

German (n.)
Revenge.

NO...

DRY.

WET.

CLEAN.

CLEAN.

CLEAN.

WET.

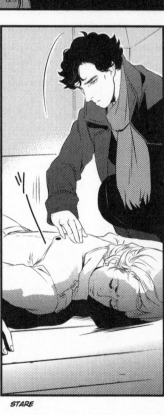

STARE

MARRIAGE.

UNHAPPILY MARRIED.

DIRTY.

... ...

SLIDE

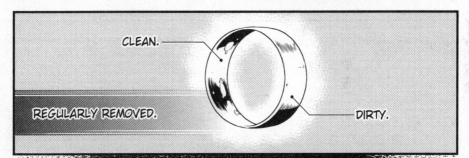

MORE THAN... TEN YEARS.

CLEAN.

REGULARLY REMOVED.

DIRTY.

SERIAL ADULTERER.

GOT ANYTHING?

NOT MUCH.

SMILE

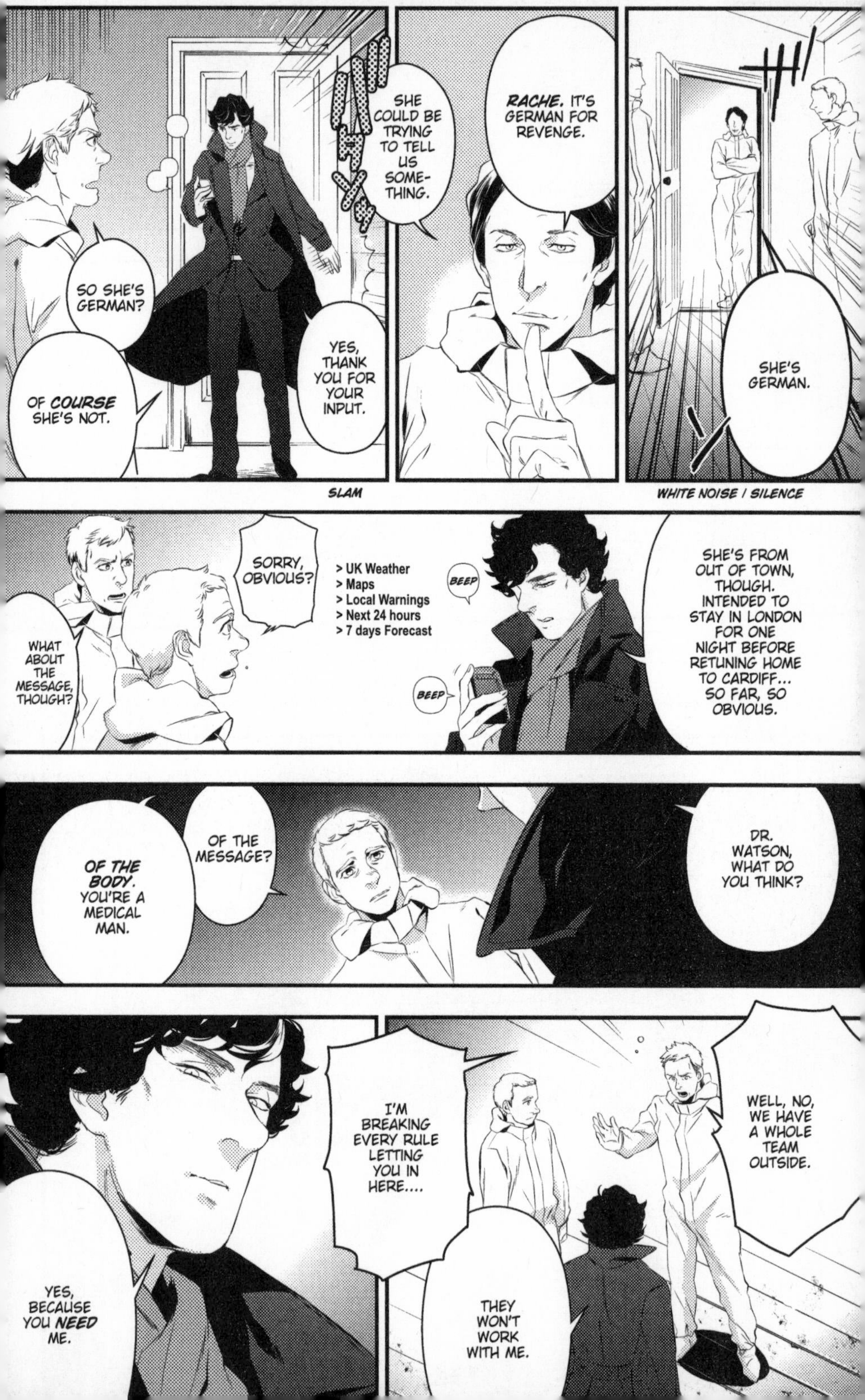
SHE'S GERMAN.
WHITE NOISE / SILENCE
RACHE. IT'S GERMAN FOR REVENGE.
SHE COULD BE TRYING TO TELL US SOME-THING.
YES, THANK YOU FOR YOUR INPUT.
SO SHE'S GERMAN?
OF ***COURSE*** SHE'S NOT.
SLAM
SHE'S FROM OUT OF TOWN, THOUGH. INTENDED TO STAY IN LONDON FOR ONE NIGHT BEFORE RETUNING HOME TO CARDIFF... SO FAR, SO OBVIOUS.
BEEP
> UK Weather
> Maps
> Local Warnings
> Next 24 hours
> 7 days Forecast
BEEP
SORRY, OBVIOUS?
WHAT ABOUT THE MESSAGE, THOUGH?
DR. WATSON, WHAT DO YOU THINK?
OF THE MESSAGE?
OF THE BODY. YOU'RE A MEDICAL MAN.
WELL, NO, WE HAVE A WHOLE TEAM OUTSIDE.
THEY WON'T WORK WITH ME.
I'M BREAKING EVERY RULE LETTING YOU IN HERE....
YES, BECAUSE YOU ***NEED*** ME.

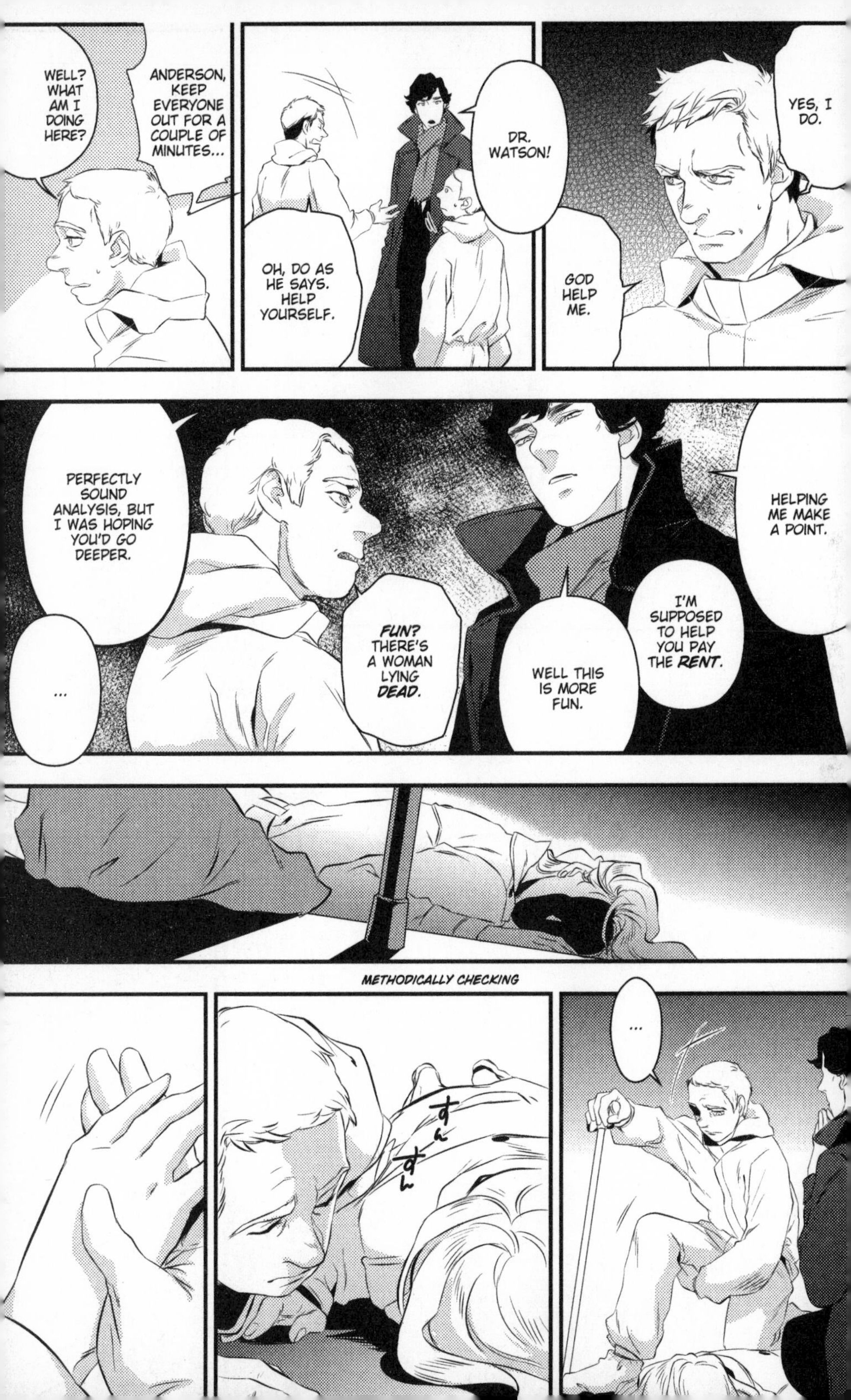
YES, I DO.
GOD HELP ME.
DR. WATSON!
OH, DO AS HE SAYS. HELP YOURSELF.
ANDERSON, KEEP EVERYONE OUT FOR A COUPLE OF MINUTES...
WELL? WHAT AM I DOING HERE?
HELPING ME MAKE A POINT.
I'M SUPPOSED TO HELP YOU PAY THE **RENT**.
WELL THIS IS MORE FUN.
FUN? THERE'S A WOMAN LYING ***DEAD***.
PERFECTLY SOUND ANALYSIS, BUT I WAS HOPING YOU'D GO DEEPER.
...
METHODICALLY CHECKING
...
すん
すん

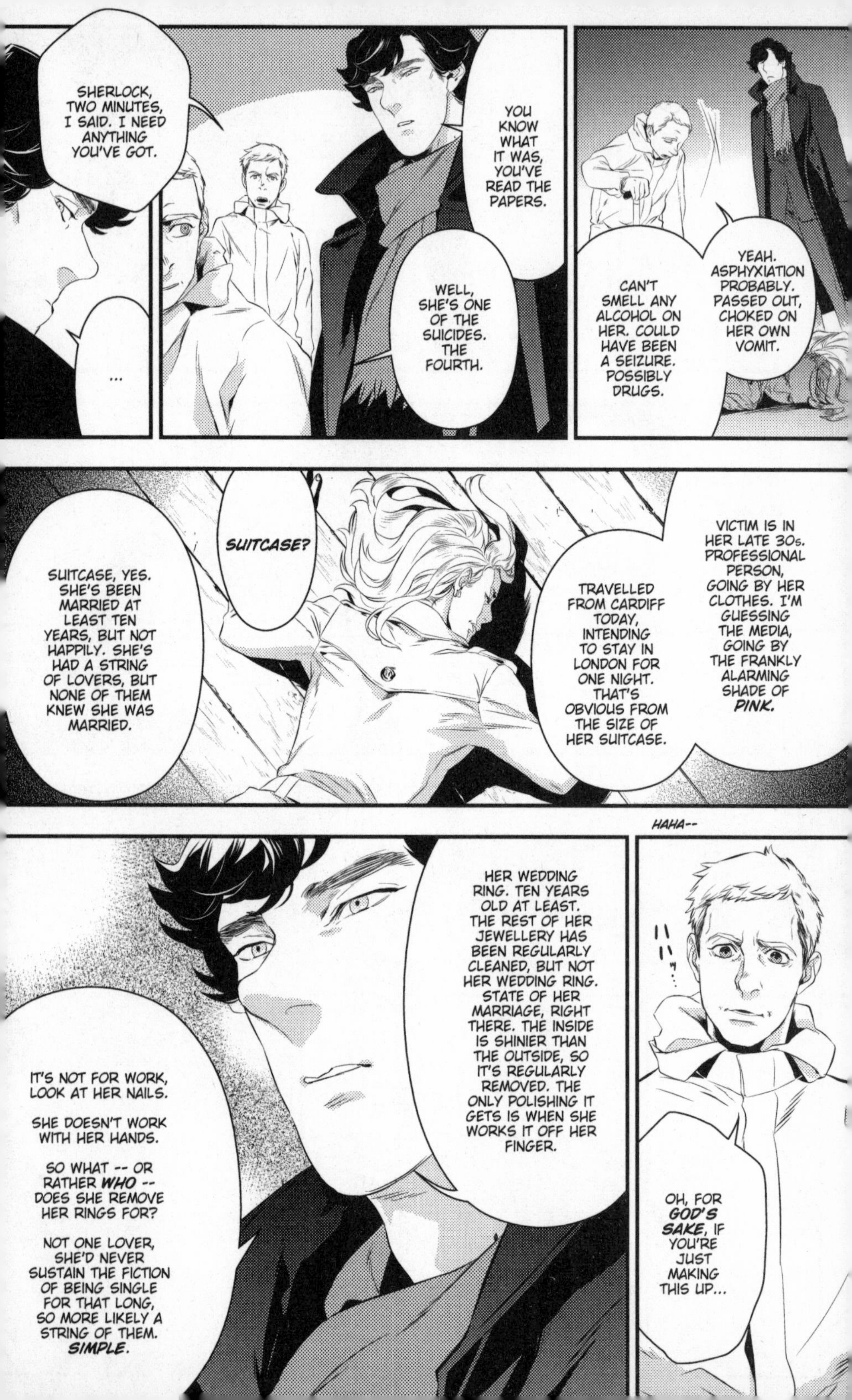
YEAH. ASPHYXIATION PROBABLY. PASSED OUT, CHOKED ON HER OWN VOMIT.
CAN'T SMELL ANY ALCOHOL ON HER. COULD HAVE BEEN A SEIZURE. POSSIBLY DRUGS.
YOU KNOW WHAT IT WAS, YOU'VE READ THE PAPERS.
WELL, SHE'S ONE OF THE SUICIDES. THE FOURTH.
SHERLOCK, TWO MINUTES, I SAID. I NEED ANYTHING YOU'VE GOT.
...
VICTIM IS IN HER LATE 30s. PROFESSIONAL PERSON, GOING BY HER CLOTHES. I'M GUESSING THE MEDIA, GOING BY THE FRANKLY ALARMING SHADE OF ***PINK.***
TRAVELLED FROM CARDIFF TODAY, INTENDING TO STAY IN LONDON FOR ONE NIGHT. THAT'S OBVIOUS FROM THE SIZE OF HER SUITCASE.
SUITCASE?
SUITCASE, YES. SHE'S BEEN MARRIED AT LEAST TEN YEARS, BUT NOT HAPPILY. SHE'S HAD A STRING OF LOVERS, BUT NONE OF THEM KNEW SHE WAS MARRIED.
HAHA--
OH, FOR ***GOD'S SAKE,*** IF YOU'RE JUST MAKING THIS UP...
HER WEDDING RING. TEN YEARS OLD AT LEAST. THE REST OF HER JEWELLERY HAS BEEN REGULARLY CLEANED, BUT NOT HER WEDDING RING. STATE OF HER MARRIAGE, RIGHT THERE. THE INSIDE IS SHINIER THAN THE OUTSIDE, SO IT'S REGULARLY REMOVED. THE ONLY POLISHING IT GETS IS WHEN SHE WORKS IT OFF HER FINGER.
IT'S NOT FOR WORK, LOOK AT HER NAILS.
SHE DOESN'T WORK WITH HER HANDS.
SO WHAT -- OR RATHER ***WHO*** -- DOES SHE REMOVE HER RINGS FOR?
NOT ONE LOVER, SHE'D NEVER SUSTAIN THE FICTION OF BEING SINGLE FOR THAT LONG, SO MORE LIKELY A STRING OF THEM. ***SIMPLE.***

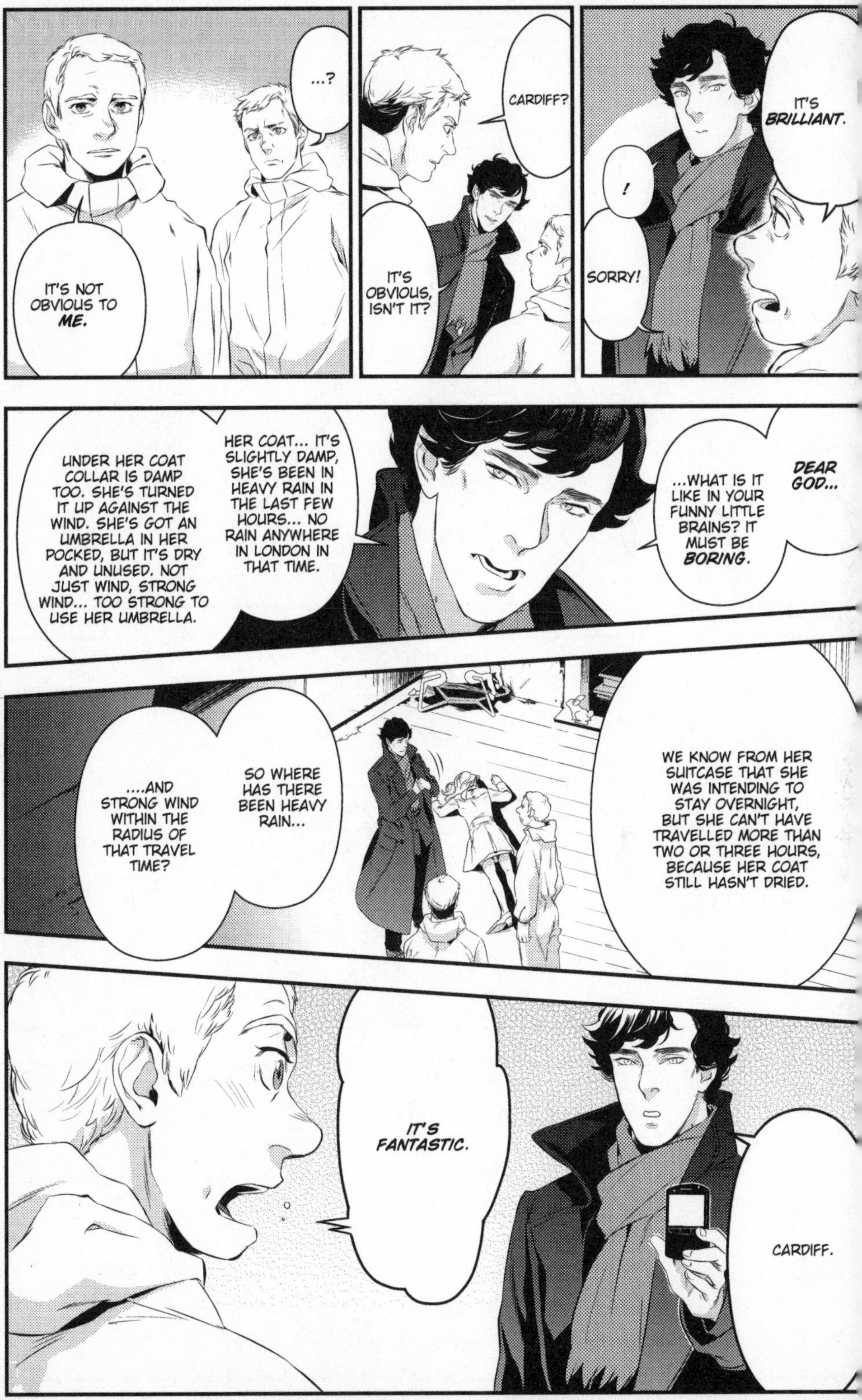
IT'S BRILLIANT.
!
SORRY!
CARDIFF?
IT'S OBVIOUS, ISN'T IT?
...?
IT'S NOT OBVIOUS TO ME.
DEAR GOD...
...WHAT IS IT LIKE IN YOUR FUNNY LITTLE BRAINS? IT MUST BE BORING.
HER COAT... IT'S SLIGHTLY DAMP, SHE'S BEEN IN HEAVY RAIN IN THE LAST FEW HOURS... NO RAIN ANYWHERE IN LONDON IN THAT TIME.
UNDER HER COAT COLLAR IS DAMP TOO. SHE'S TURNED IT UP AGAINST THE WIND. SHE'S GOT AN UMBRELLA IN HER POCKED, BUT IT'S DRY AND UNUSED. NOT JUST WIND, STRONG WIND... TOO STRONG TO USE HER UMBRELLA.
WE KNOW FROM HER SUITCASE THAT SHE WAS INTENDING TO STAY OVERNIGHT, BUT SHE CAN'T HAVE TRAVELLED MORE THAN TWO OR THREE HOURS, BECAUSE HER COAT STILL HASN'T DRIED.
SO WHERE HAS THERE BEEN HEAVY RAIN...
....AND STRONG WIND WITHIN THE RADIUS OF THAT TRAVEL TIME?
CARDIFF.
IT'S FANTASTIC.

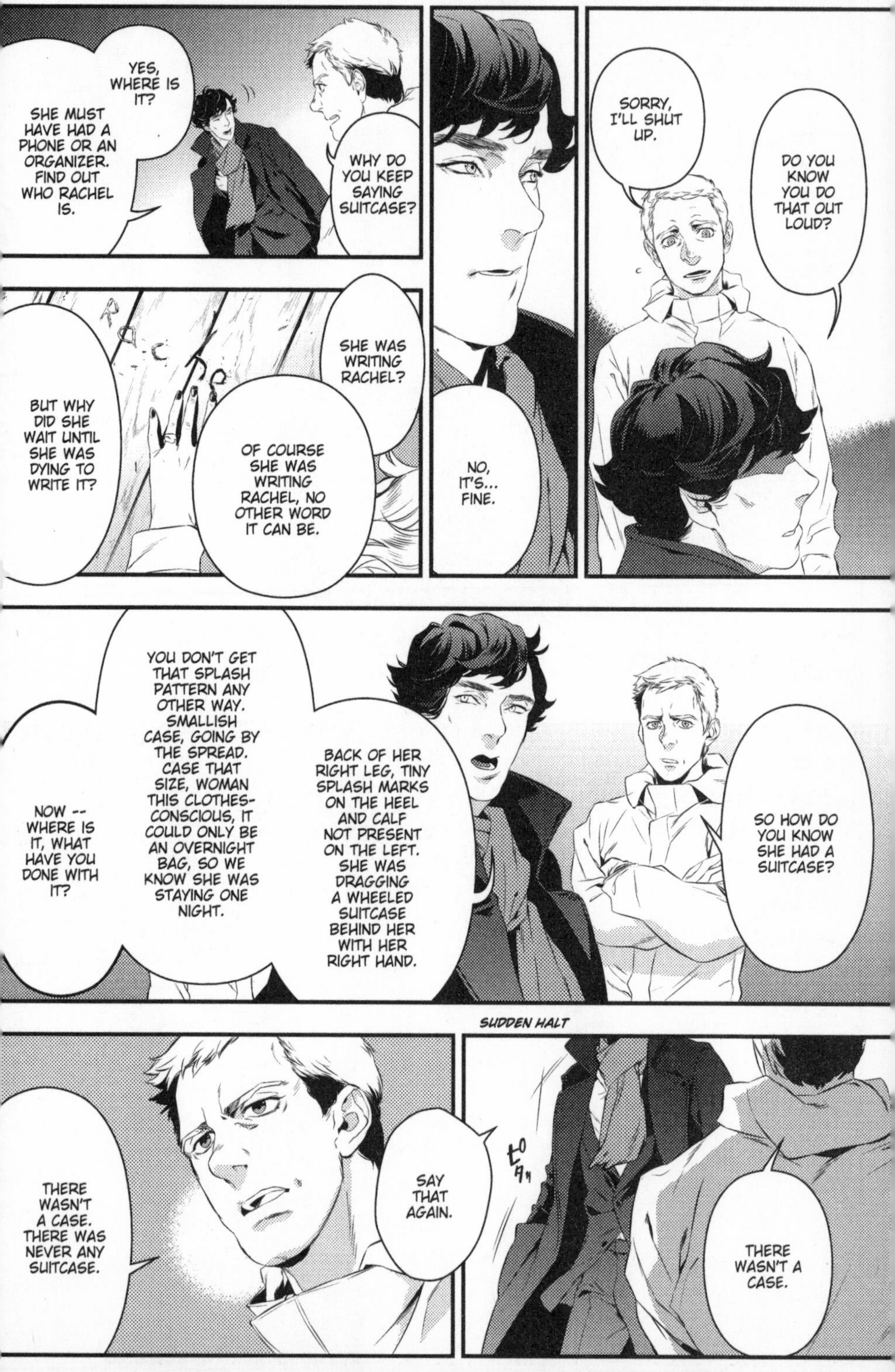
DO YOU KNOW YOU DO THAT OUT LOUD?
SORRY, I'LL SHUT UP.
NO, IT'S... FINE.
YES, WHERE IS IT?
SHE MUST HAVE HAD A PHONE OR AN ORGANIZER. FIND OUT WHO RACHEL IS.
WHY DO YOU KEEP SAYING SUITCASE?
SHE WAS WRITING RACHEL?
OF COURSE SHE WAS WRITING RACHEL, NO OTHER WORD IT CAN BE.
BUT WHY DID SHE WAIT UNTIL SHE WAS DYING TO WRITE IT?
SO HOW DO YOU KNOW SHE HAD A SUITCASE?
BACK OF HER RIGHT LEG, TINY SPLASH MARKS ON THE HEEL AND CALF NOT PRESENT ON THE LEFT. SHE WAS DRAGGING A WHEELED SUITCASE BEHIND HER WITH HER RIGHT HAND.
YOU DON'T GET THAT SPLASH PATTERN ANY OTHER WAY. SMALLISH CASE, GOING BY THE SPREAD. CASE THAT SIZE, WOMAN THIS CLOTHES-CONSCIOUS, IT COULD ONLY BE AN OVERNIGHT BAG, SO WE KNOW SHE WAS STAYING ONE NIGHT.
NOW -- WHERE IS IT, WHAT HAVE YOU DONE WITH IT?
SUDDEN HALT
THERE WASN'T A CASE.
SAY THAT AGAIN.
THERE WASN'T A CASE. THERE WAS NEVER ANY SUITCASE.

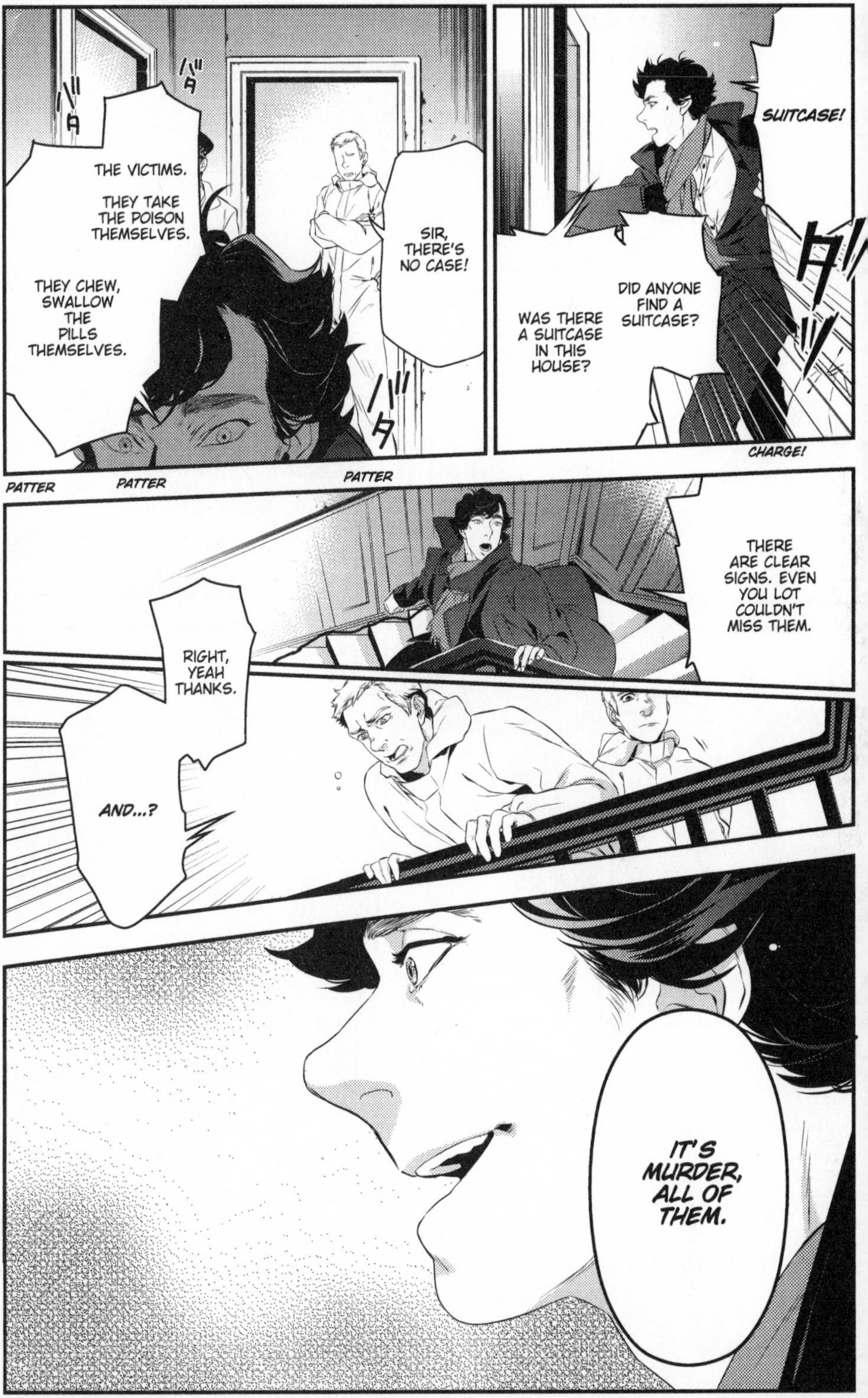
SUITCASE!
DID ANYONE FIND A SUITCASE?
WAS THERE A SUITCASE IN THIS HOUSE?
CHARGE!
SIR, THERE'S NO CASE!
THE VICTIMS.
THEY TAKE THE POISON THEMSELVES.
THEY CHEW, SWALLOW THE PILLS THEMSELVES.
PATTER
PATTER
PATTER
THERE ARE CLEAR SIGNS. EVEN YOU LOT COULDN'T MISS THEM.
RIGHT, YEAH THANKS.
AND...?
IT'S MURDER, ALL OF THEM.

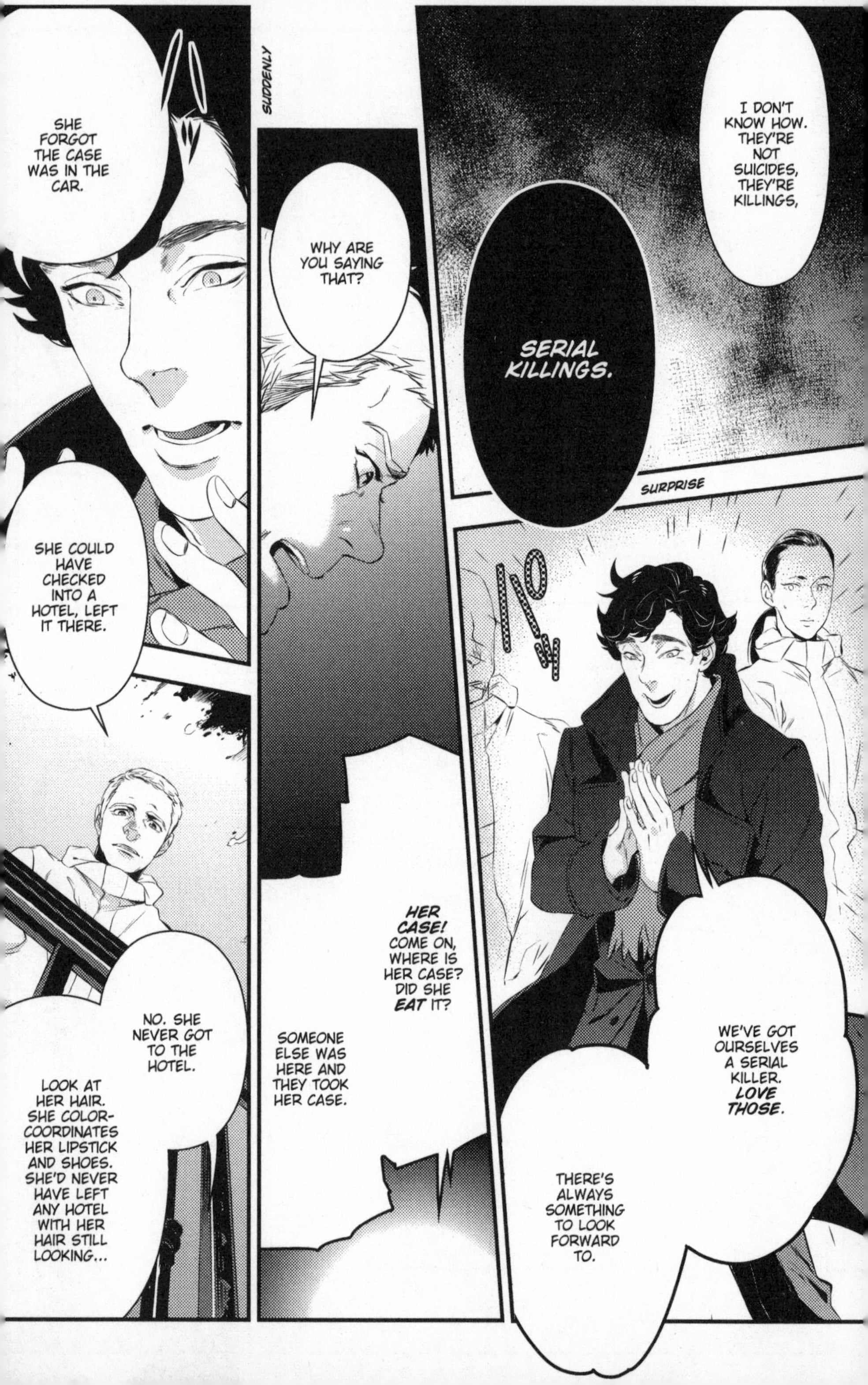

SHE FORGOT THE CASE WAS IN THE CAR.
SUDDENLY
SHE COULD HAVE CHECKED INTO A HOTEL, LEFT IT THERE.
NO. SHE NEVER GOT TO THE HOTEL.
LOOK AT HER HAIR. SHE COLOR-COORDINATES HER LIPSTICK AND SHOES. SHE'D NEVER HAVE LEFT ANY HOTEL WITH HER HAIR STILL LOOKING...
WHY ARE YOU SAYING THAT?
HER CASE! COME ON, WHERE IS HER CASE? DID SHE EAT IT?
SOMEONE ELSE WAS HERE AND THEY TOOK HER CASE.
I DON'T KNOW HOW. THEY'RE NOT SUICIDES, THEY'RE KILLINGS,
SERIAL KILLINGS.
SURPRISE
WE'VE GOT OURSELVES A SERIAL KILLER. LOVE THOSE.
THERE'S ALWAYS SOMETHING TO LOOK FORWARD TO.

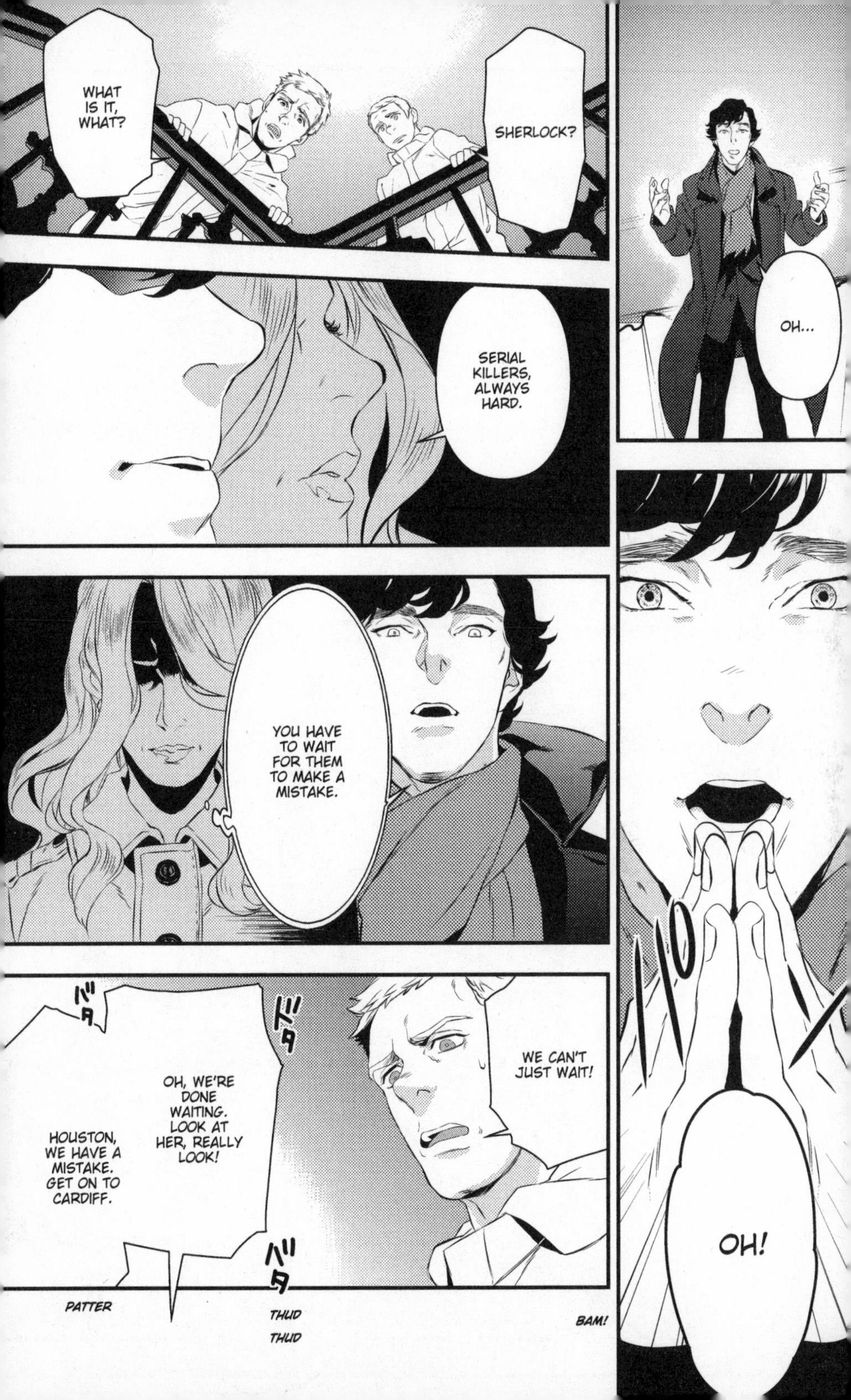

OH...
SHERLOCK?
WHAT IS IT, WHAT?
SERIAL KILLERS, ALWAYS HARD.
YOU HAVE TO WAIT FOR THEM TO MAKE A MISTAKE.
OH!
BAM!
WE CAN'T JUST WAIT!
OH, WE'RE DONE WAITING. LOOK AT HER, REALLY LOOK!
HOUSTON, WE HAVE A MISTAKE. GET ON TO CARDIFF.
THUD THUD
PATTER

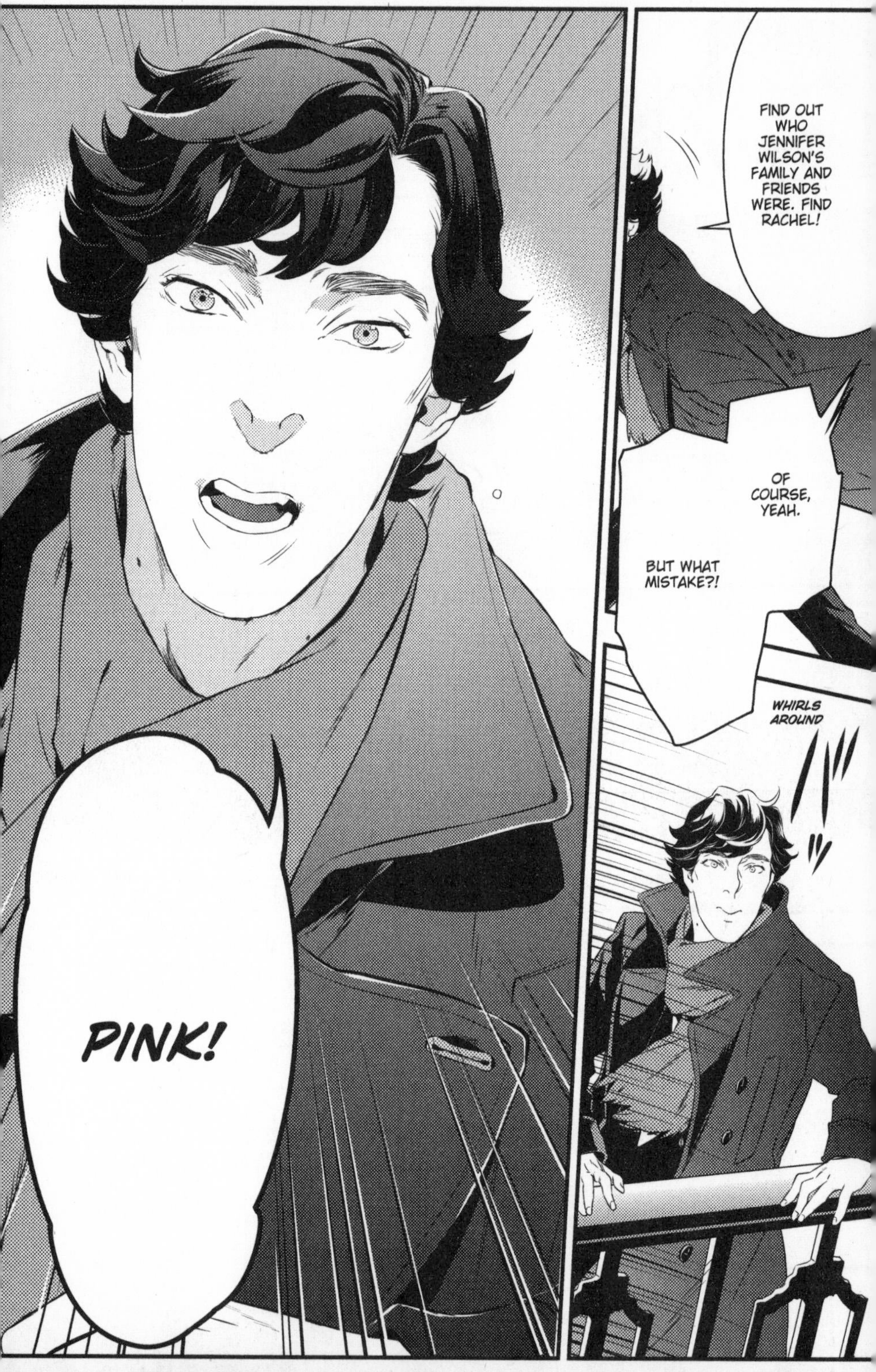
FIND OUT WHO JENNIFER WILSON'S FAMILY AND FRIENDS WERE. FIND RACHEL!
OF COURSE, YEAH.
BUT WHAT MISTAKE?!
WHIRLS AROUND
PINK!

...

...

LET'S GET ON WITH IT...

PATTER PATTER PATTER

...

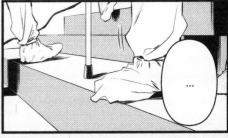

...

...

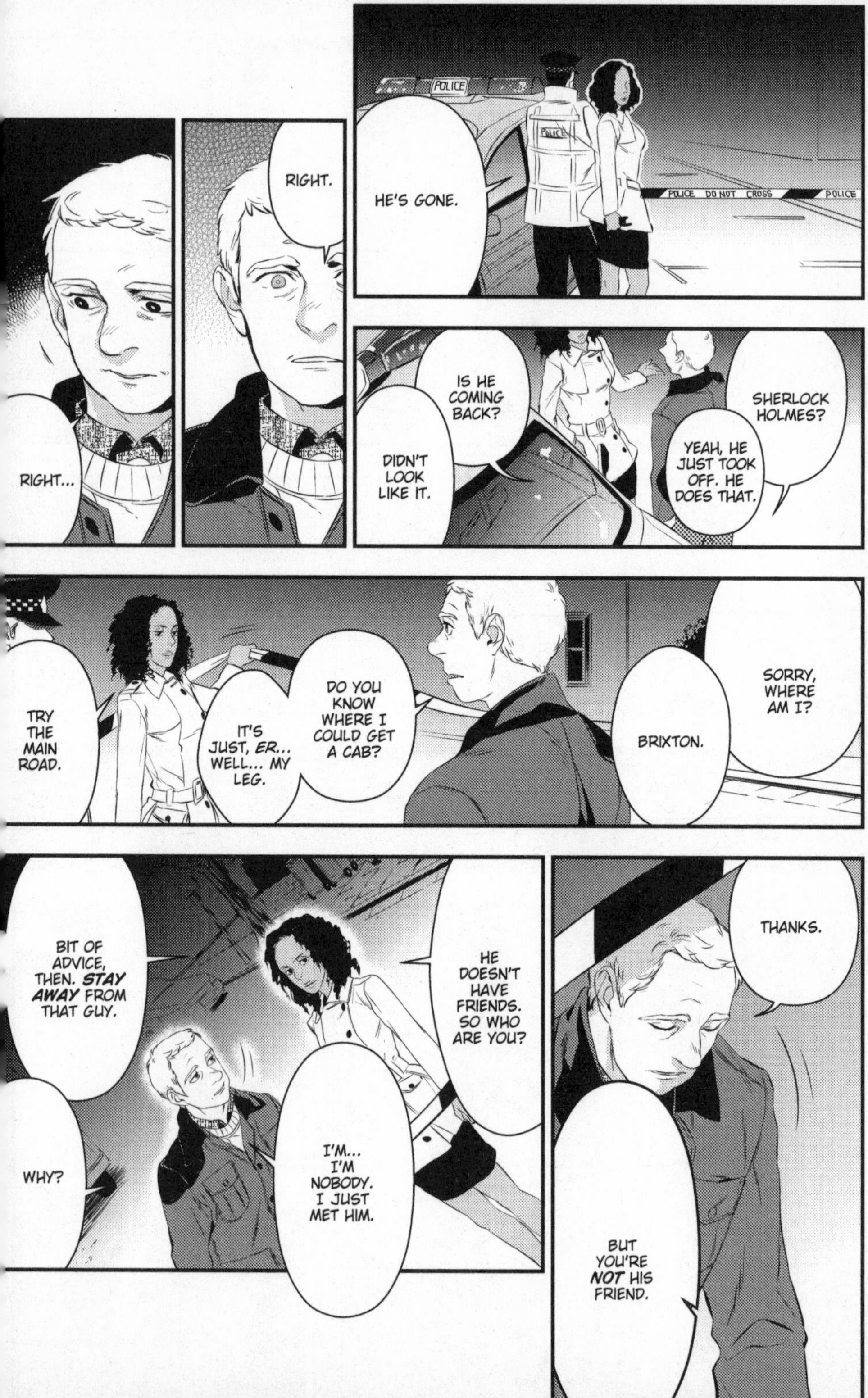
POLICE
POLICE
POLICE DO NOT CROSS
POLICE
HE'S GONE.
SHERLOCK HOLMES?
YEAH, HE JUST TOOK OFF. HE DOES THAT.
IS HE COMING BACK?
DIDN'T LOOK LIKE IT.
RIGHT.
RIGHT...
SORRY, WHERE AM I?
BRIXTON.
DO YOU KNOW WHERE I COULD GET A CAB?
IT'S JUST, *ER*... WELL... MY LEG.
TRY THE MAIN ROAD.
THANKS.
BUT YOU'RE ***NOT*** HIS FRIEND.
HE DOESN'T HAVE FRIENDS. SO WHO ARE YOU?
I'M... I'M NOBODY. I JUST MET HIM.
BIT OF ADVICE, THEN. ***STAY AWAY*** FROM THAT GUY.
WHY?

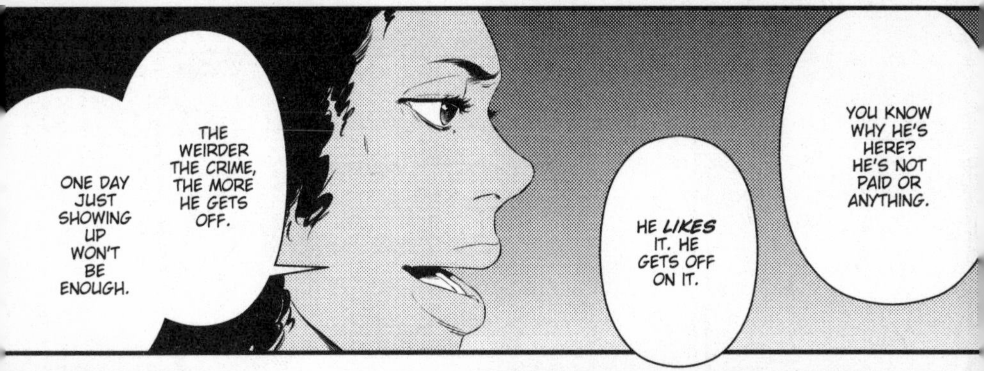
YOU KNOW WHY HE'S HERE? HE'S NOT PAID OR ANYTHING.
HE *LIKES* IT. HE GETS OFF ON IT.
THE WEIRDER THE CRIME, THE MORE HE GETS OFF.
ONE DAY JUST SHOWING UP WON'T BE ENOUGH.

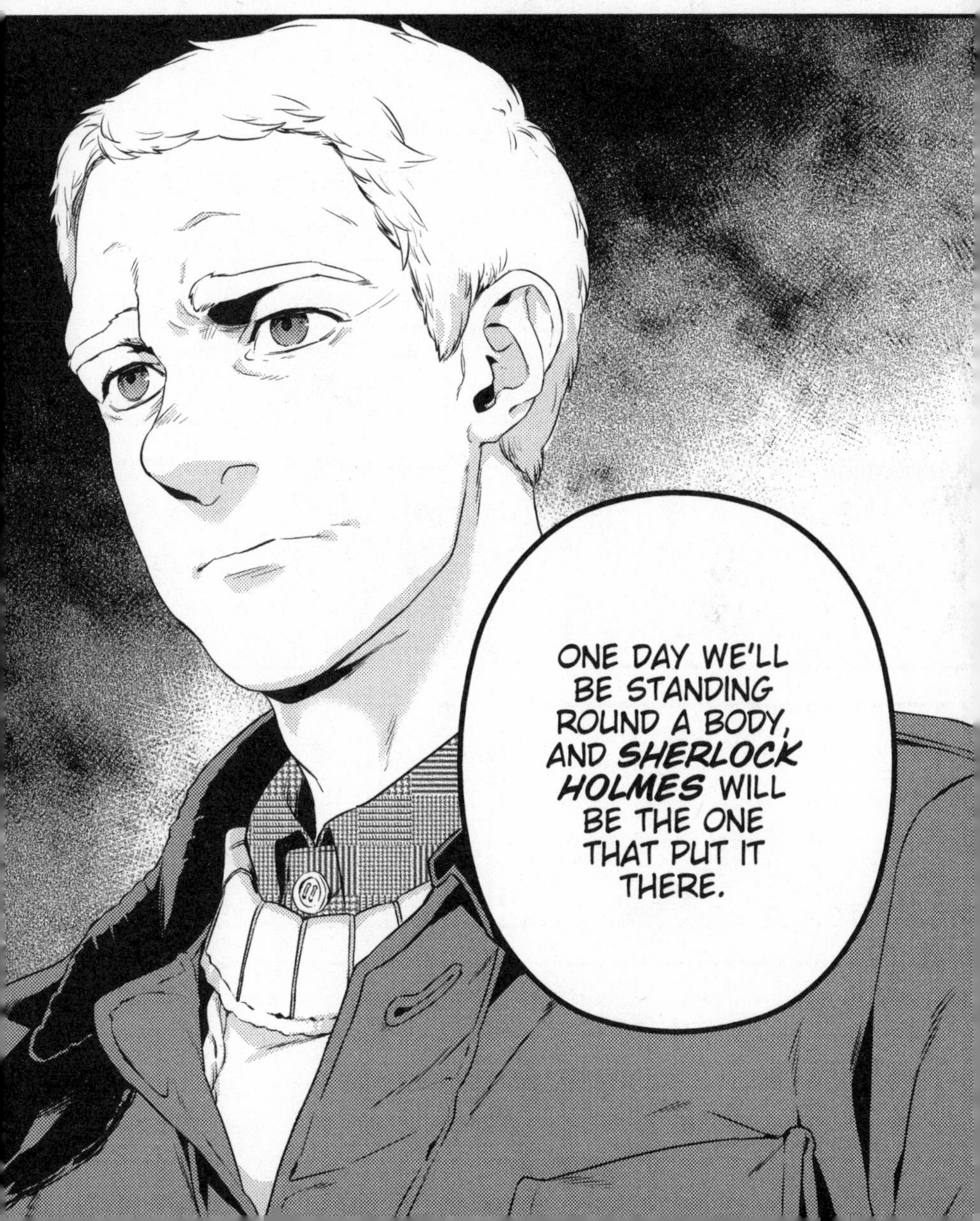
ONE DAY WE'LL BE STANDING ROUND A BODY, AND ***SHERLOCK HOLMES*** WILL BE THE ONE THAT PUT IT THERE.

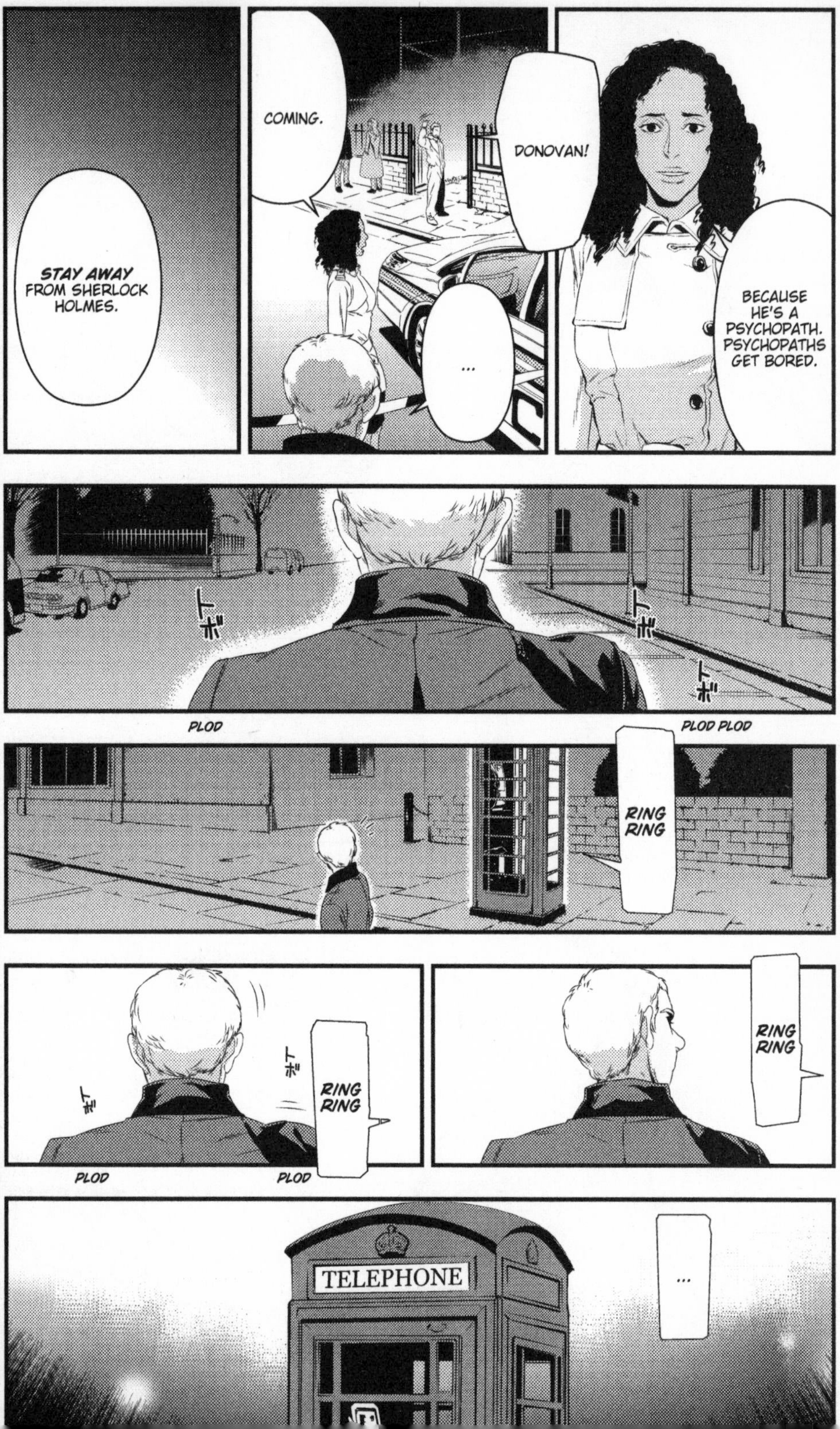
BECAUSE HE'S A PSYCHOPATH. PSYCHOPATHS GET BORED.
DONOVAN!
COMING.
...
STAY AWAY FROM SHERLOCK HOLMES.
トボ
トボ
トボ
PLOD PLOD
PLOD
RING RING
RING RING
RING RING
トボ
トボ
PLOD
PLOD
TELEPHONE
...

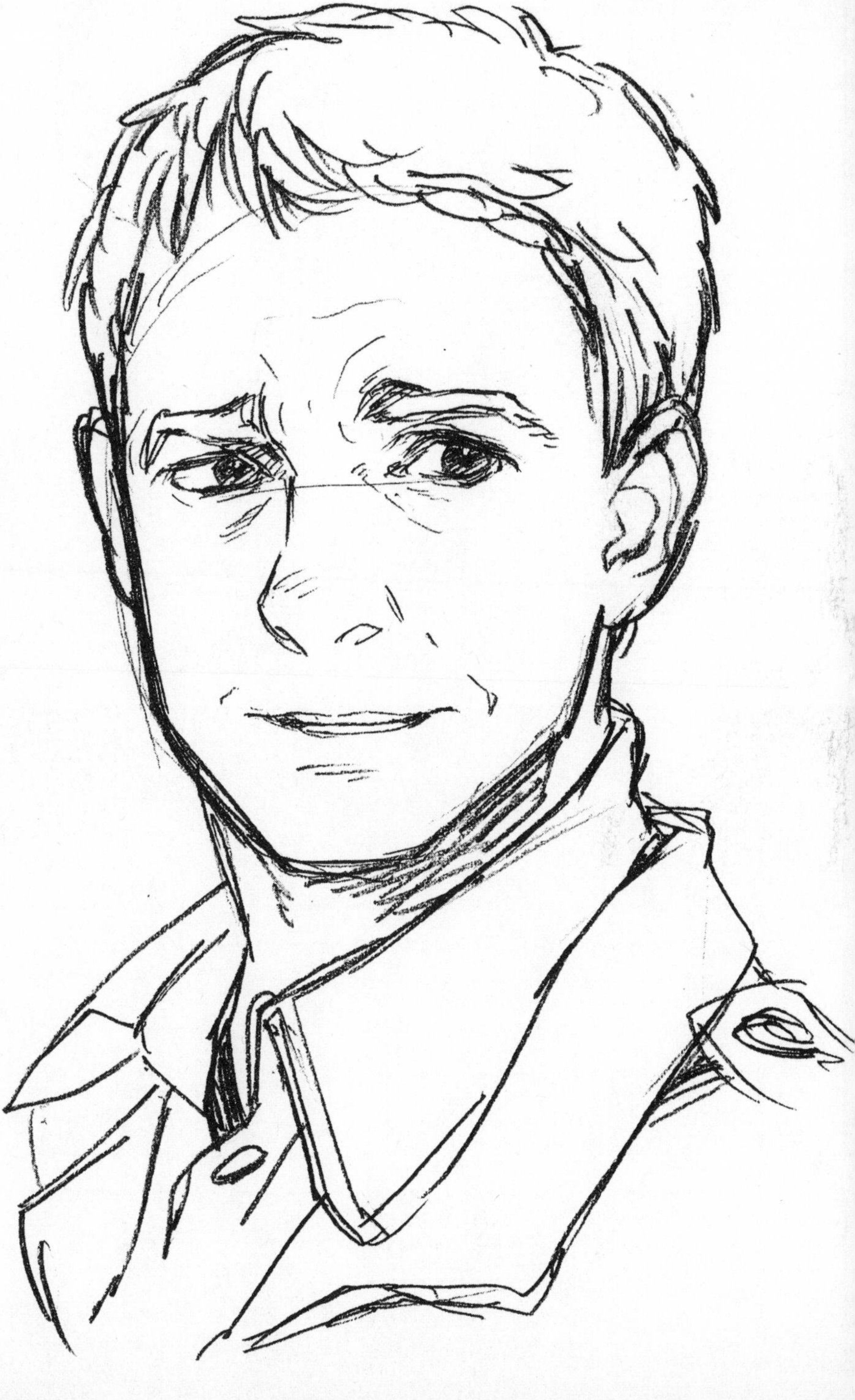

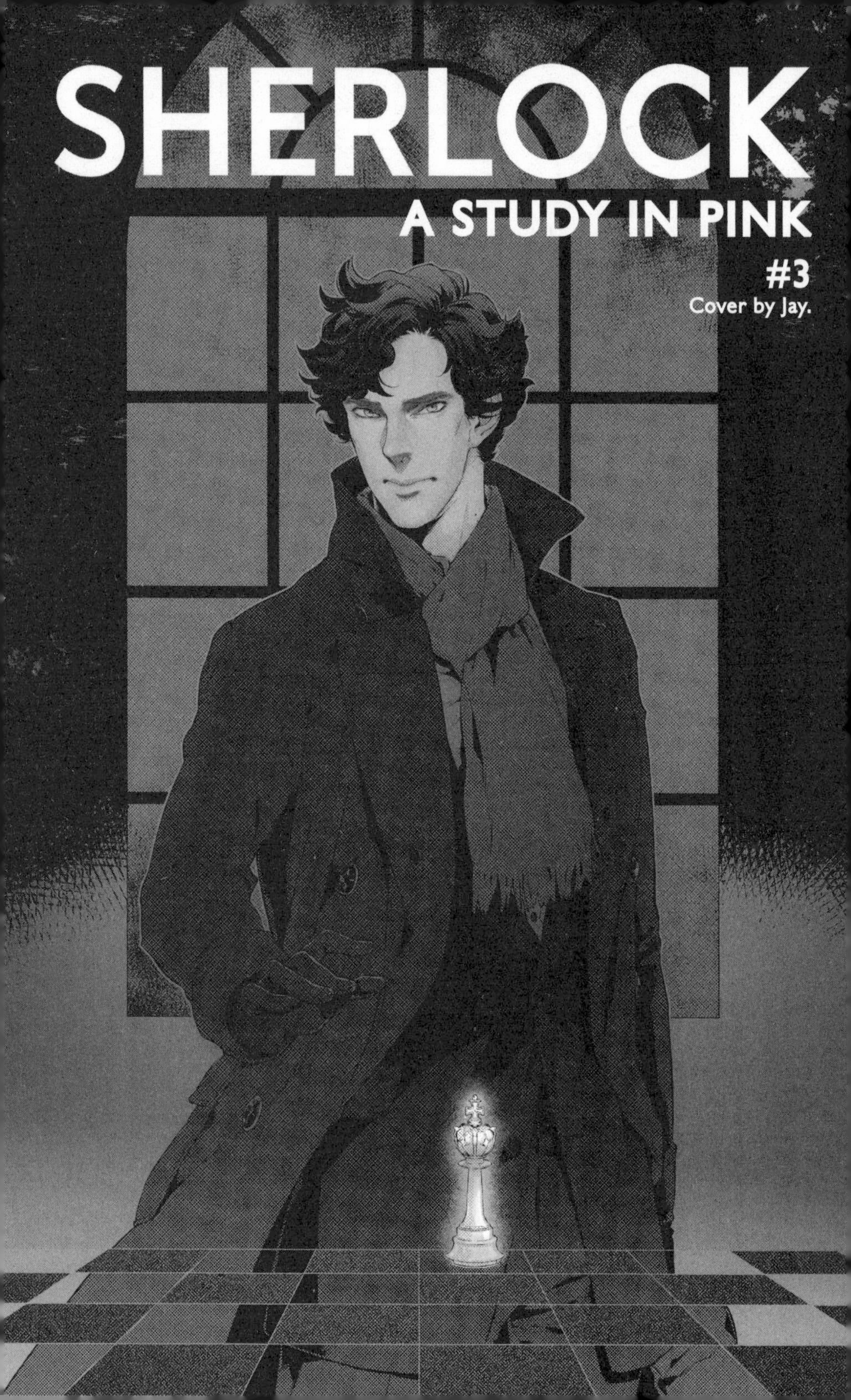
SHERLOCK
A STUDY IN PINK
#3
Cover by Jay.

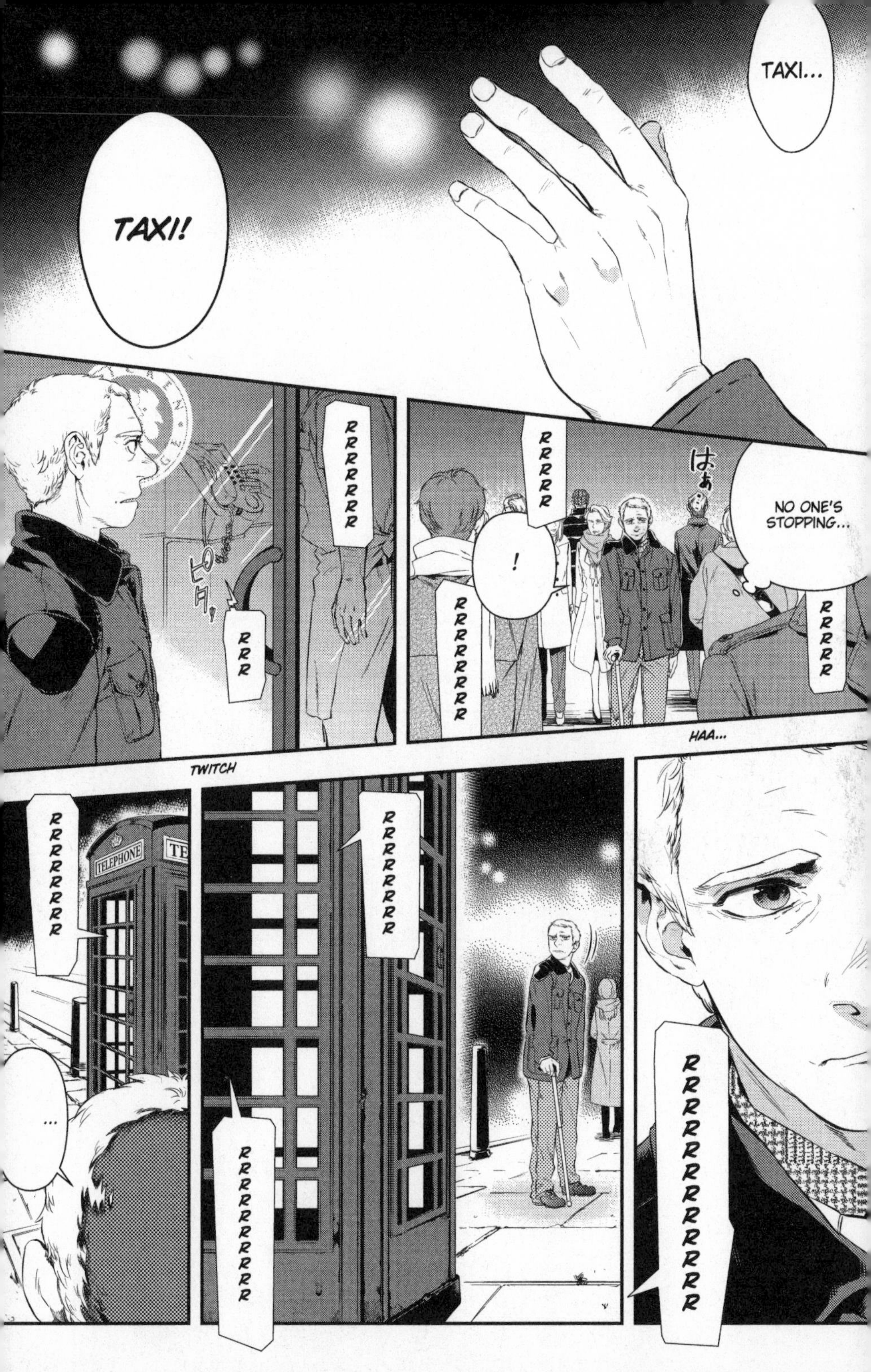
TAXI...
TAXI!
NO ONE'S STOPPING...
RRRRR
RRRRR
HAA...
!
RRRRRRRRR
RRRRRRRR
RRR
TWITCH
RRRRRRRRRRR
RRRRRRRR
RRRRRRRRRR
RRRRRRRR
...

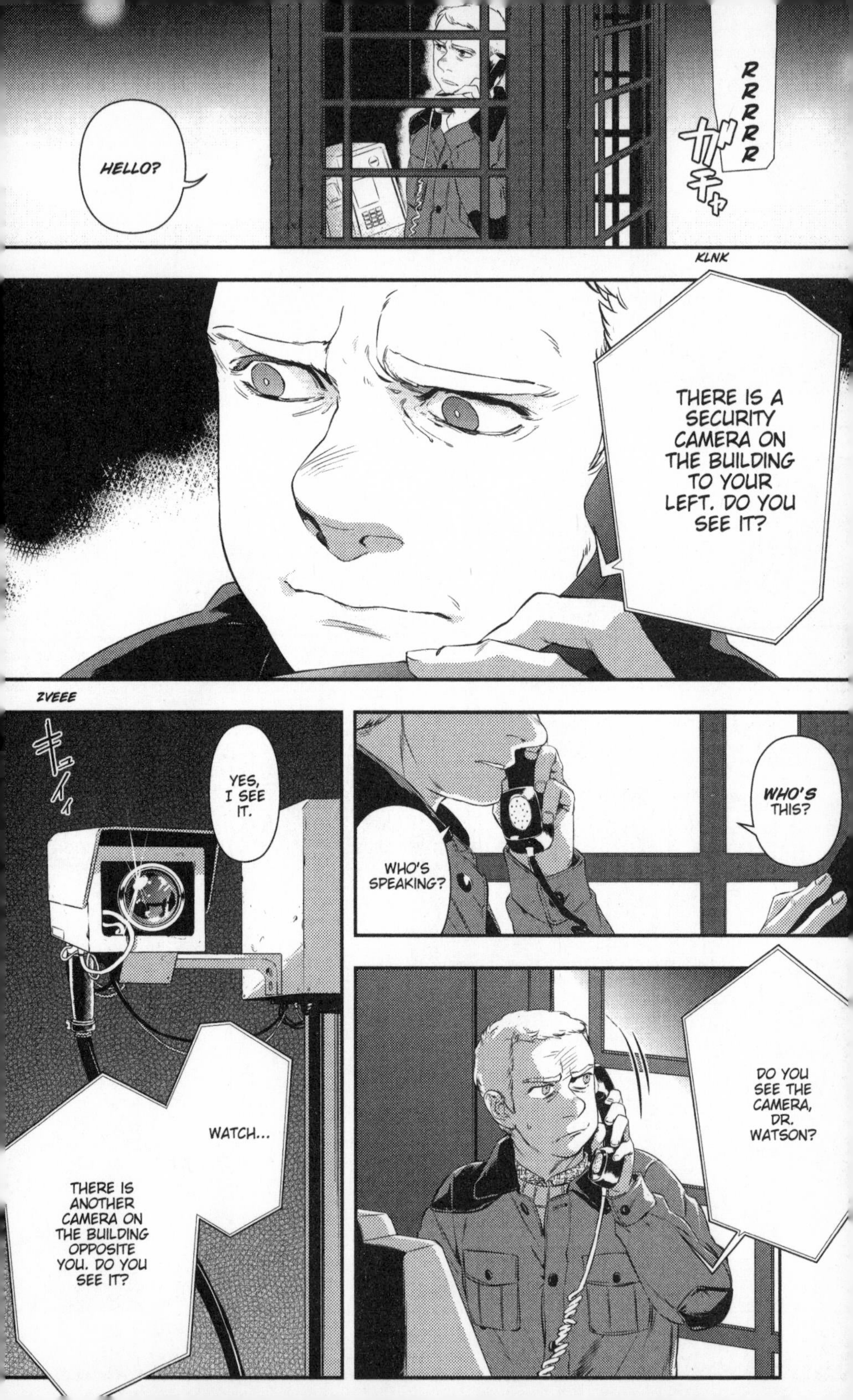
RRRR
ガチャ
HELLO?
KLNK
THERE IS A SECURITY CAMERA ON THE BUILDING TO YOUR LEFT. DO YOU SEE IT?
ZVEEE
キュイイ
WHO'S THIS?
WHO'S SPEAKING?
DO YOU SEE THE CAMERA, DR. WATSON?
YES, I SEE IT.
WATCH...
THERE IS ANOTHER CAMERA ON THE BUILDING OPPOSITE YOU. DO YOU SEE IT?

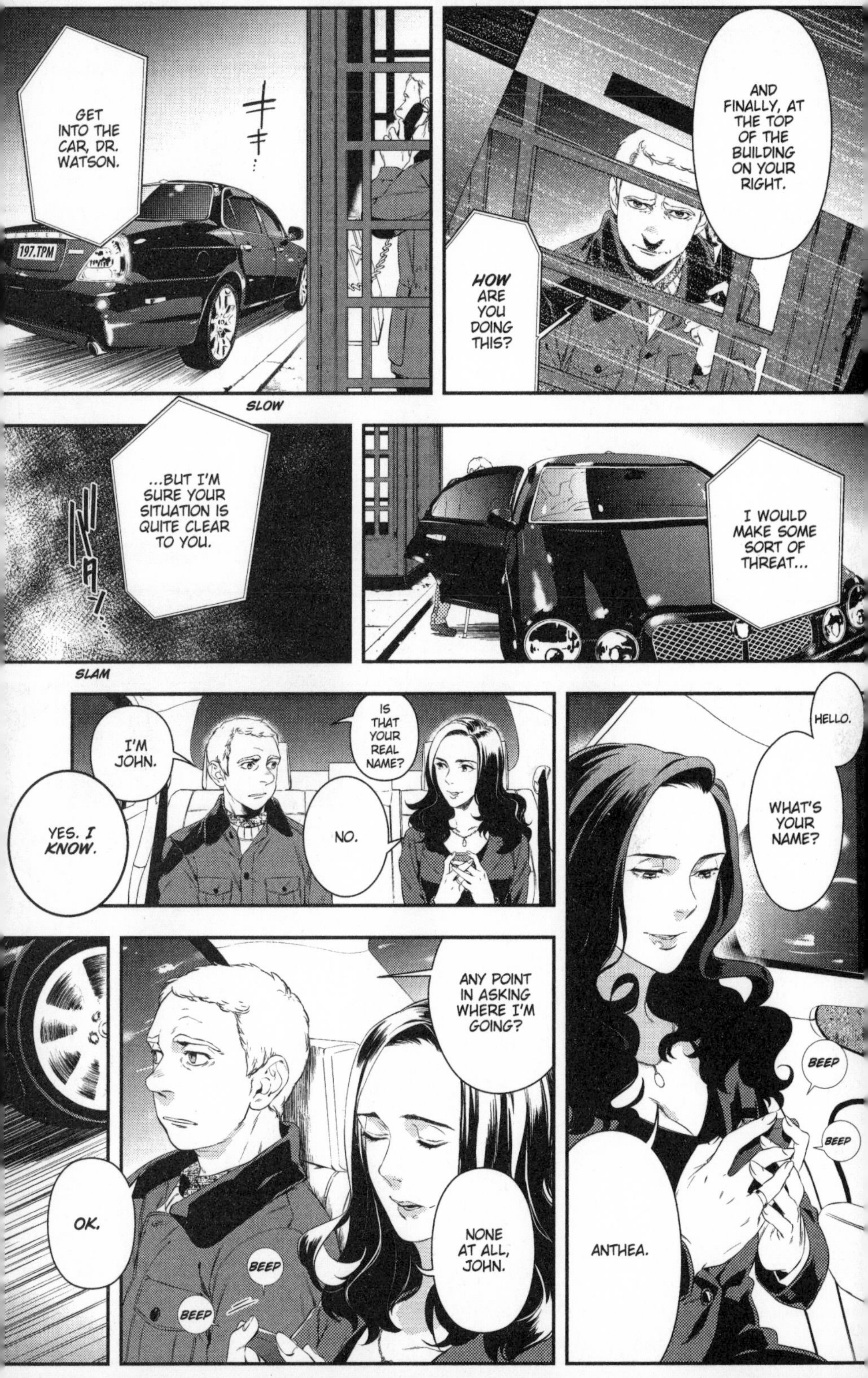
AND FINALLY, AT THE TOP OF THE BUILDING ON YOUR RIGHT.
HOW ARE YOU DOING THIS?
GET INTO THE CAR, DR. WATSON.
SLOW
I WOULD MAKE SOME SORT OF THREAT...
...BUT I'M SURE YOUR SITUATION IS QUITE CLEAR TO YOU.
SLAM
HELLO.
WHAT'S YOUR NAME?
BEEP
BEEP
ANTHEA.
IS THAT YOUR REAL NAME?
NO.
I'M JOHN.
YES. I KNOW.
ANY POINT IN ASKING WHERE I'M GOING?
NONE AT ALL, JOHN.
BEEP
BEEP
OK.

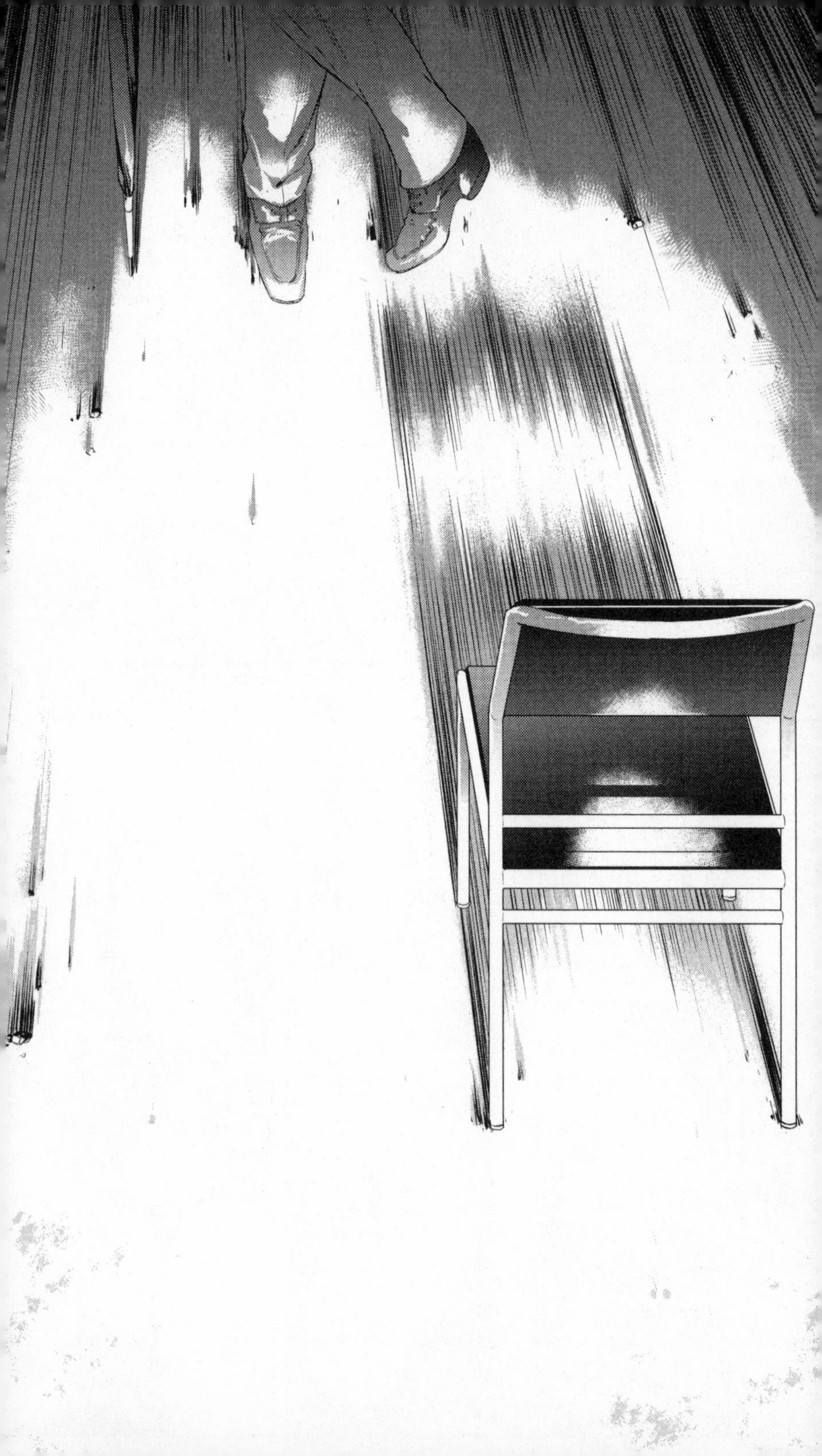

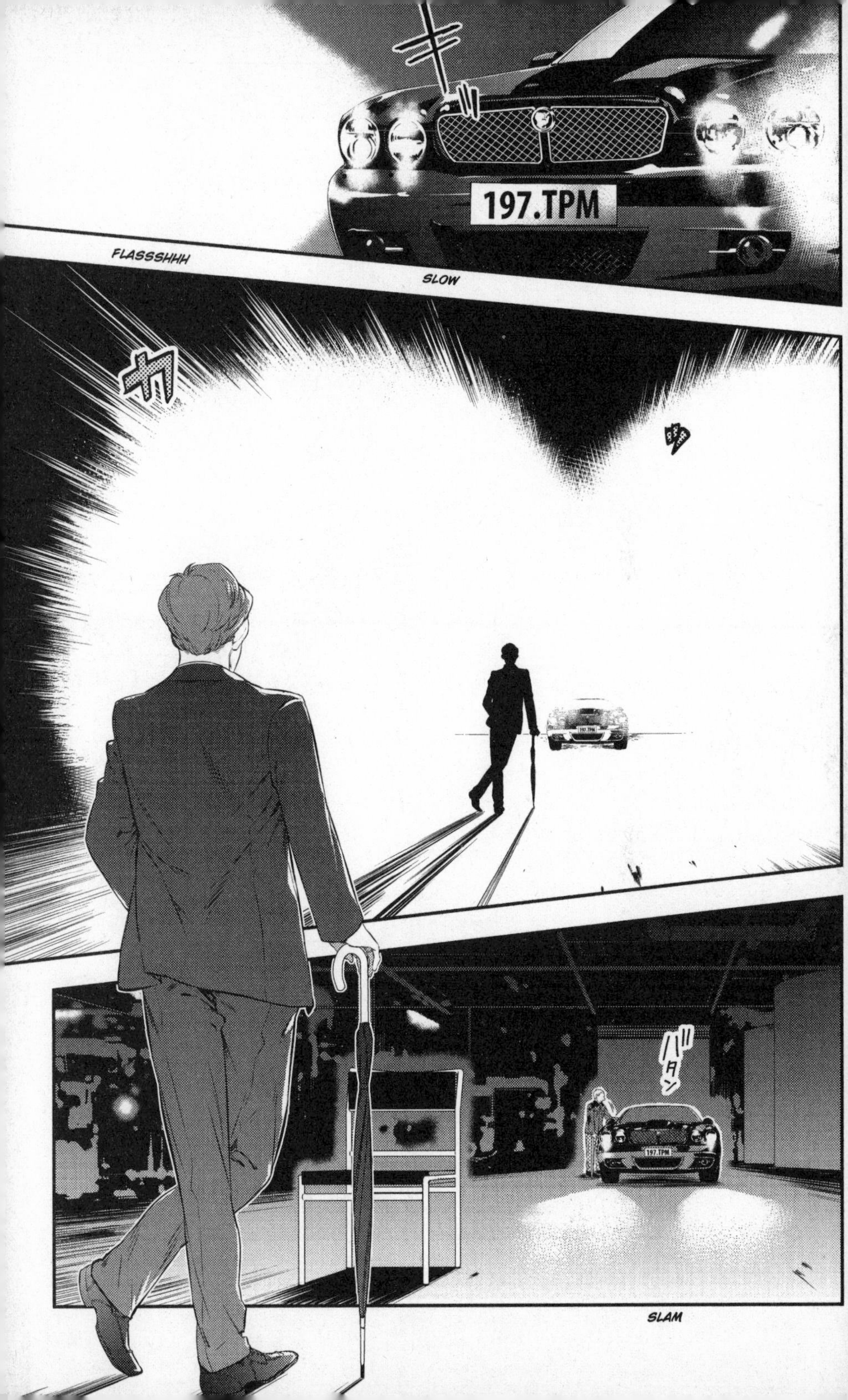
197.TPM
FLASSSHHH
SLOW
バタン
SLAM

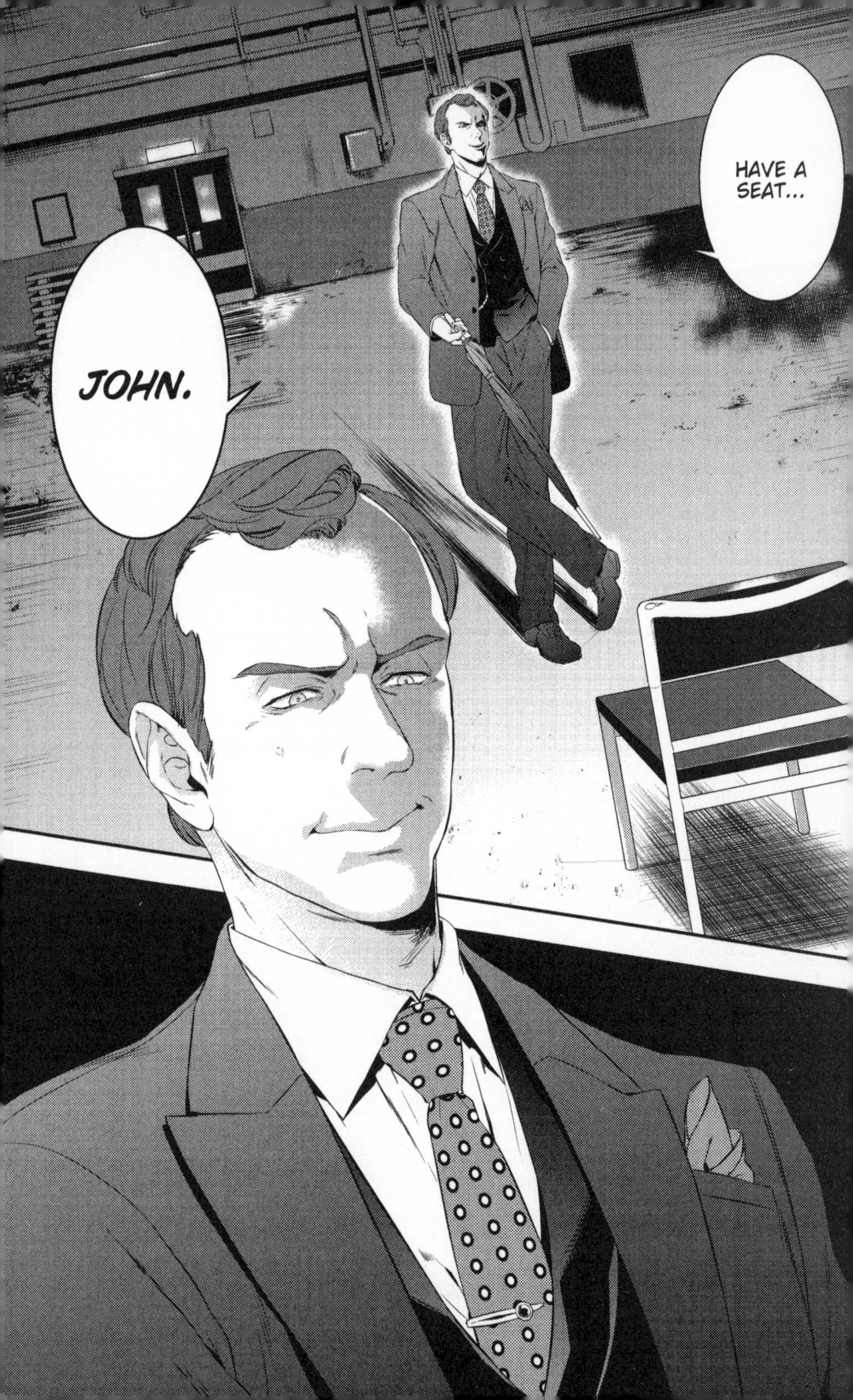
HAVE A SEAT...
JOHN.

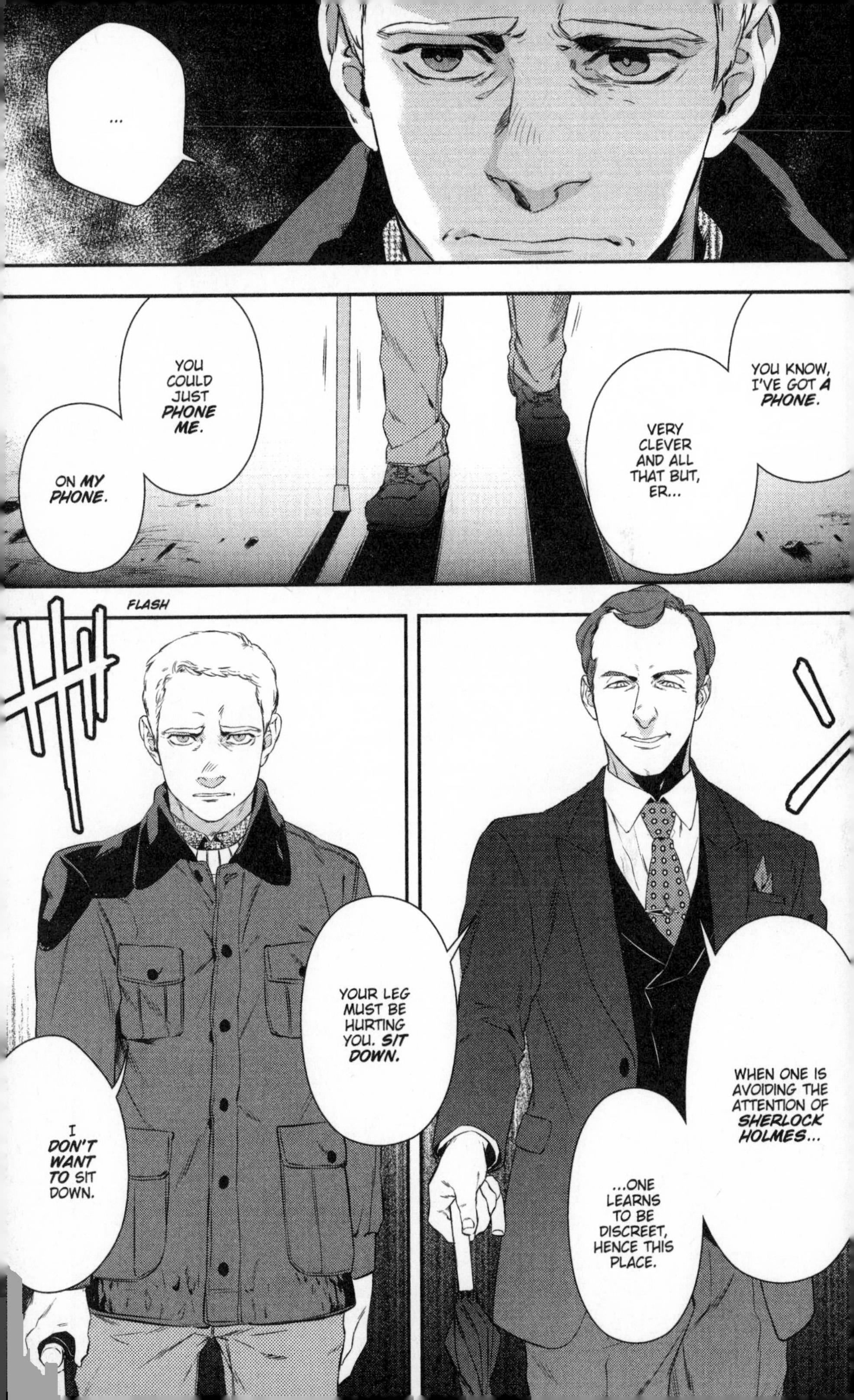
...
YOU KNOW, I'VE GOT A PHONE.
VERY CLEVER AND ALL THAT BUT, ER...
YOU COULD JUST PHONE ME.
ON MY PHONE.
WHEN ONE IS AVOIDING THE ATTENTION OF SHERLOCK HOLMES...
...ONE LEARNS TO BE DISCREET, HENCE THIS PLACE.
YOUR LEG MUST BE HURTING YOU. SIT DOWN.
FLASH
I DON'T WANT TO SIT DOWN.

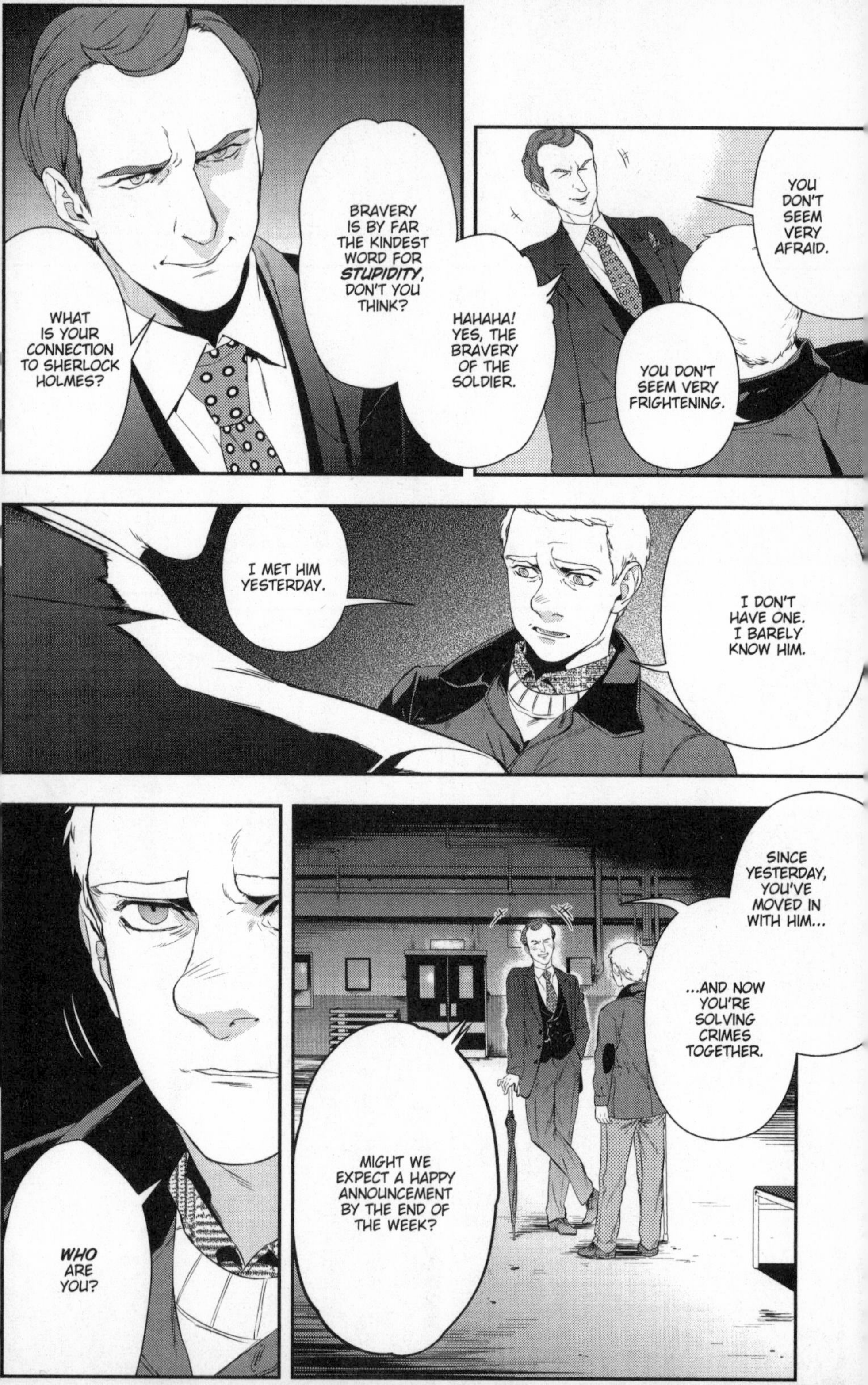
YOU DON'T SEEM VERY AFRAID.
YOU DON'T SEEM VERY FRIGHTENING.
HAHAHA! YES, THE BRAVERY OF THE SOLDIER.
BRAVERY IS BY FAR THE KINDEST WORD FOR ***STUPIDITY***, DON'T YOU THINK?
WHAT IS YOUR CONNECTION TO SHERLOCK HOLMES?
I DON'T HAVE ONE. I BARELY KNOW HIM.
I MET HIM YESTERDAY.
SINCE YESTERDAY, YOU'VE MOVED IN WITH HIM...
...AND NOW YOU'RE SOLVING CRIMES TOGETHER.
MIGHT WE EXPECT A HAPPY ANNOUNCEMENT BY THE END OF THE WEEK?
WHO ARE YOU?

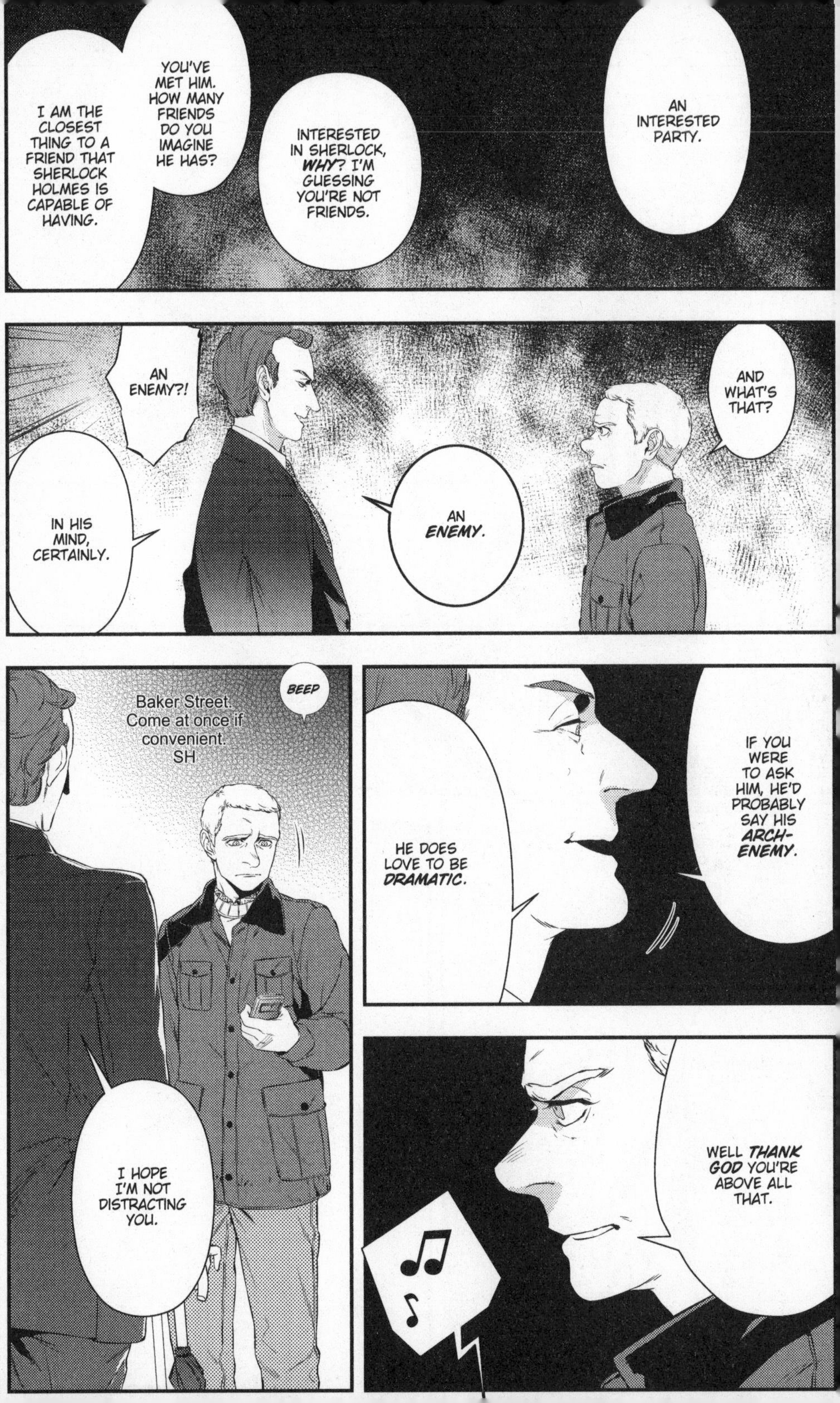
AN INTERESTED PARTY.
INTERESTED IN SHERLOCK, WHY? I'M GUESSING YOU'RE NOT FRIENDS.
YOU'VE MET HIM. HOW MANY FRIENDS DO YOU IMAGINE HE HAS?
I AM THE CLOSEST THING TO A FRIEND THAT SHERLOCK HOLMES IS CAPABLE OF HAVING.
AND WHAT'S THAT?
AN ENEMY.
AN ENEMY?!
IN HIS MIND, CERTAINLY.
IF YOU WERE TO ASK HIM, HE'D PROBABLY SAY HIS ARCH-ENEMY.
HE DOES LOVE TO BE DRAMATIC.
WELL THANK GOD YOU'RE ABOVE ALL THAT.
BEEP
Baker Street. Come at once if convenient. SH
I HOPE I'M NOT DISTRACTING YOU.

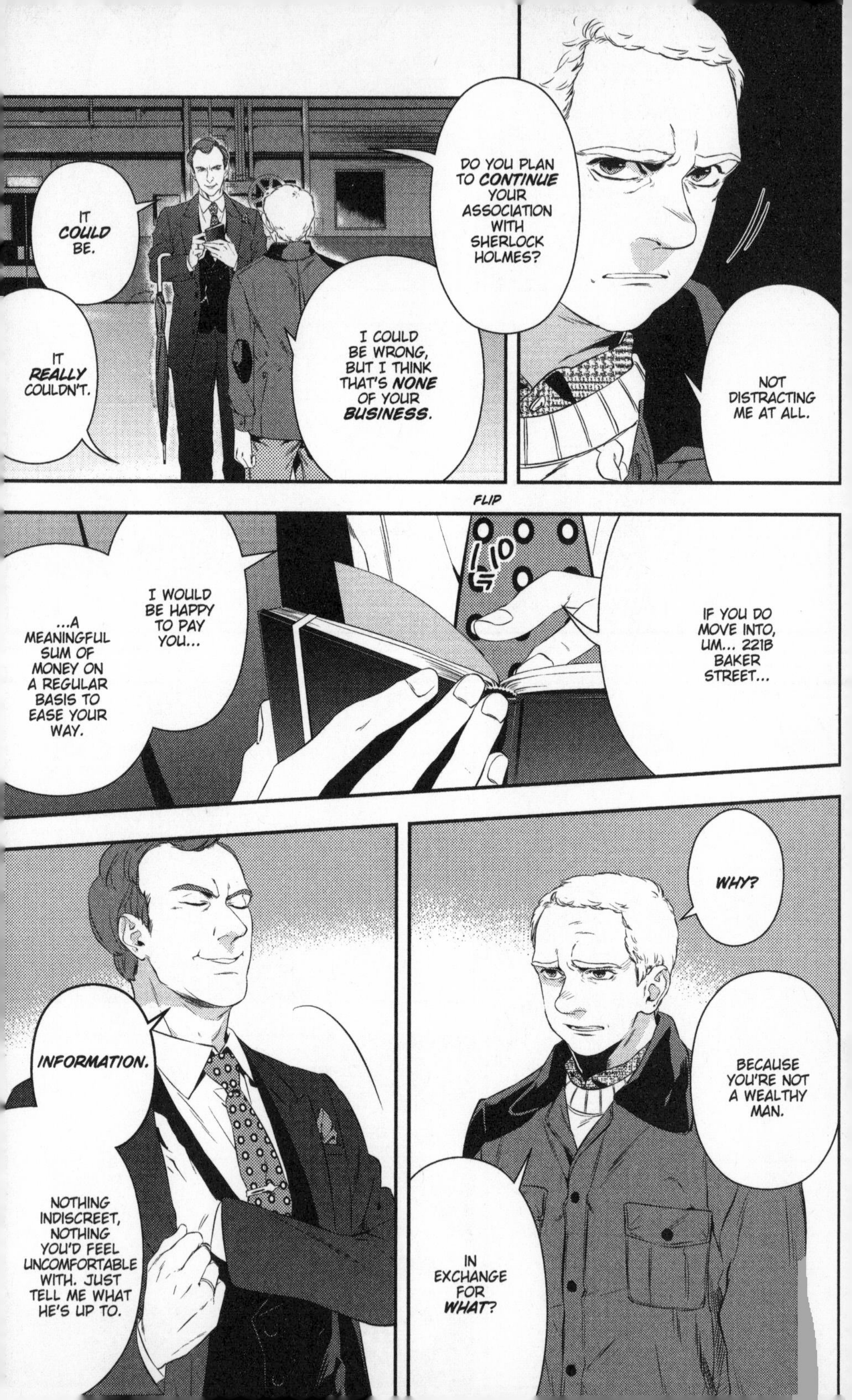
NOT DISTRACTING ME AT ALL.
DO YOU PLAN TO CONTINUE YOUR ASSOCIATION WITH SHERLOCK HOLMES?
I COULD BE WRONG, BUT I THINK THAT'S NONE OF YOUR BUSINESS.
IT COULD BE.
IT REALLY COULDN'T.
FLIP
IF YOU DO MOVE INTO, UM... 221B BAKER STREET...
I WOULD BE HAPPY TO PAY YOU...
...A MEANINGFUL SUM OF MONEY ON A REGULAR BASIS TO EASE YOUR WAY.
WHY?
BECAUSE YOU'RE NOT A WEALTHY MAN.
IN EXCHANGE FOR WHAT?
INFORMATION.
NOTHING INDISCREET, NOTHING YOU'D FEEL UNCOMFORTABLE WITH. JUST TELL ME WHAT HE'S UP TO.

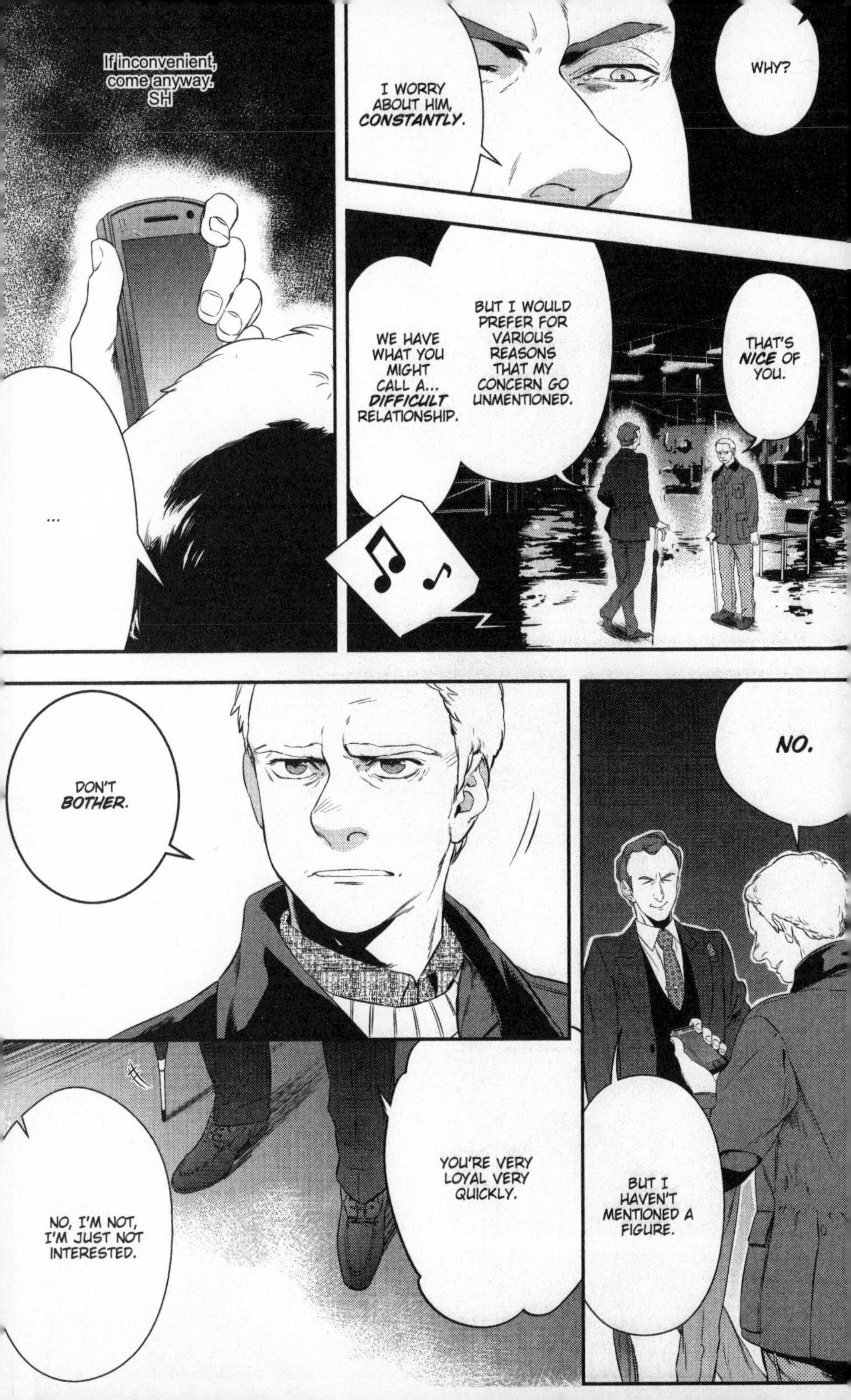
WHY?
I WORRY ABOUT HIM, CONSTANTLY.
THAT'S NICE OF YOU.
WE HAVE WHAT YOU MIGHT CALL A... DIFFICULT RELATIONSHIP.
BUT I WOULD PREFER FOR VARIOUS REASONS THAT MY CONCERN GO UNMENTIONED.
If inconvenient, come anyway. SH
...
NO.
BUT I HAVEN'T MENTIONED A FIGURE.
DON'T BOTHER.
YOU'RE VERY LOYAL VERY QUICKLY.
NO, I'M NOT, I'M JUST NOT INTERESTED.

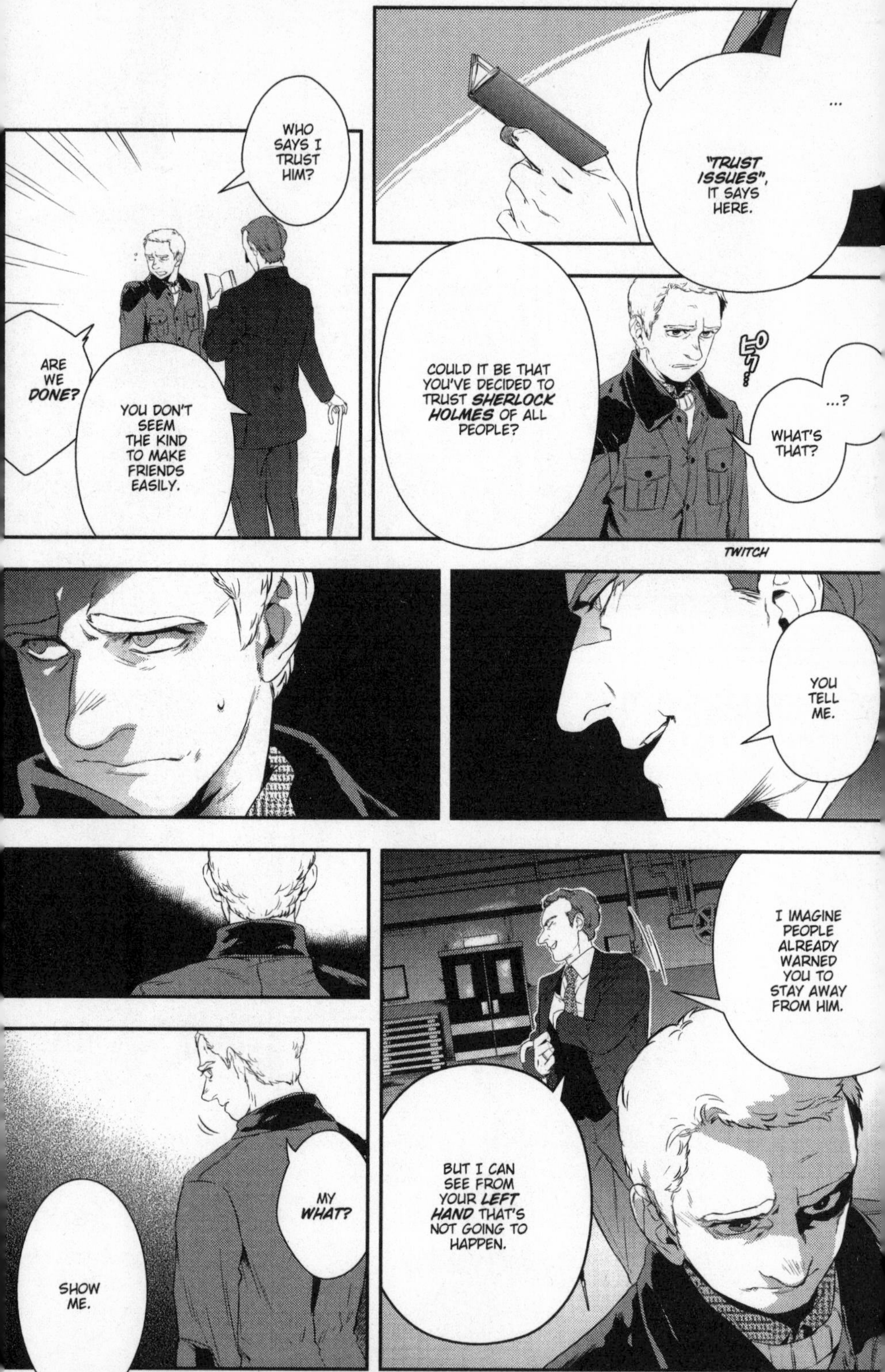
...
"TRUST ISSUES", IT SAYS HERE.
...? WHAT'S THAT?
TWITCH
COULD IT BE THAT YOU'VE DECIDED TO TRUST SHERLOCK HOLMES OF ALL PEOPLE?
WHO SAYS I TRUST HIM?
YOU DON'T SEEM THE KIND TO MAKE FRIENDS EASILY.
ARE WE DONE?
YOU TELL ME.
I IMAGINE PEOPLE ALREADY WARNED YOU TO STAY AWAY FROM HIM.
BUT I CAN SEE FROM YOUR LEFT HAND THAT'S NOT GOING TO HAPPEN.
MY WHAT?
SHOW ME.

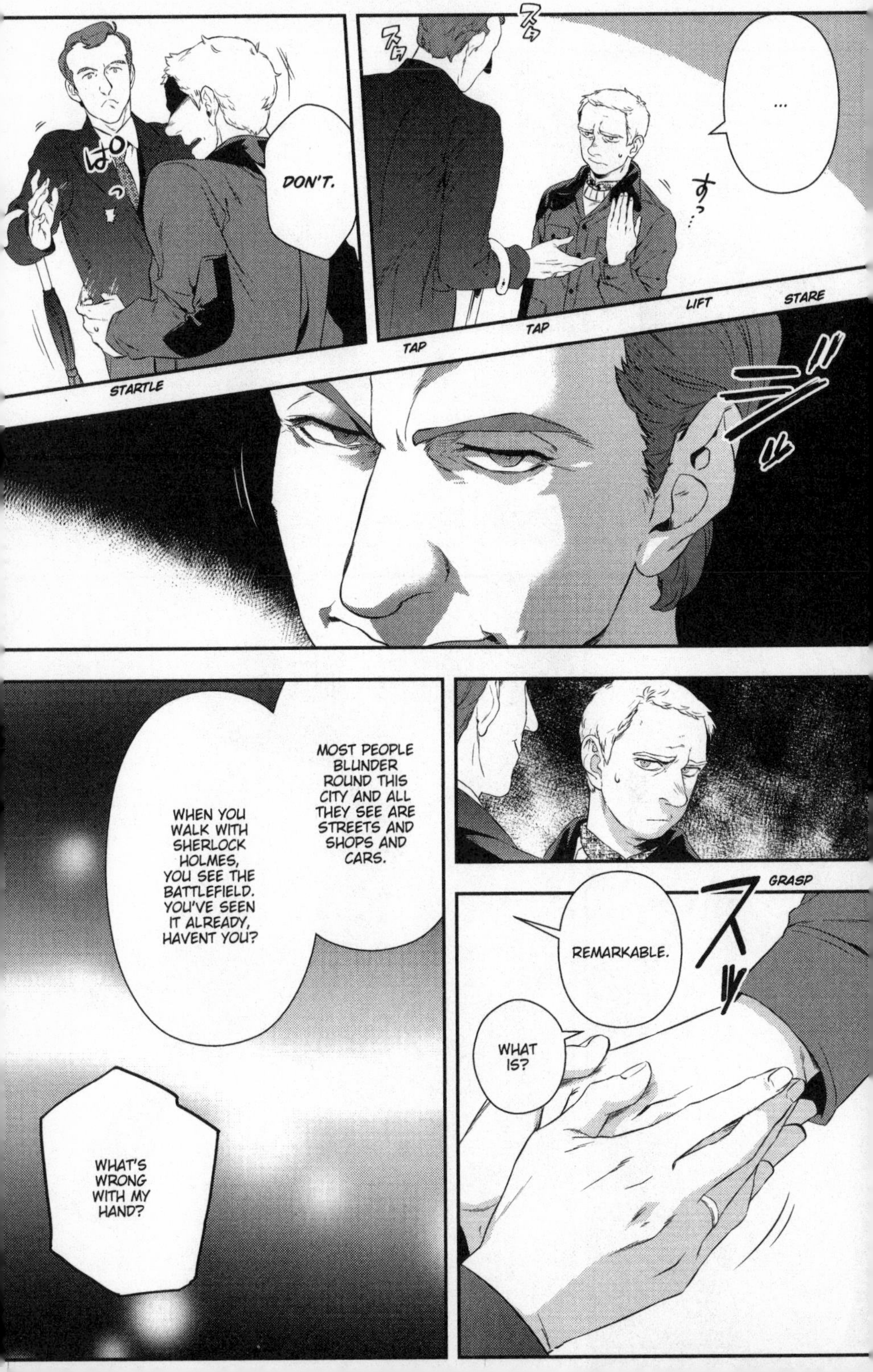
…
TAP
TAP
LIFT
DON'T.
STARTLE
STARE
GRASP
REMARKABLE.
WHAT IS?
MOST PEOPLE BLUNDER ROUND THIS CITY AND ALL THEY SEE ARE STREETS AND SHOPS AND CARS.
WHEN YOU WALK WITH SHERLOCK HOLMES, YOU SEE THE BATTLEFIELD. YOU'VE SEEN IT ALREADY, HAVENT YOU?
WHAT'S WRONG WITH MY HAND?

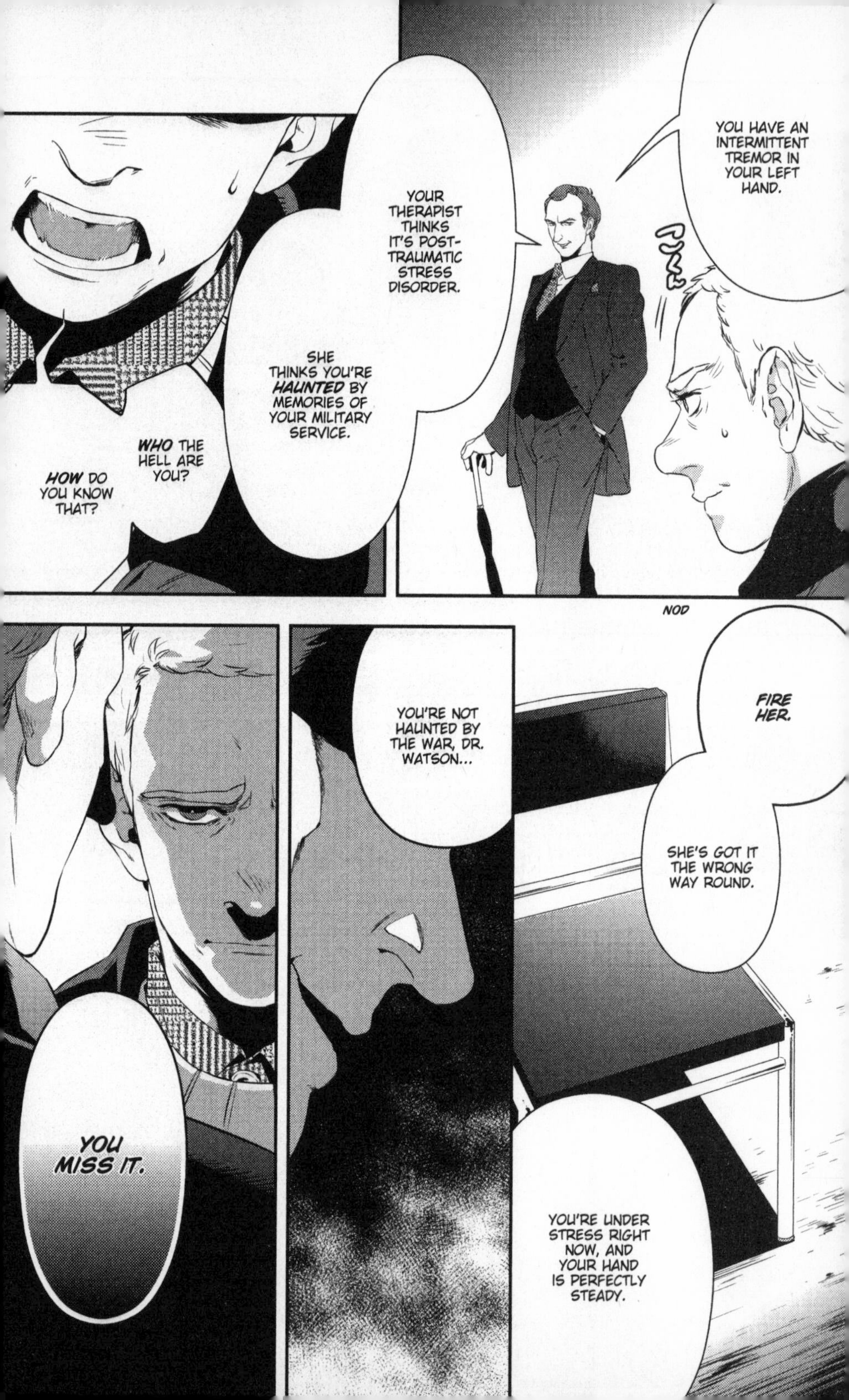
YOU HAVE AN INTERMITTENT TREMOR IN YOUR LEFT HAND.
NOD
YOUR THERAPIST THINKS IT'S POST-TRAUMATIC STRESS DISORDER.
SHE THINKS YOU'RE *HAUNTED* BY MEMORIES OF YOUR MILITARY SERVICE.
WHO THE HELL ARE YOU?
HOW DO YOU KNOW THAT?
FIRE HER.
SHE'S GOT IT THE WRONG WAY ROUND.
YOU'RE UNDER STRESS RIGHT NOW, AND YOUR HAND IS PERFECTLY STEADY.
YOU'RE NOT HAUNTED BY THE WAR, DR. WATSON...
YOU MISS IT.

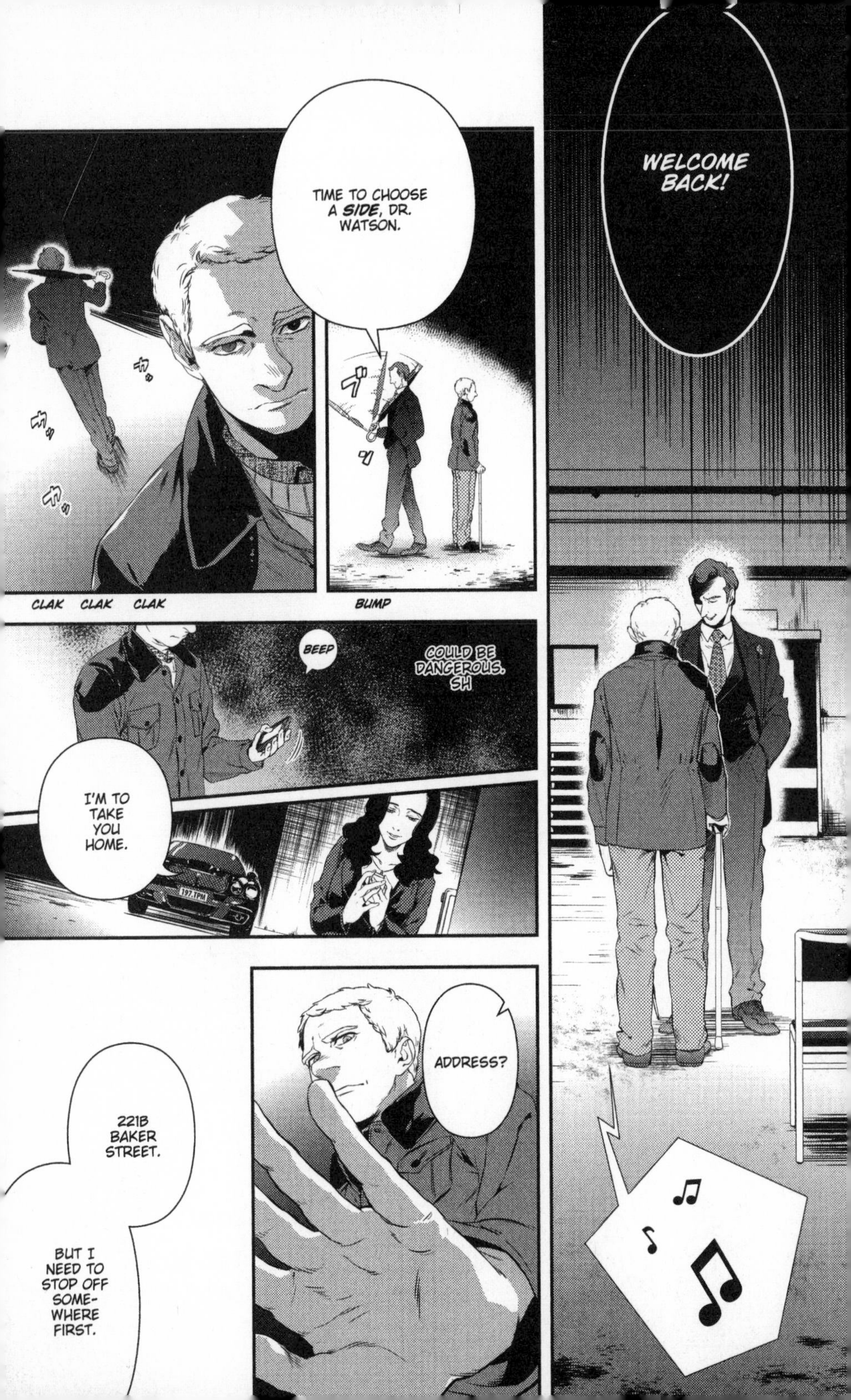
WELCOME BACK!
TIME TO CHOOSE A SIDE, DR. WATSON.
BUMP
CLAK CLAK CLAK
BEEP
COULD BE DANGEROUS. SH
I'M TO TAKE YOU HOME.
ADDRESS?
221B BAKER STREET.
BUT I NEED TO STOP OFF SOME-WHERE FIRST.

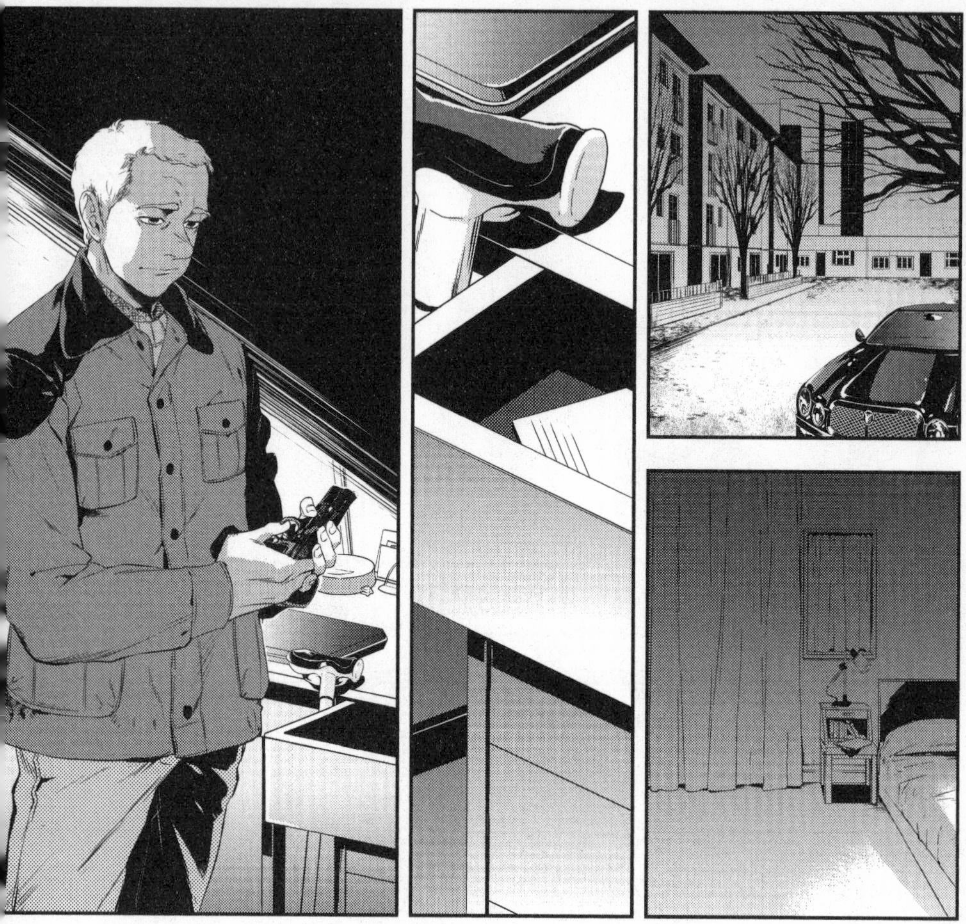

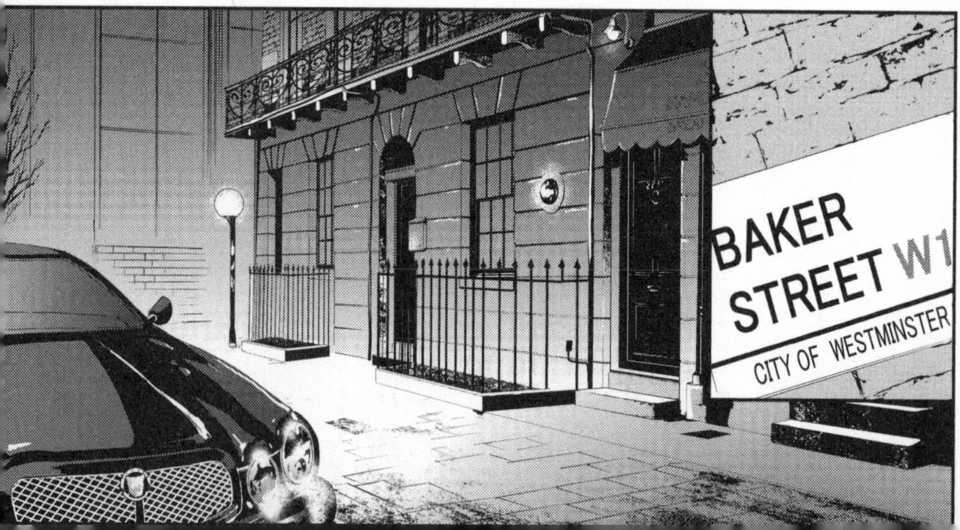
BAKER
STREET W1
CITY OF WESTMINSTER

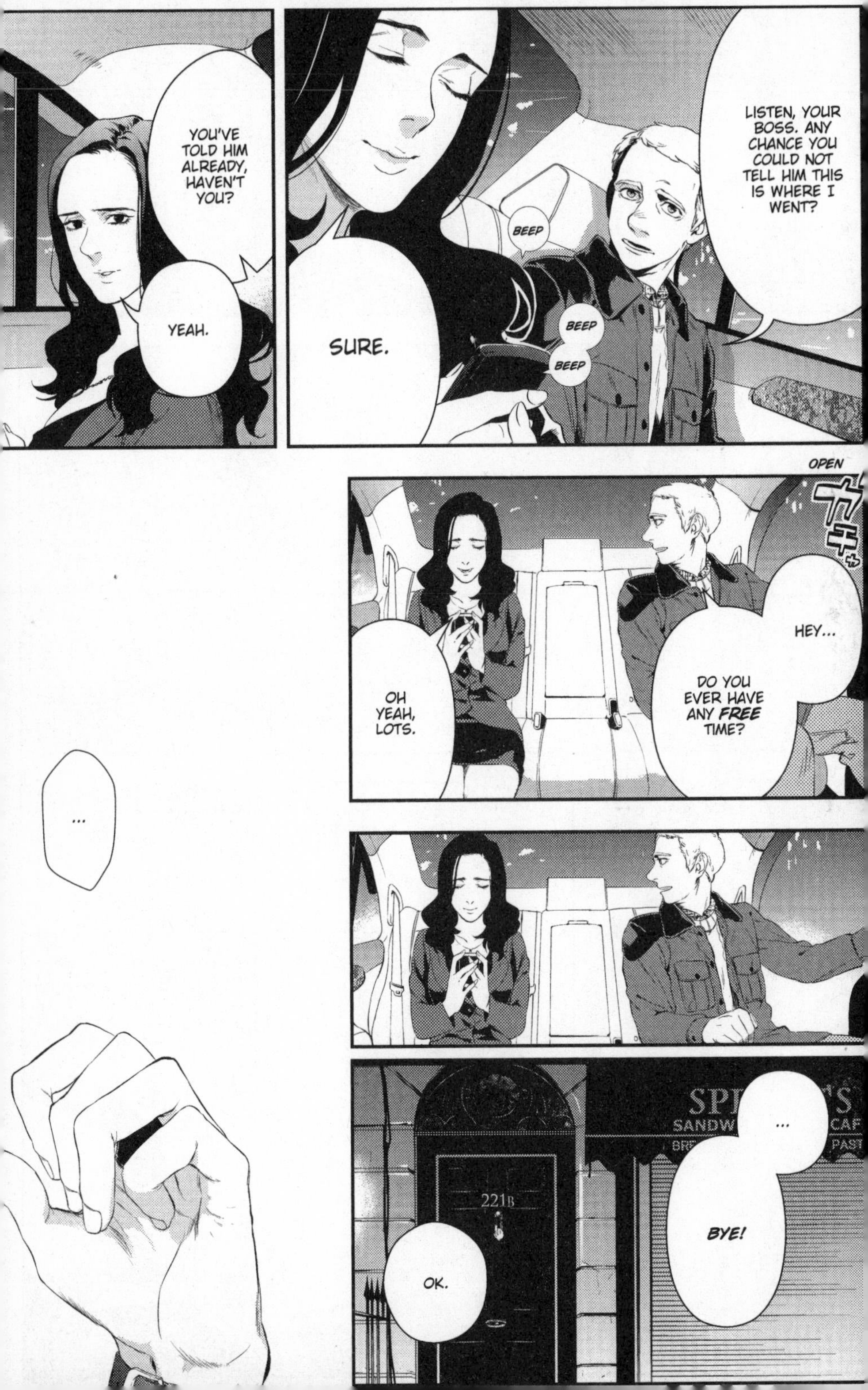
LISTEN, YOUR BOSS. ANY CHANCE YOU COULD NOT TELL HIM THIS IS WHERE I WENT?
BEEP
BEEP
BEEP
SURE.
YOU'VE TOLD HIM ALREADY, HAVEN'T YOU?
YEAH.
OPEN
HEY...
DO YOU EVER HAVE ANY FREE TIME?
OH YEAH, LOTS.
...
221B
BYE!
OK.
...

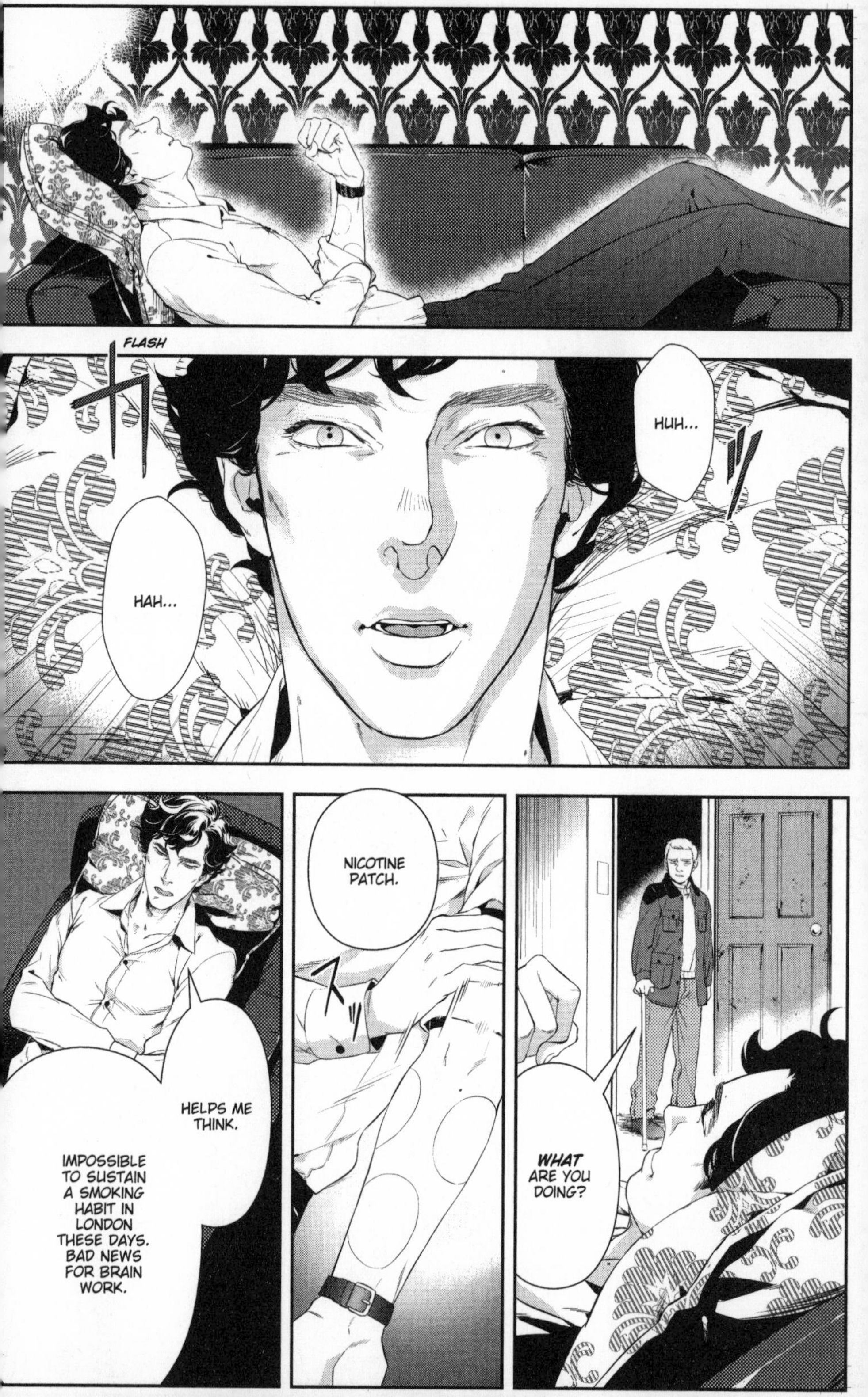
FLASH
HUH...
HAH...
WHAT ARE YOU DOING?
NICOTINE PATCH.
HELPS ME THINK.
IMPOSSIBLE TO SUSTAIN A SMOKING HABIT IN LONDON THESE DAYS. BAD NEWS FOR BRAIN WORK.

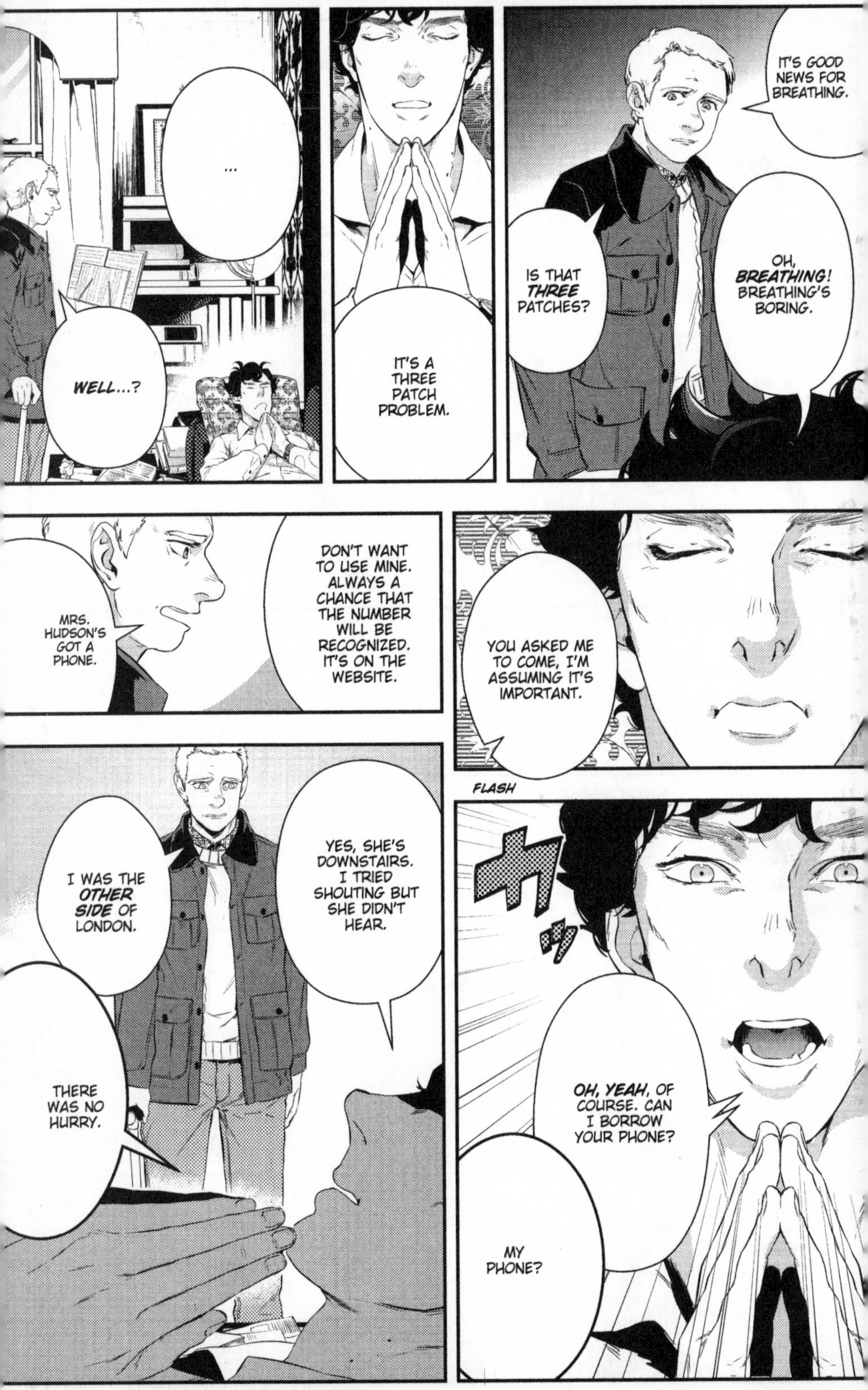
IT'S GOOD NEWS FOR BREATHING.
OH, *BREATHING*! BREATHING'S BORING.
IS THAT *THREE* PATCHES?
IT'S A THREE PATCH PROBLEM.
...
WELL...?
YOU ASKED ME TO COME, I'M ASSUMING IT'S IMPORTANT.
FLASH
OH, YEAH, OF COURSE. CAN I BORROW YOUR PHONE?
MY PHONE?
DON'T WANT TO USE MINE. ALWAYS A CHANCE THAT THE NUMBER WILL BE RECOGNIZED. IT'S ON THE WEBSITE.
MRS. HUDSON'S GOT A PHONE.
YES, SHE'S DOWNSTAIRS. I TRIED SHOUTING BUT SHE DIDN'T HEAR.
I WAS THE *OTHER SIDE* OF LONDON.
THERE WAS NO HURRY.

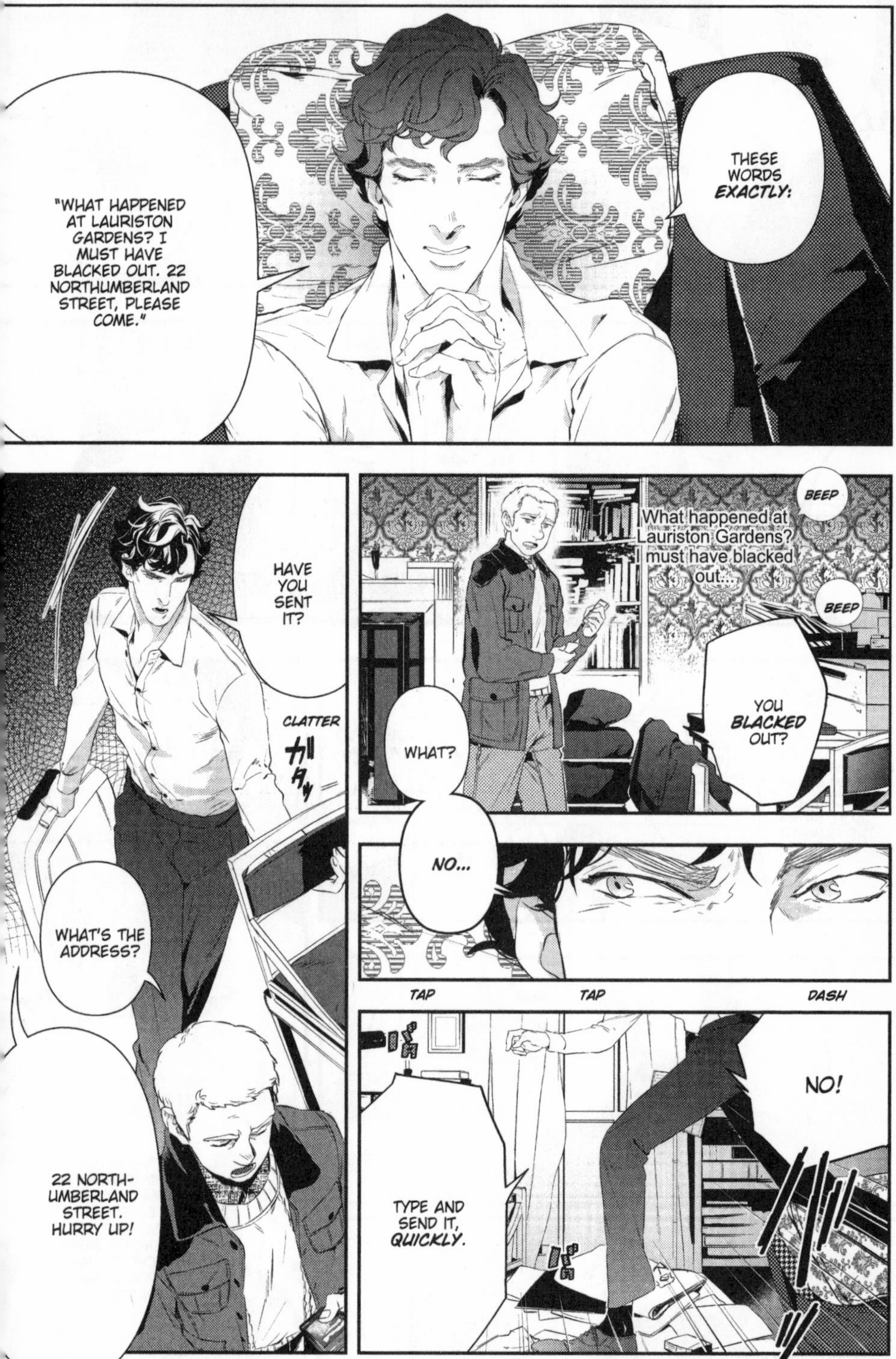

THESE WORDS *EXACTLY:*
"WHAT HAPPENED AT LAURISTON GARDENS? I MUST HAVE BLACKED OUT. 22 NORTHUMBERLAND STREET, PLEASE COME."
BEEP
What happened at Lauriston Gardens? I must have blacked out...
BEEP
YOU *BLACKED* OUT?
WHAT?
NO...
TAP
TAP
DASH
NO!
TYPE AND SEND IT, *QUICKLY*.
HAVE YOU SENT IT?
CLATTER
ガタッ
WHAT'S THE ADDRESS?
22 NORTH-UMBERLAND STREET. HURRY UP!

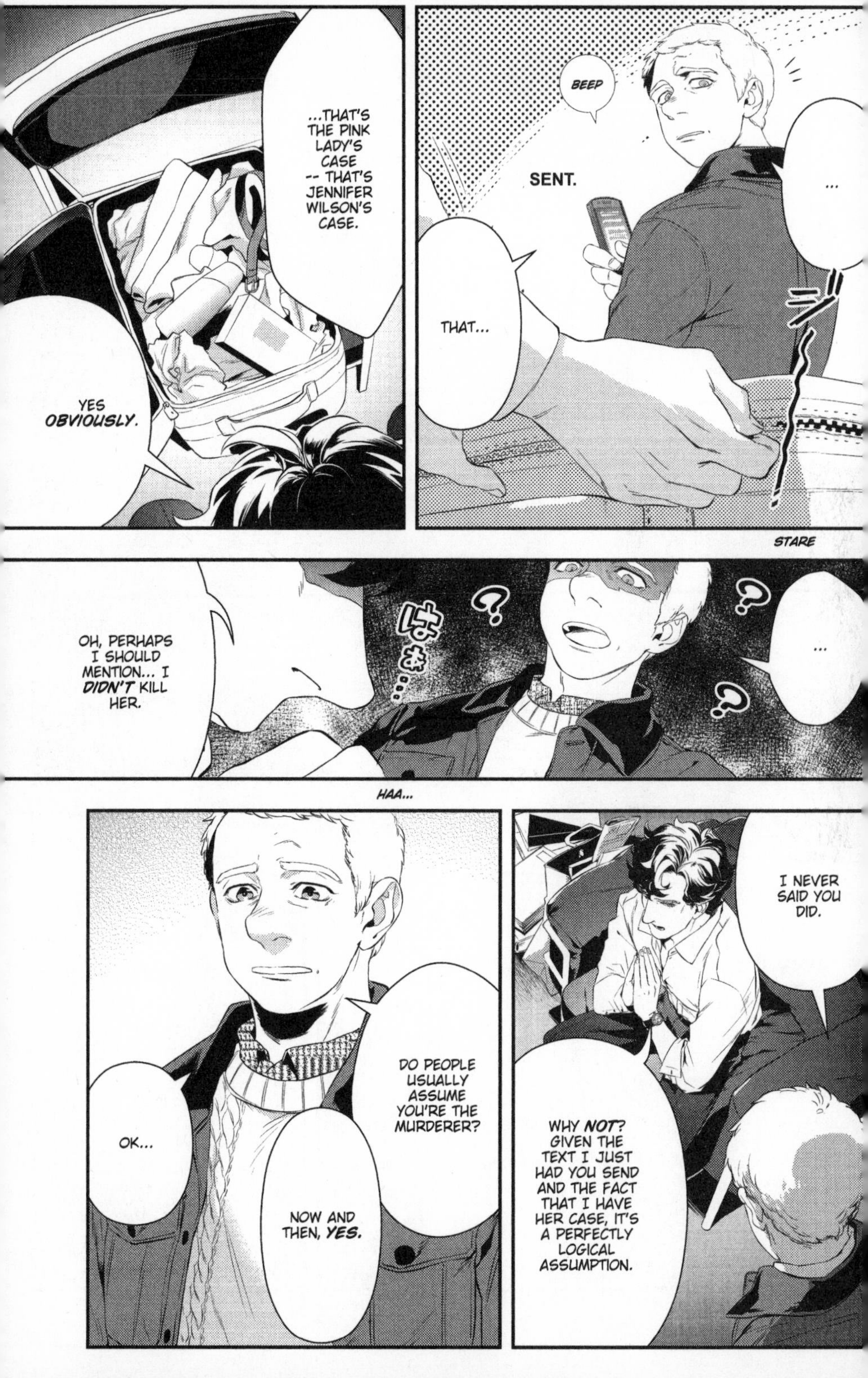

...
BEEP
SENT.
ジー
THAT...
...THAT'S THE PINK LADY'S CASE -- THAT'S JENNIFER WILSON'S CASE.
YES *OBVIOUSLY*.
STARE
...
はぁ...
OH, PERHAPS I SHOULD MENTION... I *DIDN'T* KILL HER.
HAA...
I NEVER SAID YOU DID.
WHY *NOT*? GIVEN THE TEXT I JUST HAD YOU SEND AND THE FACT THAT I HAVE HER CASE, IT'S A PERFECTLY LOGICAL ASSUMPTION.
DO PEOPLE USUALLY ASSUME YOU'RE THE MURDERER?
OK...
NOW AND THEN, *YES.*

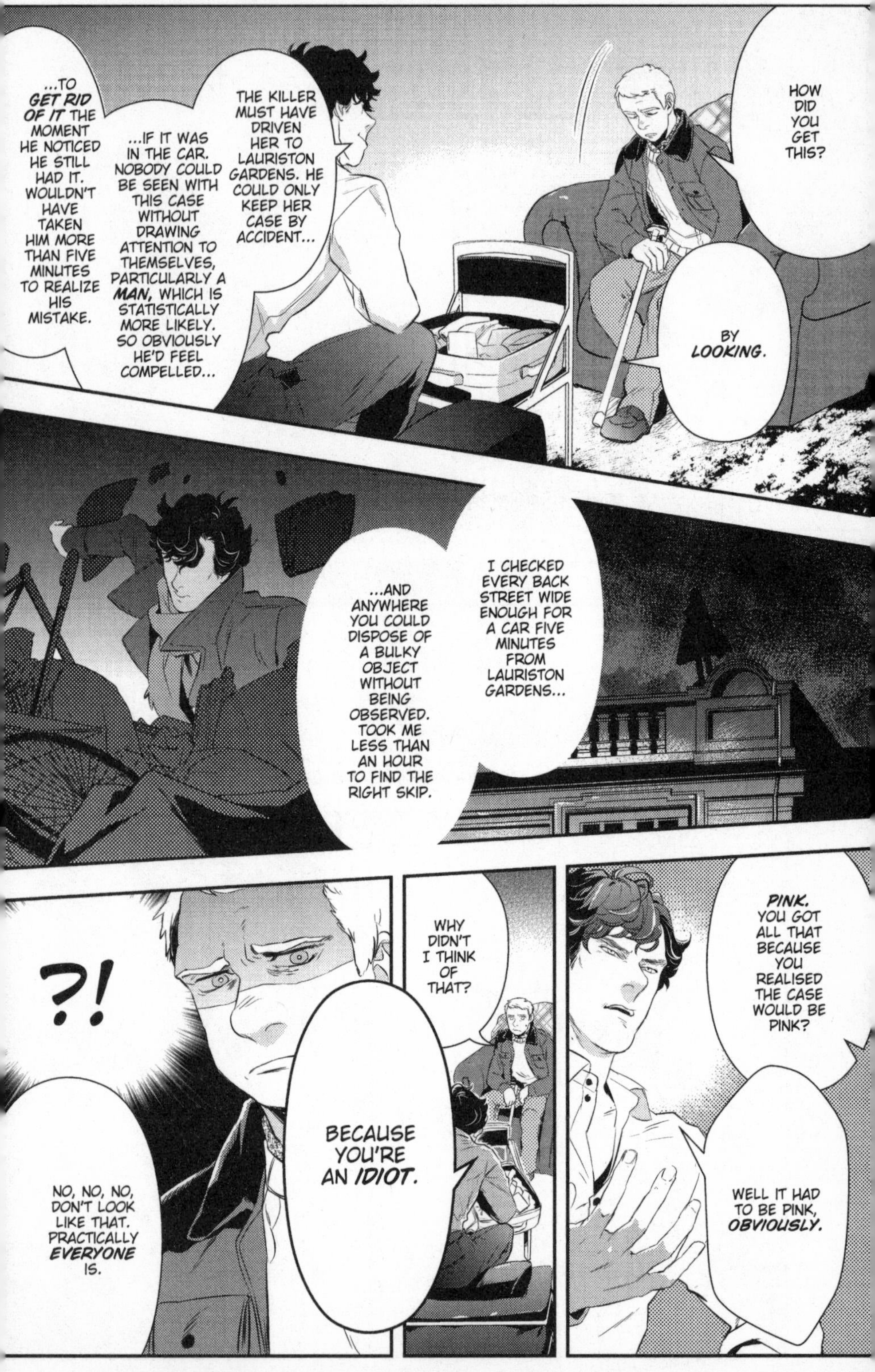
HOW DID YOU GET THIS?
BY *LOOKING*.
THE KILLER MUST HAVE DRIVEN HER TO LAURISTON GARDENS. HE COULD ONLY KEEP HER CASE BY ACCIDENT...
...IF IT WAS IN THE CAR. NOBODY COULD BE SEEN WITH THIS CASE WITHOUT DRAWING ATTENTION TO THEMSELVES, PARTICULARLY A ***MAN,*** WHICH IS STATISTICALLY MORE LIKELY. SO OBVIOUSLY HE'D FEEL COMPELLED...
...TO ***GET RID OF IT*** THE MOMENT HE NOTICED HE STILL HAD IT. WOULDN'T HAVE TAKEN HIM MORE THAN FIVE MINUTES TO REALIZE HIS MISTAKE.
I CHECKED EVERY BACK STREET WIDE ENOUGH FOR A CAR FIVE MINUTES FROM LAURISTON GARDENS...
...AND ANYWHERE YOU COULD DISPOSE OF A BULKY OBJECT WITHOUT BEING OBSERVED. TOOK ME LESS THAN AN HOUR TO FIND THE RIGHT SKIP.
PINK. YOU GOT ALL THAT BECAUSE YOU REALISED THE CASE WOULD BE PINK?
WELL IT HAD TO BE PINK, ***OBVIOUSLY.***
WHY DIDN'T I THINK OF THAT?
BECAUSE YOU'RE AN *IDIOT*.
?!
NO, NO, NO, DON'T LOOK LIKE THAT. PRACTICALLY ***EVERYONE*** IS.

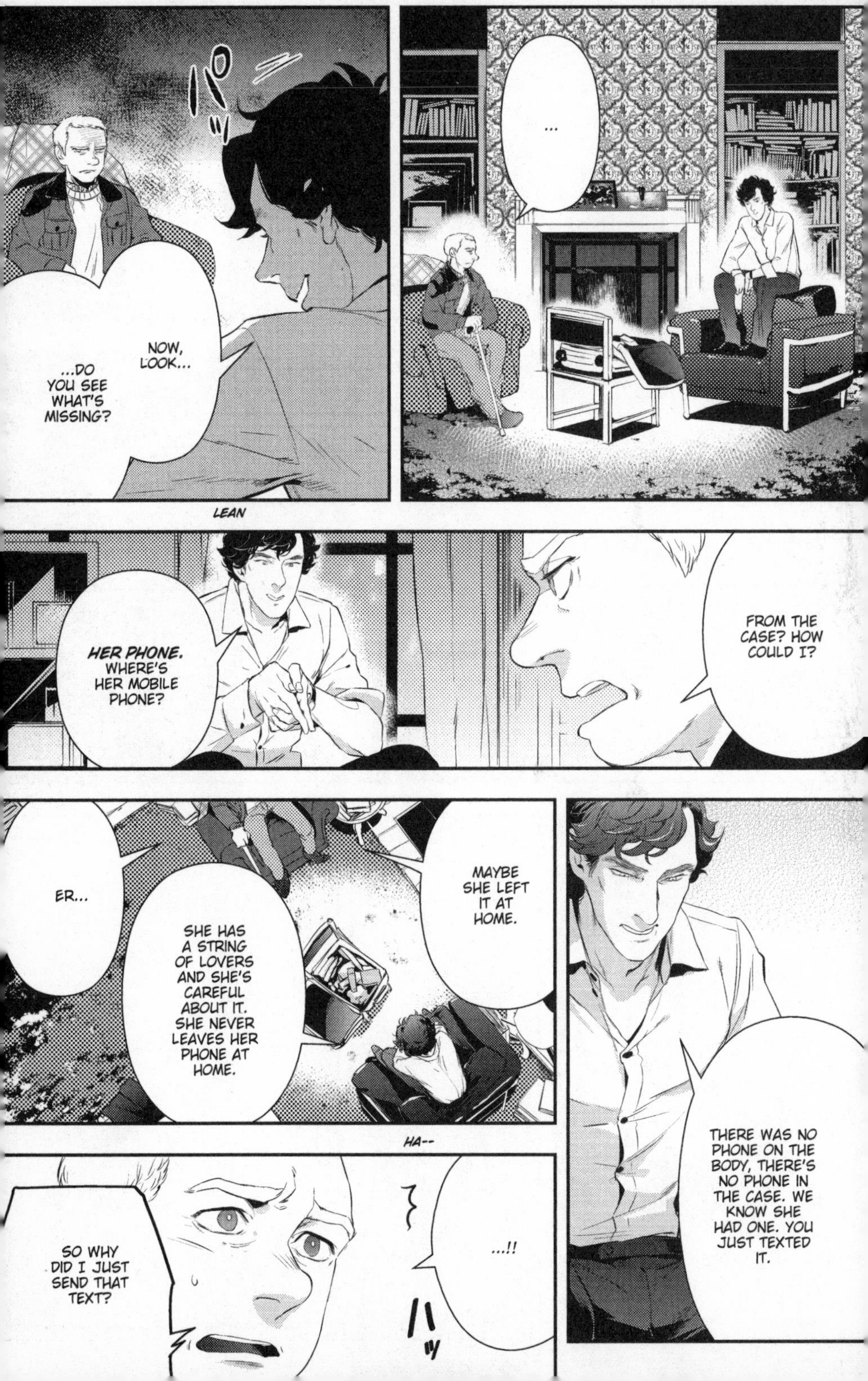

...
パッ
NOW, LOOK...
...DO YOU SEE WHAT'S MISSING?
LEAN
FROM THE CASE? HOW COULD I?
HER PHONE. WHERE'S HER MOBILE PHONE?
THERE WAS NO PHONE ON THE BODY, THERE'S NO PHONE IN THE CASE. WE KNOW SHE HAD ONE. YOU JUST TEXTED IT.
MAYBE SHE LEFT IT AT HOME.
ER...
SHE HAS A STRING OF LOVERS AND SHE'S CAREFUL ABOUT IT. SHE NEVER LEAVES HER PHONE AT HOME.
HA--
ハッ
...!!
SO WHY DID I JUST SEND THAT TEXT?

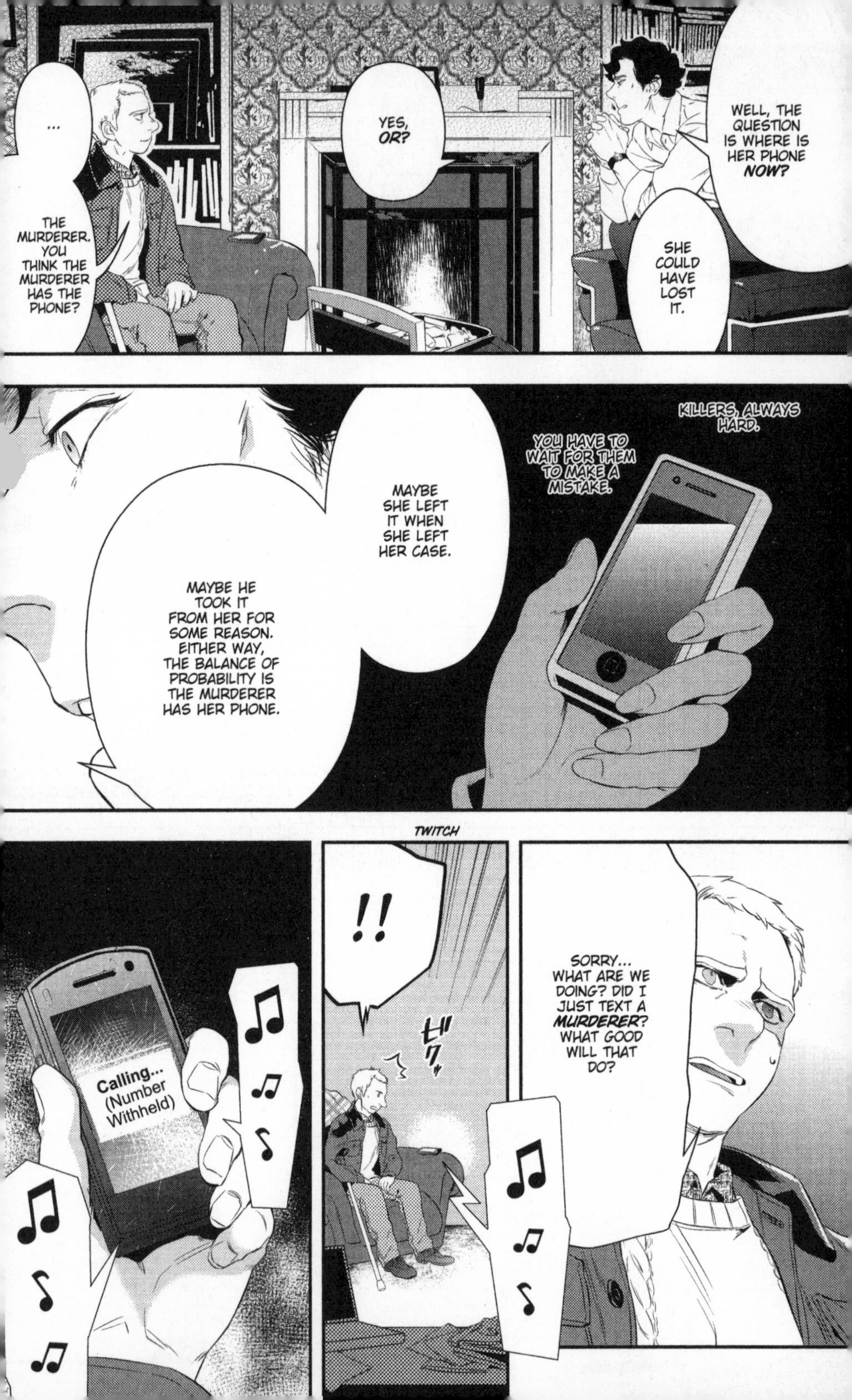
WELL, THE QUESTION IS WHERE IS HER PHONE NOW?
SHE COULD HAVE LOST IT.
YES, OR?
...
THE MURDERER. YOU THINK THE MURDERER HAS THE PHONE?
KILLERS, ALWAYS HARD.
YOU HAVE TO WAIT FOR THEM TO MAKE A MISTAKE.
MAYBE SHE LEFT IT WHEN SHE LEFT HER CASE.
MAYBE HE TOOK IT FROM HER FOR SOME REASON. EITHER WAY, THE BALANCE OF PROBABILITY IS THE MURDERER HAS HER PHONE.
SORRY... WHAT ARE WE DOING? DID I JUST TEXT A MURDERER? WHAT GOOD WILL THAT DO?
TWITCH
!!
Calling... (Number Withheld)

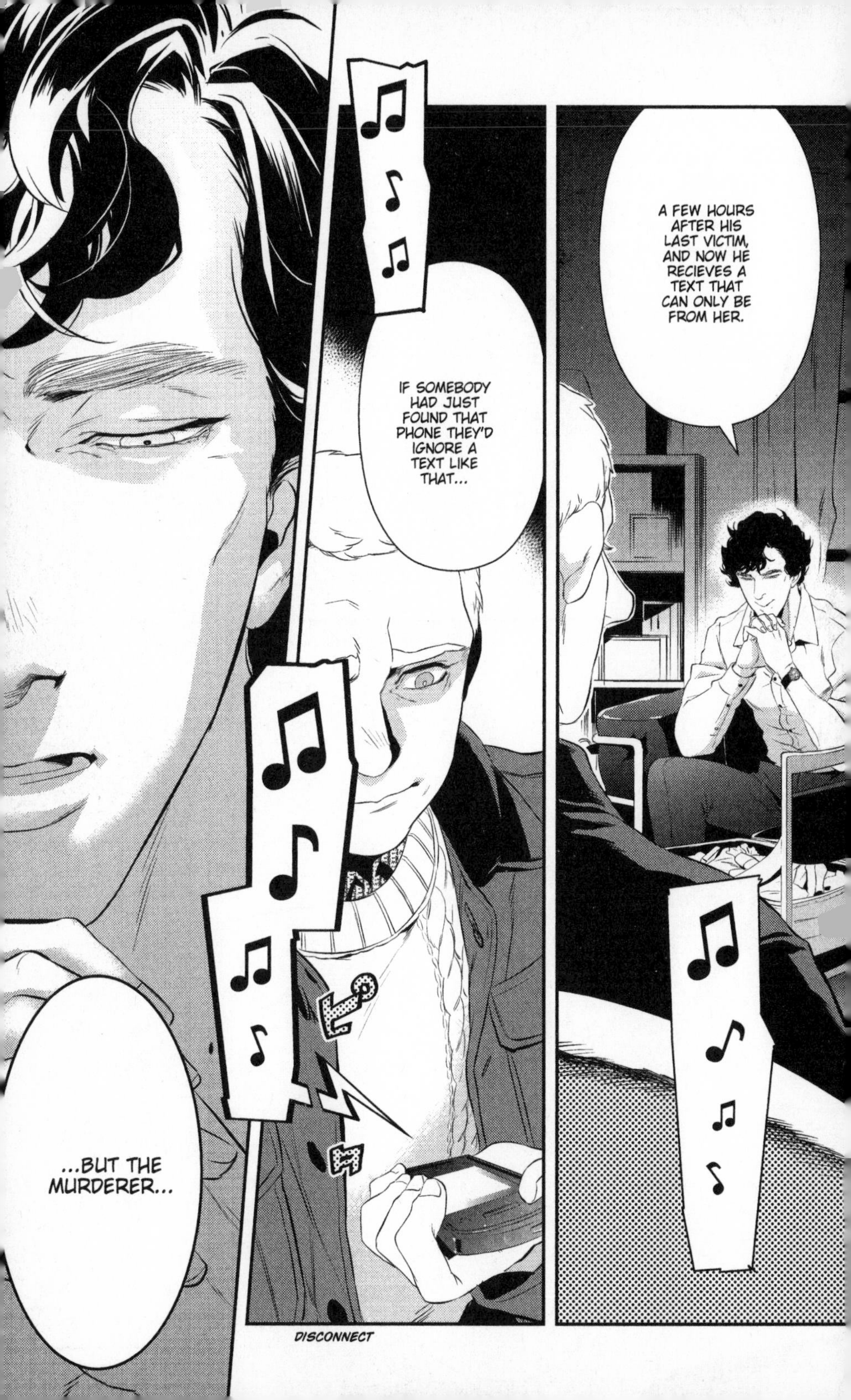
A FEW HOURS AFTER HIS LAST VICTIM, AND NOW HE RECIEVES A TEXT THAT CAN ONLY BE FROM HER.
IF SOMEBODY HAD JUST FOUND THAT PHONE THEY'D IGNORE A TEXT LIKE THAT...
DISCONNECT
...BUT THE MURDERER...

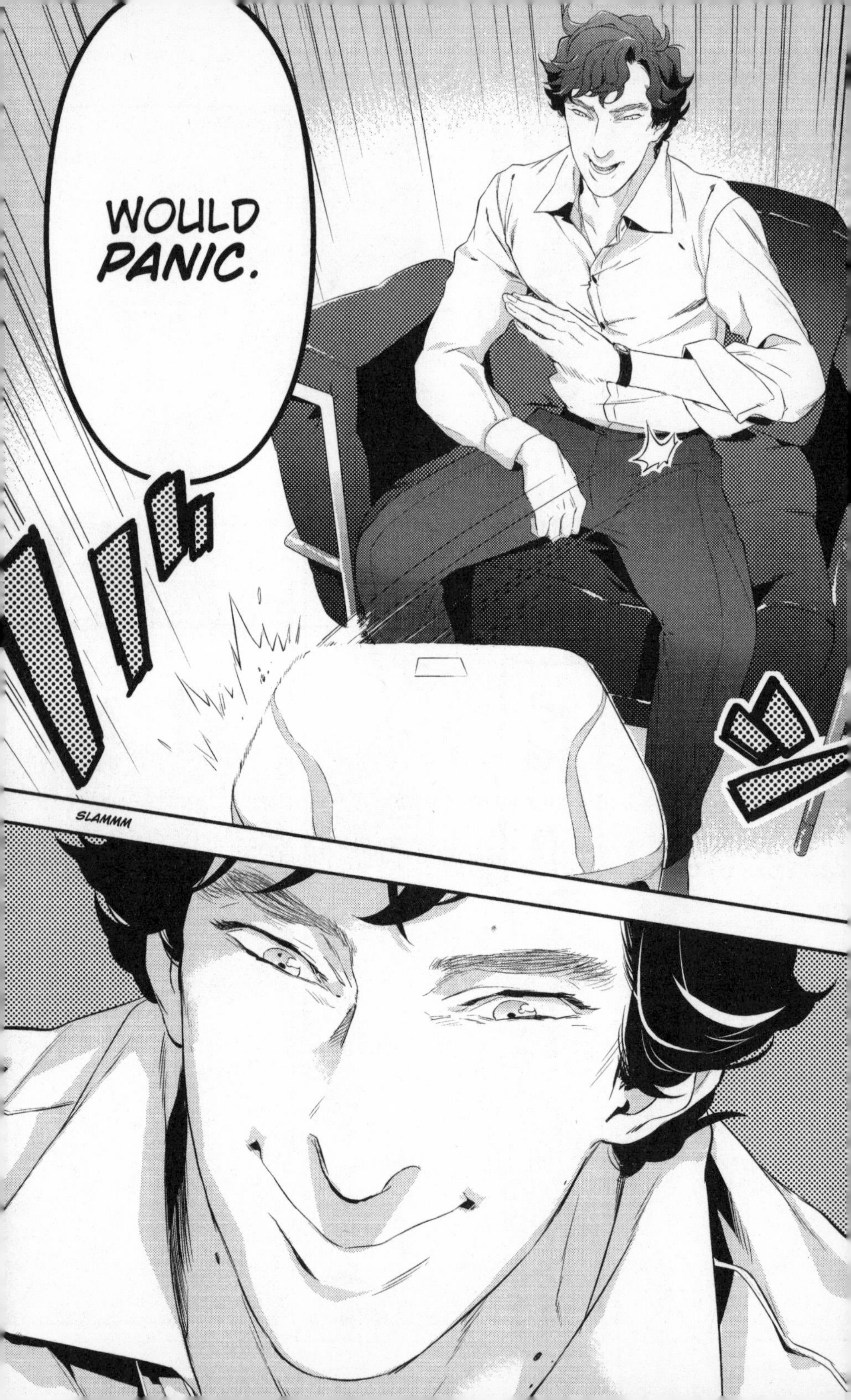
WOULD PANIC.
SLAMMM

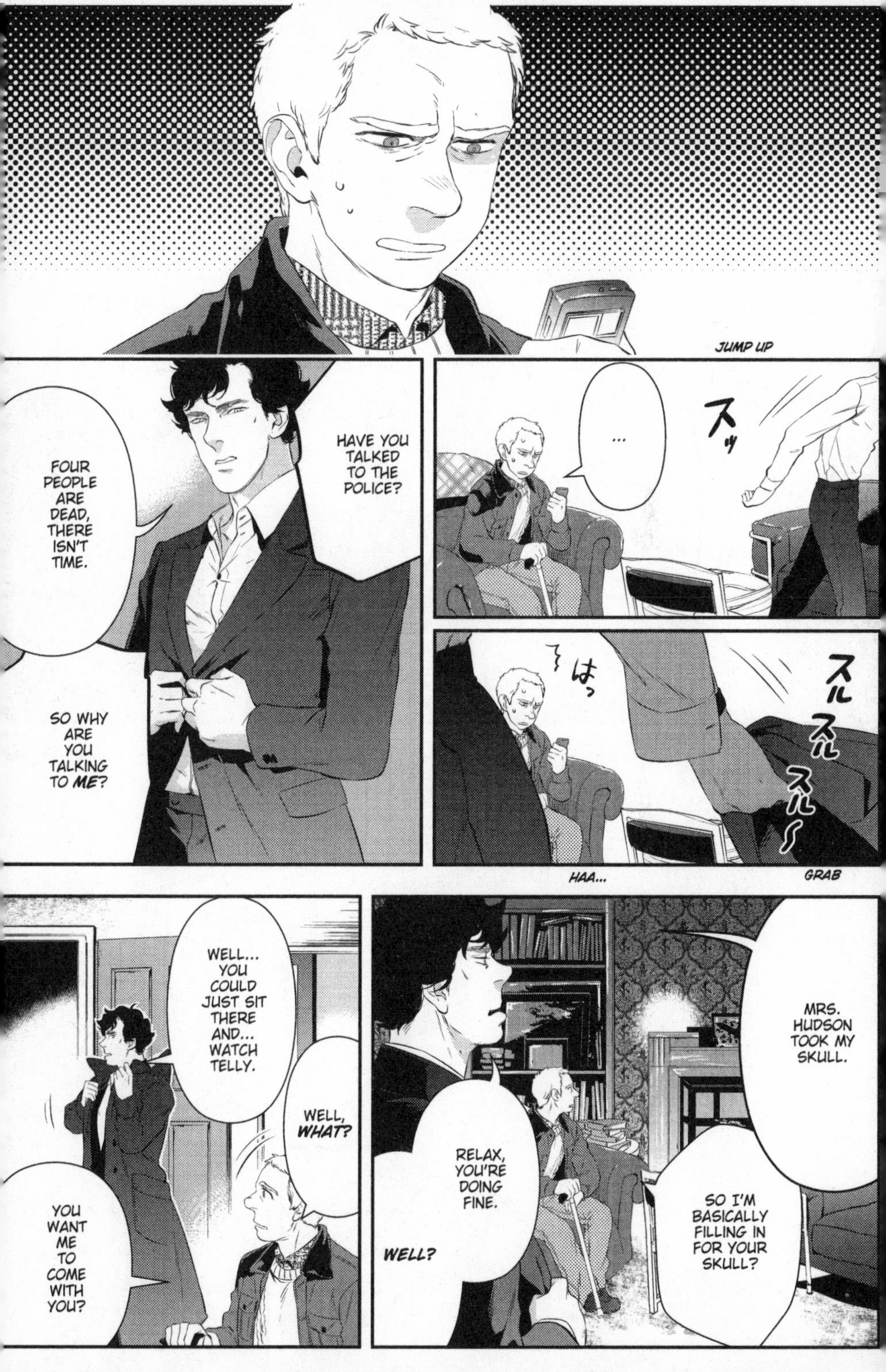
JUMP UP
…
スッ
はっ
スルスルスル～
HAA...
GRAB
HAVE YOU TALKED TO THE POLICE?
FOUR PEOPLE ARE DEAD, THERE ISN'T TIME.
SO WHY ARE YOU TALKING TO *ME*?
MRS. HUDSON TOOK MY SKULL.
SO I'M BASICALLY FILLING IN FOR YOUR SKULL?
RELAX, YOU'RE DOING FINE.
WELL?
WELL, *WHAT?*
WELL... YOU COULD JUST SIT THERE AND... WATCH TELLY.
YOU WANT ME TO COME WITH YOU?

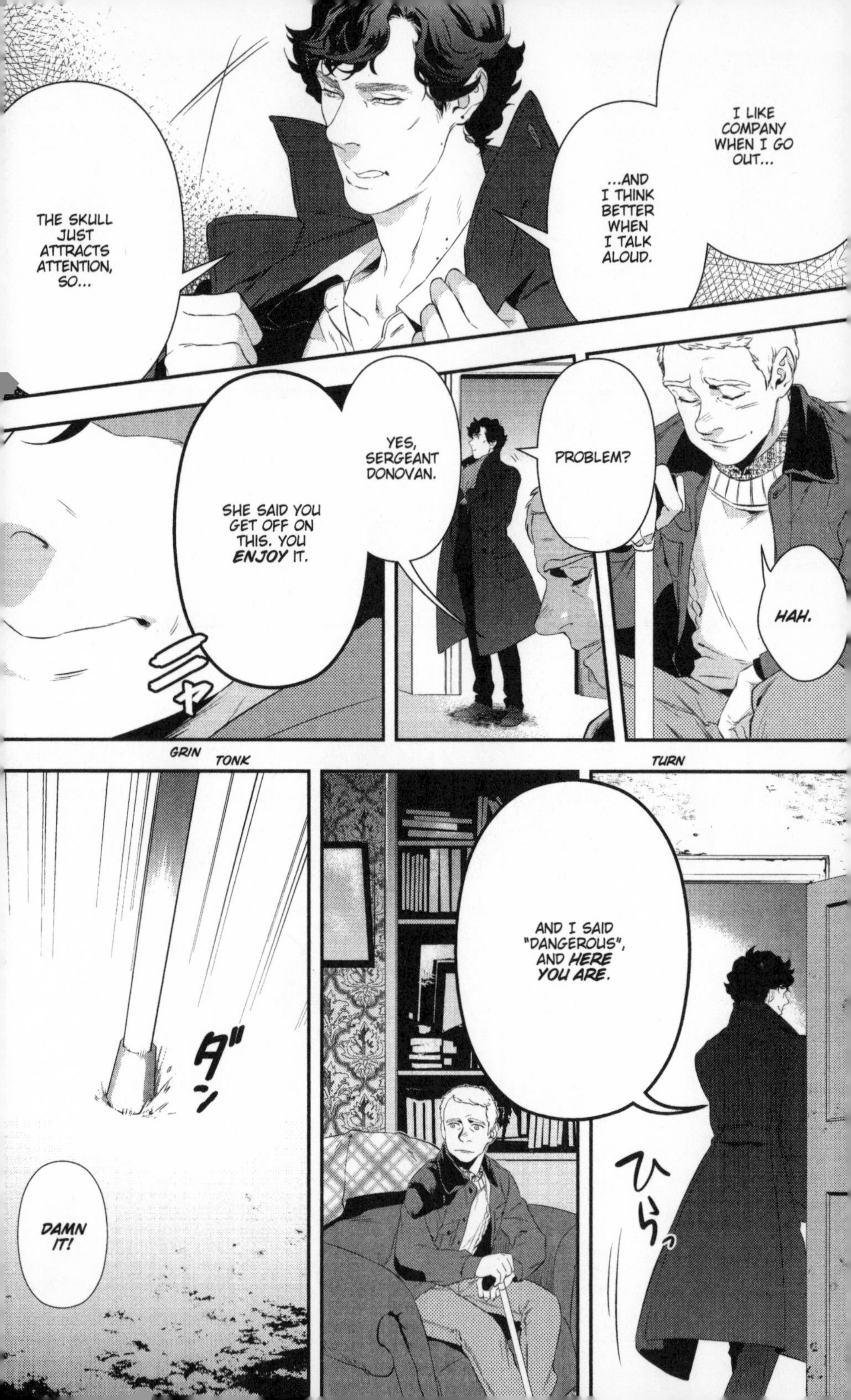
I LIKE COMPANY WHEN I GO OUT...
...AND I THINK BETTER WHEN I TALK ALOUD.
THE SKULL JUST ATTRACTS ATTENTION, SO...
HAH.
PROBLEM?
YES, SERGEANT DONOVAN.
SHE SAID YOU GET OFF ON THIS. YOU **ENJOY** IT.
ニヤ
GRIN
TURN
AND I SAID "DANGEROUS", AND **HERE YOU ARE**.
ひらっ
TONK
ダン
DAMN IT!

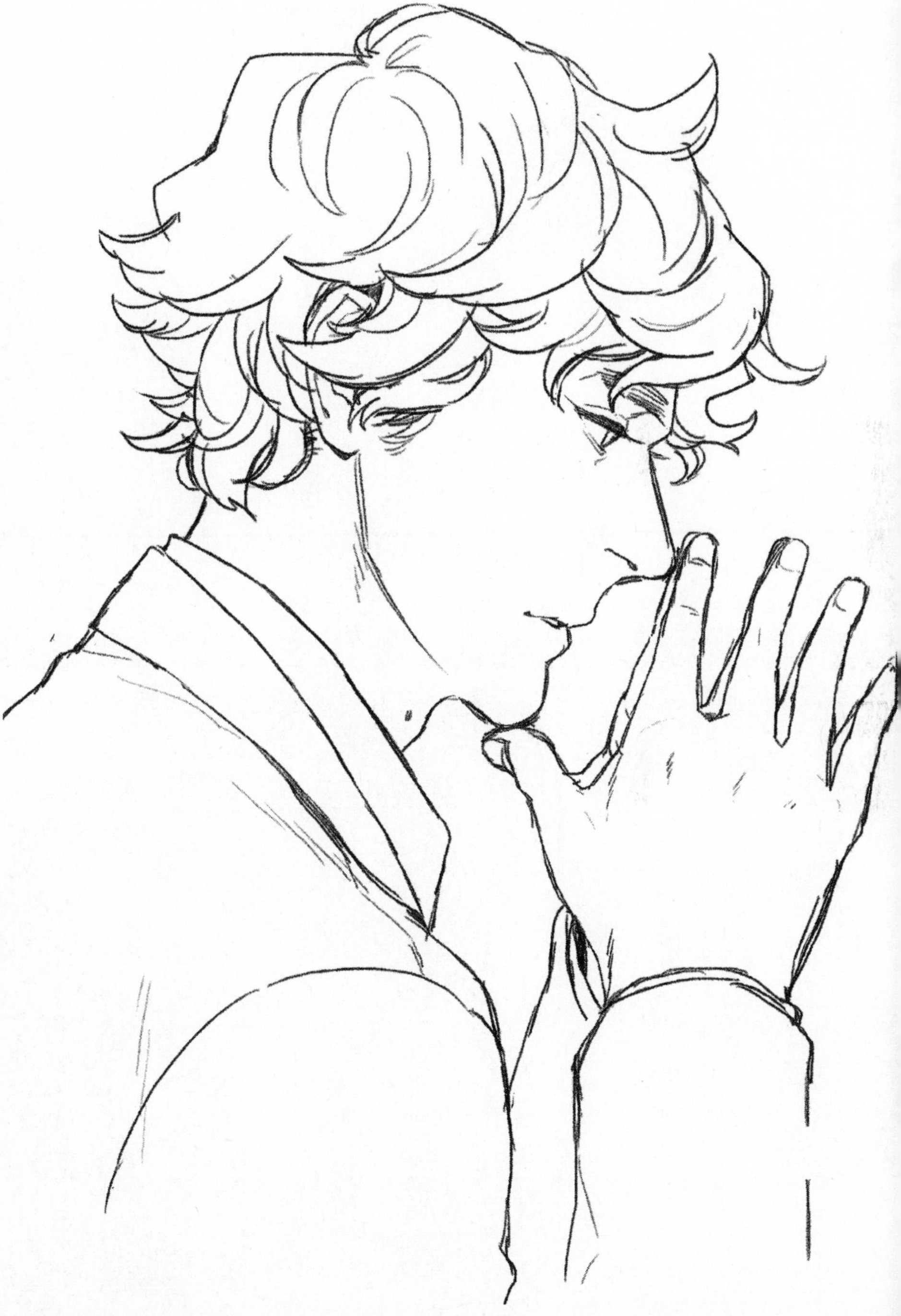

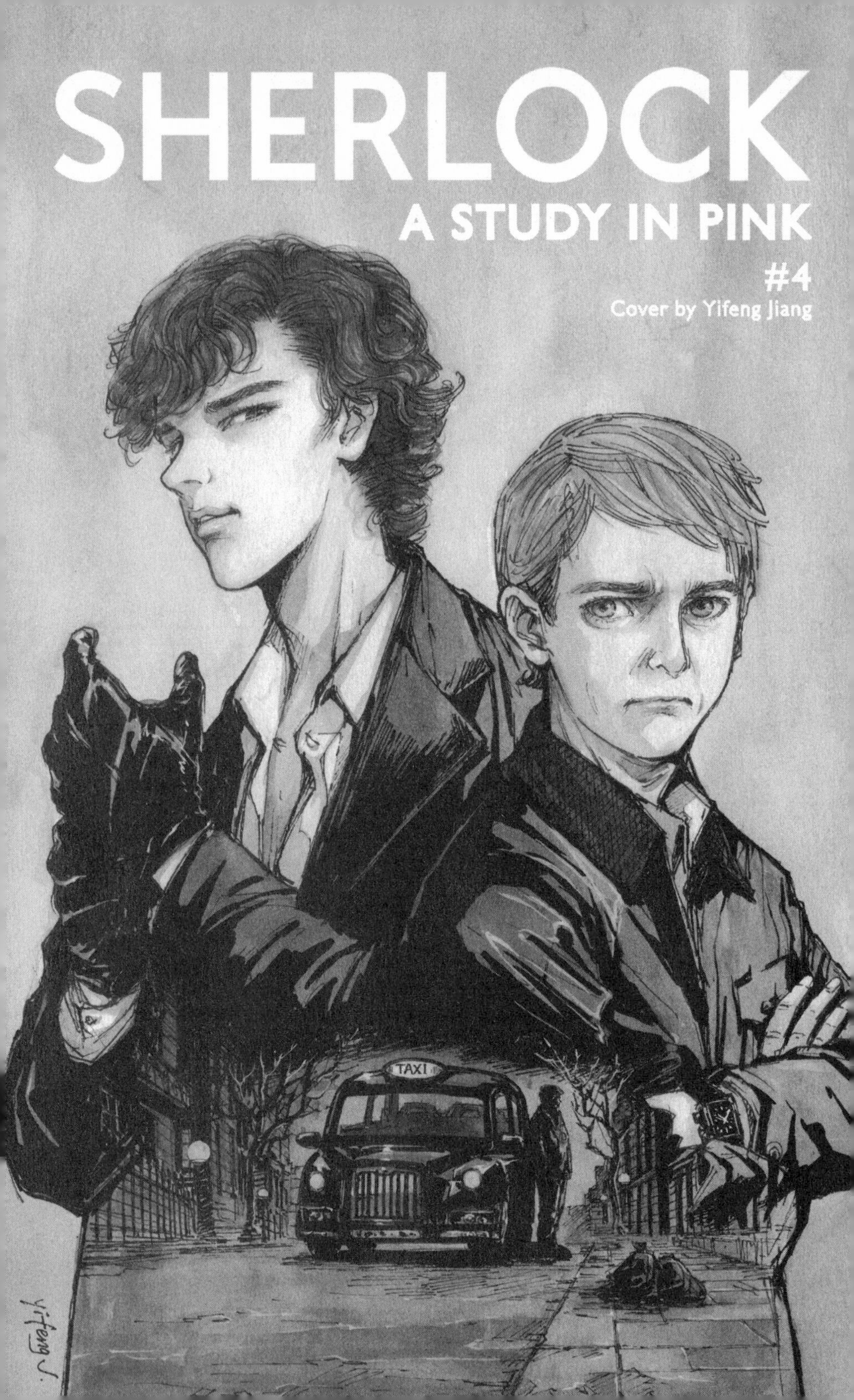
SHERLOCK
A STUDY IN PINK
#4
Cover by Yifeng Jiang
TAXI
Yifeng J.

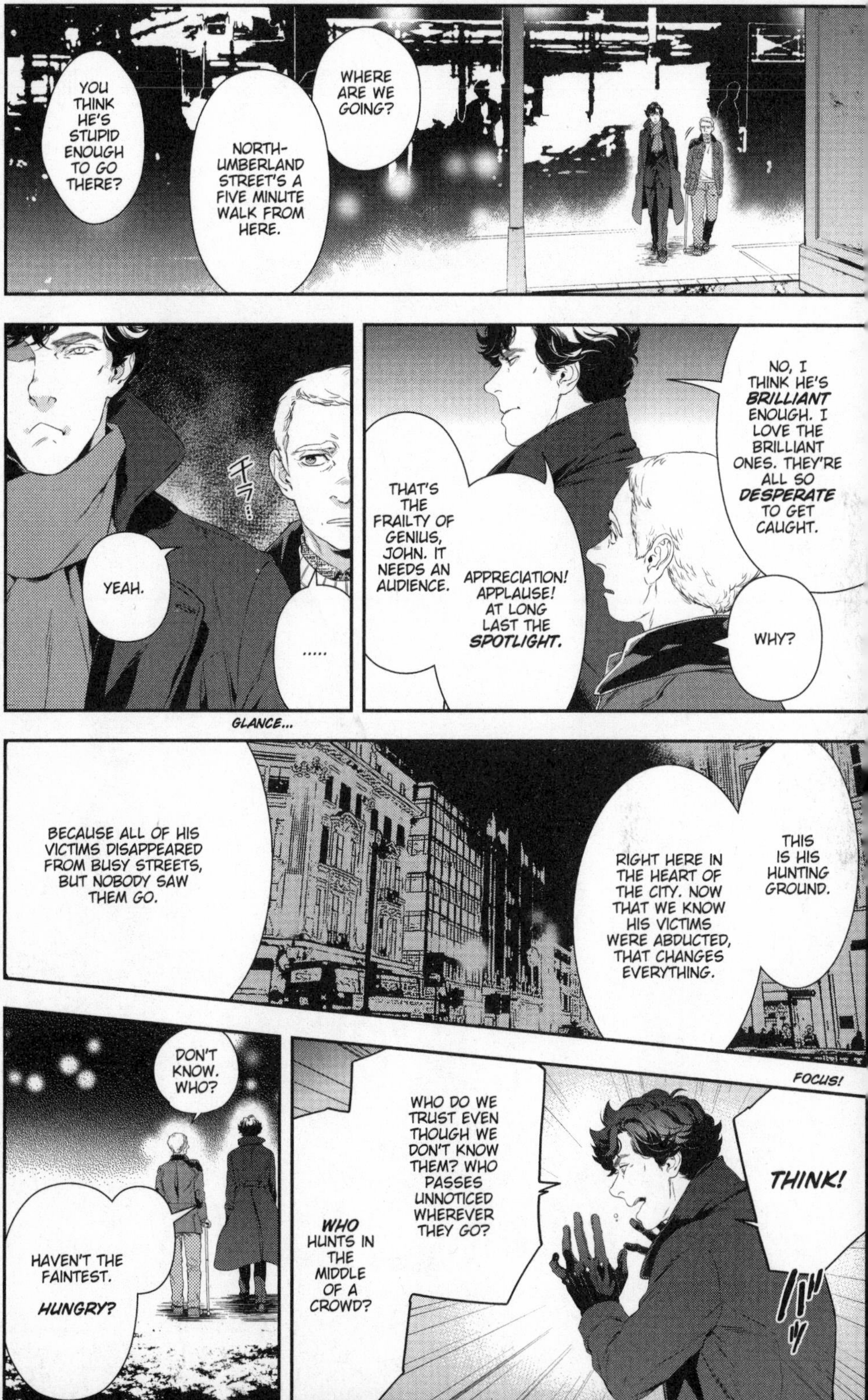

WHERE ARE WE GOING?
NORTH-UMBERLAND STREET'S A FIVE MINUTE WALK FROM HERE.
YOU THINK HE'S STUPID ENOUGH TO GO THERE?
NO, I THINK HE'S **BRILLIANT** ENOUGH. I LOVE THE BRILLIANT ONES. THEY'RE ALL SO **DESPERATE** TO GET CAUGHT.
WHY?
APPRECIATION! APPLAUSE! AT LONG LAST THE **SPOTLIGHT.**
THAT'S THE FRAILTY OF GENIUS, JOHN. IT NEEDS AN AUDIENCE.
チラ
.....
YEAH.
GLANCE...
THIS IS HIS HUNTING GROUND.
RIGHT HERE IN THE HEART OF THE CITY. NOW THAT WE KNOW HIS VICTIMS WERE ABDUCTED, THAT CHANGES EVERYTHING.
BECAUSE ALL OF HIS VICTIMS DISAPPEARED FROM BUSY STREETS, BUT NOBODY SAW THEM GO.
FOCUS!
THINK!
WHO DO WE TRUST EVEN THOUGH WE DON'T KNOW THEM? WHO PASSES UNNOTICED WHEREVER THEY GO?
WHO HUNTS IN THE MIDDLE OF A CROWD?
DON'T KNOW. WHO?
HAVEN'T THE FAINTEST.
HUNGRY?

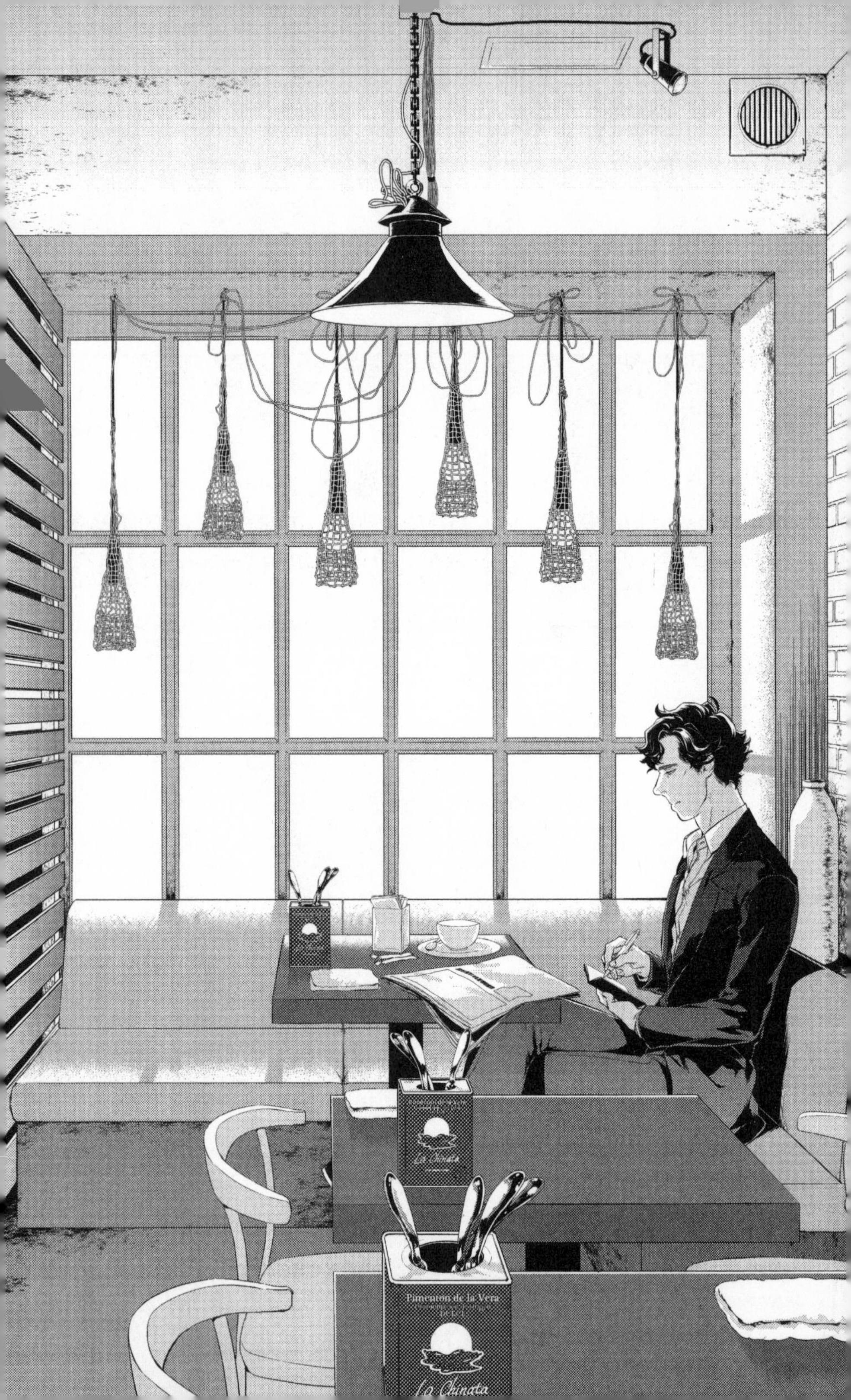
Pimenton de la Vera
La Chinata

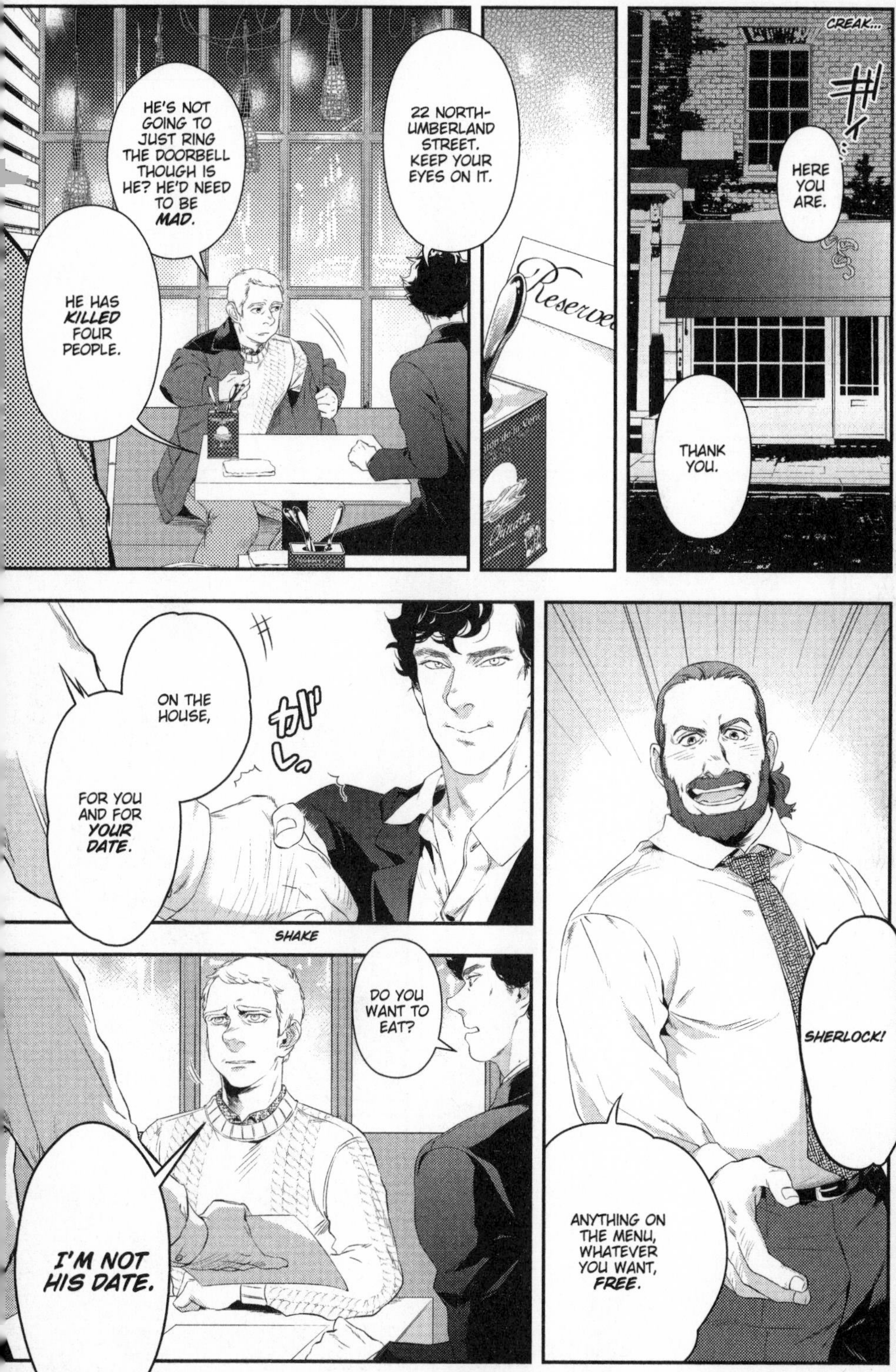
CREAK...
ギィ...
HERE YOU ARE.
THANK YOU.
22 NORTH-UMBERLAND STREET. KEEP YOUR EYES ON IT.
HE'S NOT GOING TO JUST RING THE DOORBELL THOUGH IS HE? HE'D NEED TO BE **MAD**.
HE HAS **KILLED** FOUR PEOPLE.
SHERLOCK!
ANYTHING ON THE MENU, WHATEVER YOU WANT, **FREE**.
ON THE HOUSE,
FOR YOU AND FOR **YOUR DATE**.
SHAKE
DO YOU WANT TO EAT?
I'M NOT HIS DATE.

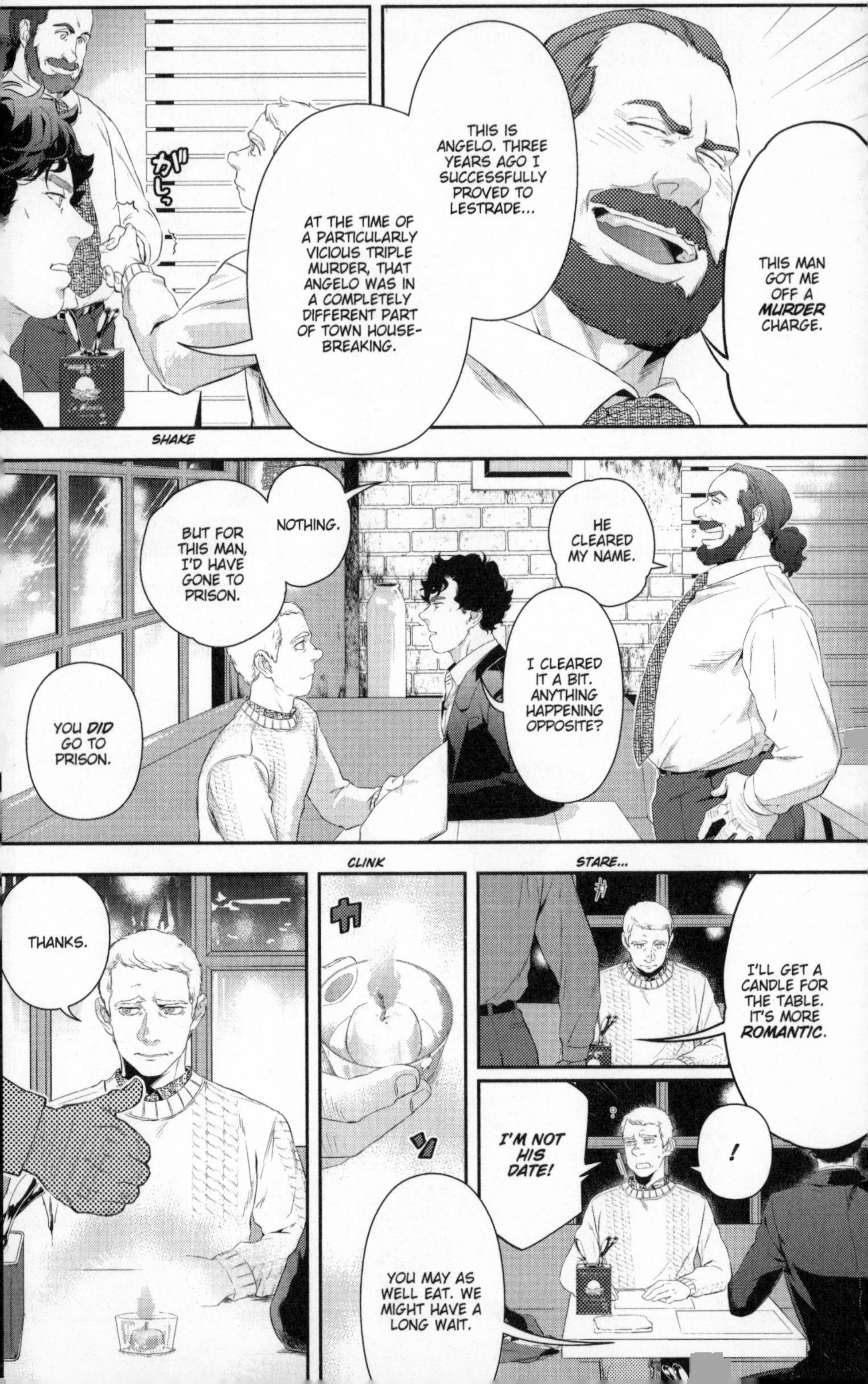
THIS MAN GOT ME OFF A *MURDER* CHARGE.
THIS IS ANGELO. THREE YEARS AGO I SUCCESSFULLY PROVED TO LESTRADE...
AT THE TIME OF A PARTICULARLY VICIOUS TRIPLE MURDER, THAT ANGELO WAS IN A COMPLETELY DIFFERENT PART OF TOWN HOUSE-BREAKING.
SHAKE
HE CLEARED MY NAME.
I CLEARED IT A BIT. ANYTHING HAPPENING OPPOSITE?
NOTHING.
BUT FOR THIS MAN, I'D HAVE GONE TO PRISON.
YOU *DID* GO TO PRISON.
STARE...
I'LL GET A CANDLE FOR THE TABLE. IT'S MORE *ROMANTIC*.
!
I'M NOT HIS DATE!
YOU MAY AS WELL EAT. WE MIGHT HAVE A LONG WAIT.
CLINK
THANKS.

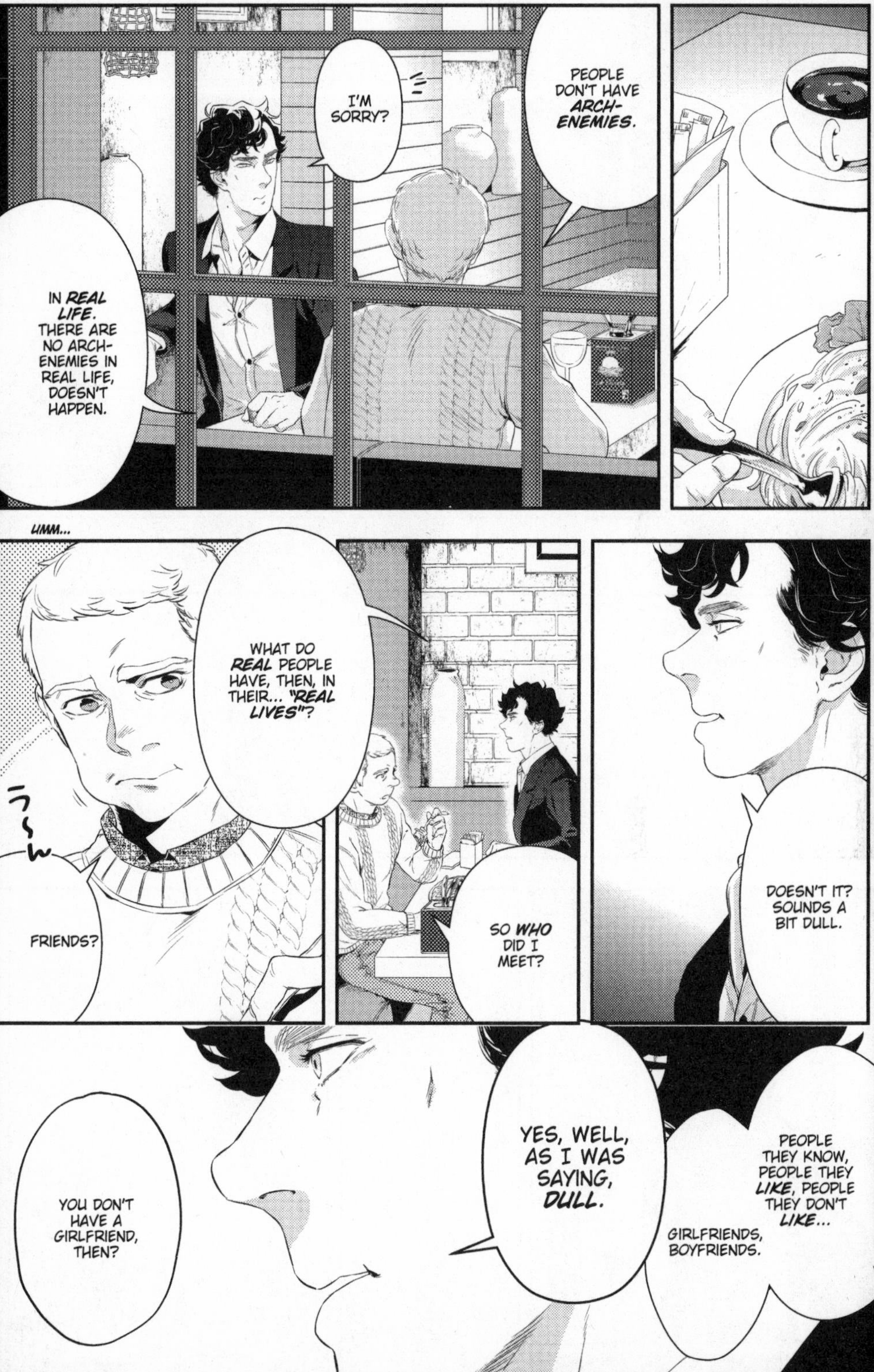
PEOPLE DON'T HAVE ARCH-ENEMIES.
I'M SORRY?
IN REAL LIFE. THERE ARE NO ARCH-ENEMIES IN REAL LIFE, DOESN'T HAPPEN.
DOESN'T IT? SOUNDS A BIT DULL.
WHAT DO REAL PEOPLE HAVE, THEN, IN THEIR... "REAL LIVES"?
SO WHO DID I MEET?
UMM...
FRIENDS?
PEOPLE THEY KNOW, PEOPLE THEY LIKE, PEOPLE THEY DON'T LIKE...
GIRLFRIENDS, BOYFRIENDS.
YES, WELL, AS I WAS SAYING, DULL.
YOU DON'T HAVE A GIRLFRIEND, THEN?

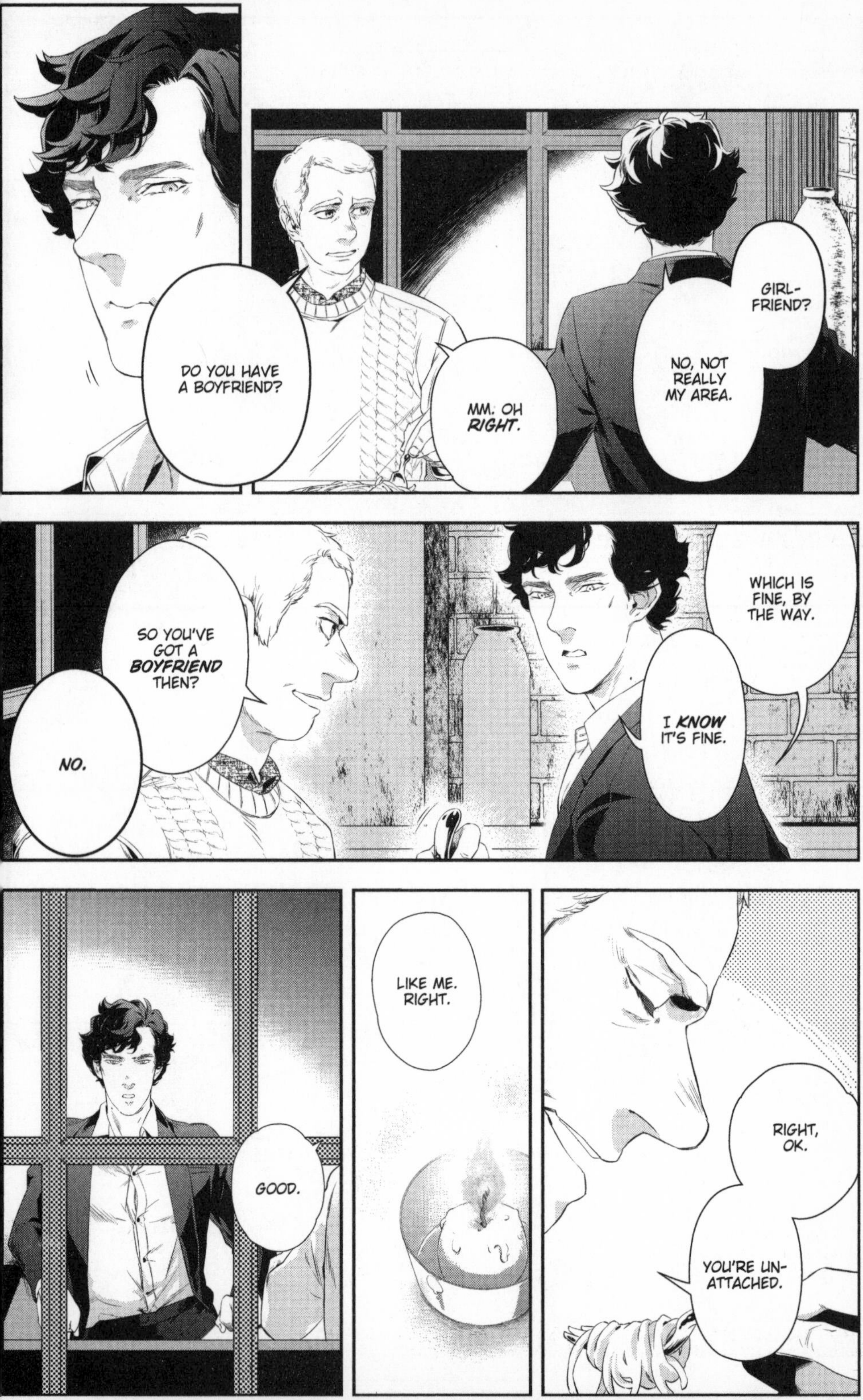
GIRL-FRIEND?
NO, NOT REALLY MY AREA.
MM. OH *RIGHT*.
DO YOU HAVE A BOYFRIEND?
WHICH IS FINE, BY THE WAY.
I *KNOW* IT'S FINE.
SO YOU'VE GOT A *BOYFRIEND* THEN?
NO.
RIGHT, OK.
YOU'RE UN-ATTACHED.
LIKE ME. RIGHT.
GOOD.

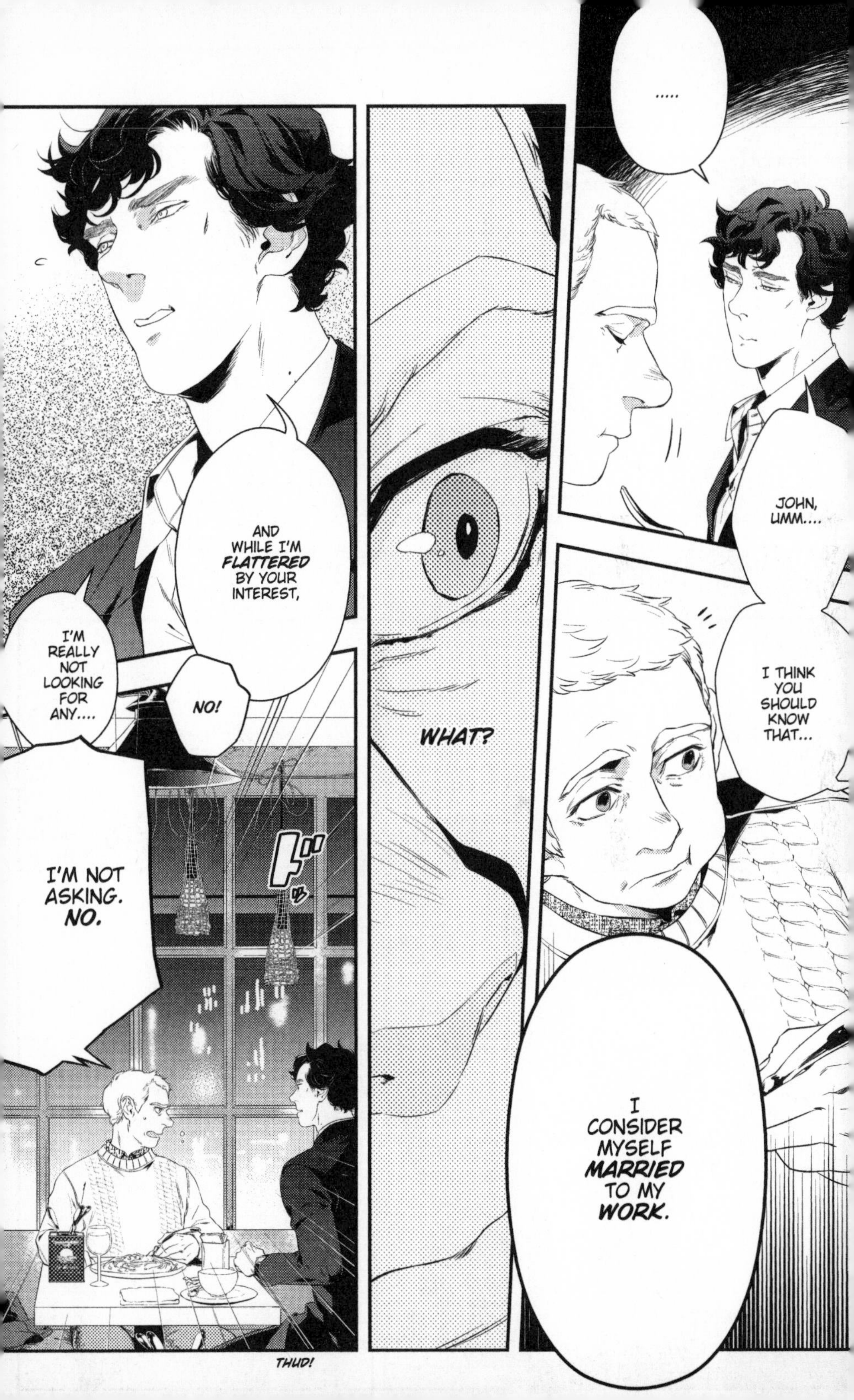
.....
JOHN, UMM....
I THINK YOU SHOULD KNOW THAT...
I CONSIDER MYSELF MARRIED TO MY WORK.
WHAT?
AND WHILE I'M FLATTERED BY YOUR INTEREST,
I'M REALLY NOT LOOKING FOR ANY....
NO!
I'M NOT ASKING. NO.
THUD!

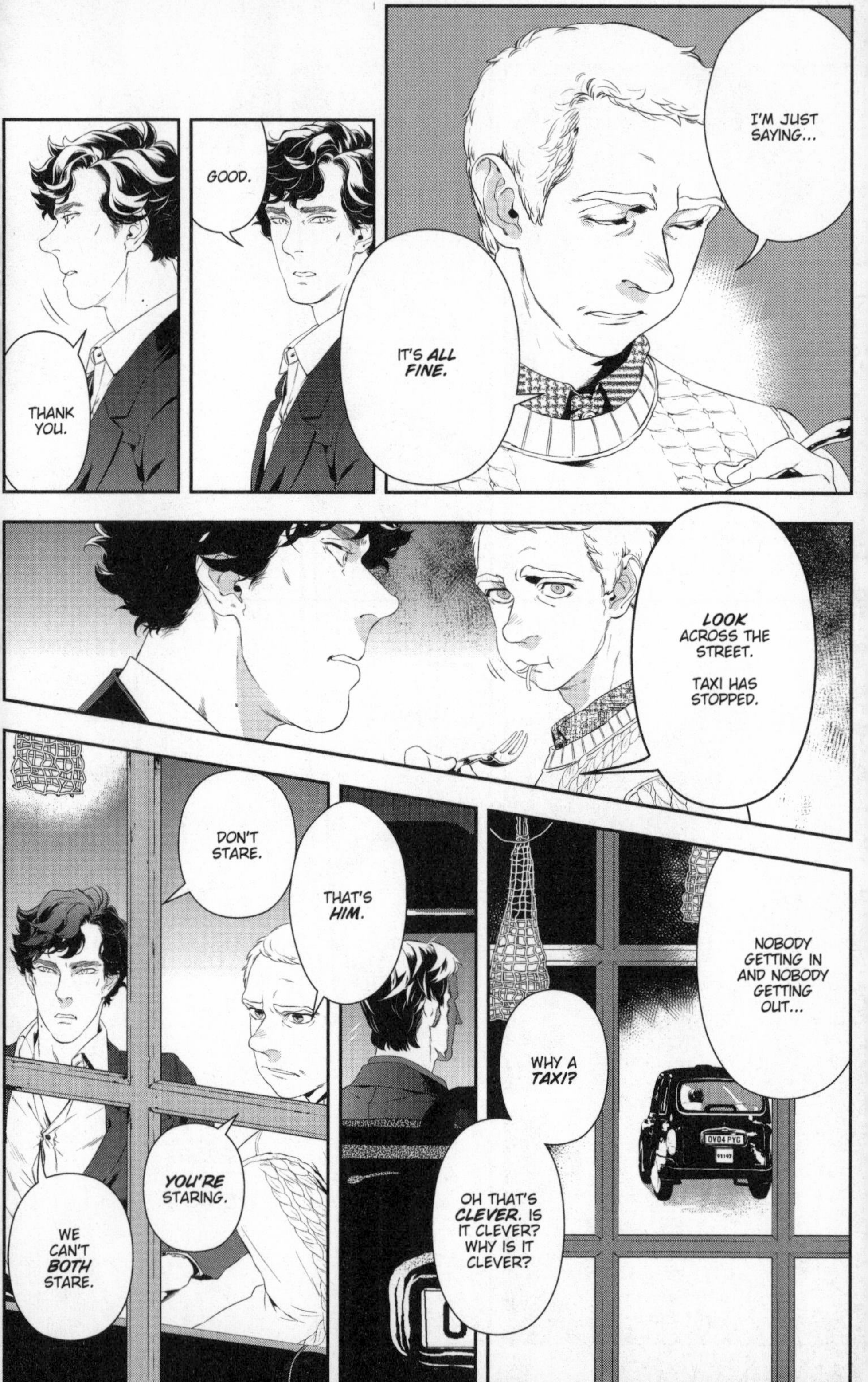
I'M JUST SAYING...
IT'S ALL FINE.
GOOD.
THANK YOU.
LOOK ACROSS THE STREET. TAXI HAS STOPPED.
NOBODY GETTING IN AND NOBODY GETTING OUT...
WHY A TAXI?
OH THAT'S CLEVER. IS IT CLEVER? WHY IS IT CLEVER?
THAT'S HIM.
DON'T STARE.
YOU'RE STARING.
WE CAN'T BOTH STARE.

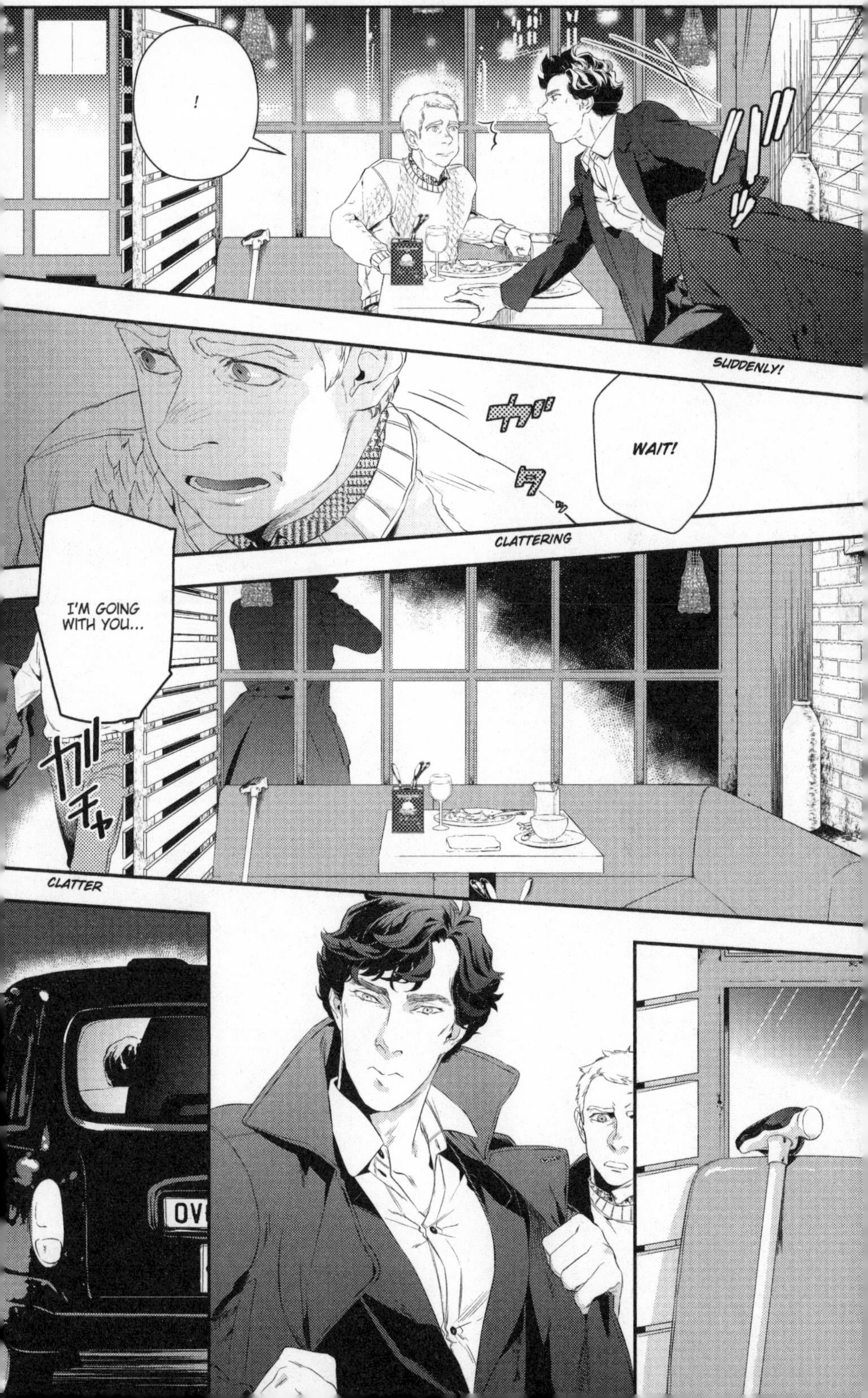
!
SUDDENLY!
WAIT!
CLATTERING
I'M GOING WITH YOU...
CLATTER
OV

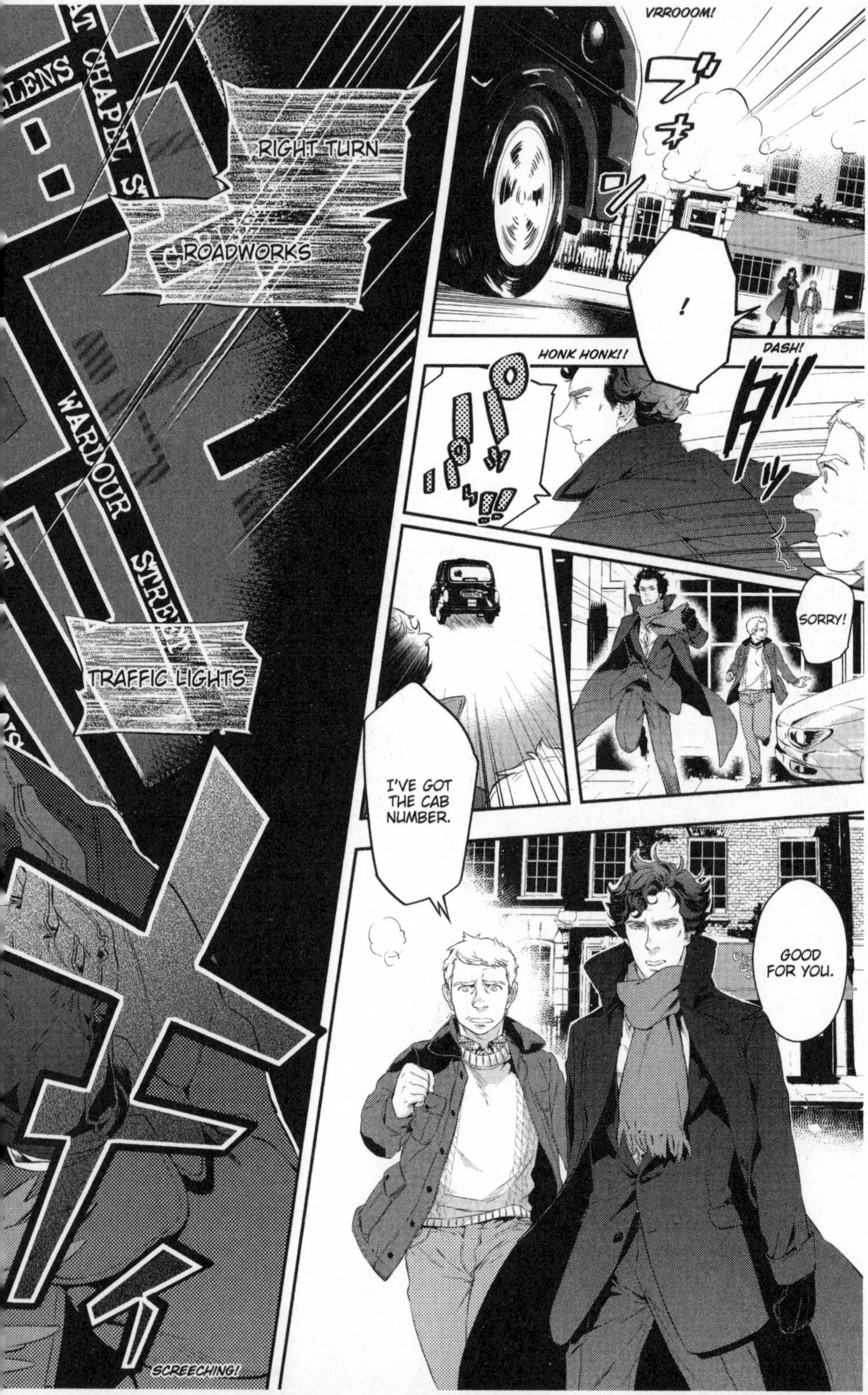
VRROOOM!
!
HONK HONK!!
DASH!
SORRY!
I'VE GOT THE CAB NUMBER.
GOOD FOR YOU.
CHAPEL
RIGHT TURN
ROADWORKS
WARDOUR
TRAFFIC LIGHTS
SCREECHING!

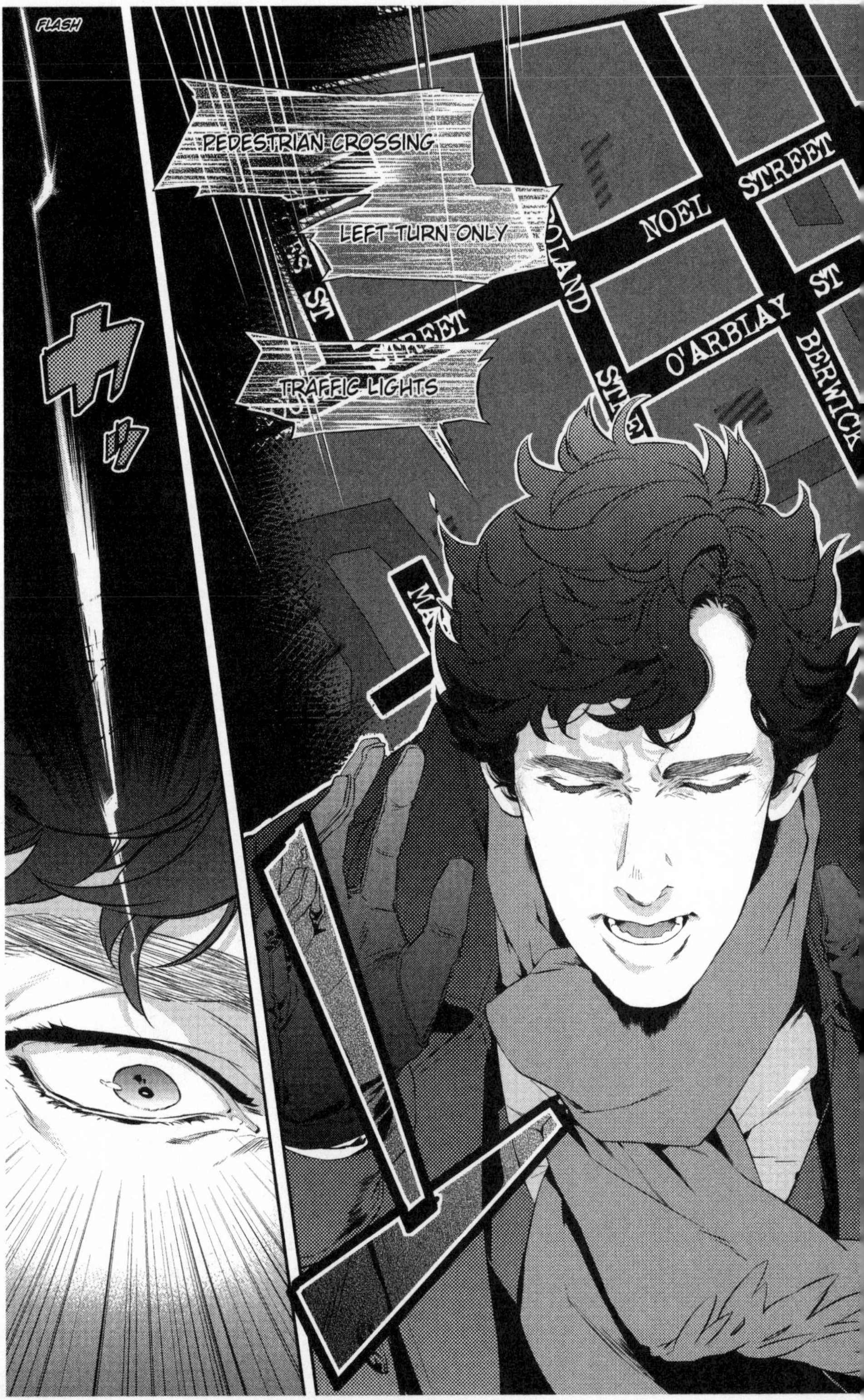
NOEL STREET
BERWICK
O'ARBLAY ST
FLASH
PEDESTRIAN CROSSING
LEFT TURN ONLY
TRAFFIC LIGHTS

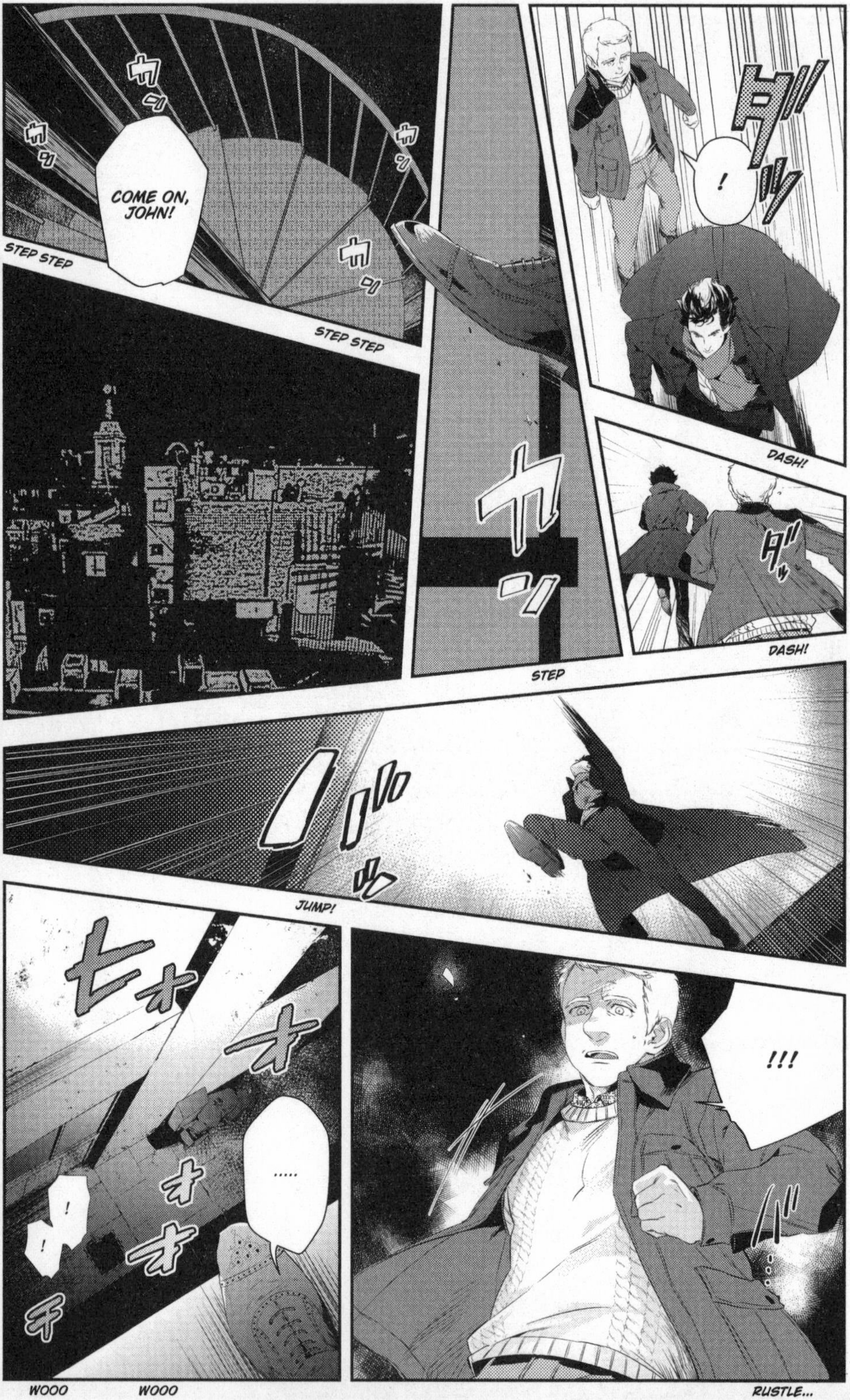
!
DASH!
DASH!
STEP
COME ON, JOHN!
STEP STEP
STEP STEP
JUMP!
!!!
RUSTLE...
......
! !
WOOO
WOOO

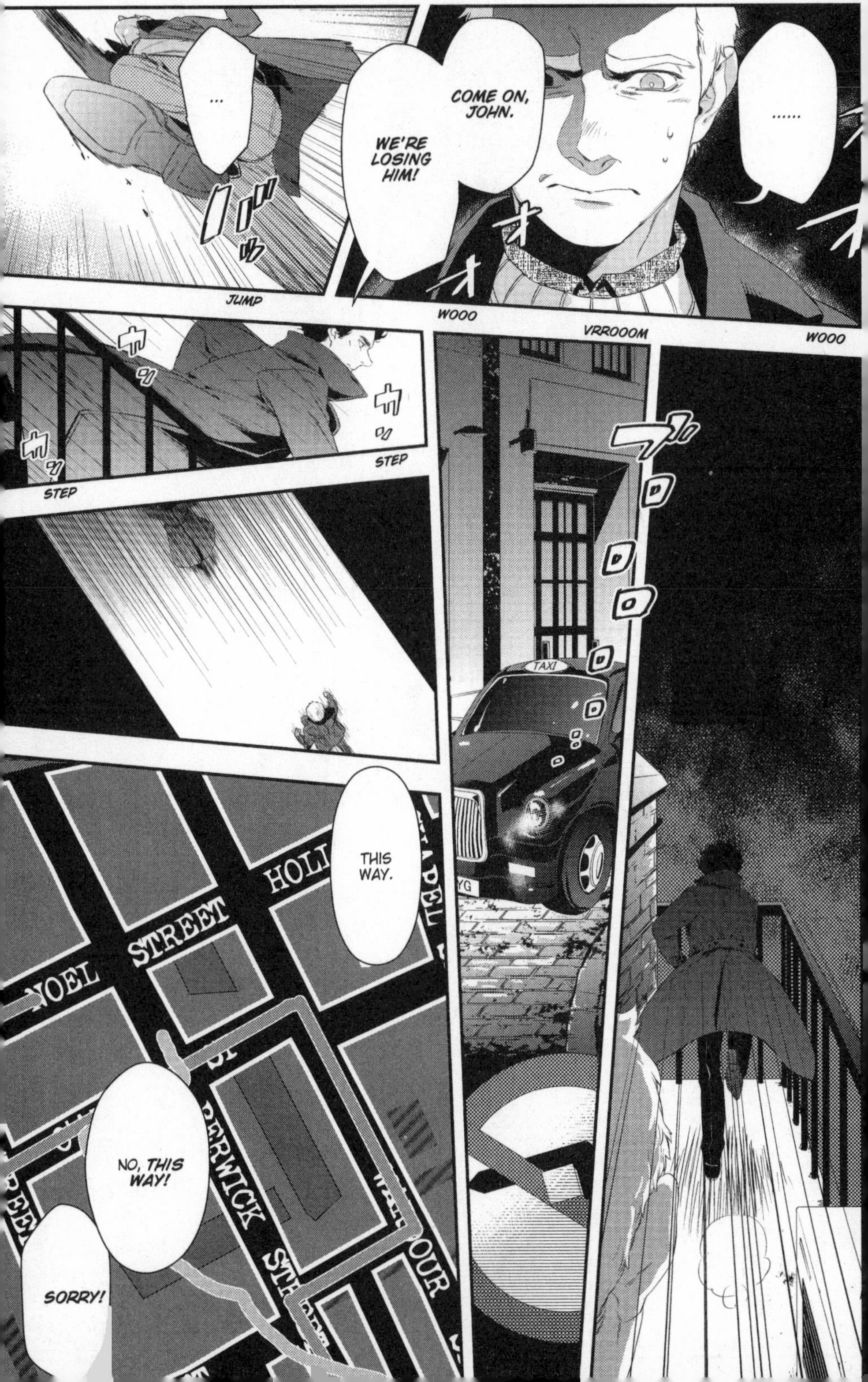
......
COME ON, JOHN.
WE'RE LOSING HIM!
WOOO
VRROOOM
WOOO
...
JUMP
STEP
STEP
THIS WAY.
NO, THIS WAY!
SORRY!
NOEL
STREET

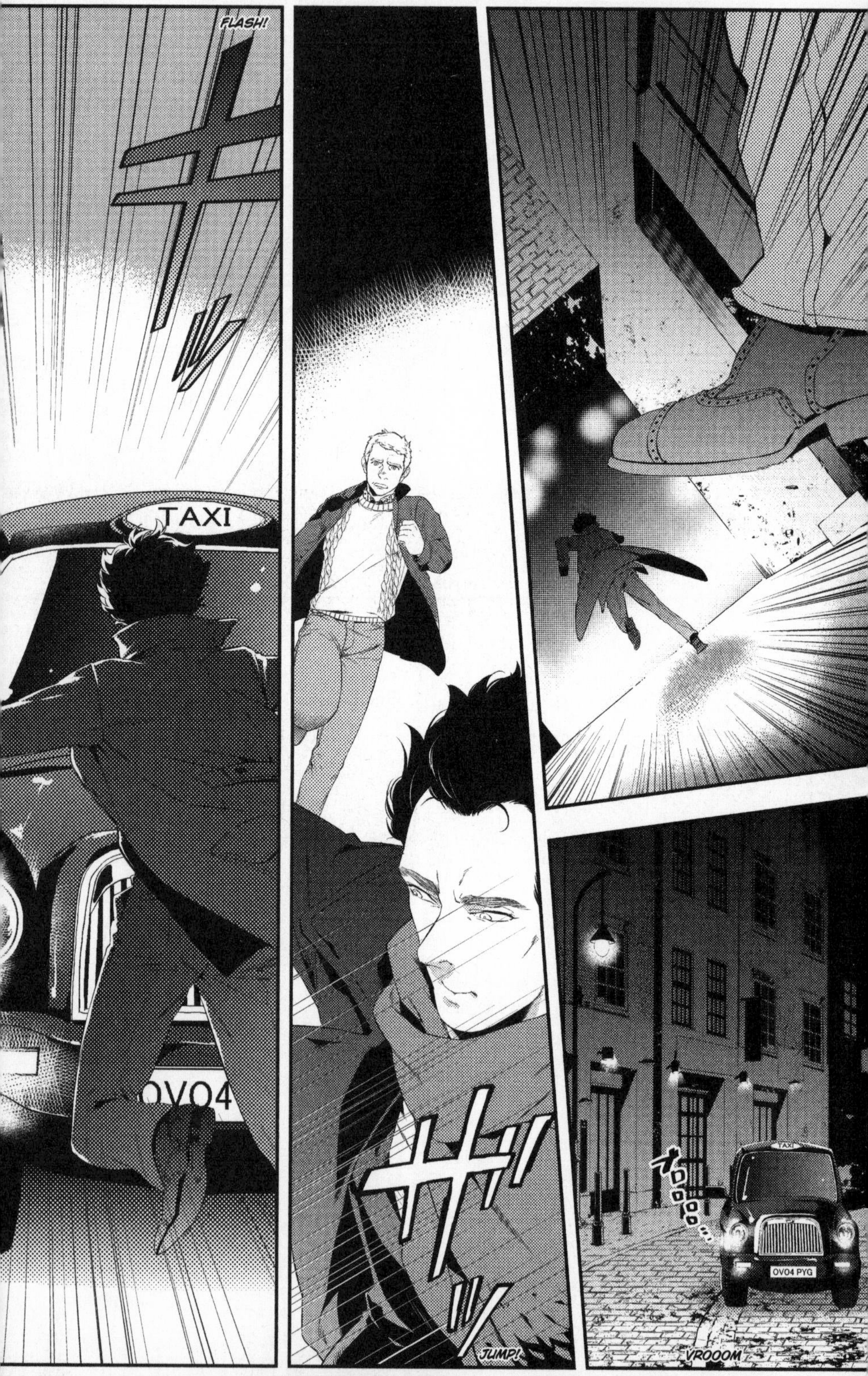
TAXI
OV04 PYG
VROOOM
JUMP!
FLASH!
TAXI
OV04

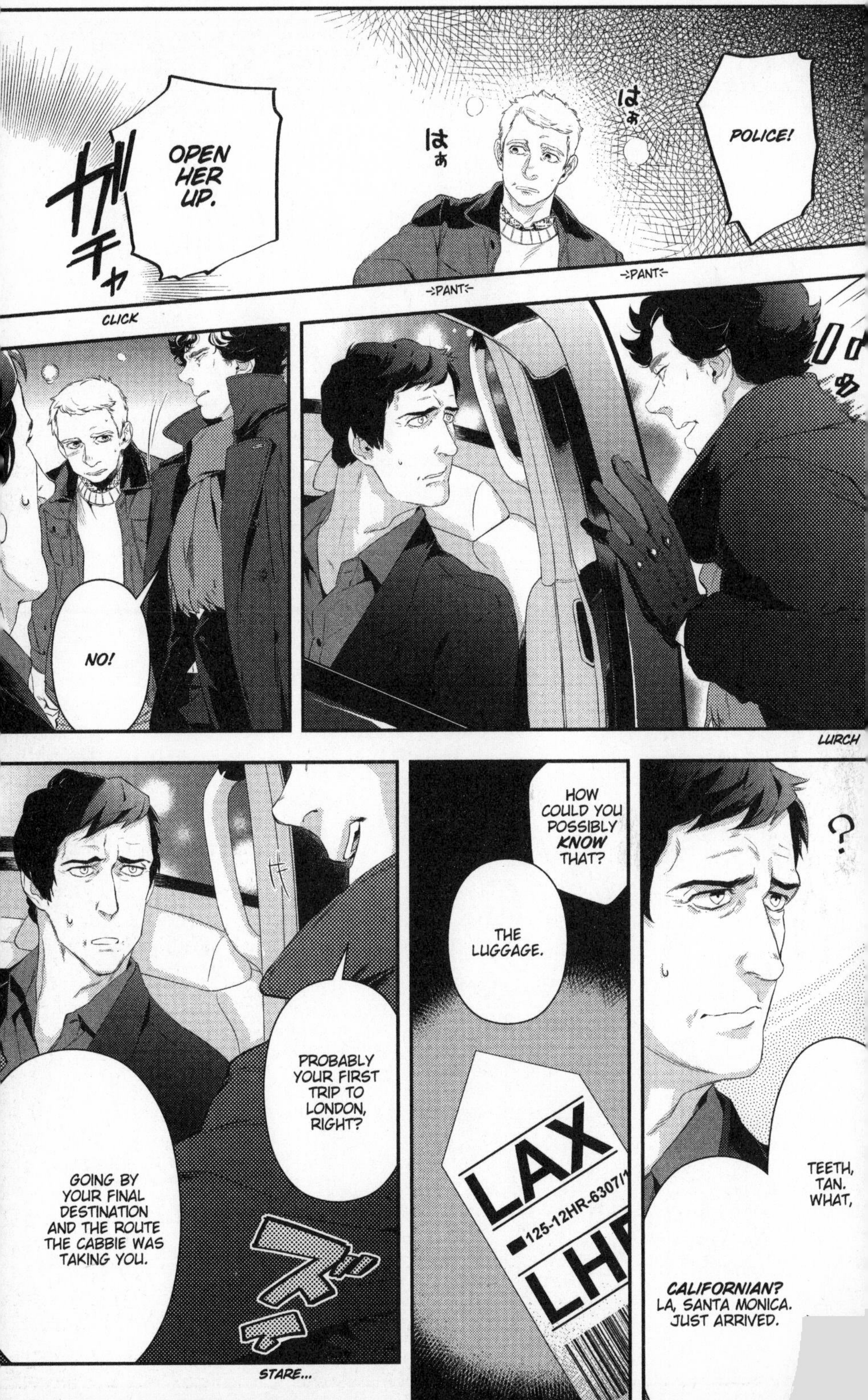
POLICE!
はぁ
はぁ
-PANT-
-PANT-
OPEN HER UP.
ガチャ
CLICK
LURCH
NO!
TEETH, TAN. WHAT,
CALIFORNIAN? LA, SANTA MONICA. JUST ARRIVED.
HOW COULD YOU POSSIBLY KNOW THAT?
THE LUGGAGE.
LAX
125-12HR-6307/1
PROBABLY YOUR FIRST TRIP TO LONDON, RIGHT?
GOING BY YOUR FINAL DESTINATION AND THE ROUTE THE CABBIE WAS TAKING YOU.
STARE...

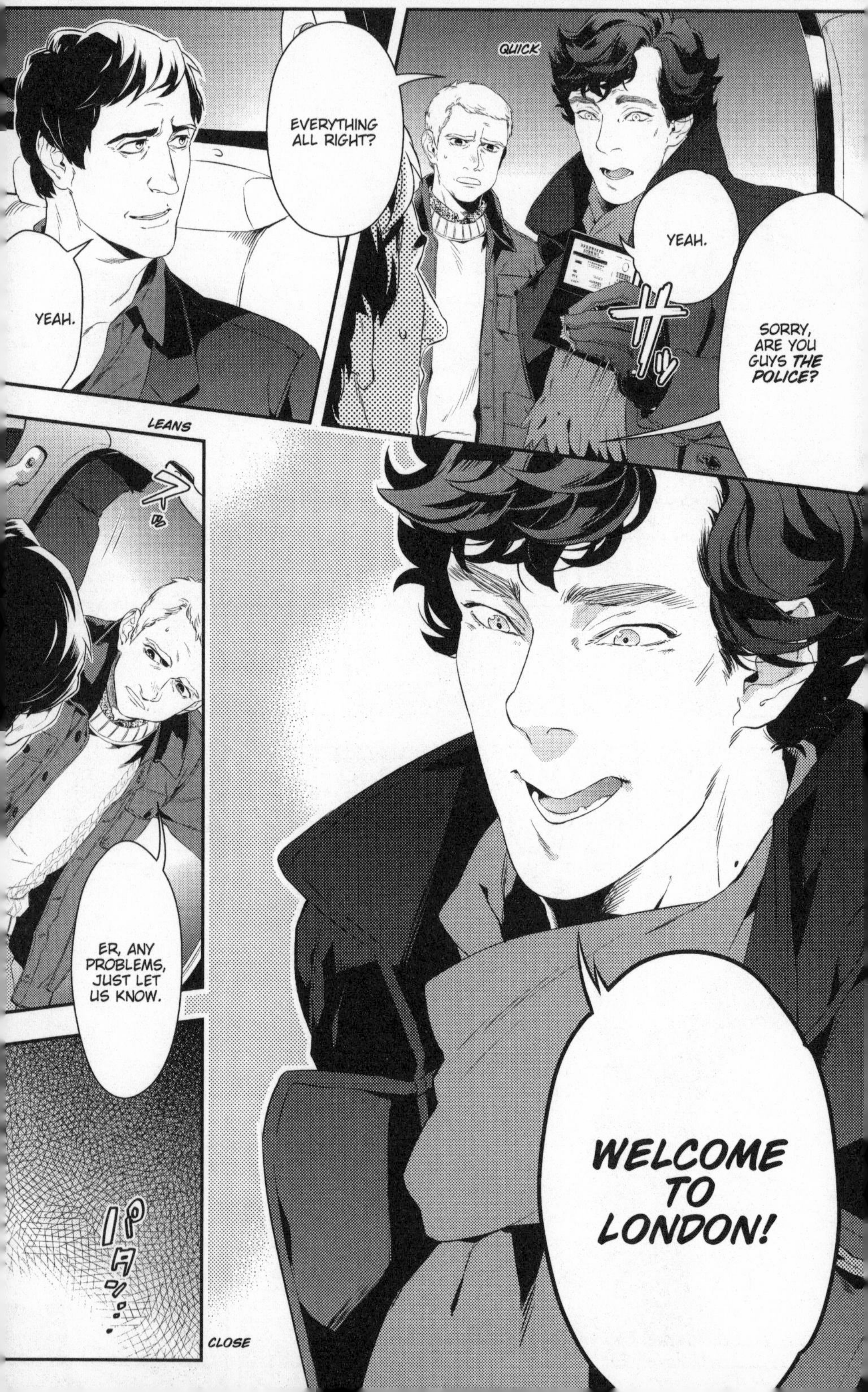
QUICK
SORRY, ARE YOU GUYS THE POLICE?
YEAH.
EVERYTHING ALL RIGHT?
YEAH.
LEANS
ER, ANY PROBLEMS, JUST LET US KNOW.
WELCOME TO LONDON!
CLOSE

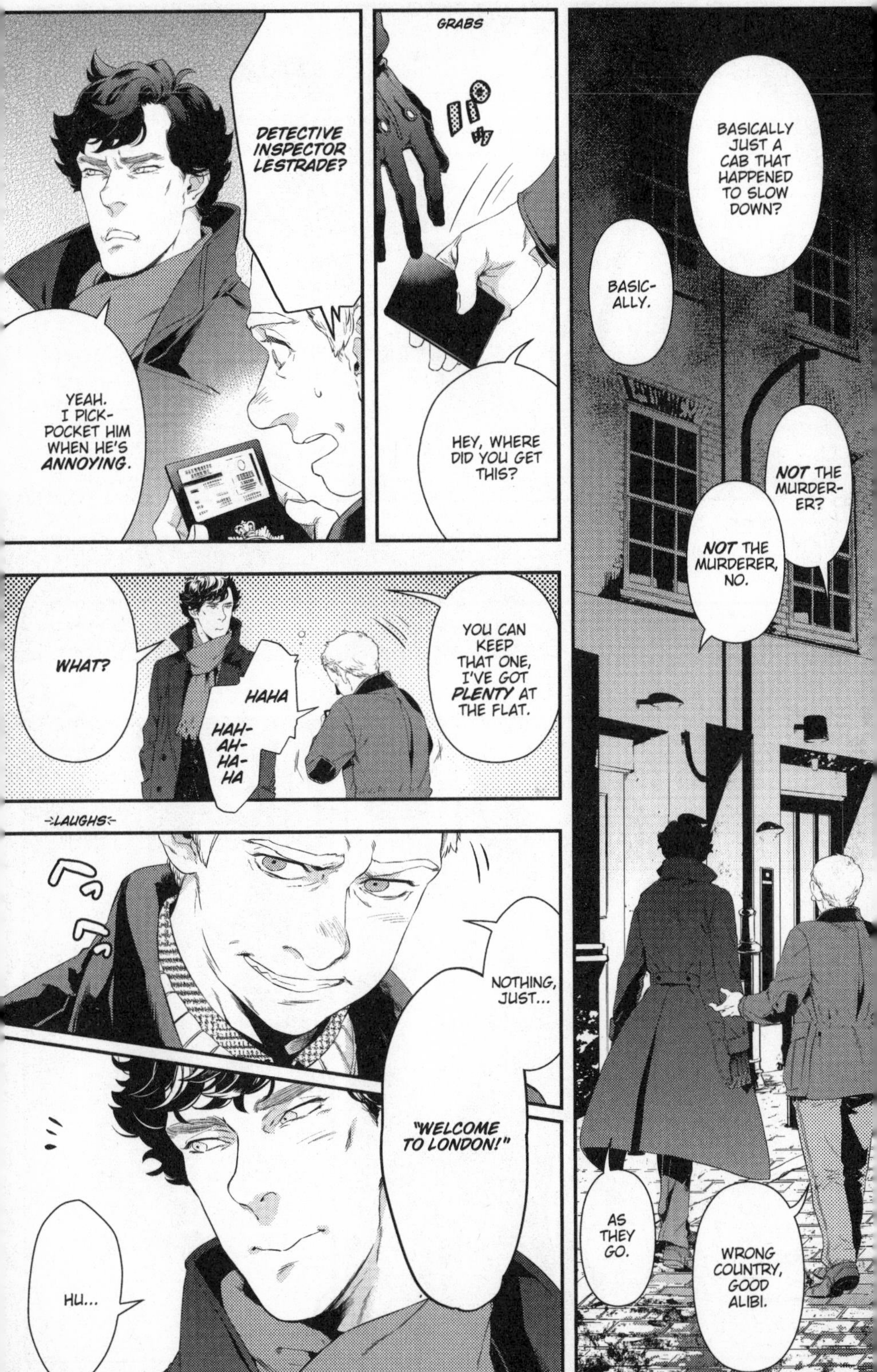

BASICALLY JUST A CAB THAT HAPPENED TO SLOW DOWN?
BASIC-ALLY.
NOT THE MURDER-ER?
NOT THE MURDERER, NO.
WRONG COUNTRY, GOOD ALIBI.
AS THEY GO.
GRABS
HEY, WHERE DID YOU GET THIS?
DETECTIVE INSPECTOR LESTRADE?
YEAH. I PICK-POCKET HIM WHEN HE'S *ANNOYING*.
YOU CAN KEEP THAT ONE, I'VE GOT *PLENTY* AT THE FLAT.
HAHA
HAH-AH-HA-HA
WHAT?
LAUGHS
NOTHING, JUST...
"WELCOME TO LONDON!"
HU...

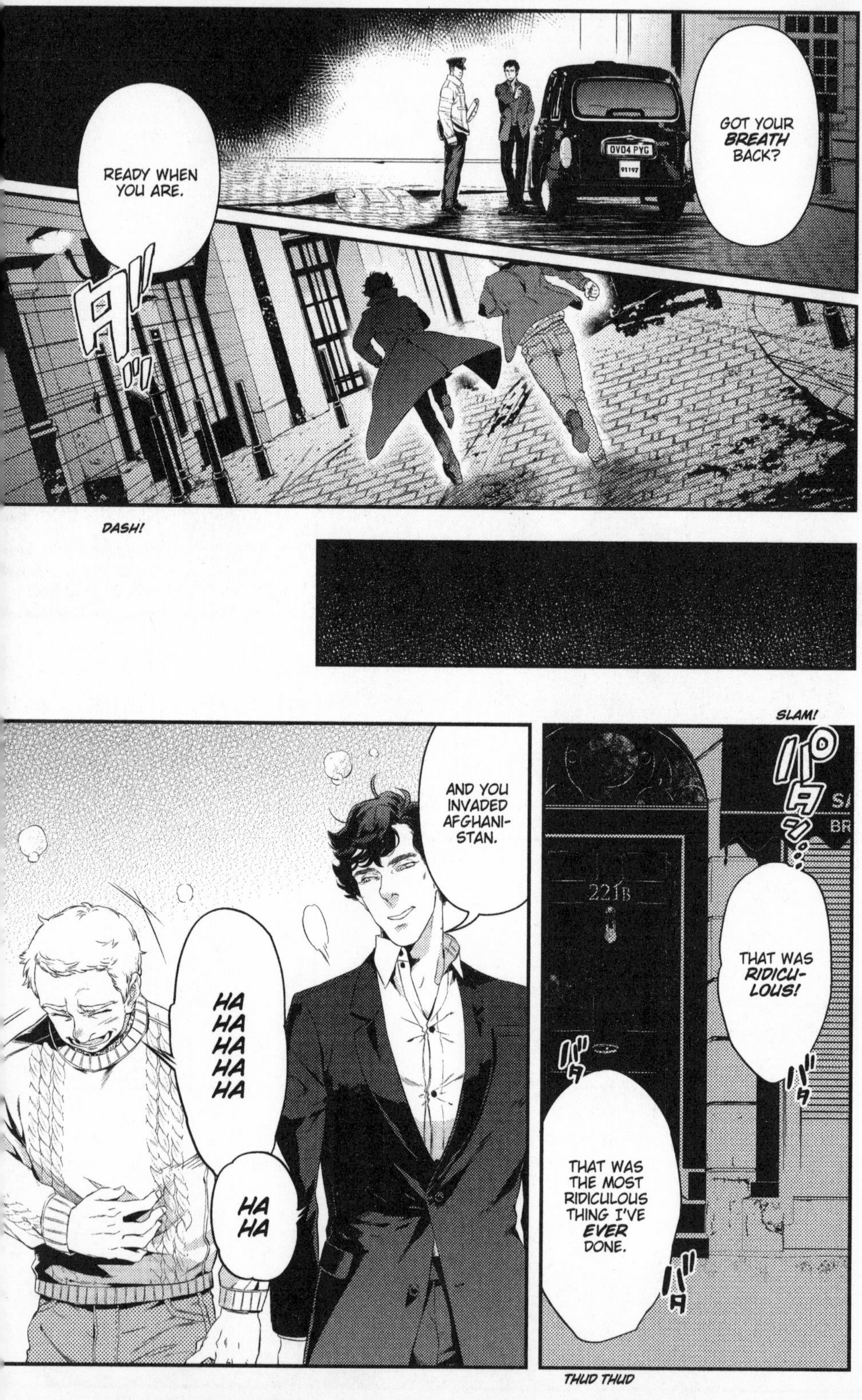
GOT YOUR BREATH BACK?
READY WHEN YOU ARE.
DASH!
SLAM!
THAT WAS RIDICULOUS!
THAT WAS THE MOST RIDICULOUS THING I'VE EVER DONE.
THUD THUD
AND YOU INVADED AFGHANISTAN.
HA HA HA HA HA
HA HA

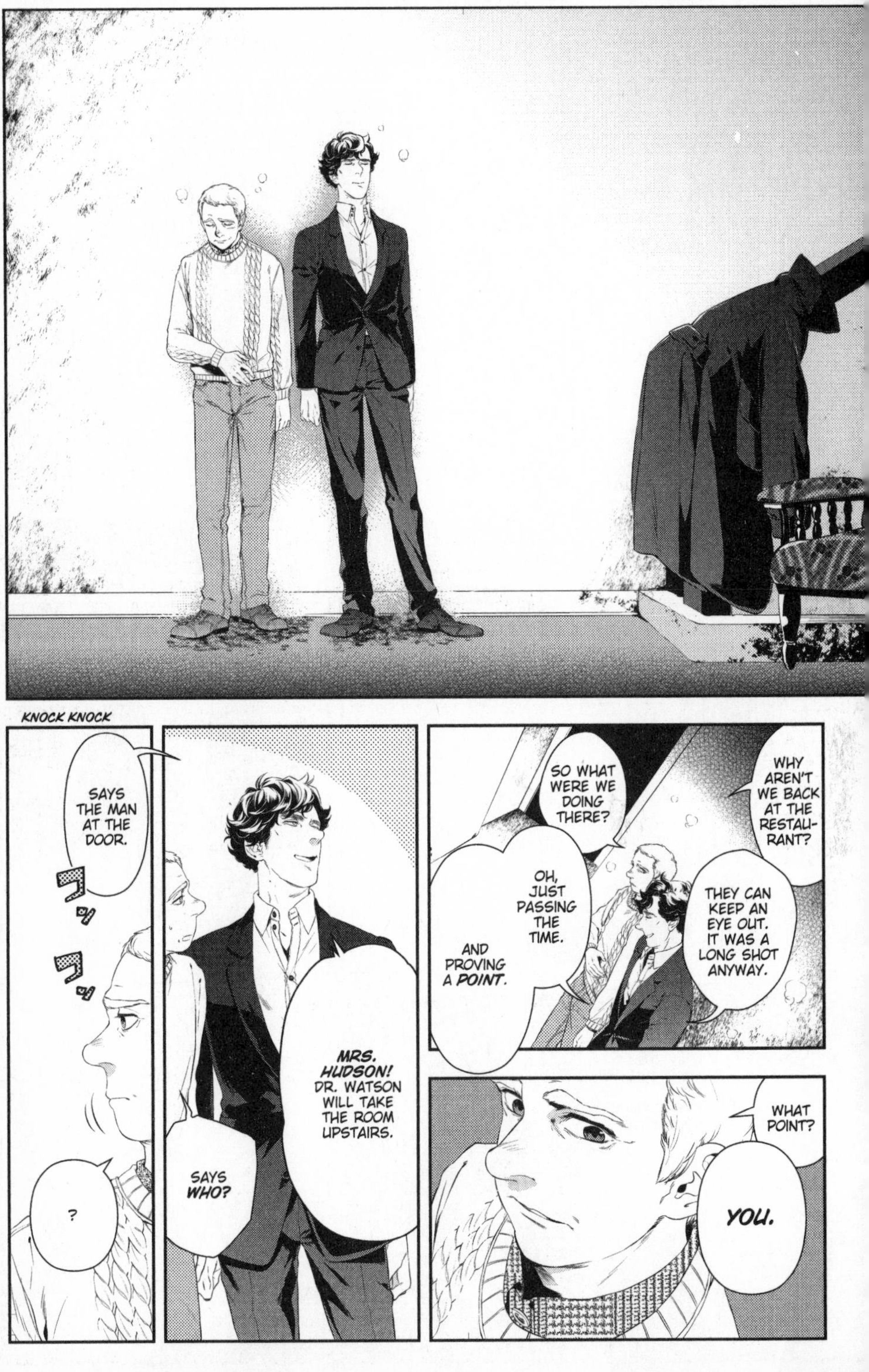
WHY AREN'T WE BACK AT THE RESTAURANT?
SO WHAT WERE WE DOING THERE?
THEY CAN KEEP AN EYE OUT. IT WAS A LONG SHOT ANYWAY.
OH, JUST PASSING THE TIME.
AND PROVING A POINT.
WHAT POINT?
YOU.
MRS. HUDSON! DR. WATSON WILL TAKE THE ROOM UPSTAIRS.
SAYS WHO?
KNOCK KNOCK
コッ
コッ
SAYS THE MAN AT THE DOOR.
?

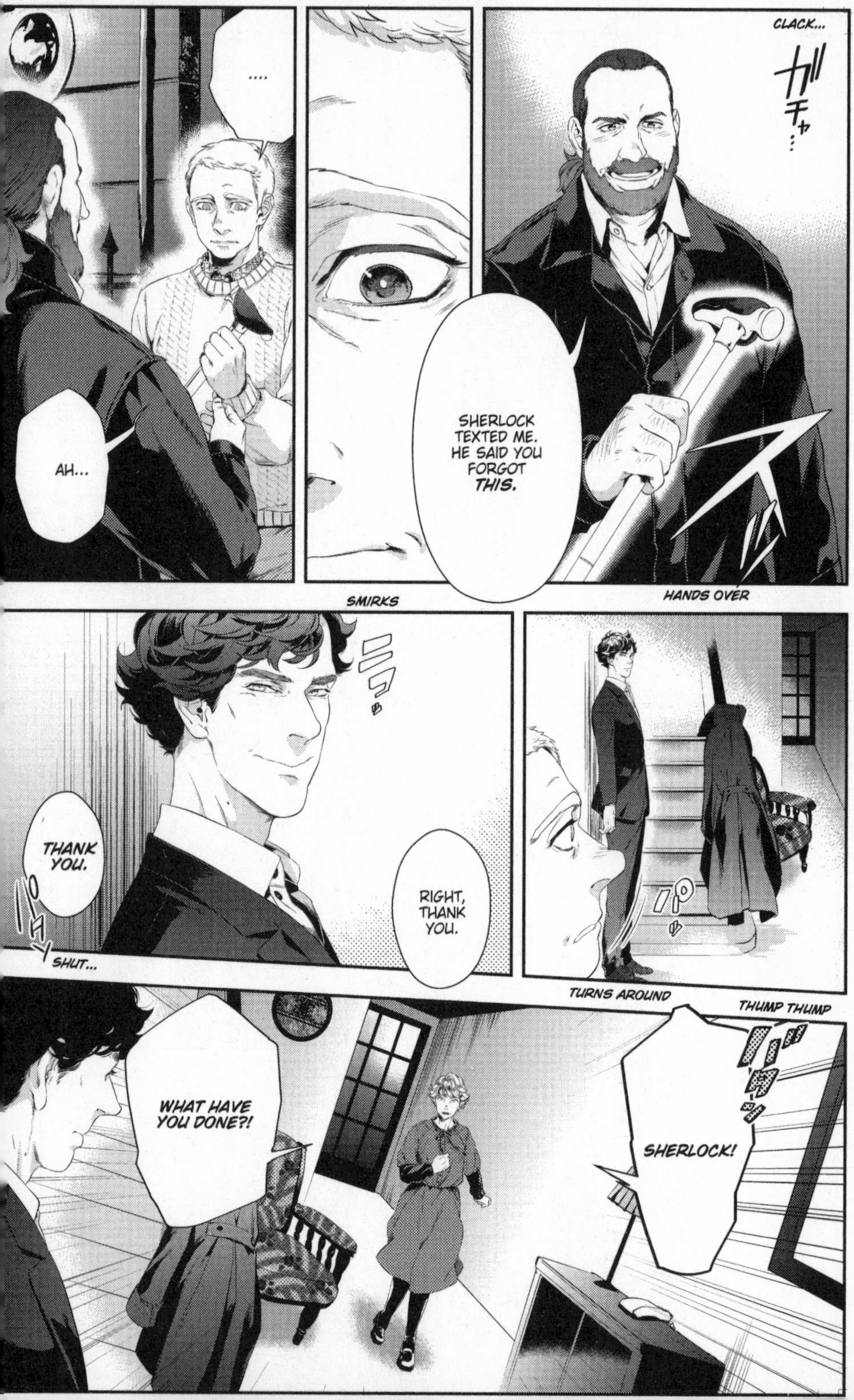
CLACK...
SHERLOCK TEXTED ME. HE SAID YOU FORGOT *THIS.*
HANDS OVER
....
AH...
TURNS AROUND
SMIRKS
RIGHT, THANK YOU.
THANK YOU.
SHUT...
THUMP THUMP
SHERLOCK!
WHAT HAVE YOU DONE?!

SHERLOCK

A STUDY IN PINK

#5

Cover by Robert Hack

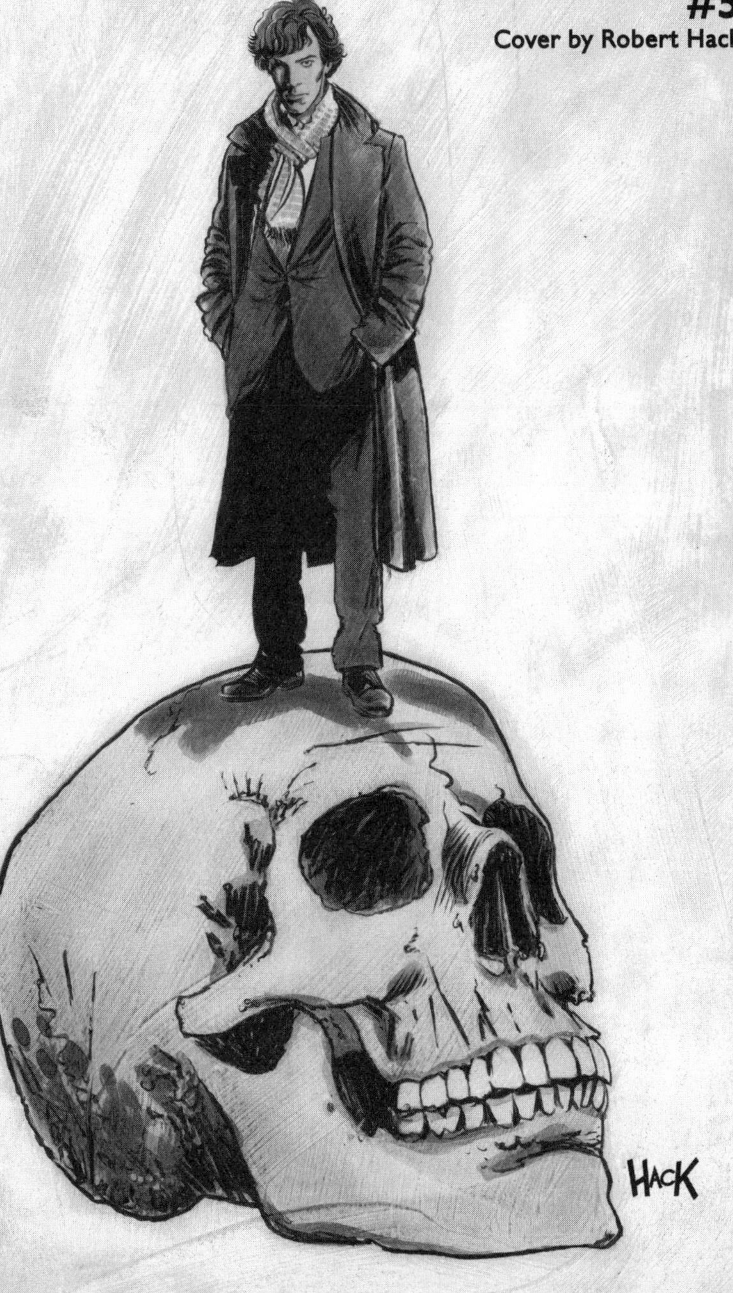
HACK

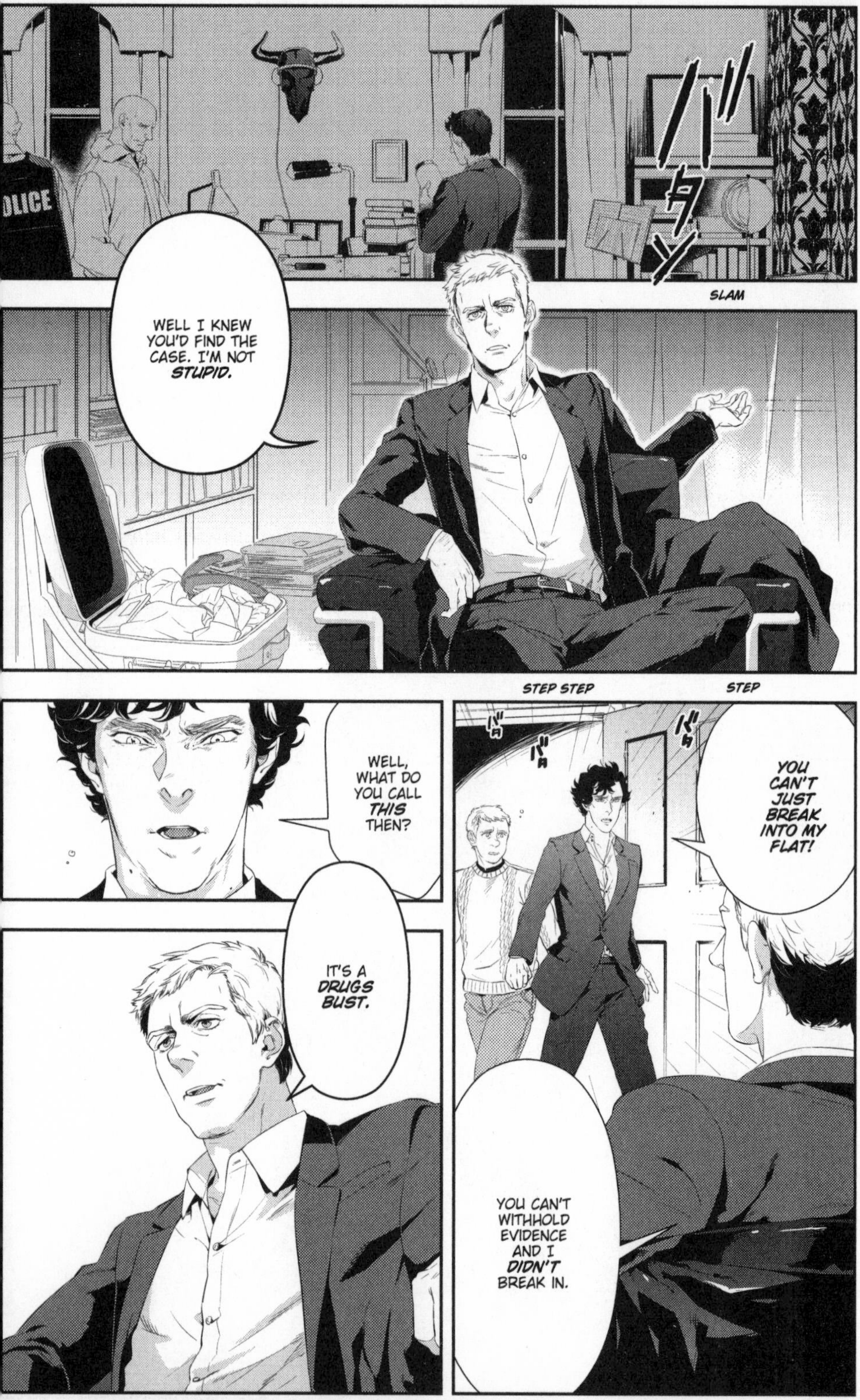
SLAM
WELL I KNEW YOU'D FIND THE CASE. I'M NOT STUPID.
STEP
STEP STEP
YOU CAN'T JUST BREAK INTO MY FLAT!
YOU CAN'T WITHHOLD EVIDENCE AND I DIDN'T BREAK IN.
WELL, WHAT DO YOU CALL THIS THEN?
IT'S A DRUGS BUST.

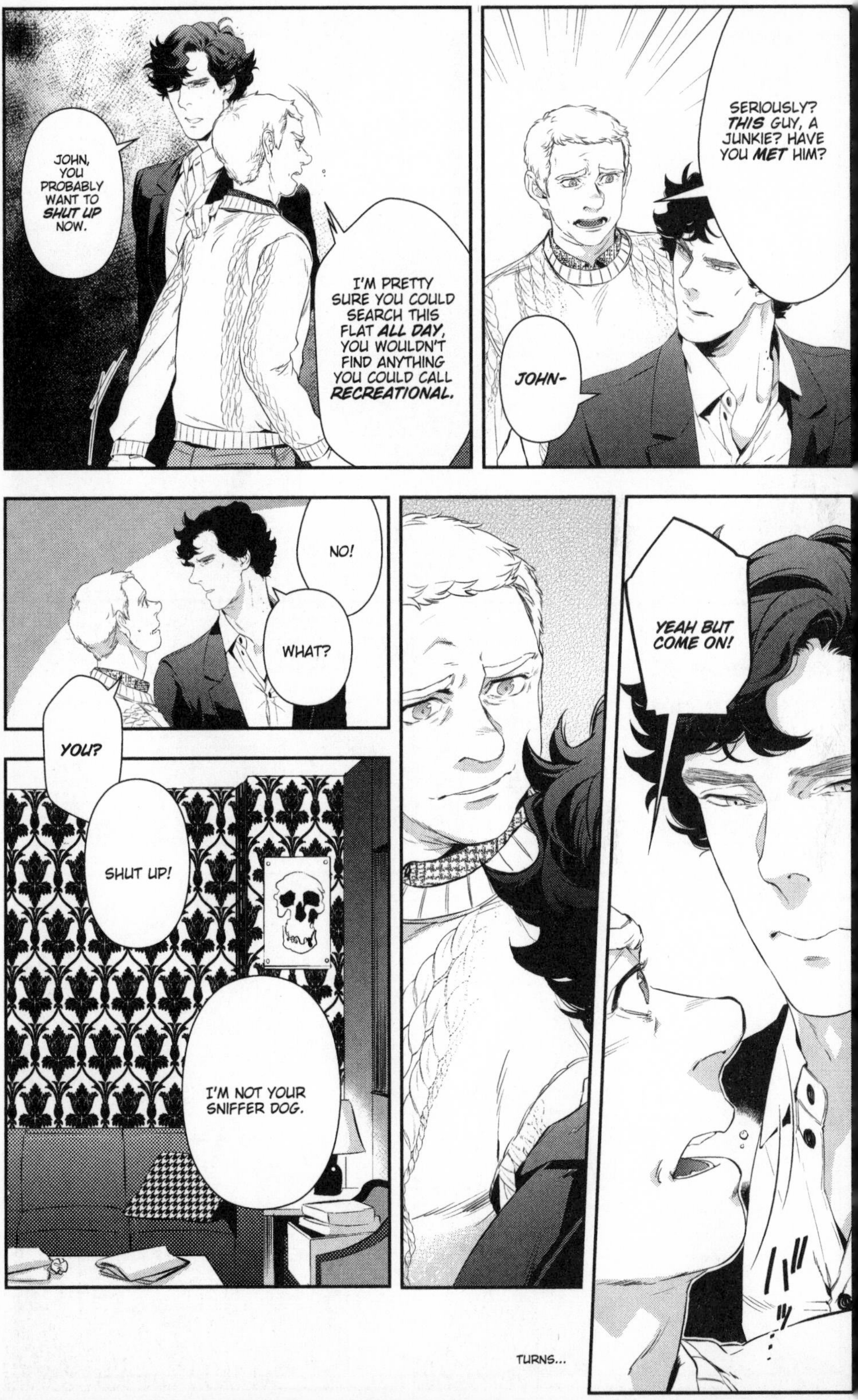
SERIOUSLY? ***THIS*** GUY, A JUNKIE? HAVE YOU ***MET*** HIM?
JOHN-
I'M PRETTY SURE YOU COULD SEARCH THIS FLAT ***ALL DAY***, YOU WOULDN'T FIND ANYTHING YOU COULD CALL ***RECREATIONAL.***
JOHN, YOU PROBABLY WANT TO ***SHUT UP*** NOW.
YEAH BUT COME ON!
NO!
WHAT?
YOU?
SHUT UP!
I'M NOT YOUR SNIFFER DOG.

TURNS...

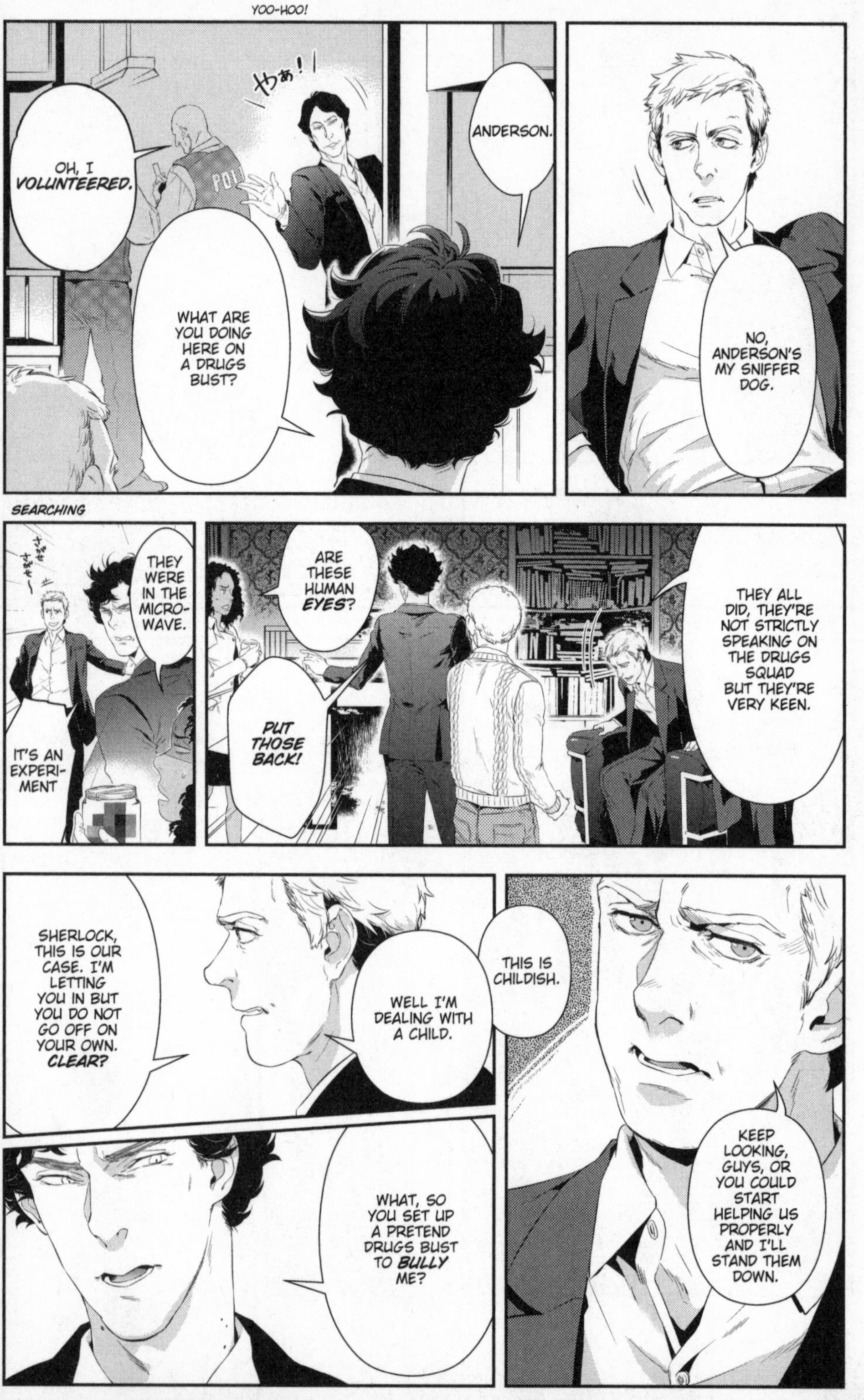
YOO-HOO!
NO, ANDERSON'S MY SNIFFER DOG.
やぁ!!
ANDERSON.
WHAT ARE YOU DOING HERE ON A DRUGS BUST?
OH, I VOLUNTEERED.
SEARCHING
THEY ALL DID, THEY'RE NOT STRICTLY SPEAKING ON THE DRUGS SQUAD BUT THEY'RE VERY KEEN.
ARE THESE HUMAN EYES?
PUT THOSE BACK!
THEY WERE IN THE MICRO-WAVE.
IT'S AN EXPERI-MENT
THIS IS CHILDISH.
KEEP LOOKING, GUYS, OR YOU COULD START HELPING US PROPERLY AND I'LL STAND THEM DOWN.
SHERLOCK, THIS IS OUR CASE. I'M LETTING YOU IN BUT YOU DO NOT GO OFF ON YOUR OWN. CLEAR?
WELL I'M DEALING WITH A CHILD.
WHAT, SO YOU SET UP A PRETEND DRUGS BUST TO BULLY ME?

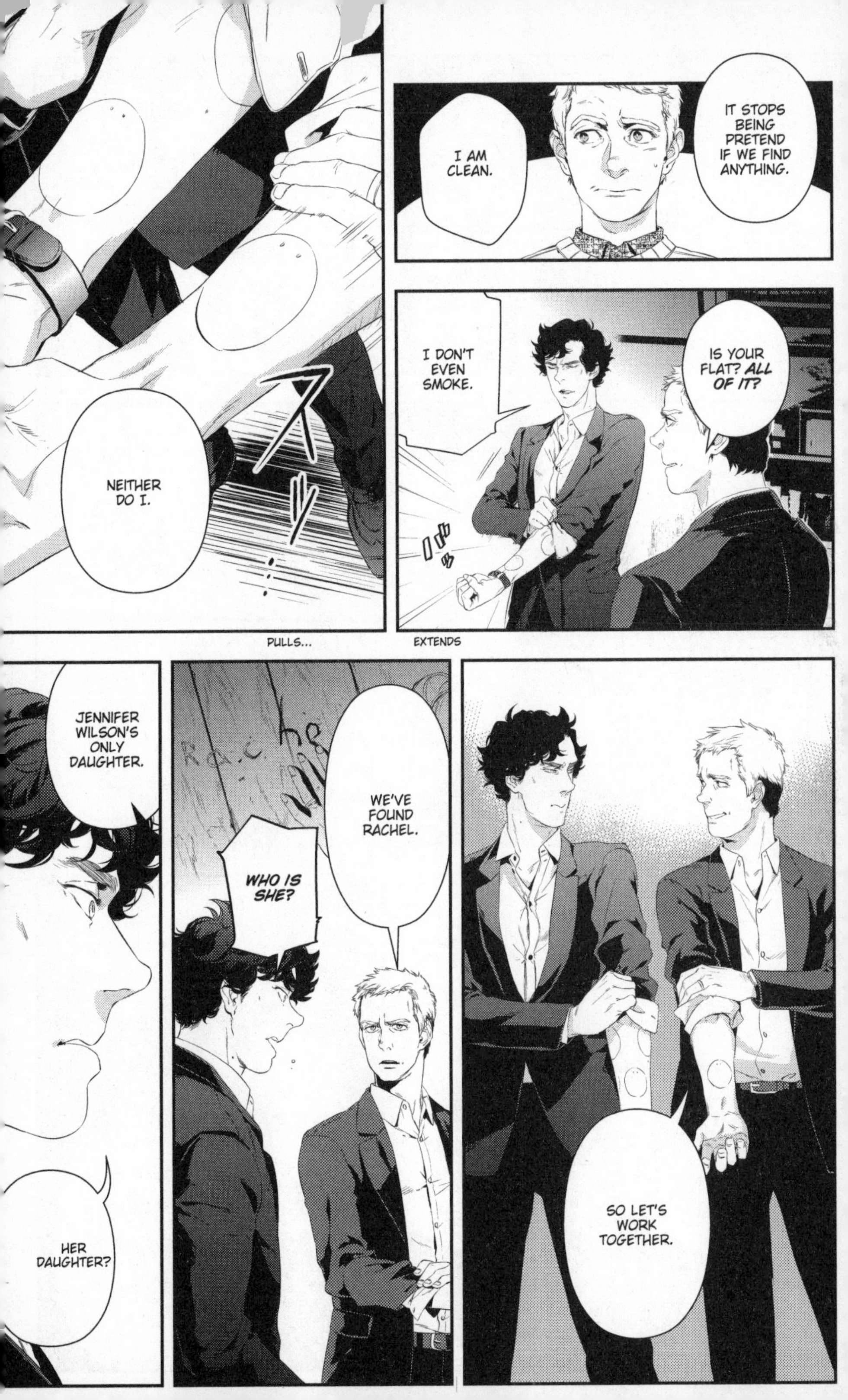
IT STOPS BEING PRETEND IF WE FIND ANYTHING.
I AM CLEAN.
IS YOUR FLAT? ALL OF IT?
I DON'T EVEN SMOKE.
EXTENDS
NEITHER DO I.
PULLS...
SO LET'S WORK TOGETHER.
WE'VE FOUND RACHEL.
WHO IS SHE?
JENNIFER WILSON'S ONLY DAUGHTER.
HER DAUGHTER?

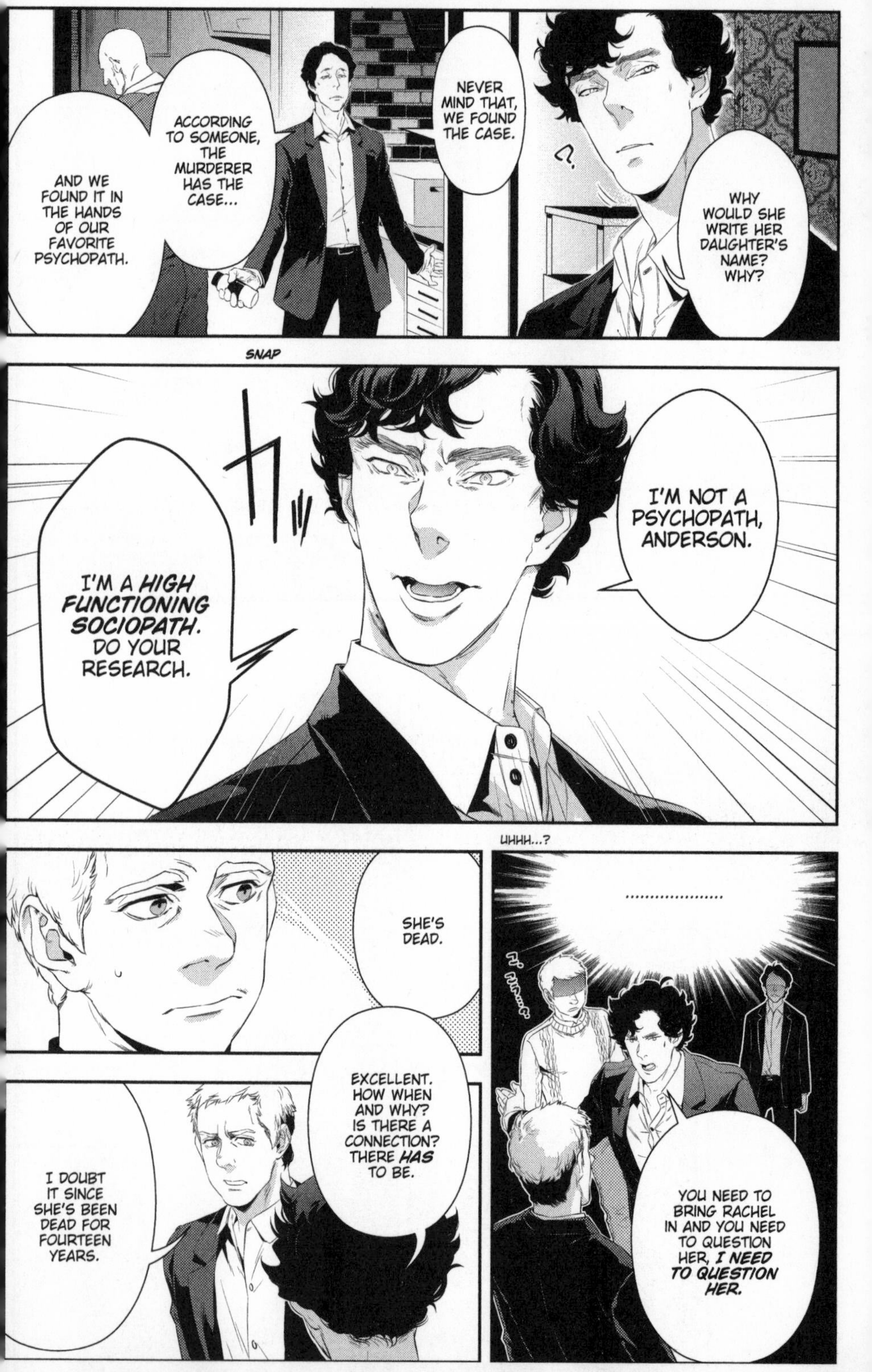

?
WHY WOULD SHE WRITE HER DAUGHTER'S NAME? WHY?
NEVER MIND THAT, WE FOUND THE CASE.
ACCORDING TO SOMEONE, THE MURDERER HAS THE CASE...
AND WE FOUND IT IN THE HANDS OF OUR FAVORITE PSYCHOPATH.
SNAP
I'M NOT A PSYCHOPATH, ANDERSON.
I'M A *HIGH FUNCTIONING SOCIOPATH*. DO YOUR RESEARCH.
UHHH...?
....
YOU NEED TO BRING RACHEL IN AND YOU NEED TO QUESTION HER, ***I NEED TO QUESTION HER.***
SHE'S DEAD.
EXCELLENT. HOW WHEN AND WHY? IS THERE A CONNECTION? THERE ***HAS*** TO BE.
I DOUBT IT SINCE SHE'S BEEN DEAD FOR FOURTEEN YEARS.

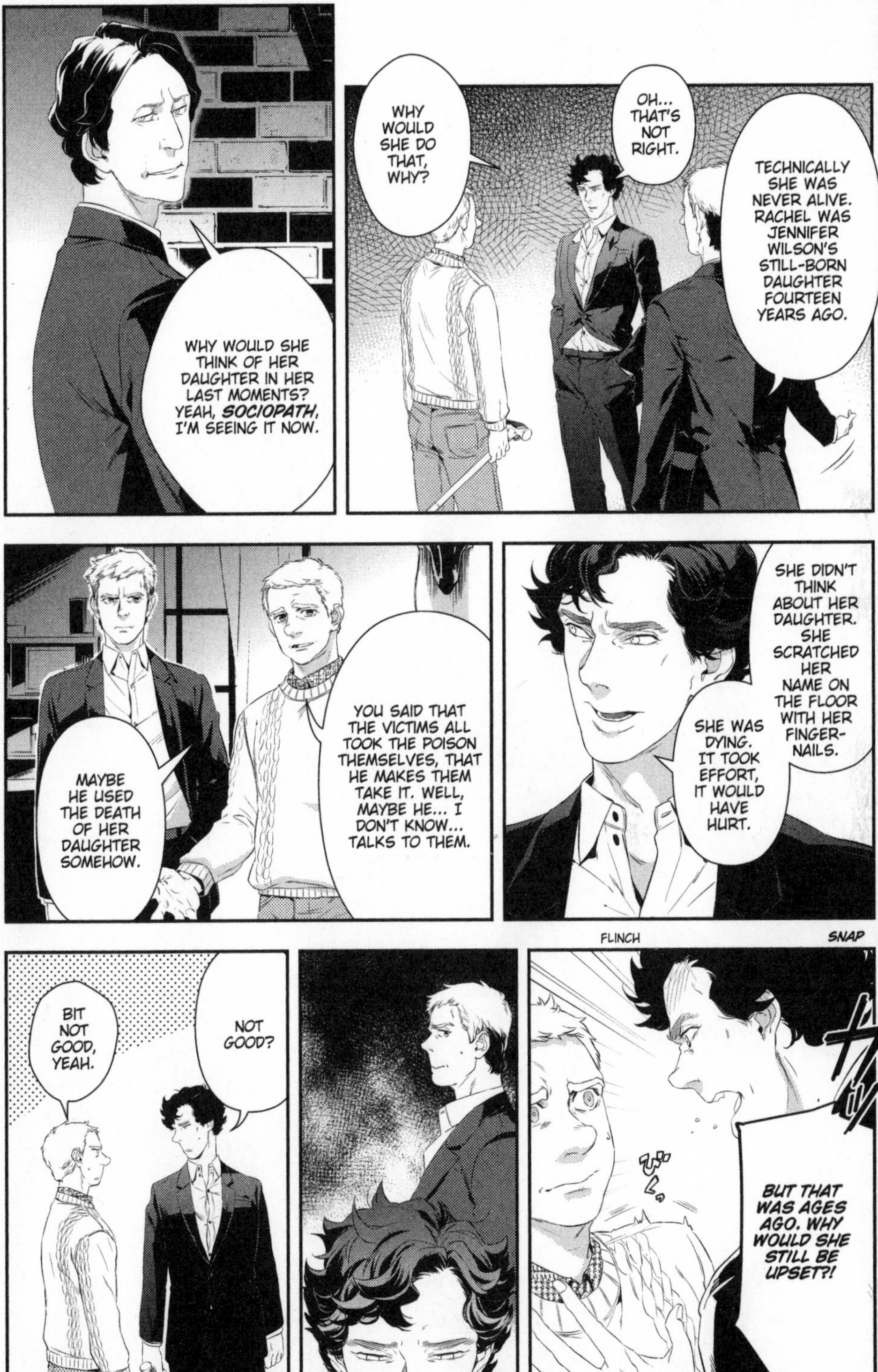
OH... THAT'S NOT RIGHT.
WHY WOULD SHE DO THAT, WHY?
TECHNICALLY SHE WAS NEVER ALIVE. RACHEL WAS JENNIFER WILSON'S STILL-BORN DAUGHTER FOURTEEN YEARS AGO.
WHY WOULD SHE THINK OF HER DAUGHTER IN HER LAST MOMENTS? YEAH, SOCIOPATH, I'M SEEING IT NOW.
SHE DIDN'T THINK ABOUT HER DAUGHTER. SHE SCRATCHED HER NAME ON THE FLOOR WITH HER FINGER-NAILS.
SHE WAS DYING. IT TOOK EFFORT, IT WOULD HAVE HURT.
YOU SAID THAT THE VICTIMS ALL TOOK THE POISON THEMSELVES, THAT HE MAKES THEM TAKE IT. WELL, MAYBE HE... I DON'T KNOW... TALKS TO THEM.
MAYBE HE USED THE DEATH OF HER DAUGHTER SOMEHOW.
SNAP
BUT THAT WAS AGES AGO. WHY WOULD SHE STILL BE UPSET?!
FLINCH
NOT GOOD?
BIT NOT GOOD, YEAH.

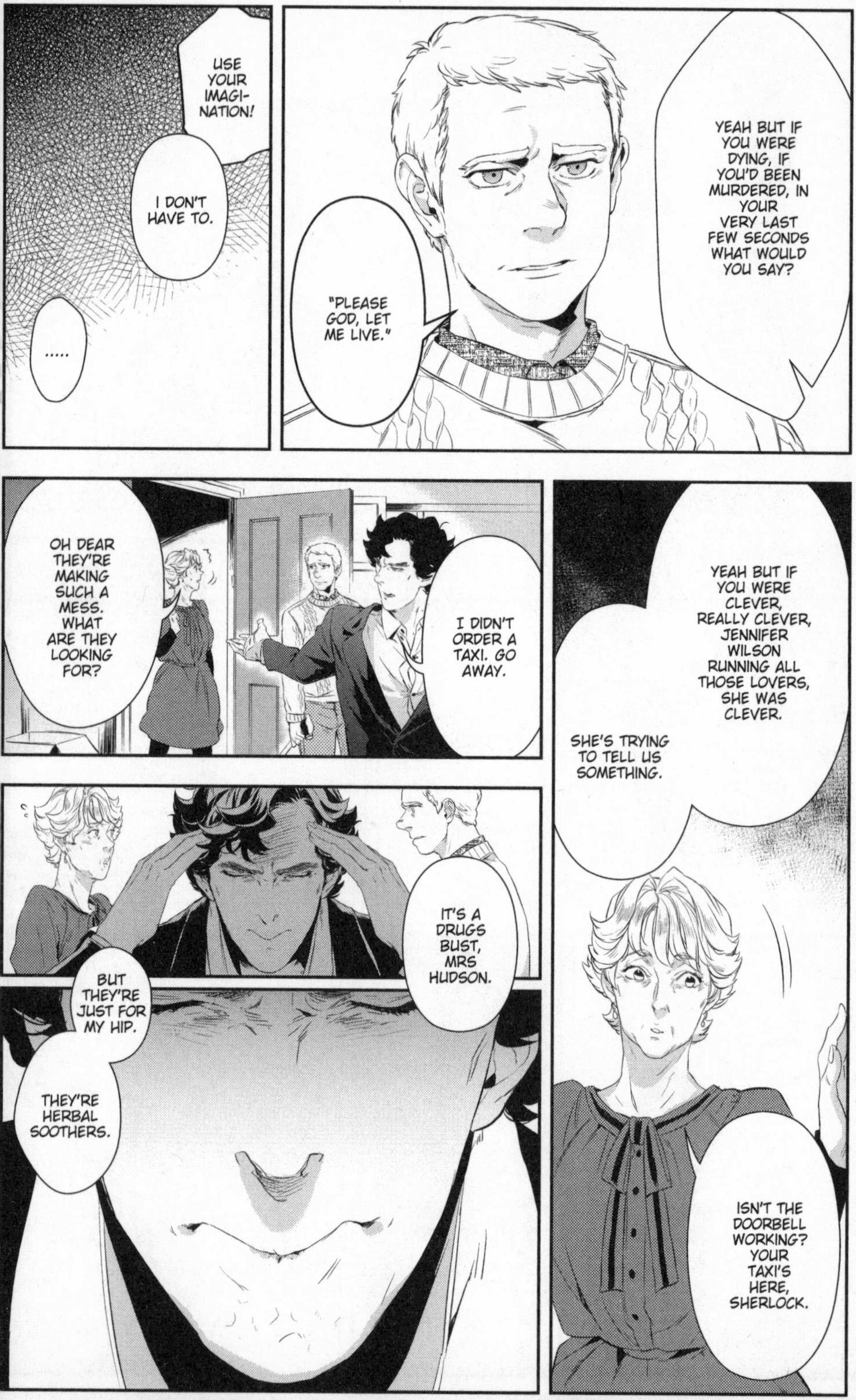
YEAH BUT IF YOU WERE DYING, IF YOU'D BEEN MURDERED, IN YOUR VERY LAST FEW SECONDS WHAT WOULD YOU SAY?
"PLEASE GOD, LET ME LIVE."
USE YOUR IMAGI-NATION!
I DON'T HAVE TO.
.....
YEAH BUT IF YOU WERE CLEVER, REALLY CLEVER, JENNIFER WILSON RUNNING ALL THOSE LOVERS, SHE WAS CLEVER.
SHE'S TRYING TO TELL US SOMETHING.
ISN'T THE DOORBELL WORKING? YOUR TAXI'S HERE, SHERLOCK.
I DIDN'T ORDER A TAXI. GO AWAY.
OH DEAR THEY'RE MAKING SUCH A MESS. WHAT ARE THEY LOOKING FOR?
IT'S A DRUGS BUST, MRS HUDSON.
BUT THEY'RE JUST FOR MY HIP.
THEY'RE HERBAL SOOTHERS.

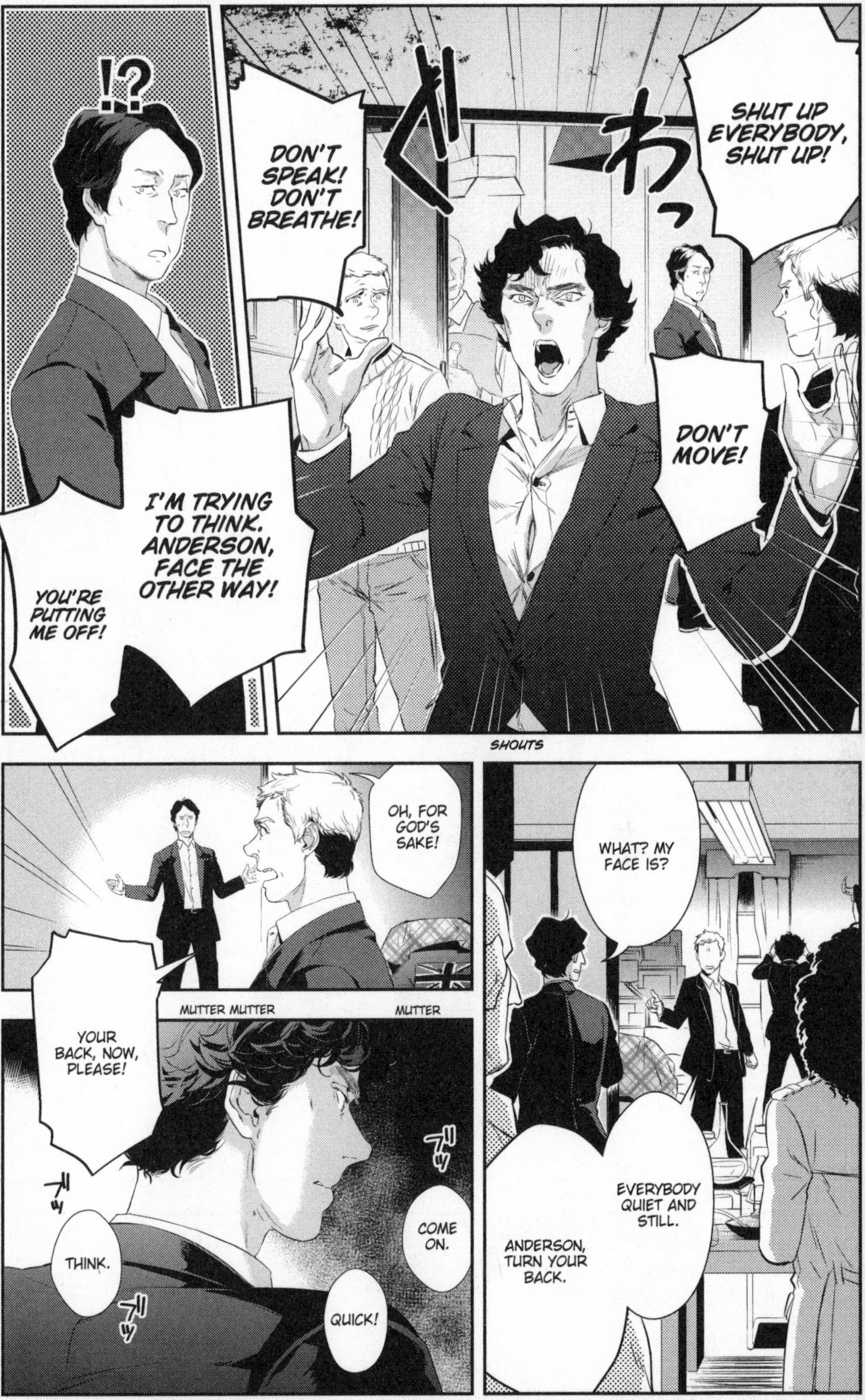
SHUT UP EVERYBODY, SHUT UP!
DON'T MOVE!
DON'T SPEAK! DON'T BREATHE!
I'M TRYING TO THINK. ANDERSON, FACE THE OTHER WAY!
YOU'RE PUTTING ME OFF!
SHOUTS
!?
WHAT? MY FACE IS?
EVERYBODY QUIET AND STILL.
ANDERSON, TURN YOUR BACK.
OH, FOR GOD'S SAKE!
YOUR BACK, NOW, PLEASE!
MUTTER
MUTTER MUTTER
COME ON.
THINK.
QUICK!

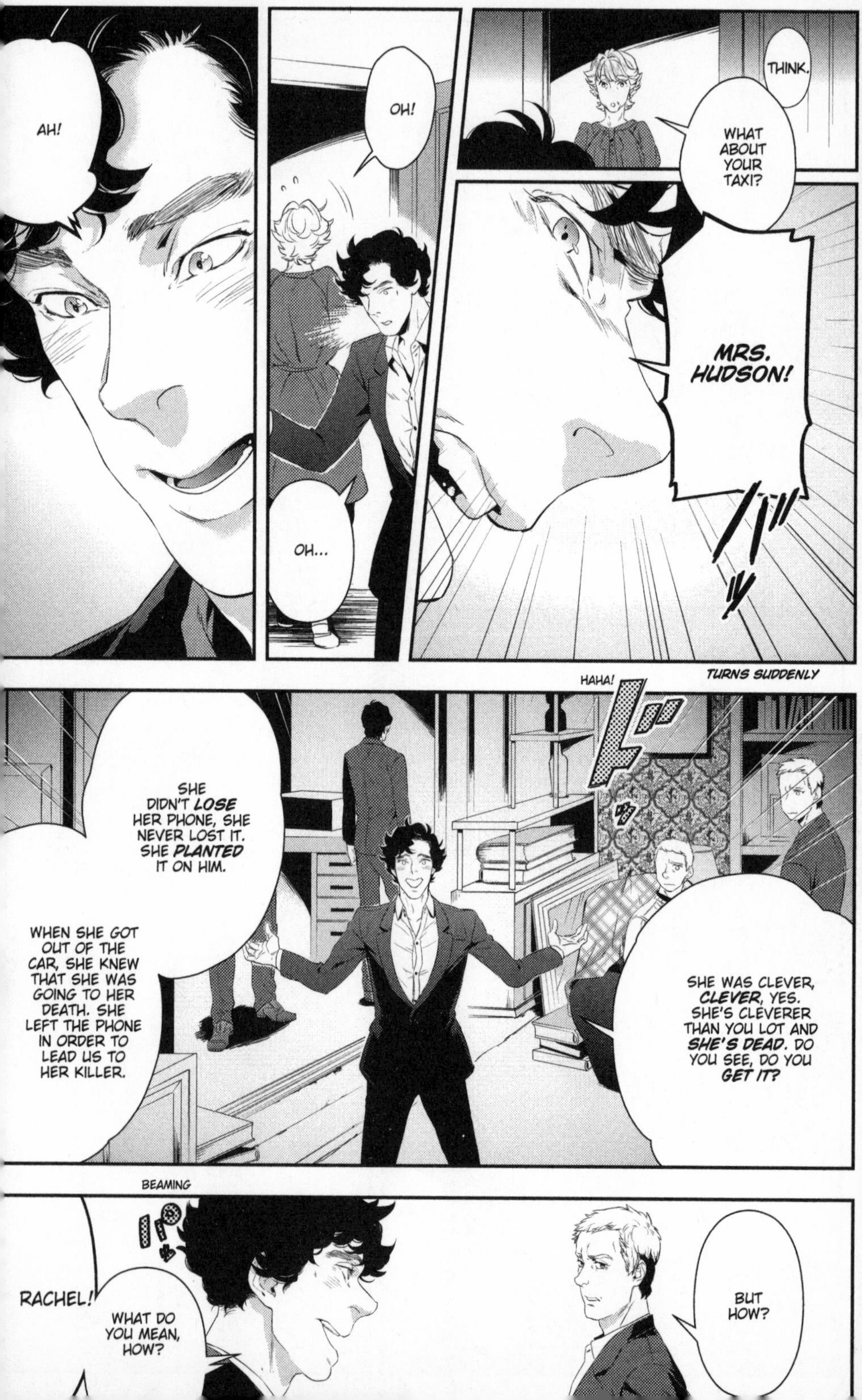
THINK.
WHAT ABOUT YOUR TAXI?
MRS. HUDSON!
OH!
OH...
AH!
TURNS SUDDENLY
HAHA!
SHE DIDN'T *LOSE* HER PHONE, SHE NEVER LOST IT. SHE *PLANTED* IT ON HIM.
WHEN SHE GOT OUT OF THE CAR, SHE KNEW THAT SHE WAS GOING TO HER DEATH. SHE LEFT THE PHONE IN ORDER TO LEAD US TO HER KILLER.
SHE WAS CLEVER, *CLEVER*, YES. SHE'S CLEVERER THAN YOU LOT AND *SHE'S DEAD*. DO YOU SEE, DO YOU *GET IT?*
BEAMING
BUT HOW?
WHAT DO YOU MEAN, HOW?
RACHEL!

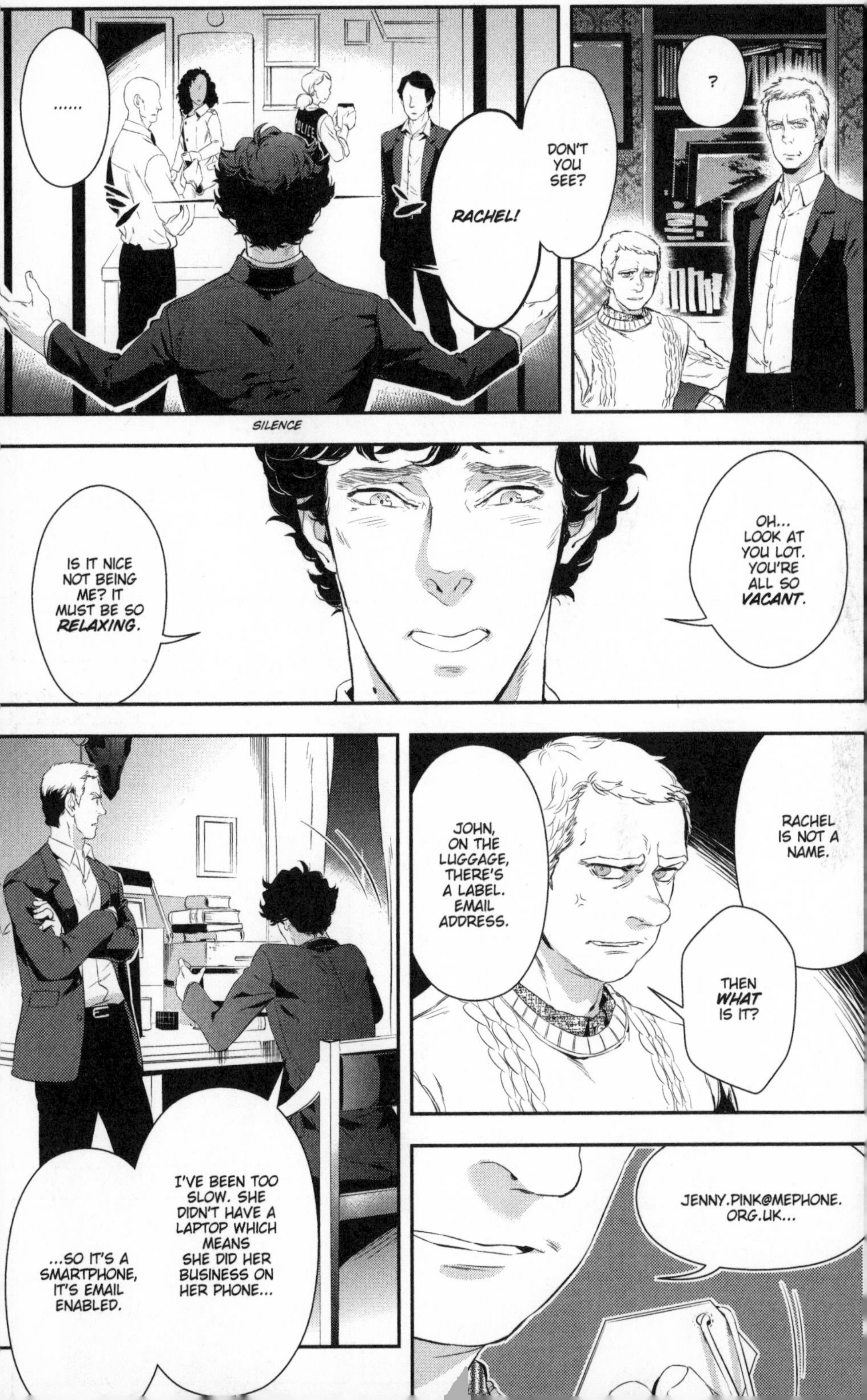

?
DON'T YOU SEE? RACHEL!
......
SILENCE
OH... LOOK AT YOU LOT. YOU'RE ALL SO **VACANT**.
IS IT NICE NOT BEING ME? IT MUST BE SO **RELAXING**.
RACHEL IS NOT A NAME.
THEN **WHAT** IS IT?
JOHN, ON THE LUGGAGE, THERE'S A LABEL. EMAIL ADDRESS.
JENNY.PINK@MEPHONE. ORG.UK...
I'VE BEEN TOO SLOW. SHE DIDN'T HAVE A LAPTOP WHICH MEANS SHE DID HER BUSINESS ON HER PHONE...
...SO IT'S A SMARTPHONE, IT'S EMAIL ENABLED.

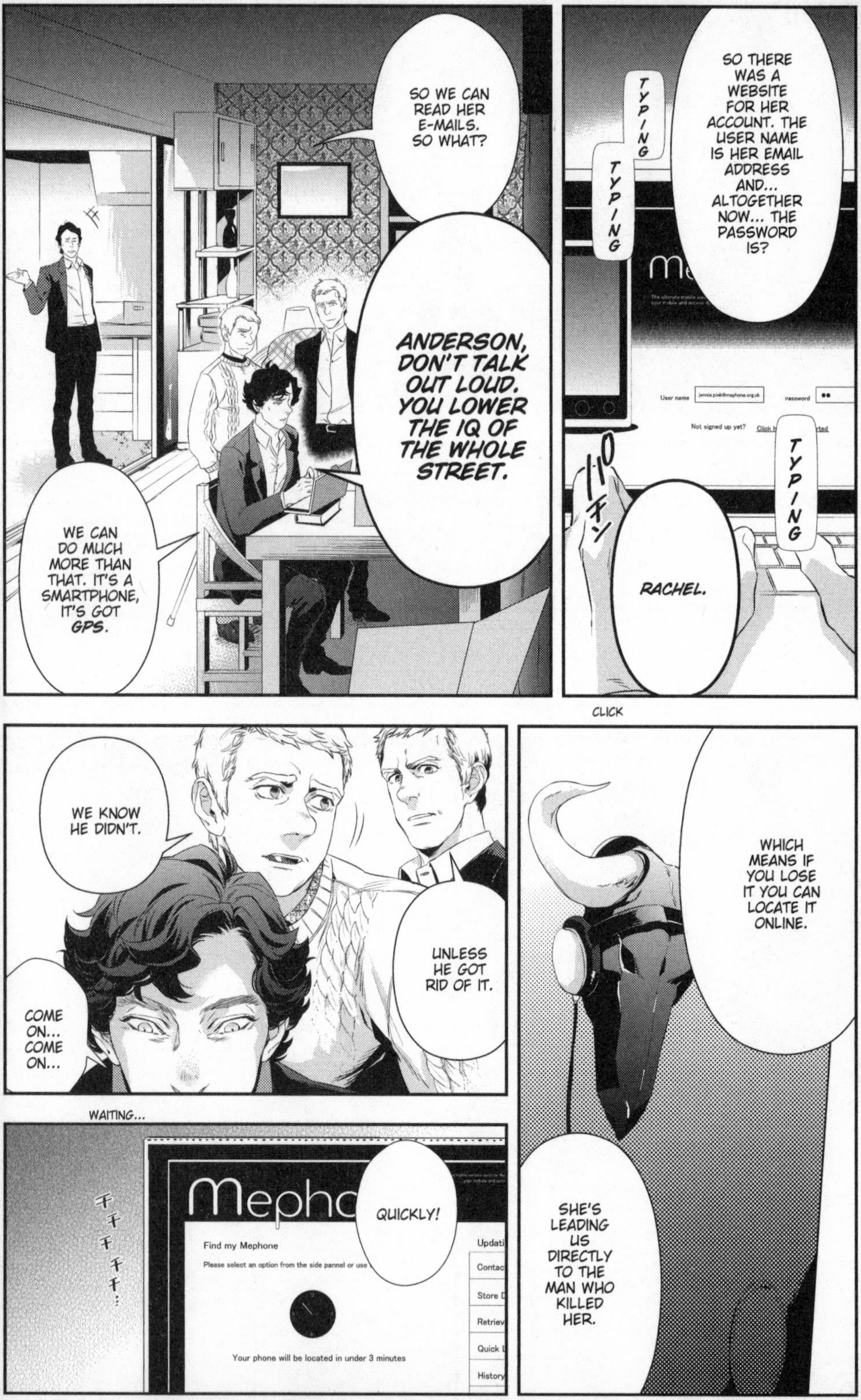
SO WE CAN READ HER E-MAILS. SO WHAT?
ANDERSON, DON'T TALK OUT LOUD. YOU LOWER THE IQ OF THE WHOLE STREET.
WE CAN DO MUCH MORE THAN THAT. IT'S A SMARTPHONE, IT'S GOT GPS.
TYPING
TYPING
SO THERE WAS A WEBSITE FOR HER ACCOUNT. THE USER NAME IS HER EMAIL ADDRESS AND... ALTOGETHER NOW... THE PASSWORD IS?
User name jennie.pink@mephone.org.uk
Password ●●
Not signed up yet?
TYPING
RACHEL.
CLICK
UNLESS HE GOT RID OF IT.
WE KNOW HE DIDN'T.
COME ON... COME ON...
WHICH MEANS IF YOU LOSE IT YOU CAN LOCATE IT ONLINE.
SHE'S LEADING US DIRECTLY TO THE MAN WHO KILLED HER.
WAITING...
Find my Mephone
Please select an option from the side pannel or use
Your phone will be located in under 3 minutes
QUICKLY!

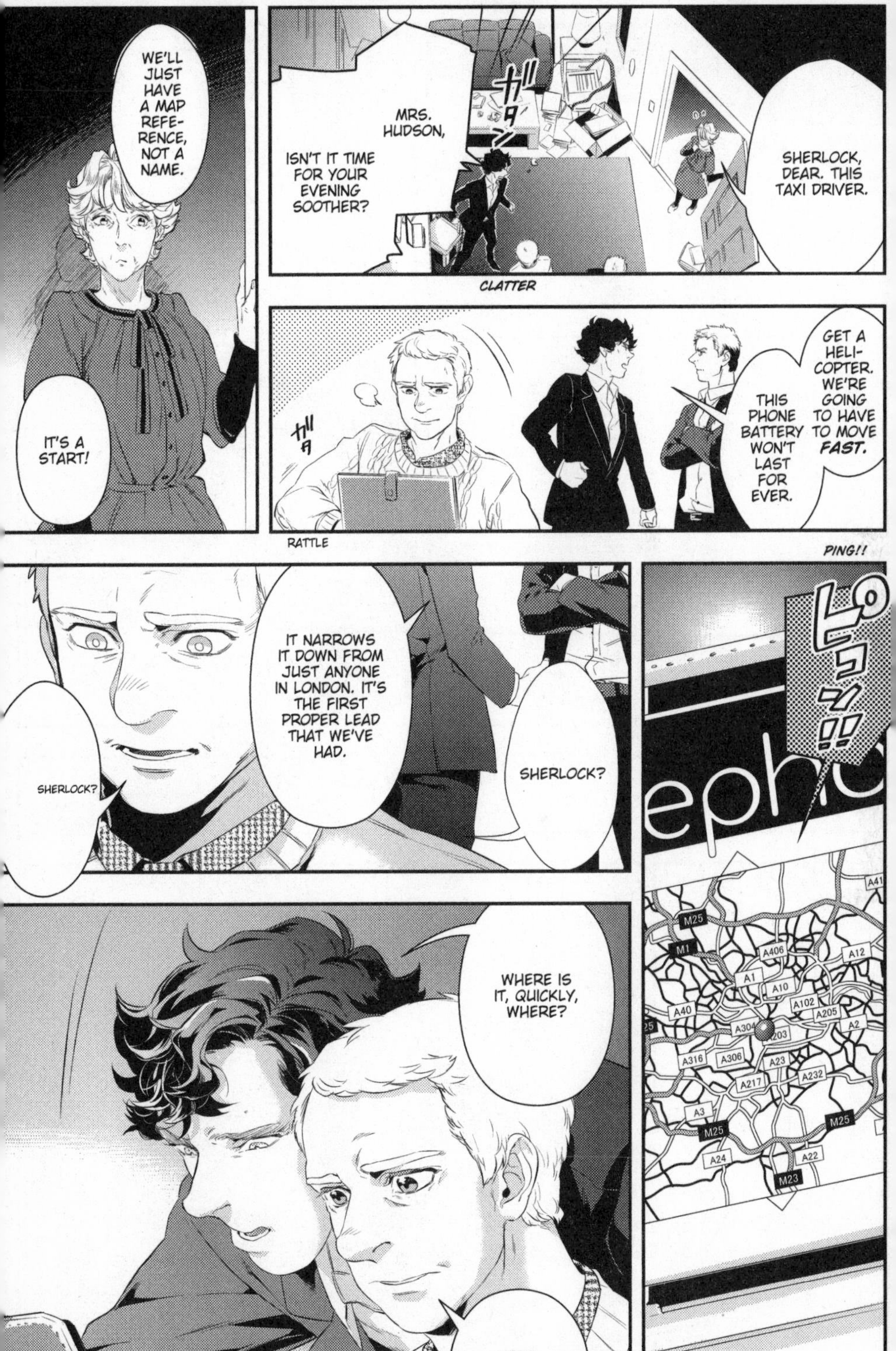
SHERLOCK, DEAR. THIS TAXI DRIVER.
MRS. HUDSON,
ISN'T IT TIME FOR YOUR EVENING SOOTHER?
CLATTER
GET A HELICOPTER. WE'RE GOING TO HAVE TO MOVE *FAST.*
THIS PHONE BATTERY WON'T LAST FOR EVER.
RATTLE
WE'LL JUST HAVE A MAP REFERENCE, NOT A NAME.
IT'S A START!
PING!!
M25
M1
A406
A12
A1
A10
A40
A102
A205
A2
A304
A316
A306
A23
A232
A217
A3
M25
M25
A24
A22
M23
IT NARROWS IT DOWN FROM JUST ANYONE IN LONDON. IT'S THE FIRST PROPER LEAD THAT WE'VE HAD.
SHERLOCK?
SHERLOCK?
WHERE IS IT, QUICKLY, WHERE?
HERE. IT'S...

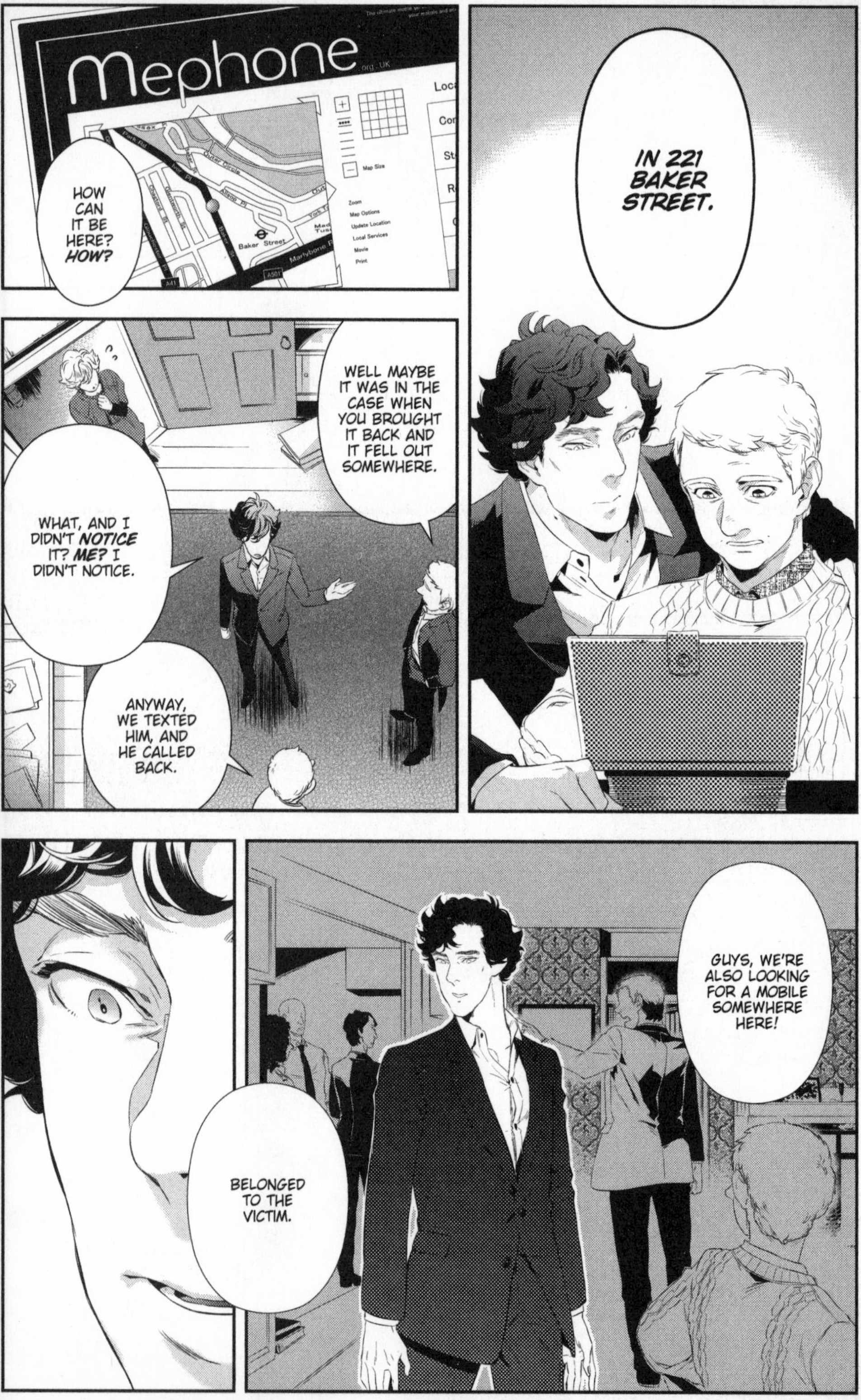
IN 221 BAKER STREET.
Mephone
.org.UK
Map Size
Zoom
Map Options
Update Location
Local Services
Movie
Print
Baker Street
HOW CAN IT BE HERE? *HOW?*
WELL MAYBE IT WAS IN THE CASE WHEN YOU BROUGHT IT BACK AND IT FELL OUT SOMEWHERE.
WHAT, AND I DIDN'T *NOTICE* IT? *ME?* I DIDN'T NOTICE.
ANYWAY, WE TEXTED HIM, AND HE CALLED BACK.
GUYS, WE'RE ALSO LOOKING FOR A MOBILE SOMEWHERE HERE!
BELONGED TO THE VICTIM.

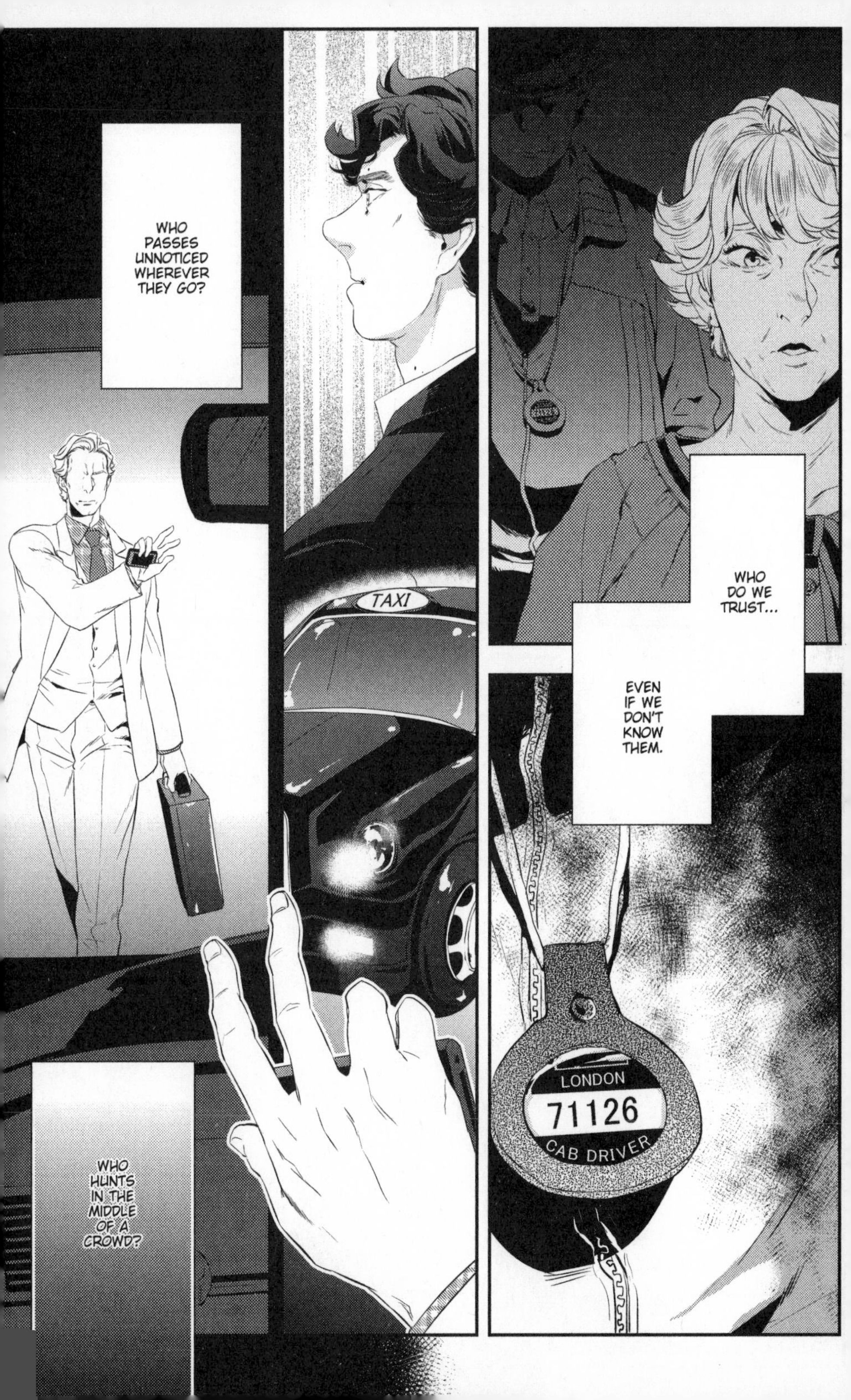
WHO DO WE TRUST...
EVEN IF WE DON'T KNOW THEM.
LONDON
71126
CAB DRIVER
TAXI
WHO PASSES UNNOTICED WHEREVER THEY GO?
WHO HUNTS IN THE MIDDLE OF A CROWD?

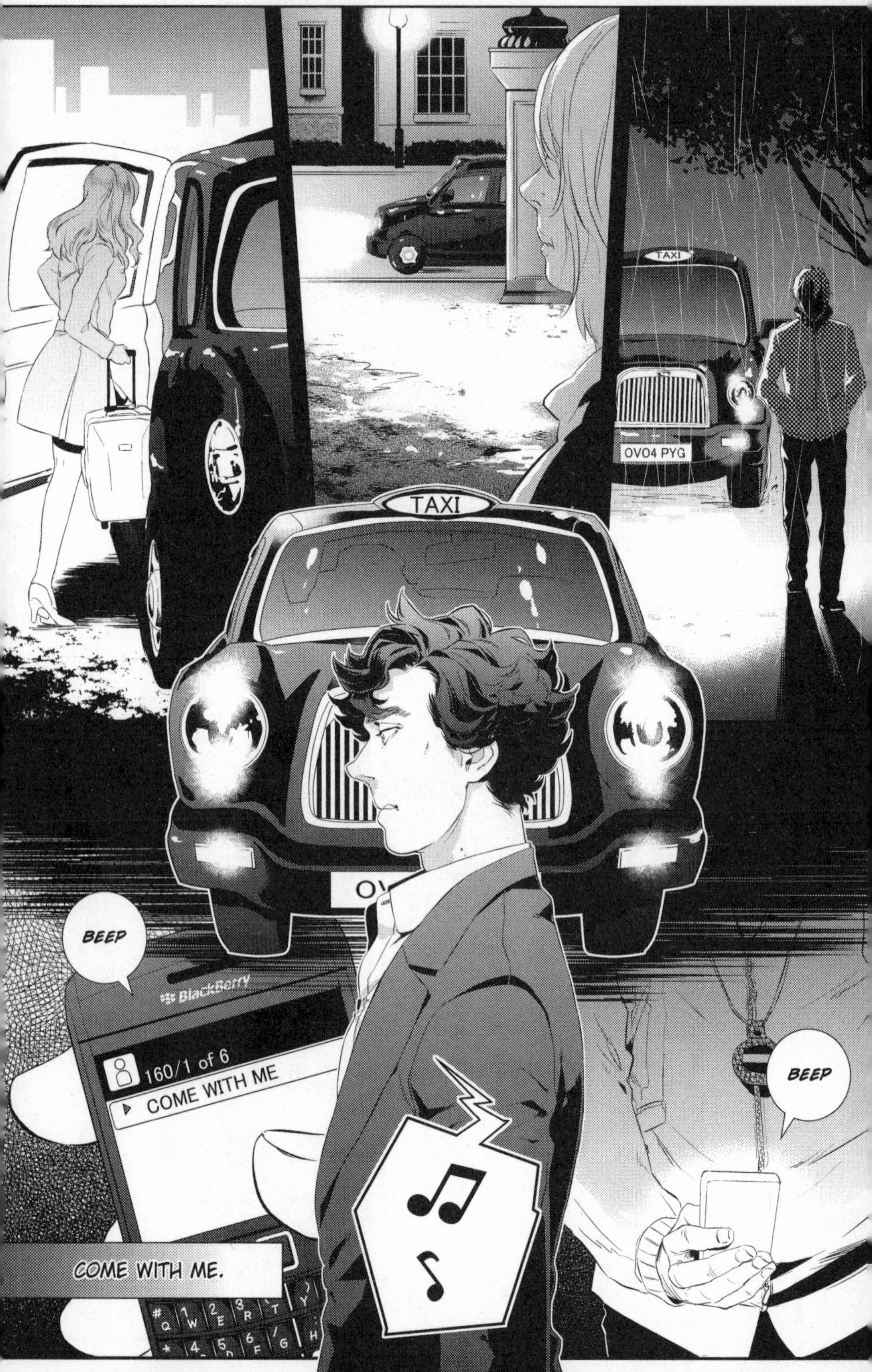
TAXI
OV04 PYG
TAXI
BEEP
BEEP
BlackBerry
160/1 of 6
COME WITH ME
COME WITH ME.

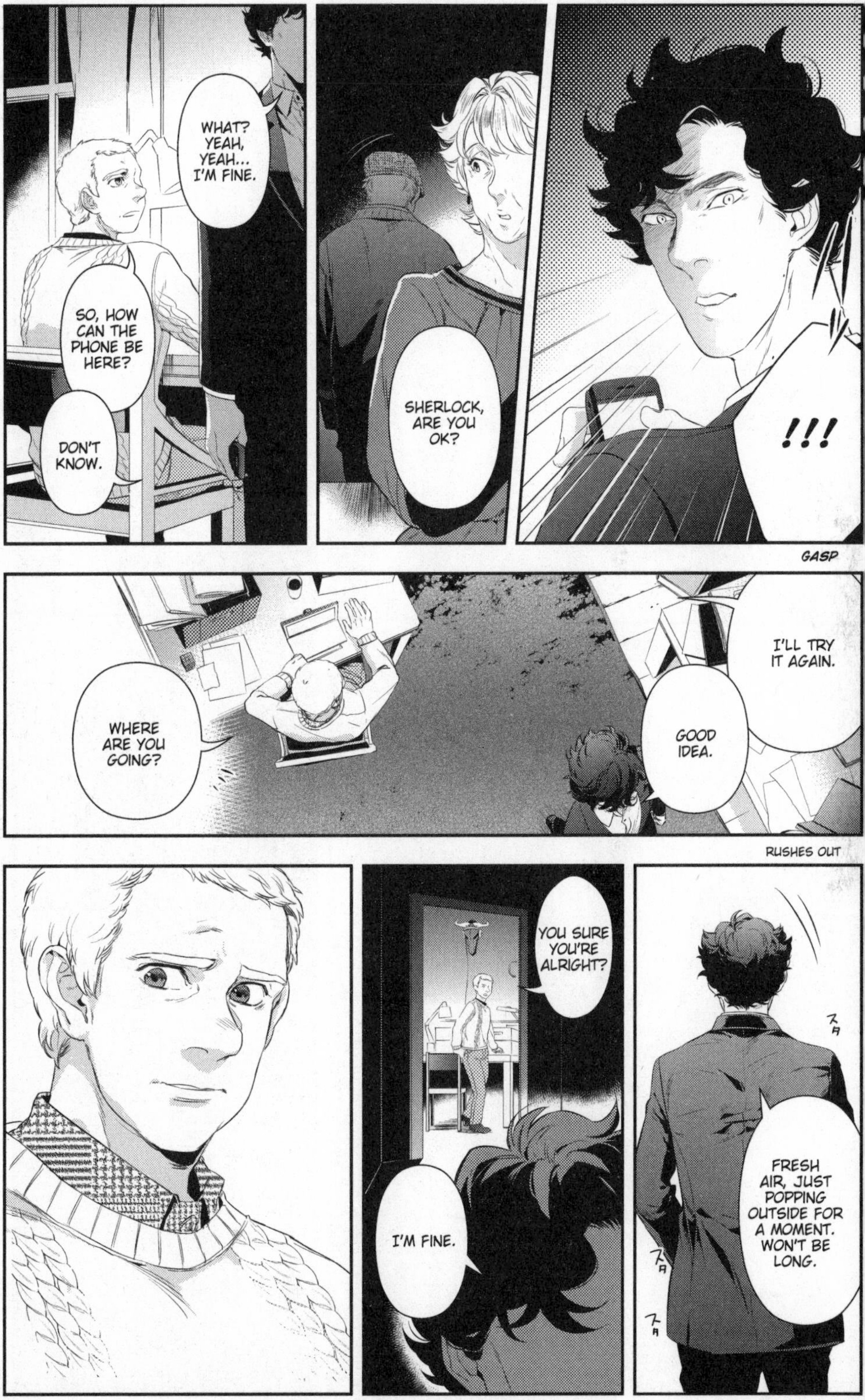
!!!
SHERLOCK, ARE YOU OK?
WHAT? YEAH, YEAH... I'M FINE.
SO, HOW CAN THE PHONE BE HERE?
DON'T KNOW.
GASP
I'LL TRY IT AGAIN.
GOOD IDEA.
WHERE ARE YOU GOING?
RUSHES OUT
FRESH AIR, JUST POPPING OUTSIDE FOR A MOMENT. WON'T BE LONG.
YOU SURE YOU'RE ALRIGHT?
I'M FINE.

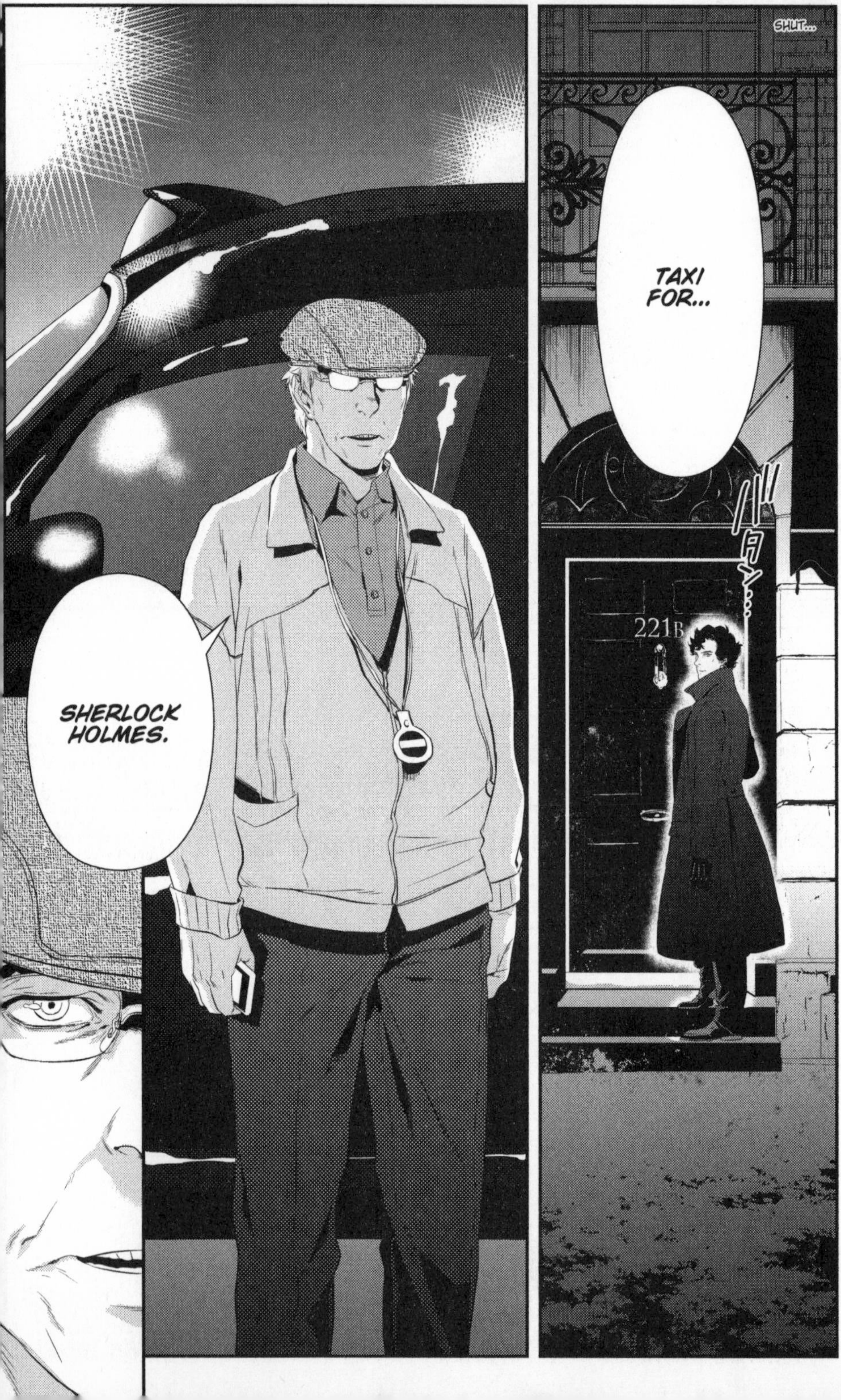
SHUT...
TAXI FOR...
バタン…
SHERLOCK HOLMES.

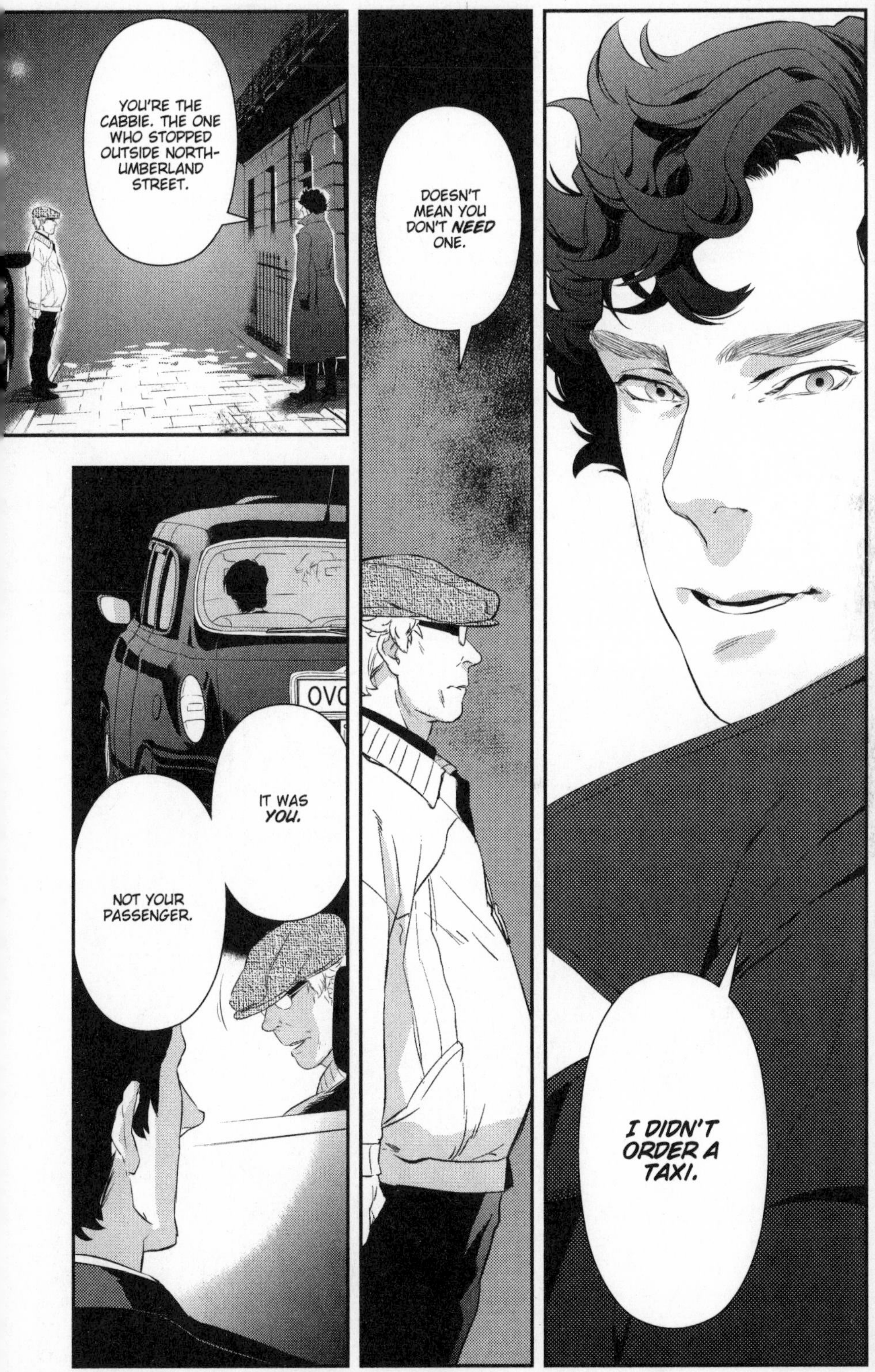
I DIDN'T ORDER A TAXI.
DOESN'T MEAN YOU DON'T NEED ONE.
YOU'RE THE CABBIE. THE ONE WHO STOPPED OUTSIDE NORTH-UMBERLAND STREET.
IT WAS YOU.
NOT YOUR PASSENGER.

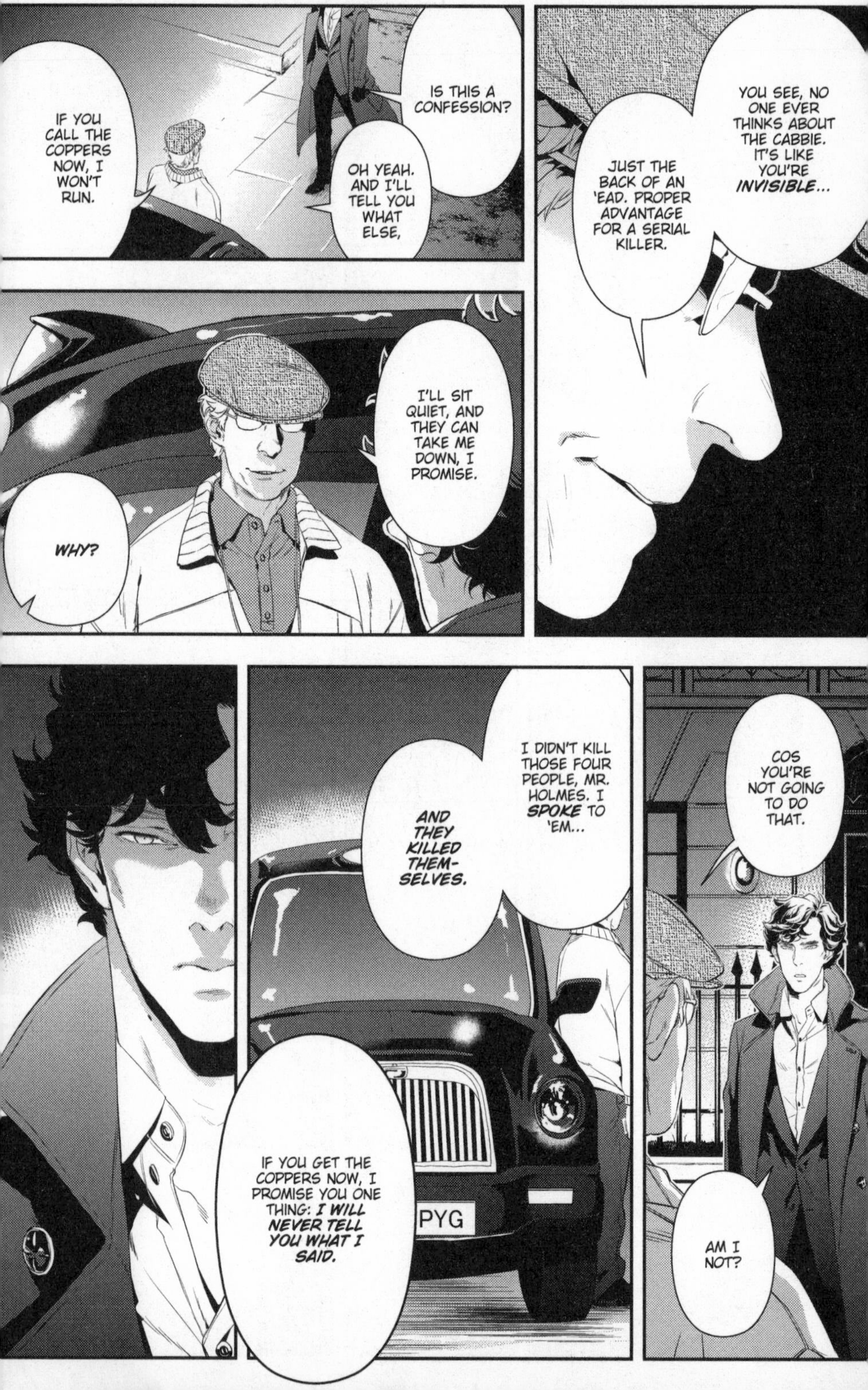
YOU SEE, NO ONE EVER THINKS ABOUT THE CABBIE. IT'S LIKE YOU'RE ***INVISIBLE***...
JUST THE BACK OF AN 'EAD. PROPER ADVANTAGE FOR A SERIAL KILLER.
IS THIS A CONFESSION?
OH YEAH. AND I'LL TELL YOU WHAT ELSE,
IF YOU CALL THE COPPERS NOW, I WON'T RUN.
I'LL SIT QUIET, AND THEY CAN TAKE ME DOWN, I PROMISE.
WHY?
COS YOU'RE NOT GOING TO DO THAT.
AM I NOT?
I DIDN'T KILL THOSE FOUR PEOPLE, MR. HOLMES. I ***SPOKE*** TO 'EM...
AND THEY KILLED THEM-SELVES.
IF YOU GET THE COPPERS NOW, I PROMISE YOU ONE THING: ***I WILL NEVER TELL YOU WHAT I SAID.***
PYG

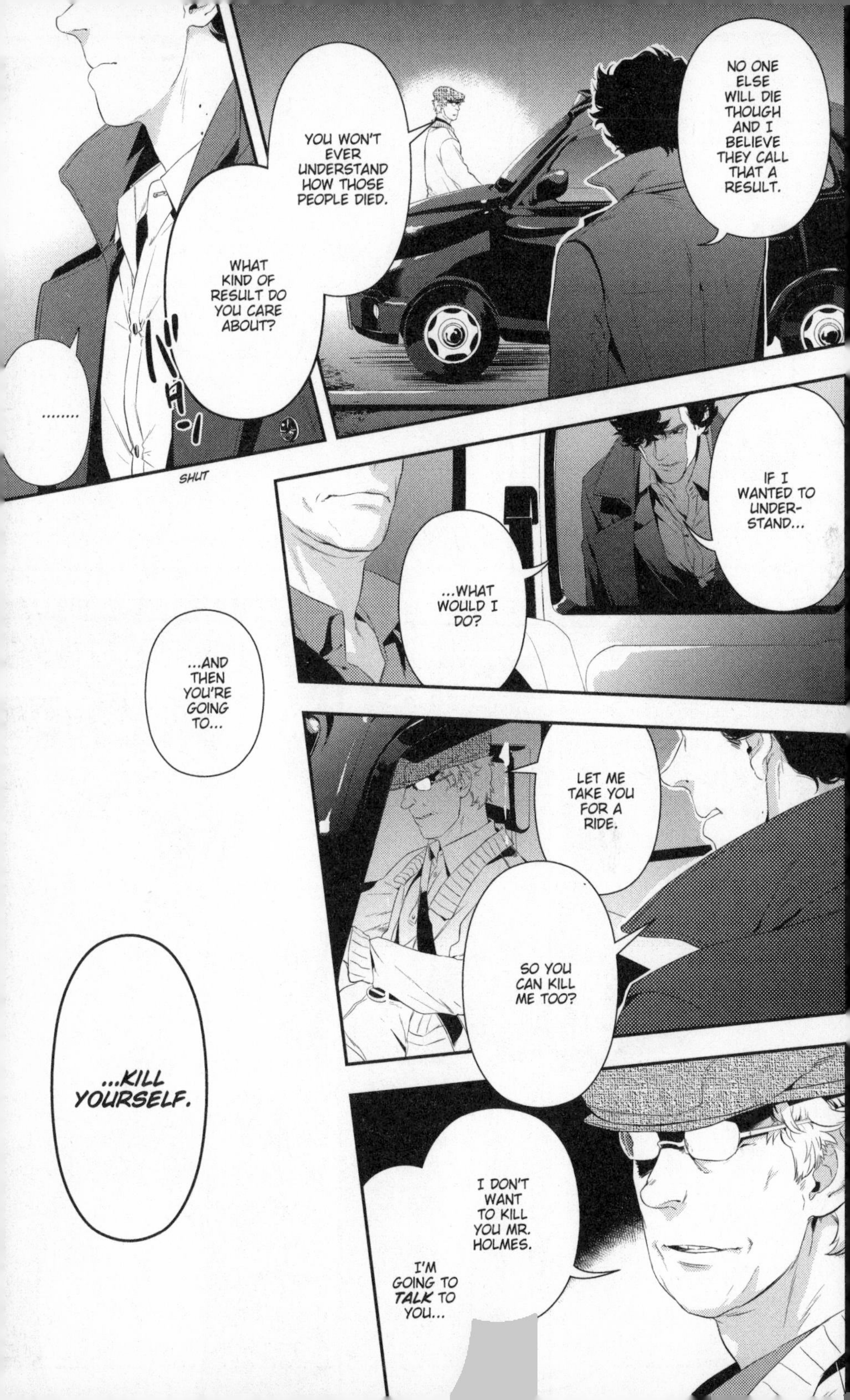
NO ONE ELSE WILL DIE THOUGH AND I BELIEVE THEY CALL THAT A RESULT.
YOU WON'T EVER UNDERSTAND HOW THOSE PEOPLE DIED.
WHAT KIND OF RESULT DO YOU CARE ABOUT?
....
SHUT
IF I WANTED TO UNDER-STAND...
...WHAT WOULD I DO?
...AND THEN YOU'RE GOING TO...
LET ME TAKE YOU FOR A RIDE.
SO YOU CAN KILL ME TOO?
I DON'T WANT TO KILL YOU MR. HOLMES.
I'M GOING TO *TALK* TO YOU...
...KILL YOURSELF.

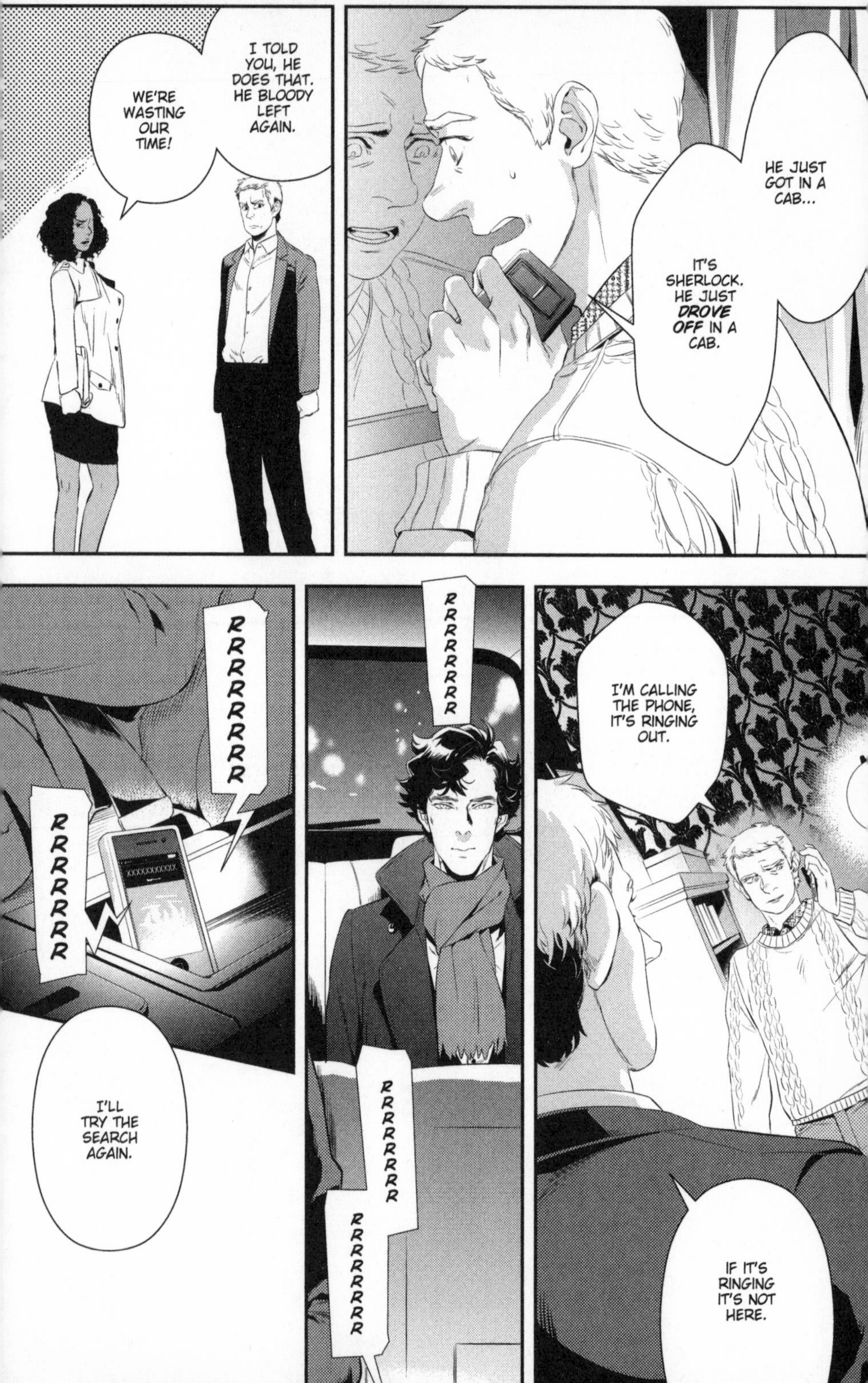
HE JUST GOT IN A CAB...
IT'S SHERLOCK. HE JUST **DROVE OFF** IN A CAB.
I TOLD YOU, HE DOES THAT. HE BLOODY LEFT AGAIN.
WE'RE WASTING OUR TIME!
I'M CALLING THE PHONE, IT'S RINGING OUT.
IF IT'S RINGING IT'S NOT HERE.
RRRRRRRR
RRRRRRRR
RRRRRRRRR
RRRRRRRRR
RRRRRRR
I'LL TRY THE SEARCH AGAIN.

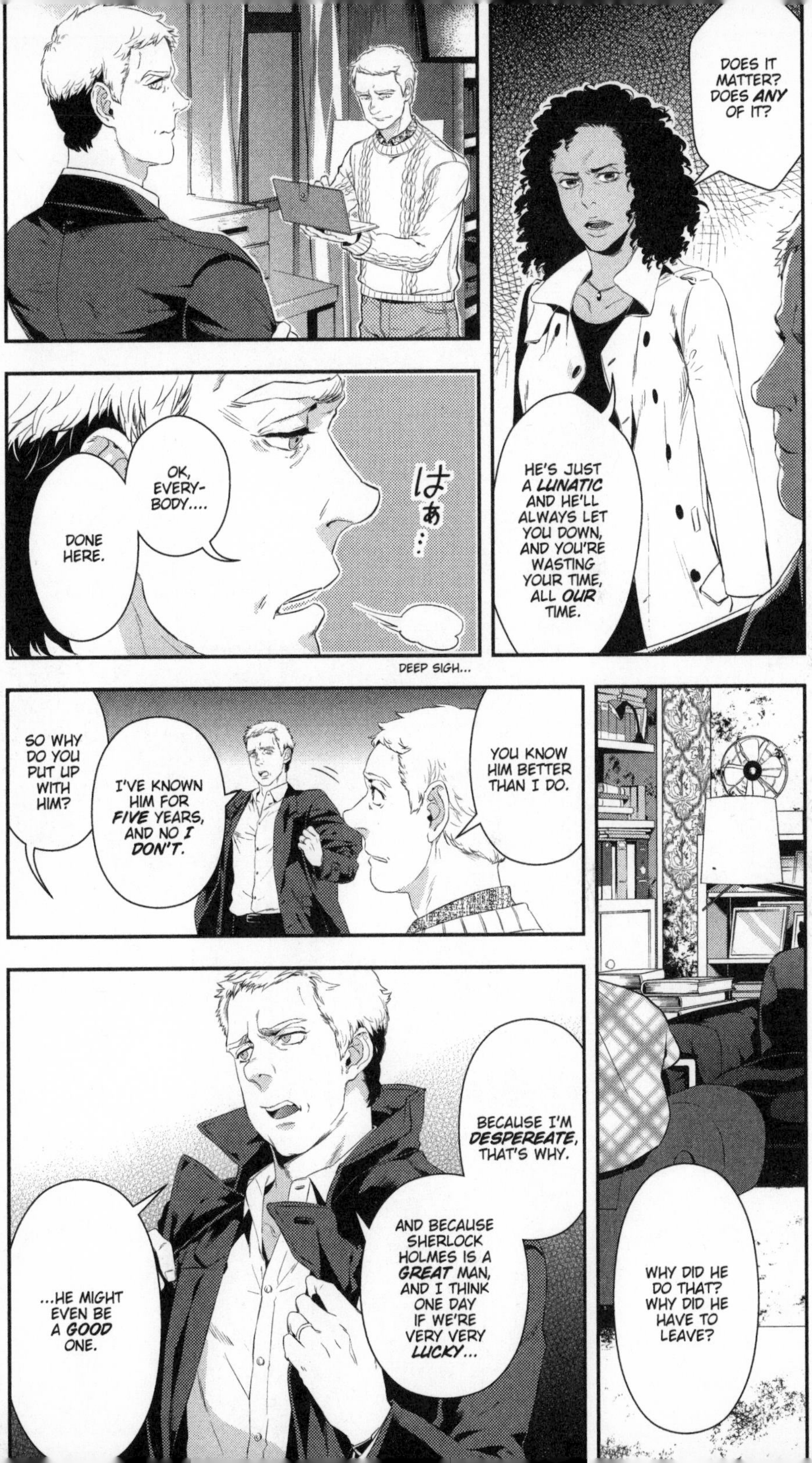
DOES IT MATTER? DOES ANY OF IT?
HE'S JUST A LUNATIC AND HE'LL ALWAYS LET YOU DOWN, AND YOU'RE WASTING YOUR TIME, ALL OUR TIME.
OK, EVERYBODY....
DONE HERE.
はぁ…
DEEP SIGH...
WHY DID HE DO THAT? WHY DID HE HAVE TO LEAVE?
YOU KNOW HIM BETTER THAN I DO.
I'VE KNOWN HIM FOR FIVE YEARS, AND NO I DON'T.
SO WHY DO YOU PUT UP WITH HIM?
BECAUSE I'M DESPEREATE, THAT'S WHY.
AND BECAUSE SHERLOCK HOLMES IS A GREAT MAN, AND I THINK ONE DAY IF WE'RE VERY VERY LUCKY...
...HE MIGHT EVEN BE A GOOD ONE.

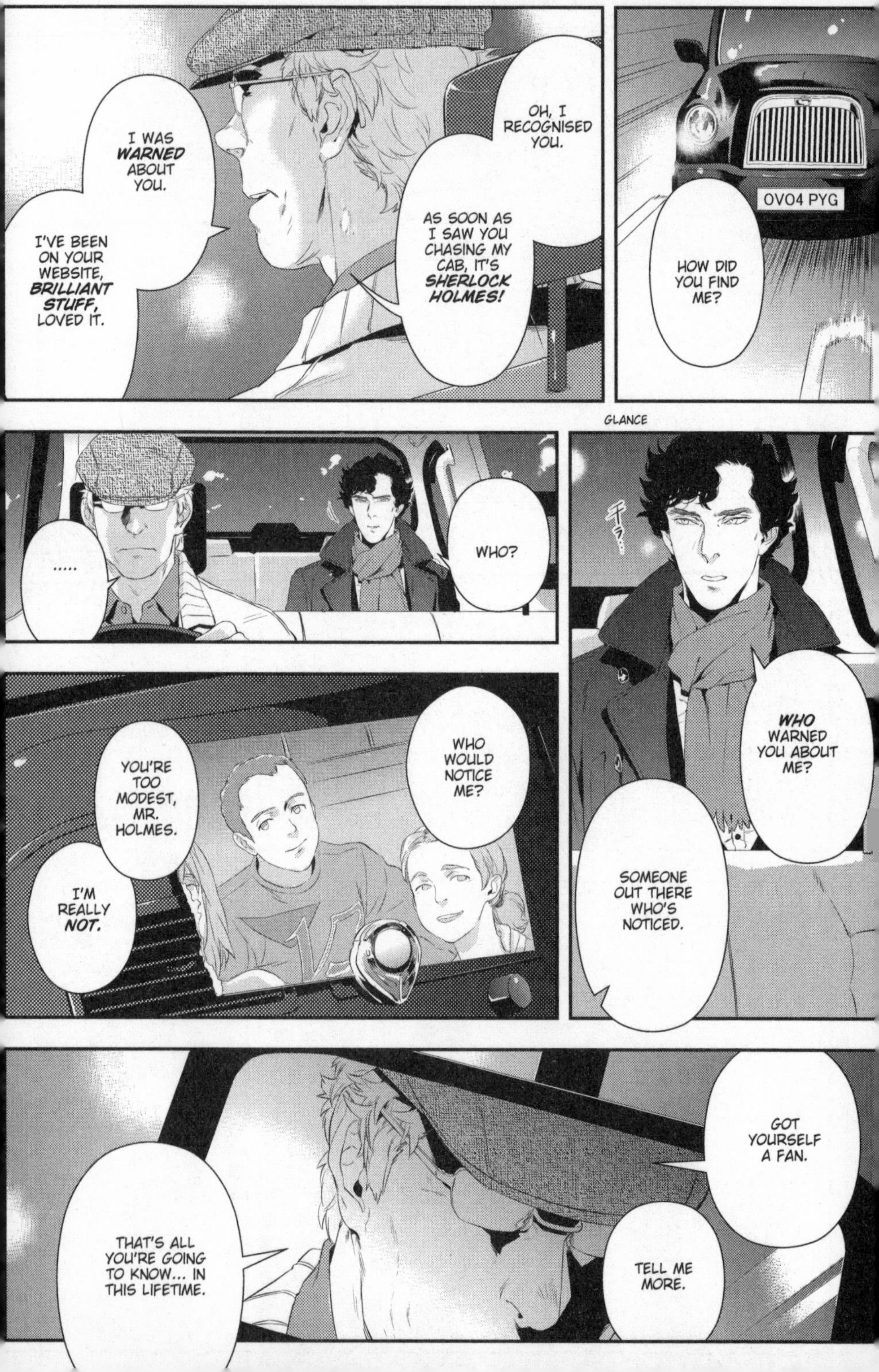
HOW DID YOU FIND ME?
OH, I RECOGNISED YOU.
AS SOON AS I SAW YOU CHASING MY CAB, IT'S **SHERLOCK HOLMES!**
I WAS **WARNED** ABOUT YOU.
I'VE BEEN ON YOUR WEBSITE, **BRILLIANT STUFF,** LOVED IT.
GLANCE
WHO WARNED YOU ABOUT ME?
SOMEONE OUT THERE WHO'S NOTICED.
WHO?
.....
WHO WOULD NOTICE ME?
YOU'RE TOO MODEST, MR. HOLMES.
I'M REALLY ***NOT.***
GOT YOURSELF A FAN.
TELL ME MORE.
THAT'S ALL YOU'RE GOING TO KNOW... IN THIS LIFETIME.

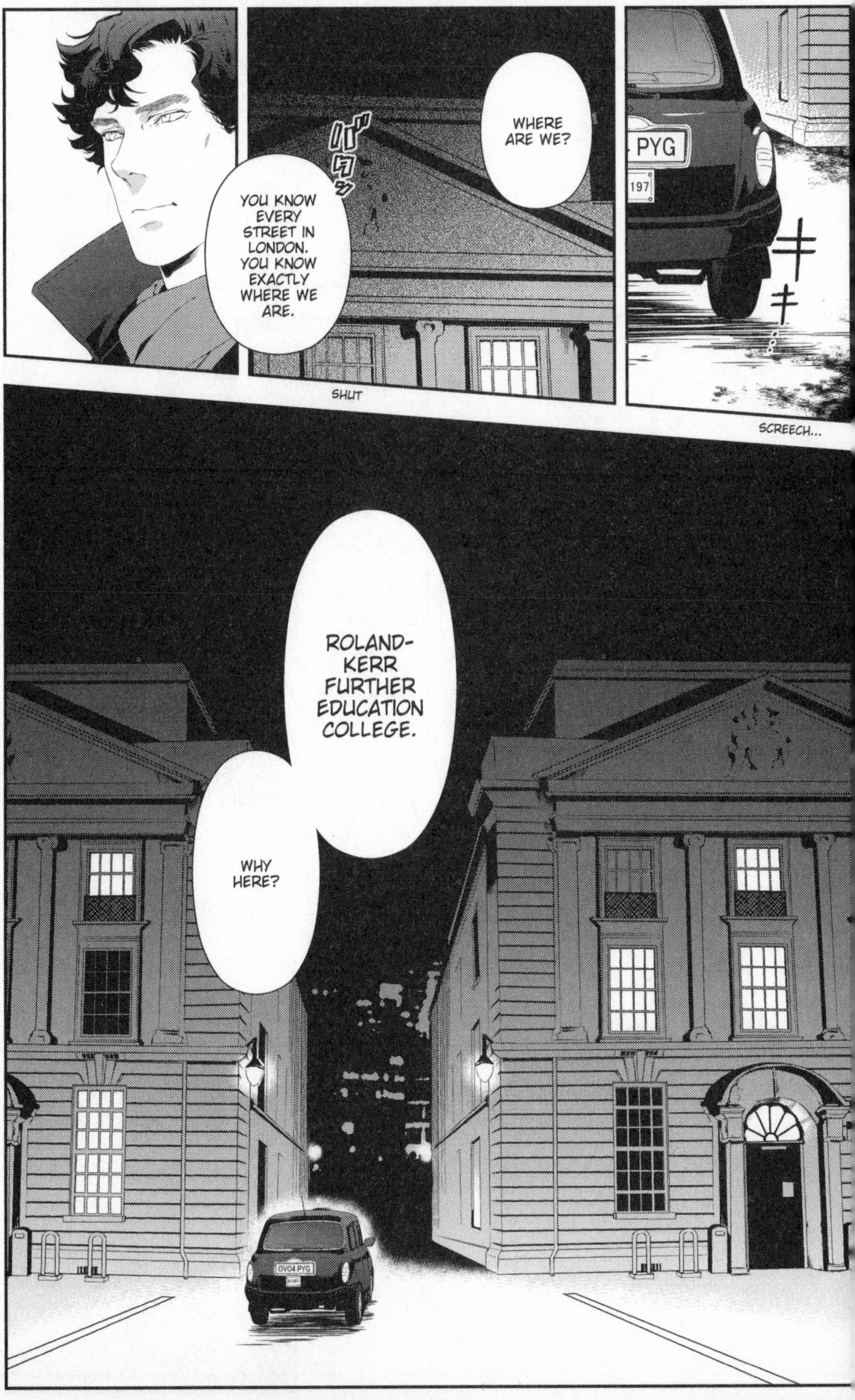
SCREECH...
WHERE ARE WE?
YOU KNOW EVERY STREET IN LONDON. YOU KNOW EXACTLY WHERE WE ARE.
SHUT
ROLAND-KERR FURTHER EDUCATION COLLEGE.
WHY HERE?

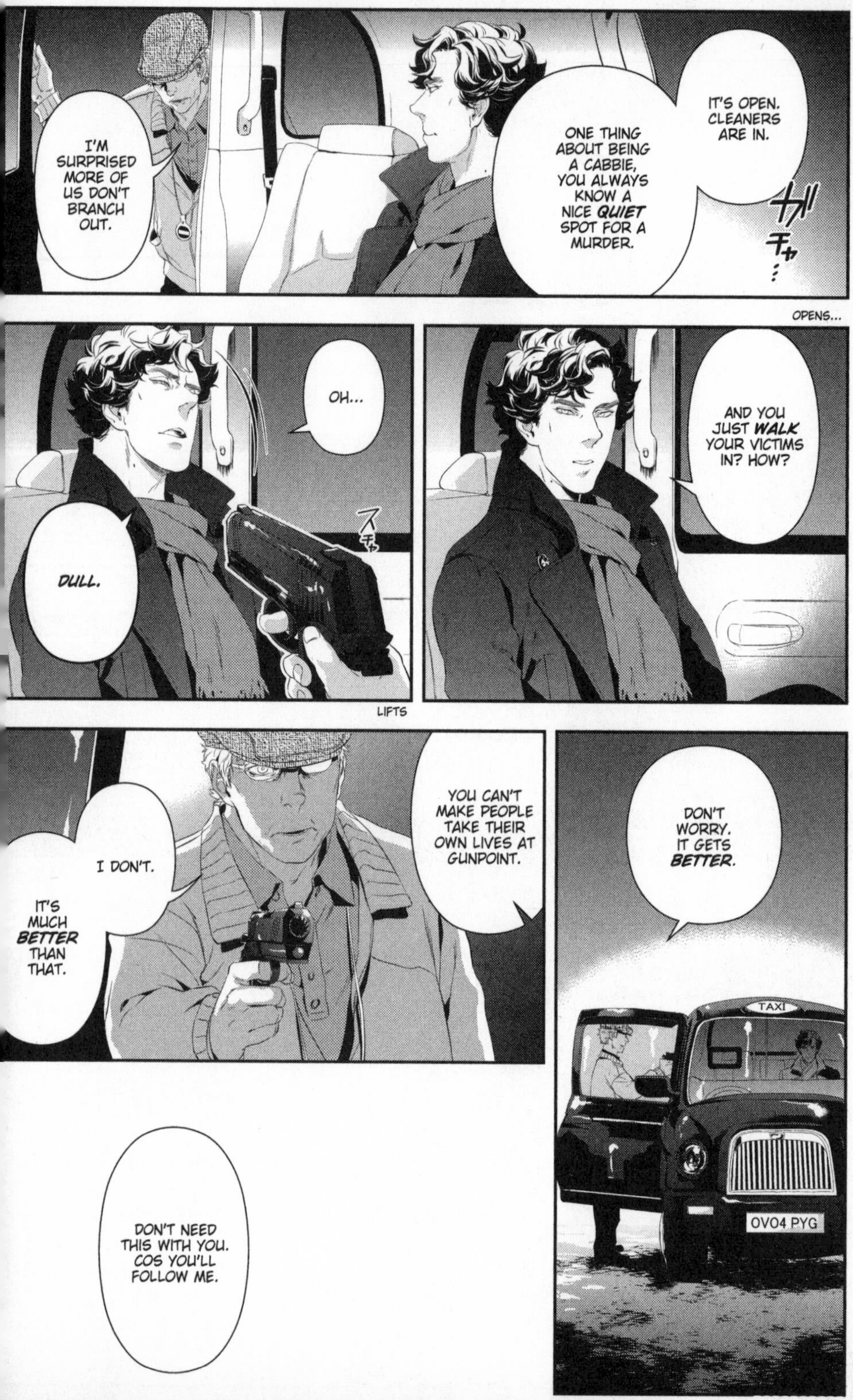
IT'S OPEN. CLEANERS ARE IN.
ONE THING ABOUT BEING A CABBIE, YOU ALWAYS KNOW A NICE ***QUIET*** SPOT FOR A MURDER.
ガチャ…
OPENS...
I'M SURPRISED MORE OF US DON'T BRANCH OUT.
AND YOU JUST ***WALK*** YOUR VICTIMS IN? HOW?
OH...
スチャ
DULL.
LIFTS
DON'T WORRY. IT GETS ***BETTER***.
TAXI
OV04 PYG
YOU CAN'T MAKE PEOPLE TAKE THEIR OWN LIVES AT GUNPOINT.
I DON'T.
IT'S MUCH ***BETTER*** THAN THAT.
DON'T NEED THIS WITH YOU. COS YOU'LL FOLLOW ME.

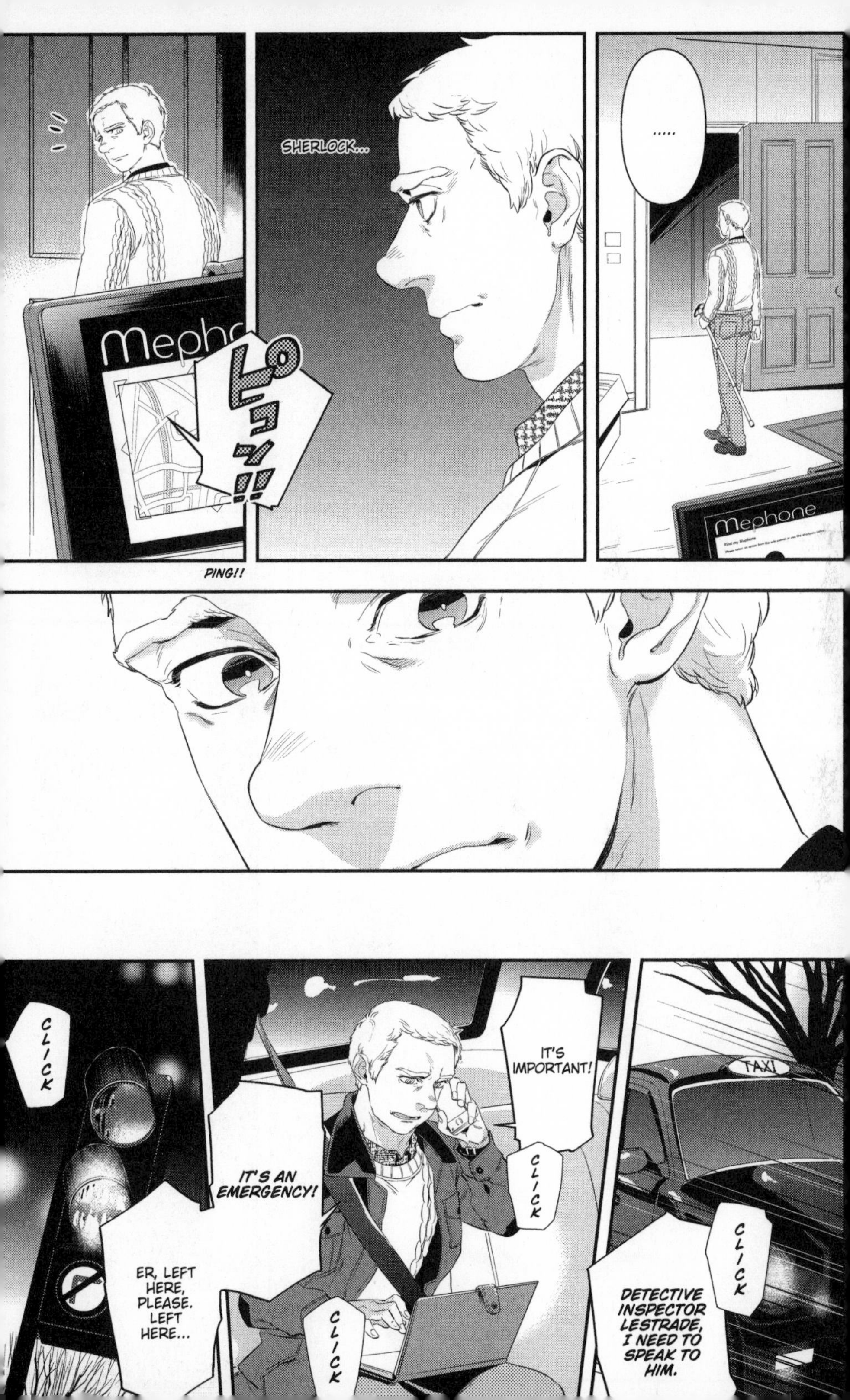
.....
Mephone
SHERLOCK...
Mephone
ピコッ!!
PING!!
TAXI
CLICK
DETECTIVE INSPECTOR LESTRADE, I NEED TO SPEAK TO HIM.
IT'S IMPORTANT!
CLICK
IT'S AN EMERGENCY!
ER, LEFT HERE, PLEASE. LEFT HERE...
CLICK
CLICK

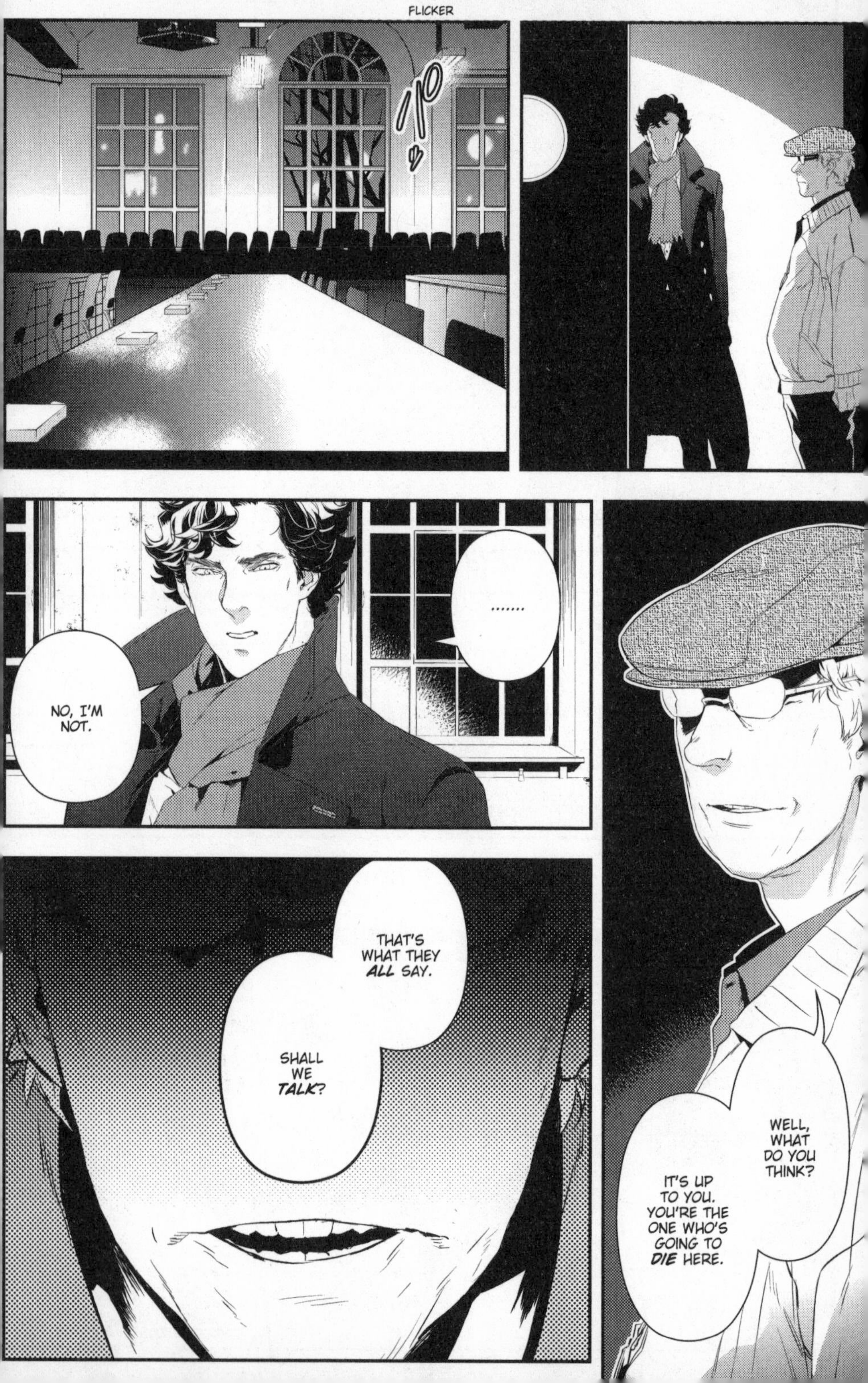
FLICKER
WELL, WHAT DO YOU THINK?
IT'S UP TO YOU. YOU'RE THE ONE WHO'S GOING TO *DIE* HERE.
....
NO, I'M NOT.
THAT'S WHAT THEY *ALL* SAY.
SHALL WE *TALK*?

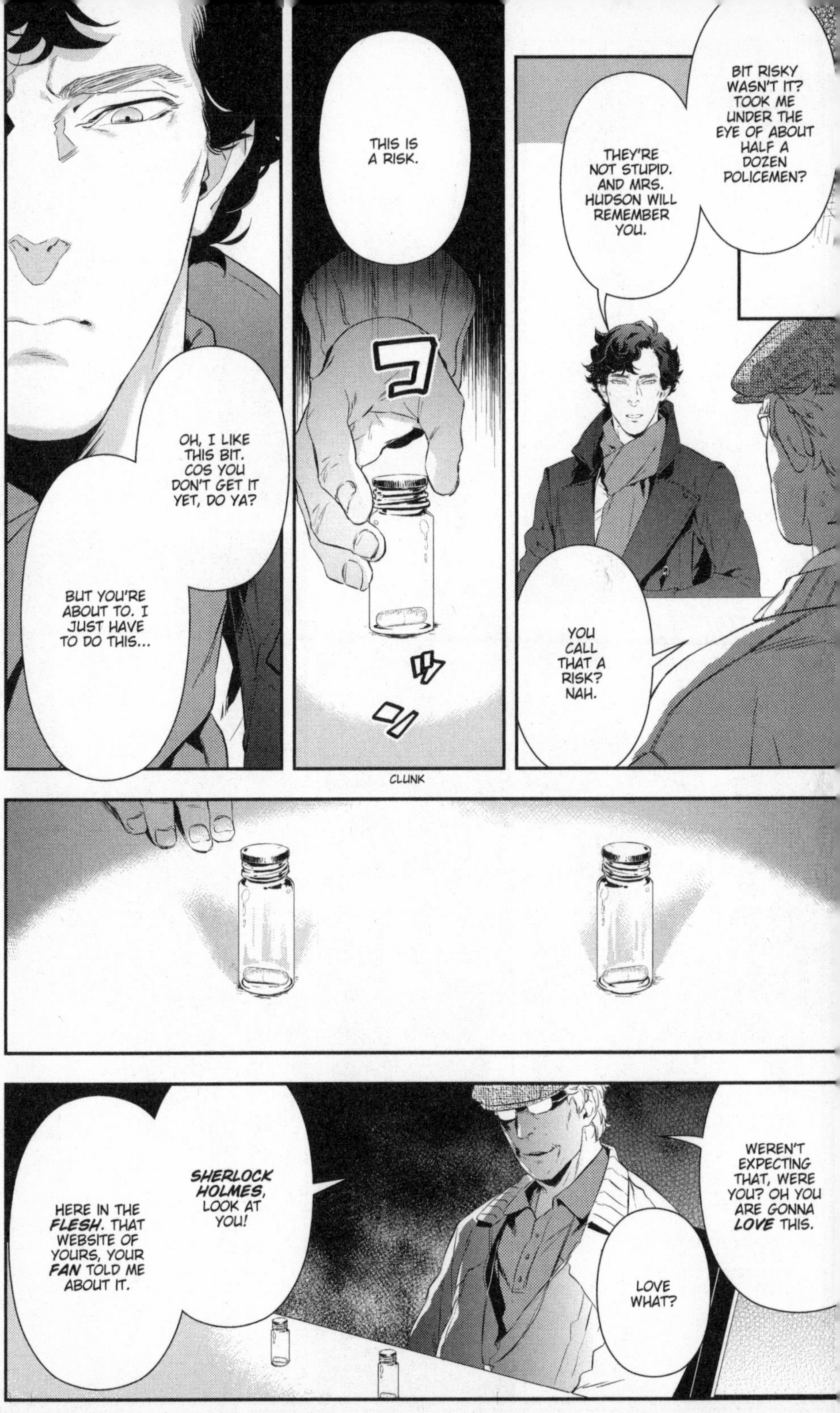
BIT RISKY WASN'T IT? TOOK ME UNDER THE EYE OF ABOUT HALF A DOZEN POLICEMEN?
THEY'RE NOT STUPID. AND MRS. HUDSON WILL REMEMBER YOU.
YOU CALL THAT A RISK? NAH.
THIS IS A RISK.
OH, I LIKE THIS BIT. COS YOU DON'T GET IT YET, DO YA?
BUT YOU'RE ABOUT TO. I JUST HAVE TO DO THIS...
CLUNK
WEREN'T EXPECTING THAT, WERE YOU? OH YOU ARE GONNA **LOVE** THIS.
LOVE WHAT?
SHERLOCK HOLMES, LOOK AT YOU!
HERE IN THE ***FLESH***. THAT WEBSITE OF YOURS, YOUR ***FAN*** TOLD ME ABOUT IT.

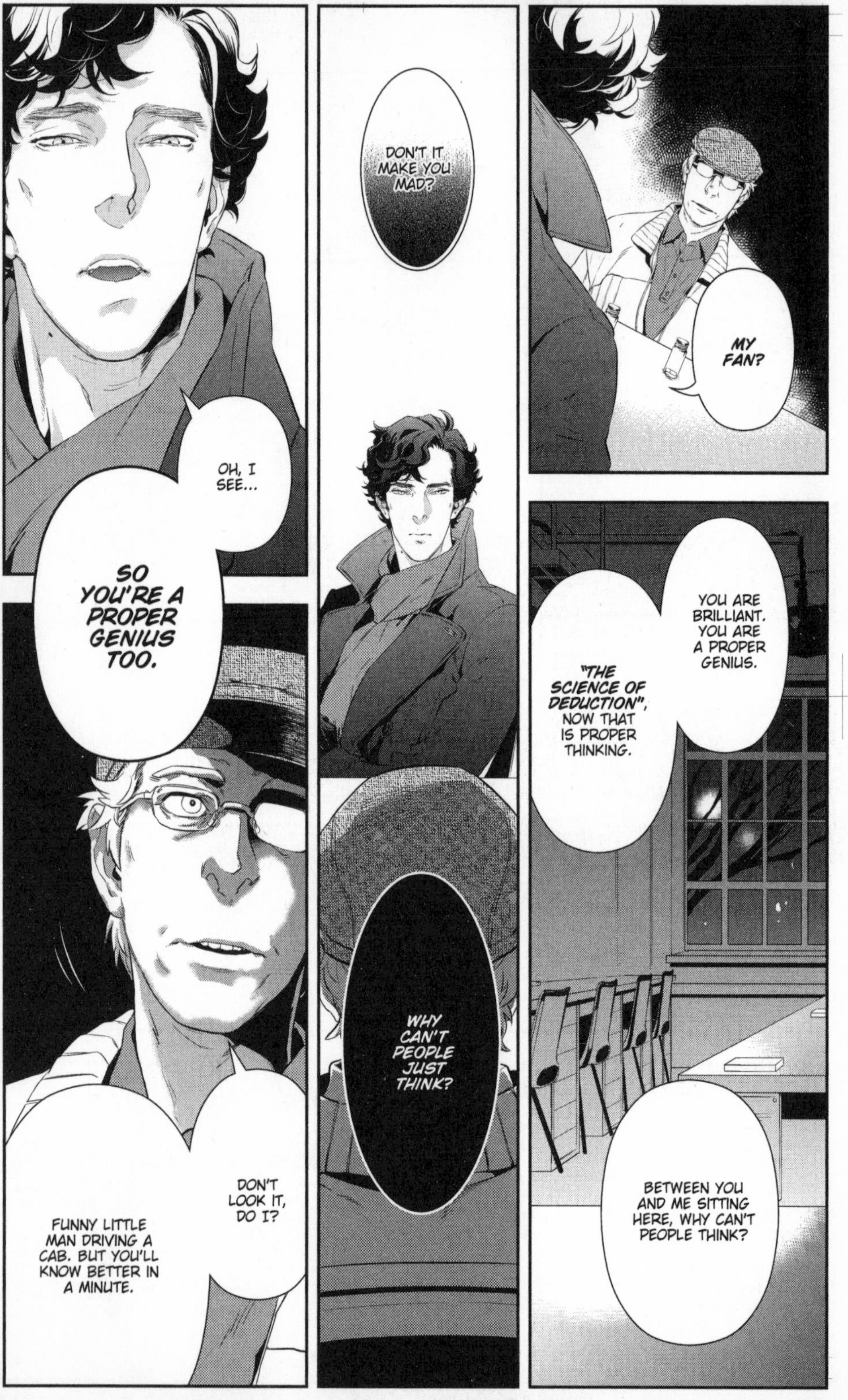
MY FAN?
YOU ARE BRILLIANT. YOU ARE A PROPER GENIUS.
"THE SCIENCE OF DEDUCTION", NOW THAT IS PROPER THINKING.
BETWEEN YOU AND ME SITTING HERE, WHY CAN'T PEOPLE THINK?
DON'T IT MAKE YOU MAD?
WHY CAN'T PEOPLE JUST THINK?
OH, I SEE...
SO YOU'RE A PROPER GENIUS TOO.
DON'T LOOK IT, DO I?
FUNNY LITTLE MAN DRIVING A CAB. BUT YOU'LL KNOW BETTER IN A MINUTE.

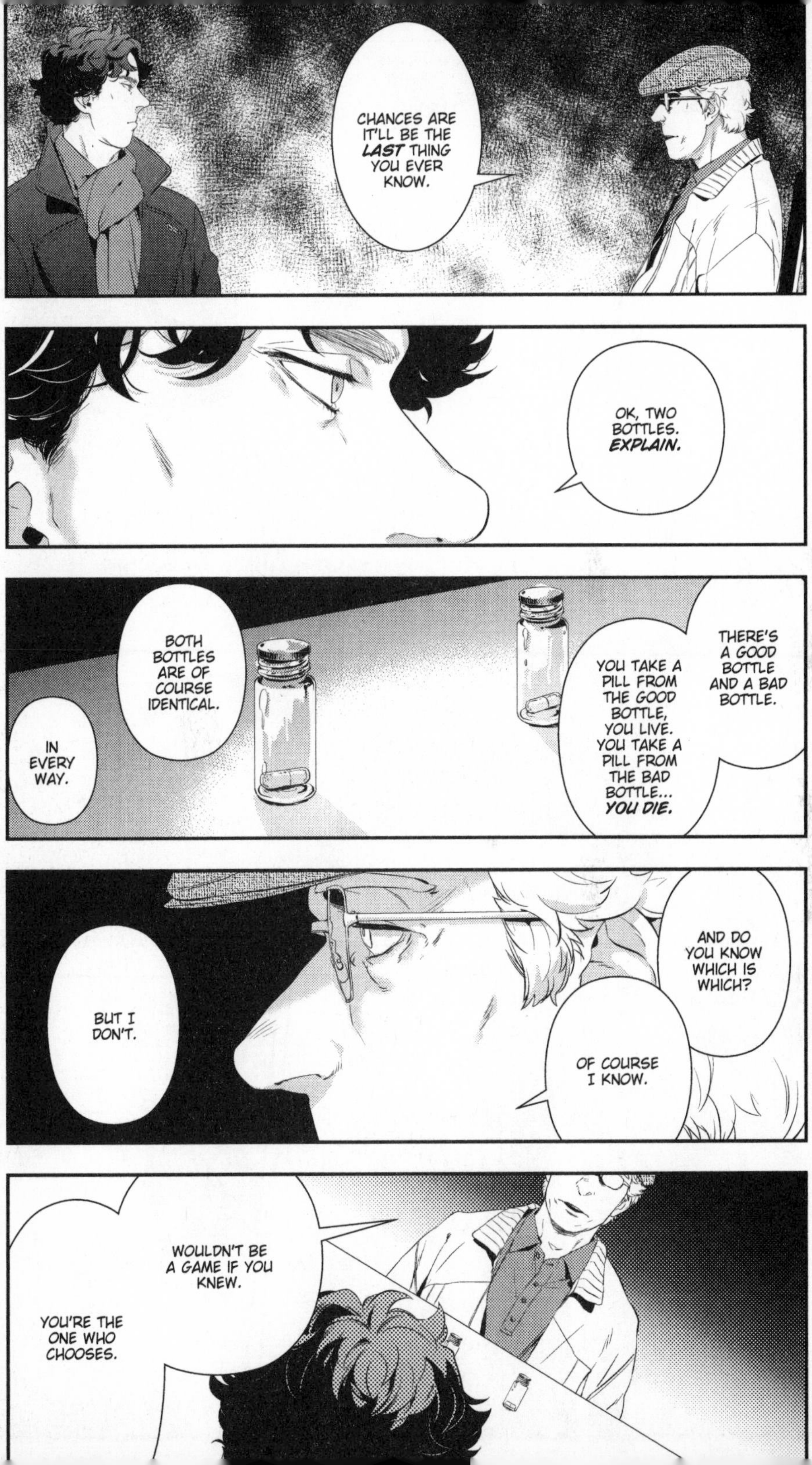
CHANCES ARE IT'LL BE THE ***LAST*** THING YOU EVER KNOW.
OK, TWO BOTTLES. ***EXPLAIN.***
THERE'S A GOOD BOTTLE AND A BAD BOTTLE.
YOU TAKE A PILL FROM THE GOOD BOTTLE, YOU LIVE. YOU TAKE A PILL FROM THE BAD BOTTLE... ***YOU DIE.***
BOTH BOTTLES ARE OF COURSE IDENTICAL.
IN EVERY WAY.
AND DO YOU KNOW WHICH IS WHICH?
OF COURSE I KNOW.
BUT I DON'T.
WOULDN'T BE A GAME IF YOU KNEW.
YOU'RE THE ONE WHO CHOOSES.

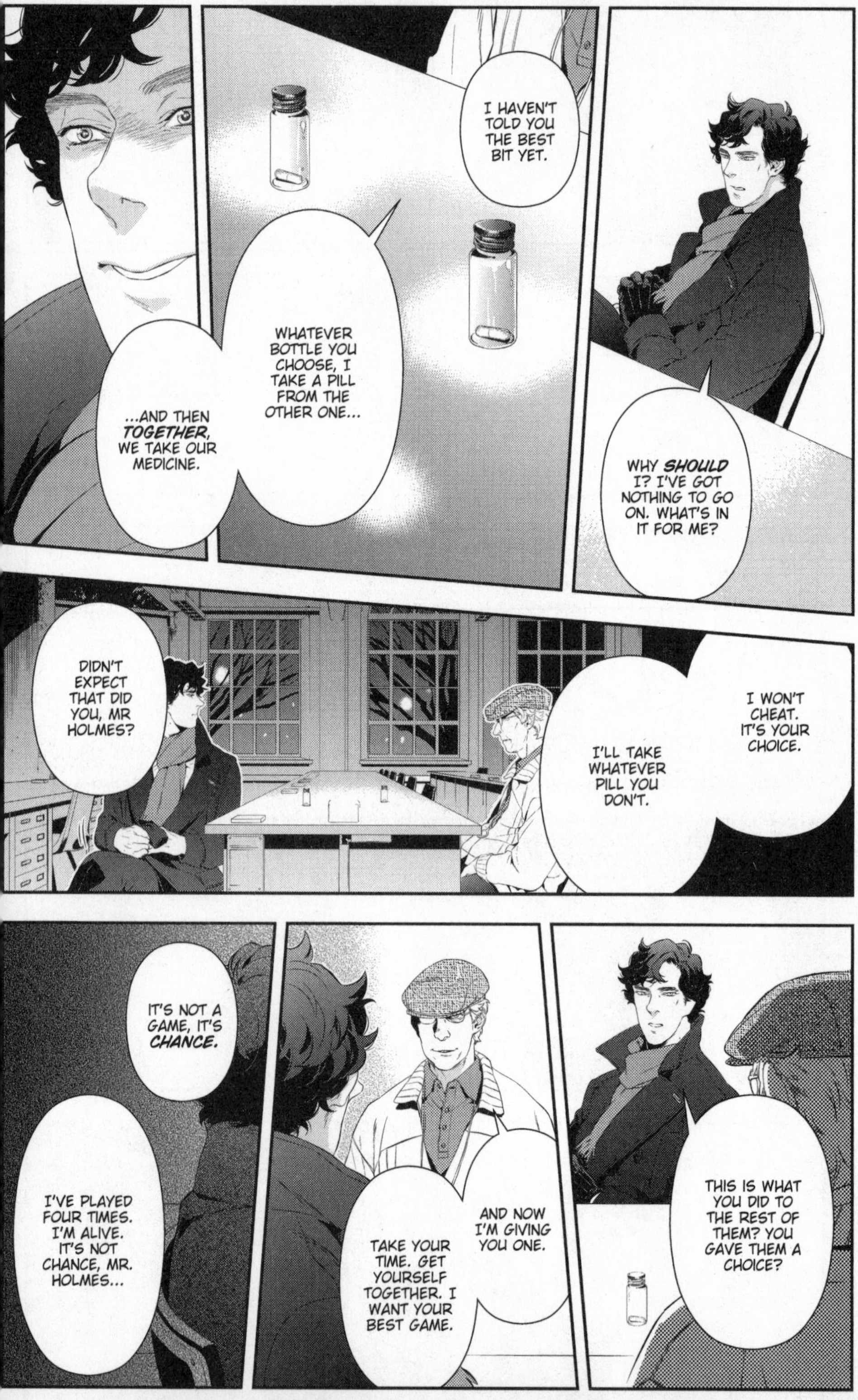
WHY **SHOULD** I? I'VE GOT NOTHING TO GO ON. WHAT'S IN IT FOR ME?
I HAVEN'T TOLD YOU THE BEST BIT YET.
WHATEVER BOTTLE YOU CHOOSE, I TAKE A PILL FROM THE OTHER ONE...
...AND THEN **TOGETHER**, WE TAKE OUR MEDICINE.
I WON'T CHEAT. IT'S YOUR CHOICE.
I'LL TAKE WHATEVER PILL YOU DON'T.
DIDN'T EXPECT THAT DID YOU, MR HOLMES?
THIS IS WHAT YOU DID TO THE REST OF THEM? YOU GAVE THEM A CHOICE?
AND NOW I'M GIVING YOU ONE.
TAKE YOUR TIME. GET YOURSELF TOGETHER. I WANT YOUR BEST GAME.
IT'S NOT A GAME, IT'S **CHANCE.**
I'VE PLAYED FOUR TIMES. I'M ALIVE. IT'S NOT CHANCE, MR. HOLMES...

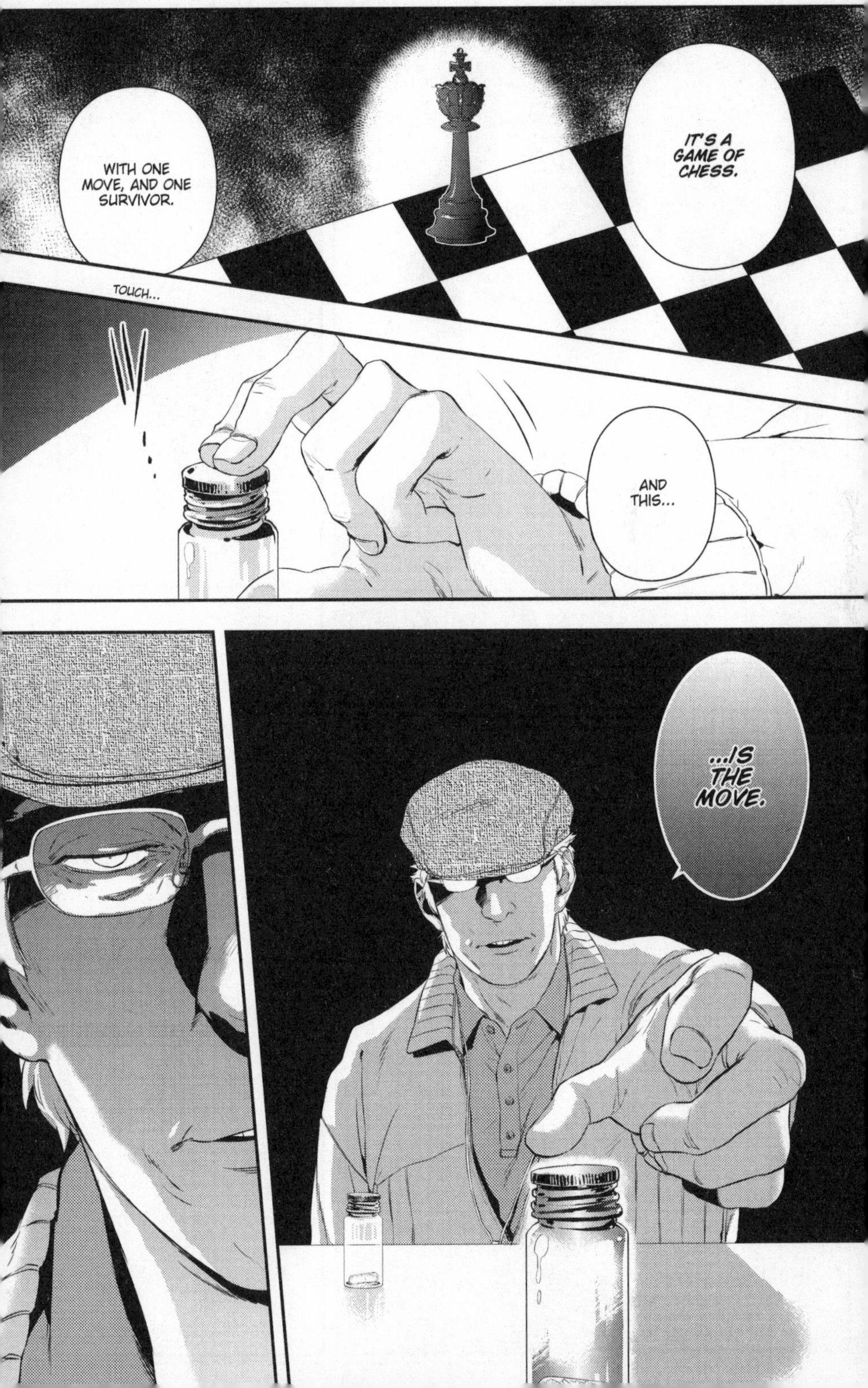
IT'S A GAME OF CHESS.
WITH ONE MOVE, AND ONE SURVIVOR.
TOUCH...
AND THIS...
...IS THE MOVE.

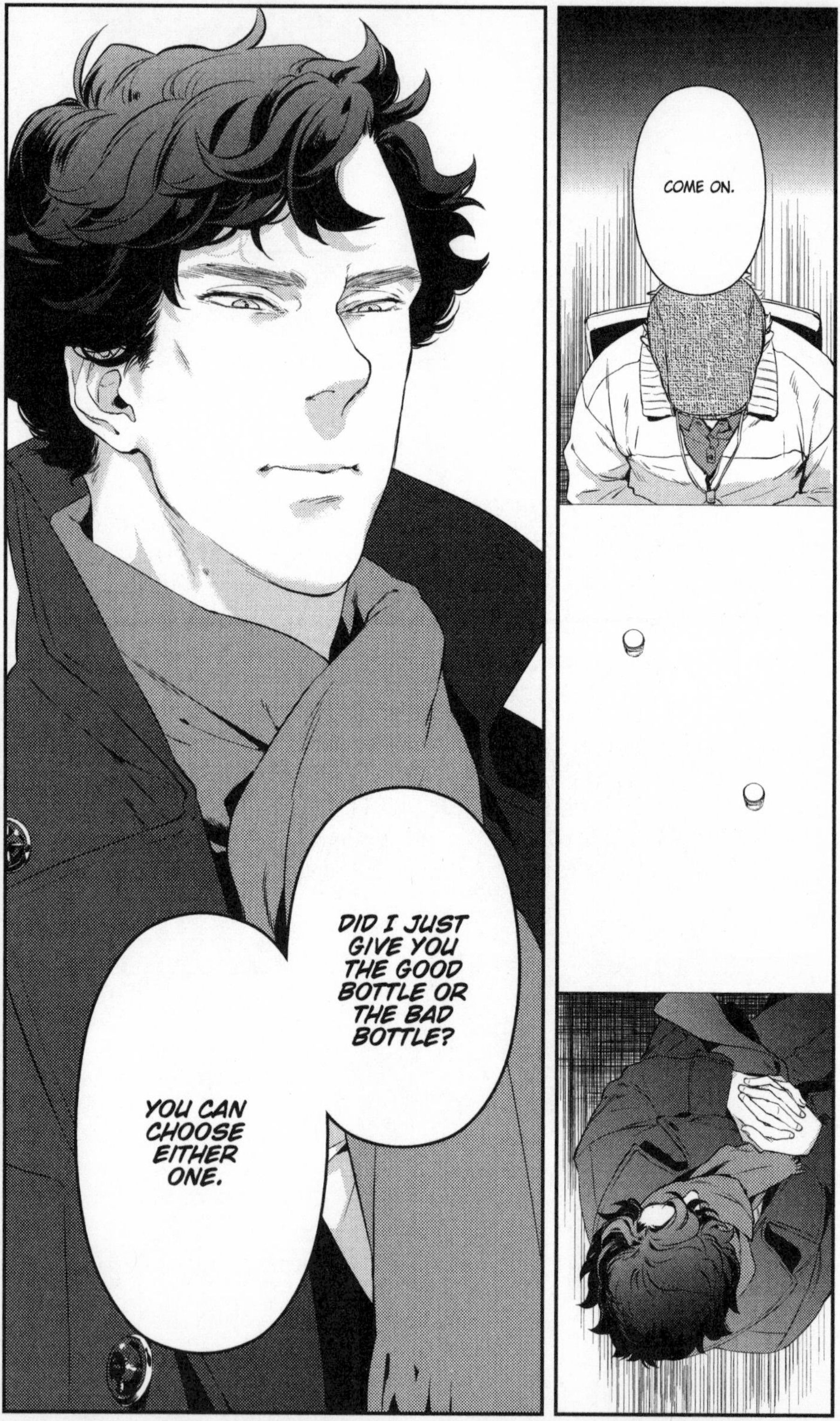
COME ON.
DID I JUST GIVE YOU THE GOOD BOTTLE OR THE BAD BOTTLE?
YOU CAN CHOOSE EITHER ONE.

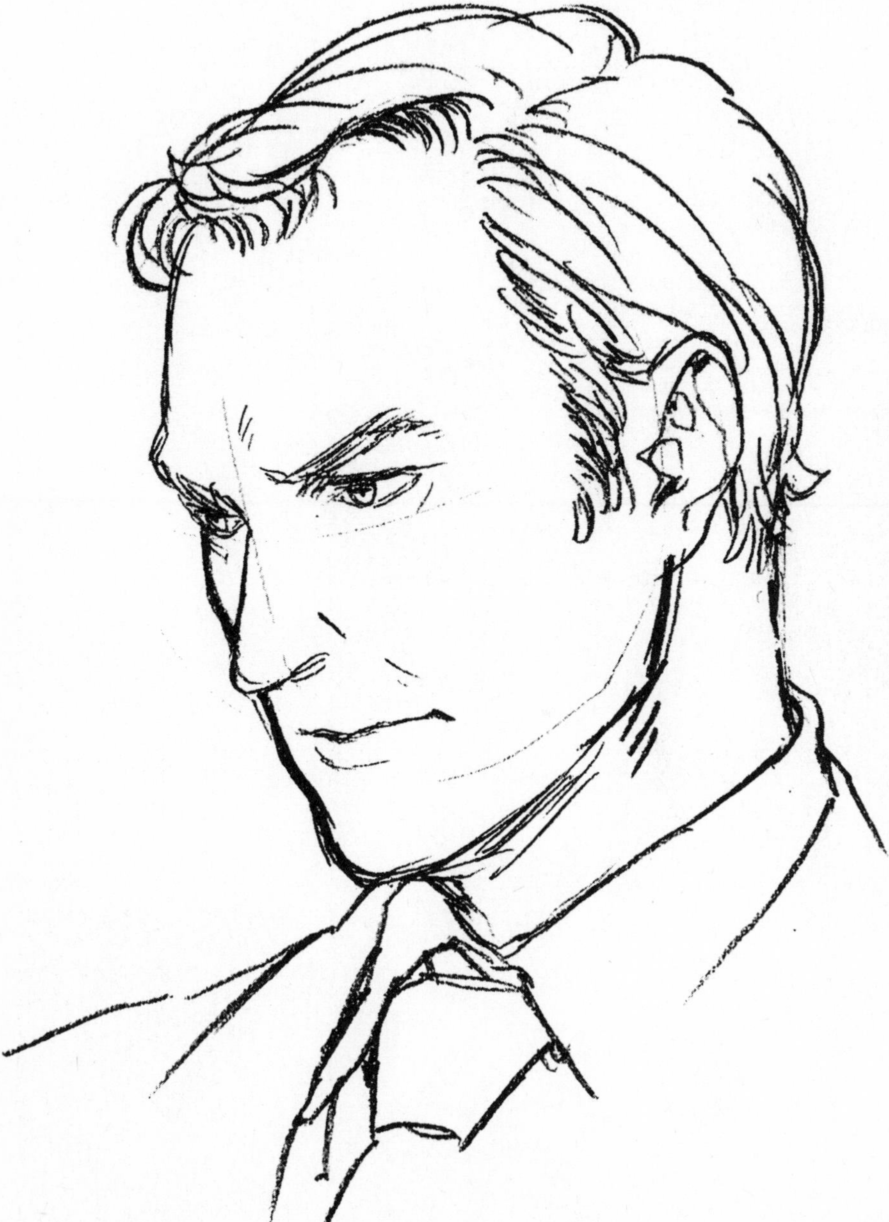

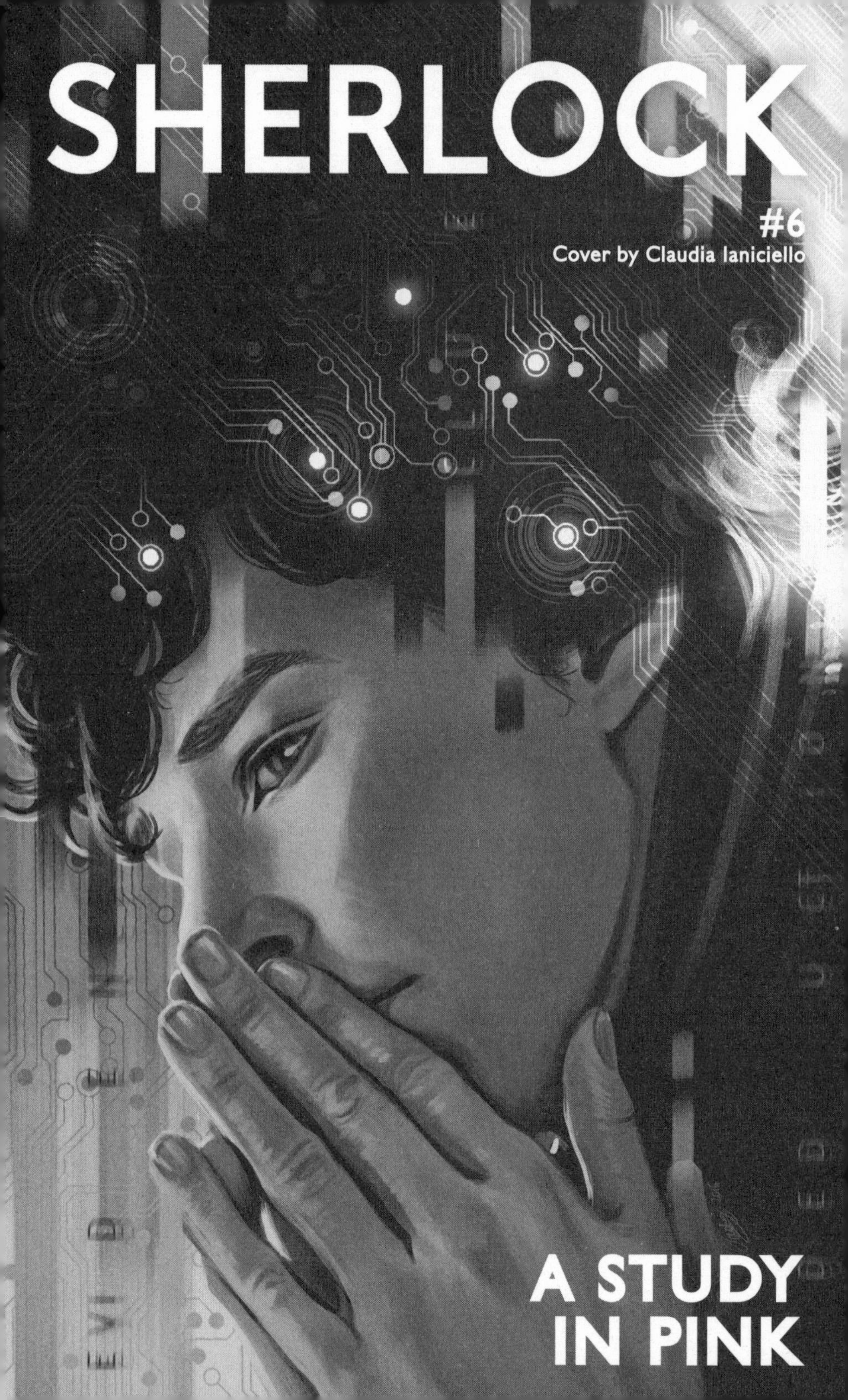
SHERLOCK
#6
Cover by Claudia Ianiciello
A STUDY
IN PINK

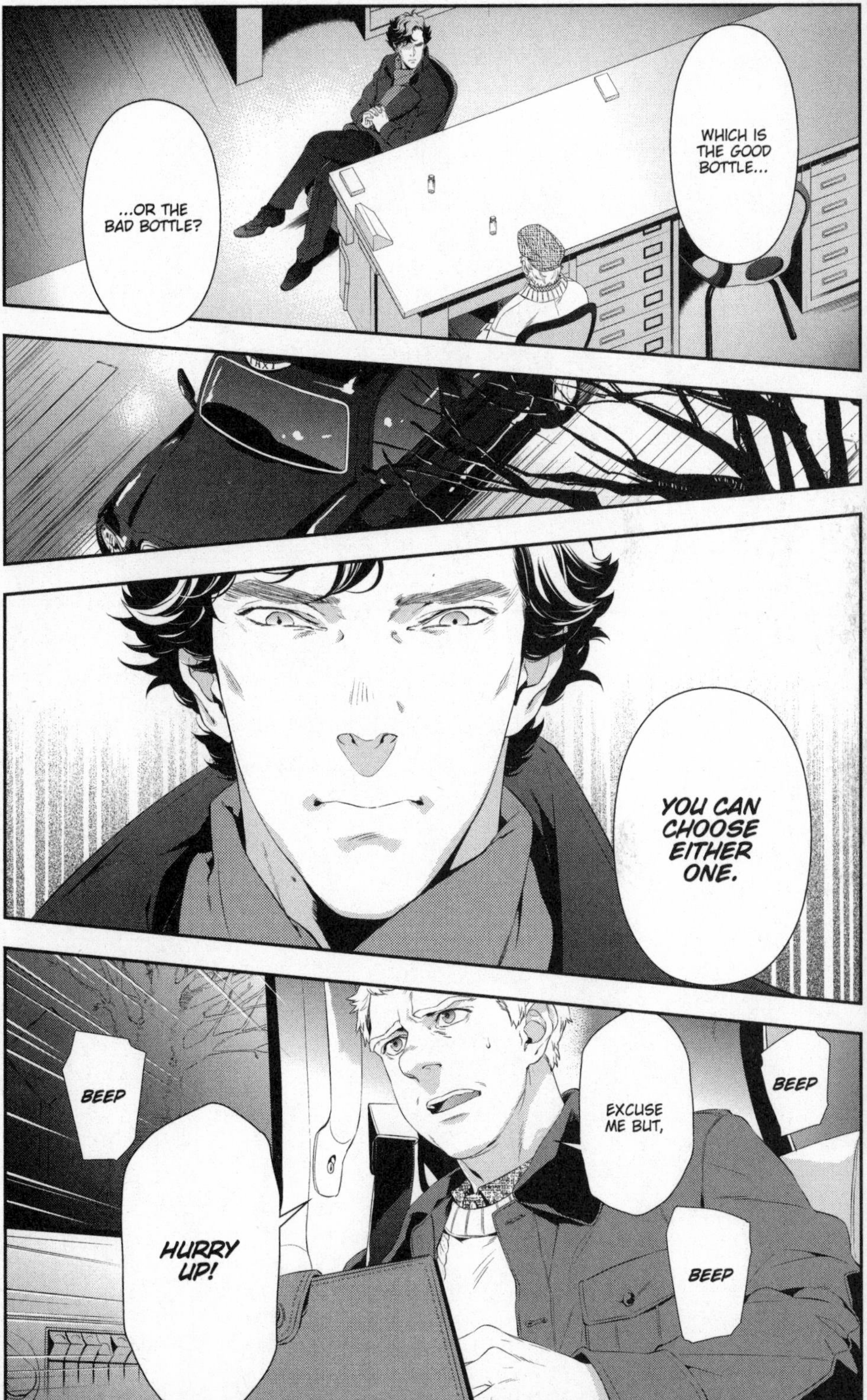
WHICH IS THE GOOD BOTTLE...
...OR THE BAD BOTTLE?
YOU CAN CHOOSE EITHER ONE.
BEEP
EXCUSE ME BUT,
BEEP
BEEP
HURRY UP!

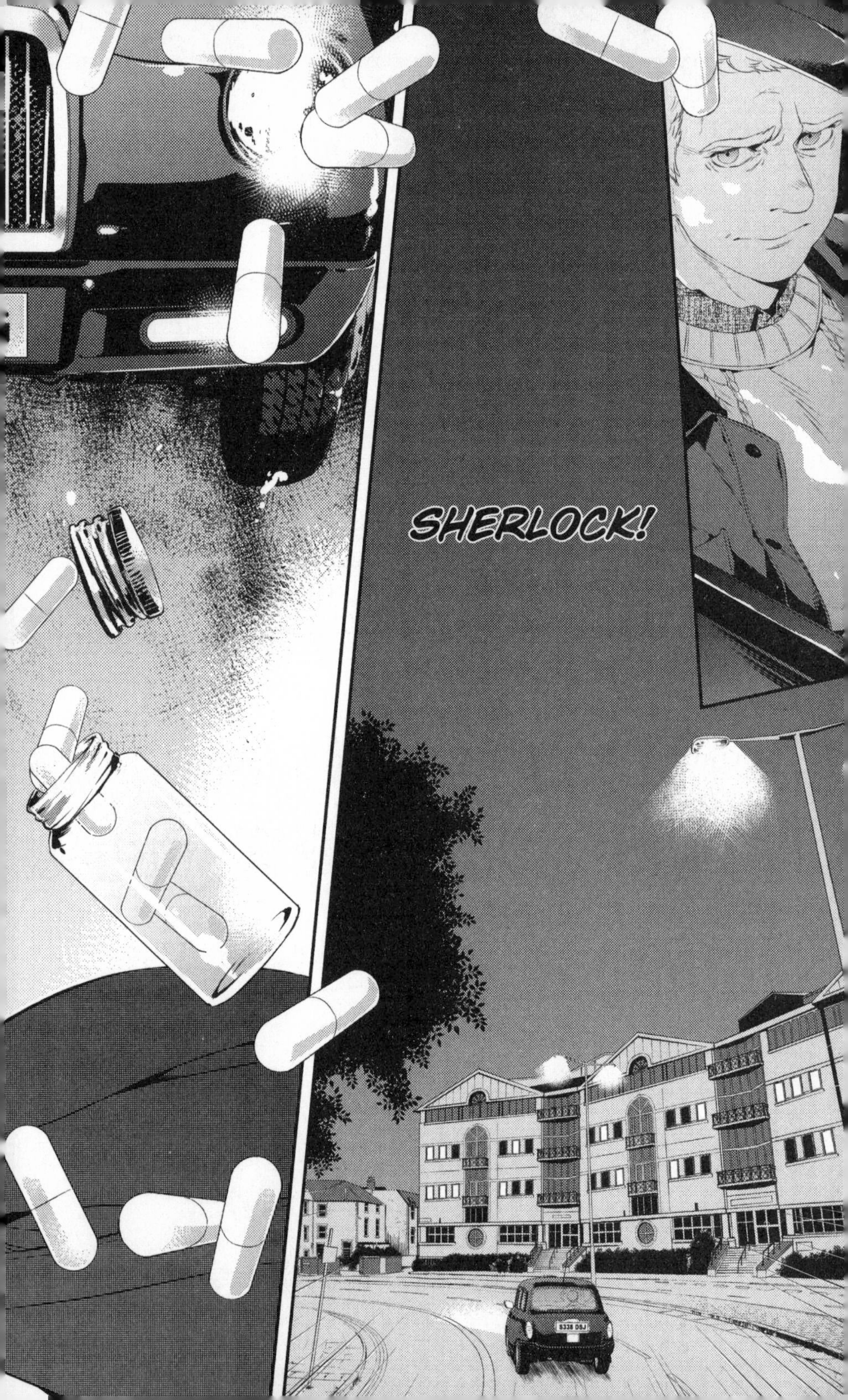
SHERLOCK!

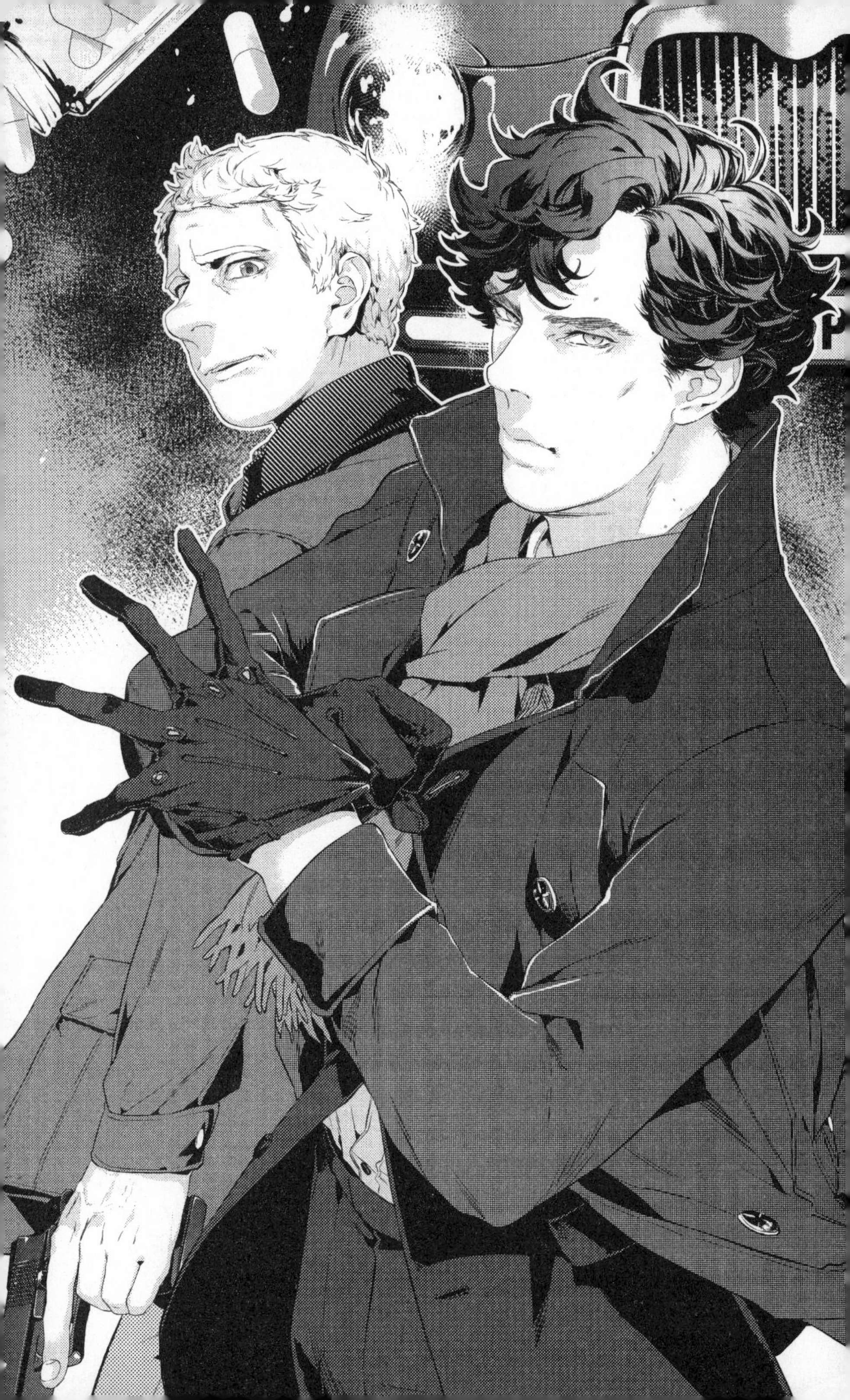

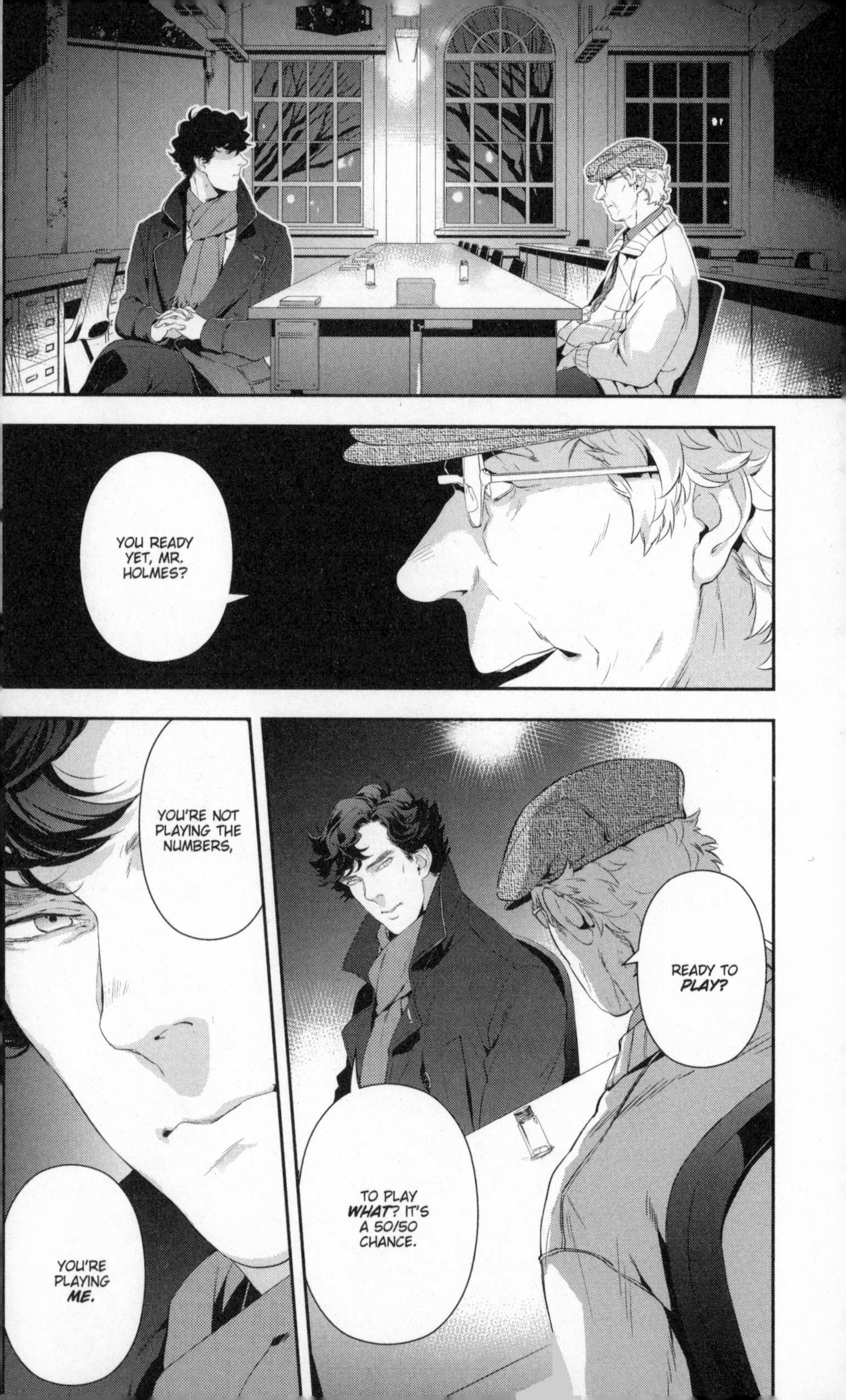
YOU READY YET, MR. HOLMES?
READY TO PLAY?
TO PLAY WHAT? IT'S A 50/50 CHANCE.
YOU'RE NOT PLAYING THE NUMBERS,
YOU'RE PLAYING ME.

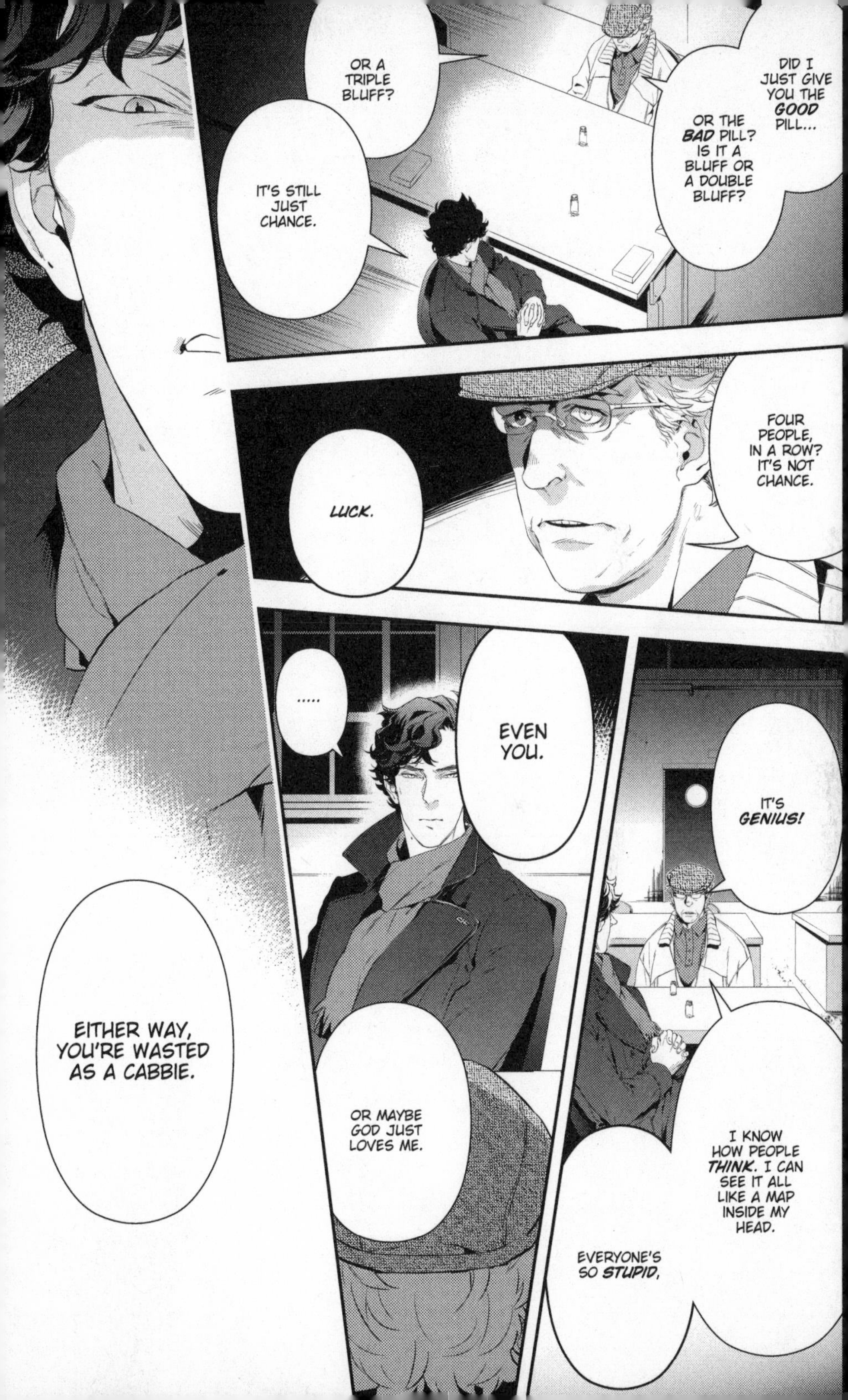
DID I JUST GIVE YOU THE **GOOD** PILL...
OR THE **BAD** PILL? IS IT A BLUFF OR A DOUBLE BLUFF?
OR A TRIPLE BLUFF?
IT'S STILL JUST CHANCE.
FOUR PEOPLE, IN A ROW? IT'S NOT CHANCE.
LUCK.
IT'S **GENIUS!**
I KNOW HOW PEOPLE **THINK**. I CAN SEE IT ALL LIKE A MAP INSIDE MY HEAD.
EVERYONE'S SO **STUPID**,
EVEN YOU.
......
OR MAYBE GOD JUST LOVES ME.
EITHER WAY, YOU'RE WASTED AS A CABBIE.

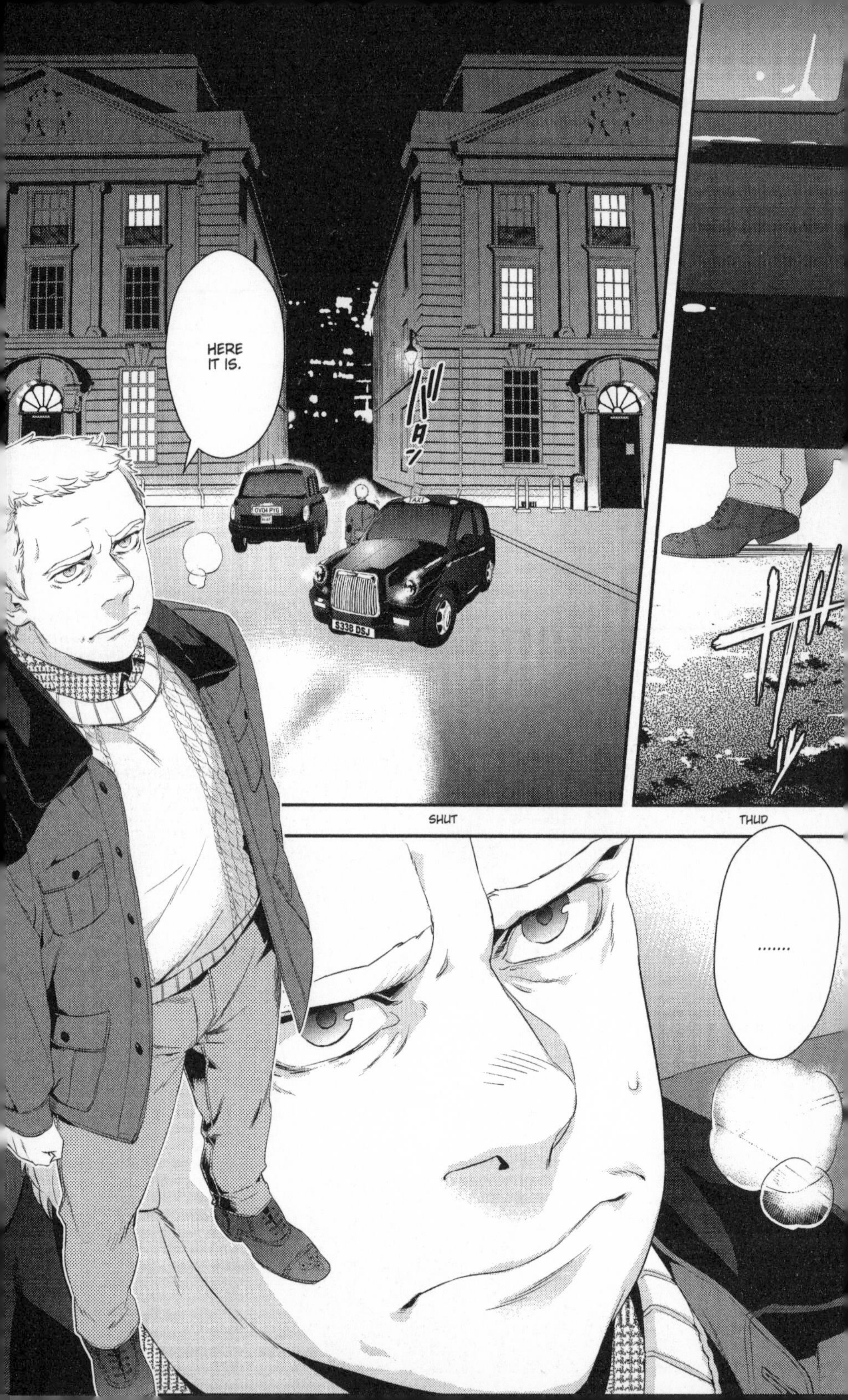
THUD
HERE IT IS.
バタン
SHUT
....

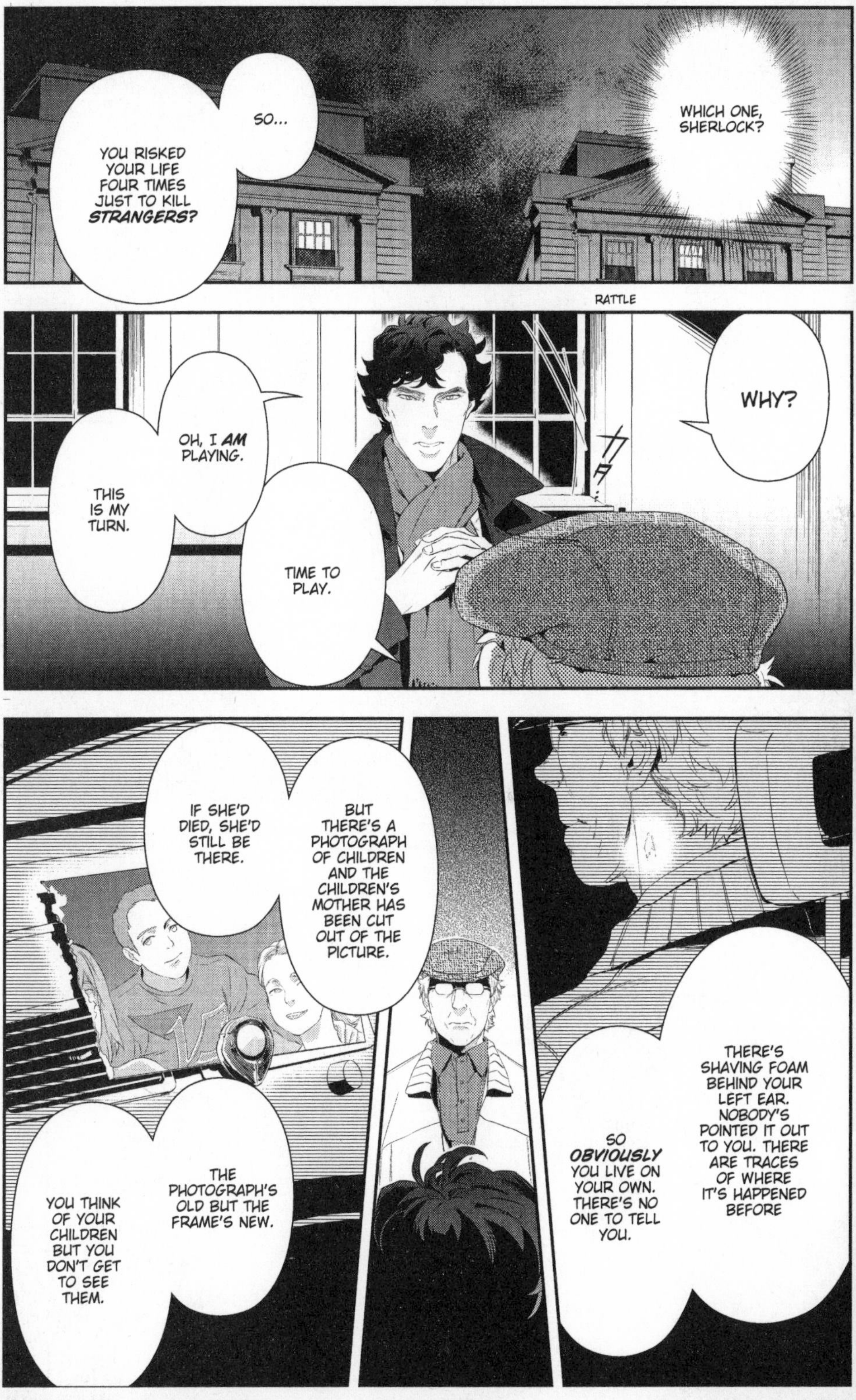
WHICH ONE, SHERLOCK?
SO...
YOU RISKED YOUR LIFE FOUR TIMES JUST TO KILL ***STRANGERS?***
RATTLE
WHY?
TIME TO PLAY.
OH, I ***AM*** PLAYING.
THIS IS MY TURN.
THERE'S SHAVING FOAM BEHIND YOUR LEFT EAR. NOBODY'S POINTED IT OUT TO YOU. THERE ARE TRACES OF WHERE IT'S HAPPENED BEFORE
SO ***OBVIOUSLY*** YOU LIVE ON YOUR OWN. THERE'S NO ONE TO TELL YOU.
BUT THERE'S A PHOTOGRAPH OF CHILDREN AND THE CHILDREN'S MOTHER HAS BEEN CUT OUT OF THE PICTURE.
IF SHE'D DIED, SHE'D STILL BE THERE.
THE PHOTOGRAPH'S OLD BUT THE FRAME'S NEW.
YOU THINK OF YOUR CHILDREN BUT YOU DON'T GET TO SEE THEM.

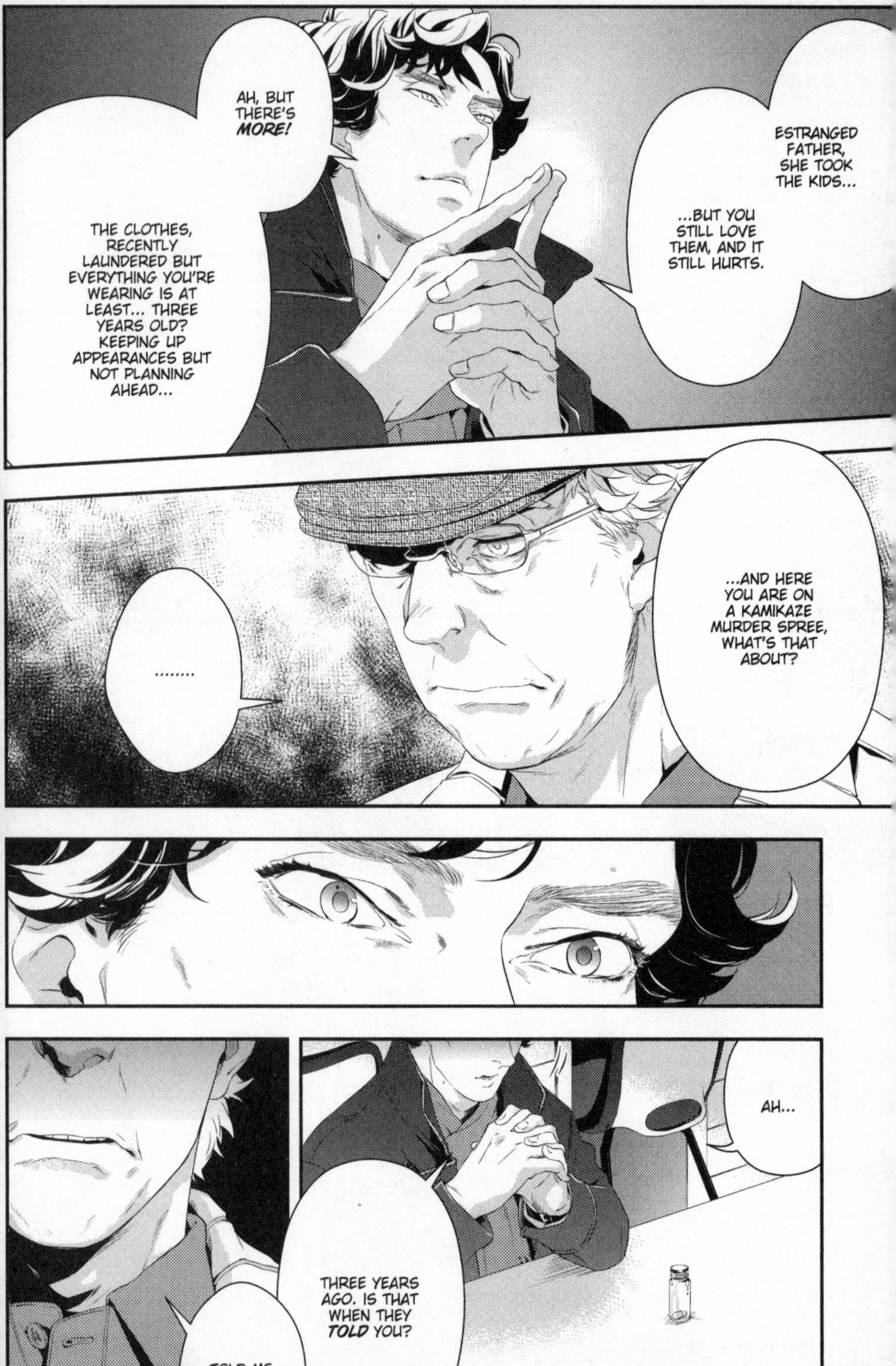

ESTRANGED FATHER, SHE TOOK THE KIDS...
...BUT YOU STILL LOVE THEM, AND IT STILL HURTS.
AH, BUT THERE'S ***MORE!***
THE CLOTHES, RECENTLY LAUNDERED BUT EVERYTHING YOU'RE WEARING IS AT LEAST... THREE YEARS OLD? KEEPING UP APPEARANCES BUT NOT PLANNING AHEAD...
...AND HERE YOU ARE ON A KAMIKAZE MURDER SPREE, WHAT'S THAT ABOUT?
....
AH...
THREE YEARS AGO. IS THAT WHEN THEY ***TOLD*** YOU?
TOLD ME ***WHAT?***

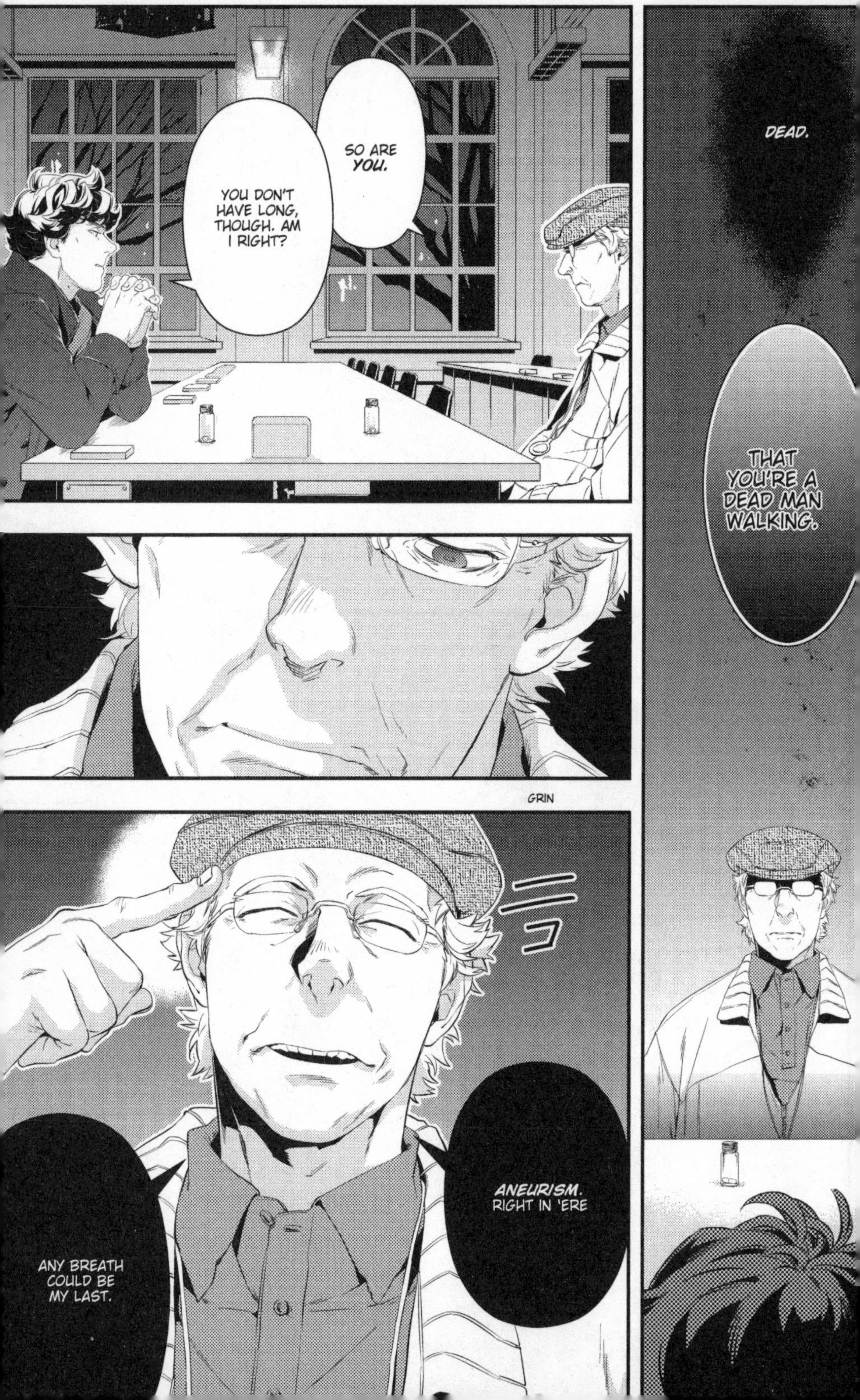
DEAD.
THAT YOU'RE A DEAD MAN WALKING.
SO ARE YOU.
YOU DON'T HAVE LONG, THOUGH. AM I RIGHT?
GRIN
ANEURISM. RIGHT IN 'ERE
ANY BREATH COULD BE MY LAST.

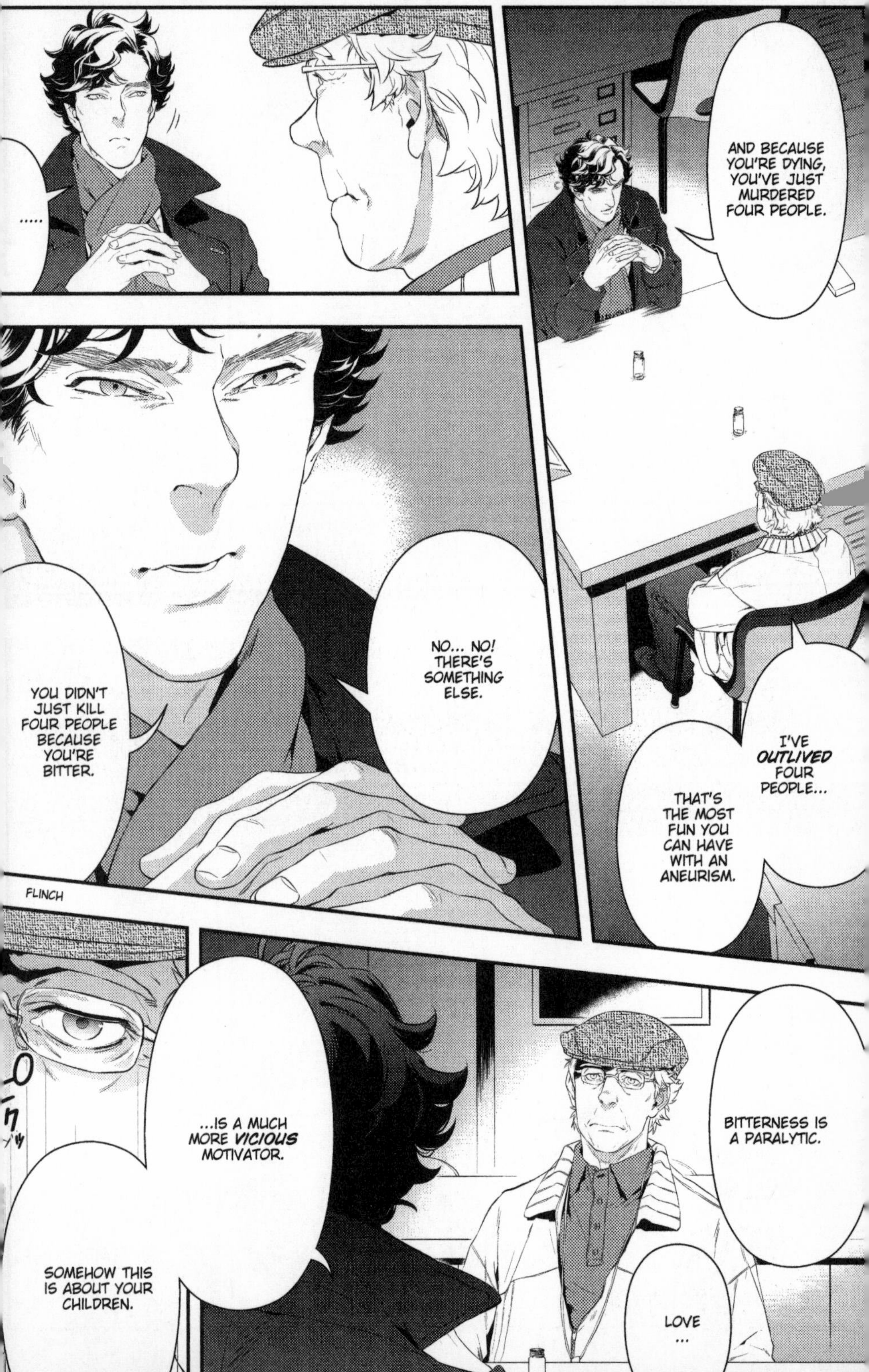
AND BECAUSE YOU'RE DYING, YOU'VE JUST MURDERED FOUR PEOPLE.
I'VE OUTLIVED FOUR PEOPLE...
THAT'S THE MOST FUN YOU CAN HAVE WITH AN ANEURISM.
.....
NO... NO! THERE'S SOMETHING ELSE.
YOU DIDN'T JUST KILL FOUR PEOPLE BECAUSE YOU'RE BITTER.
FLINCH
BITTERNESS IS A PARALYTIC.
LOVE ...
...IS A MUCH MORE VICIOUS MOTIVATOR.
SOMEHOW THIS IS ABOUT YOUR CHILDREN.

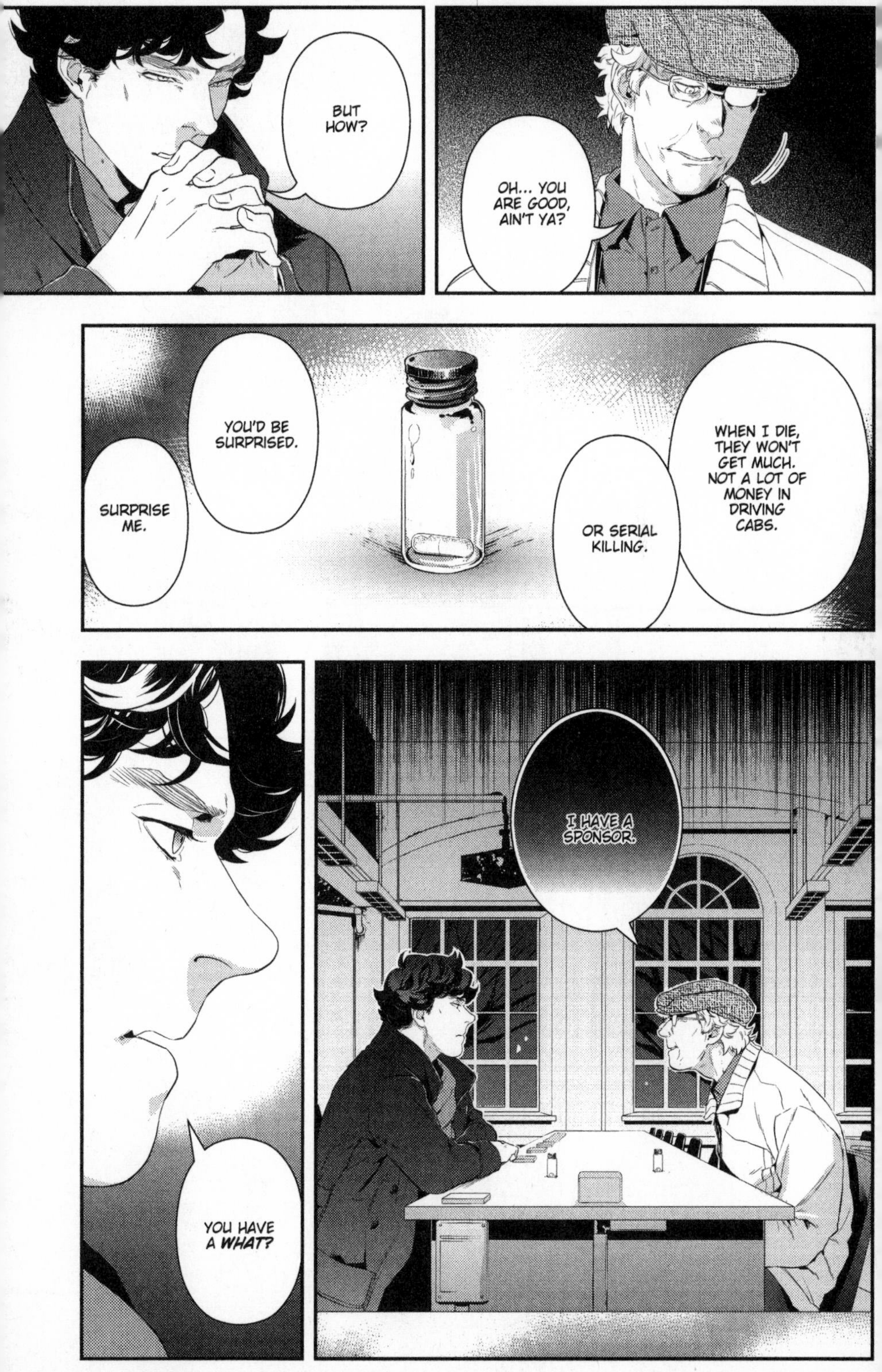
OH... YOU ARE GOOD, AIN'T YA?
BUT HOW?
WHEN I DIE, THEY WON'T GET MUCH. NOT A LOT OF MONEY IN DRIVING CABS.
OR SERIAL KILLING.
YOU'D BE SURPRISED.
SURPRISE ME.
I HAVE A SPONSOR.
YOU HAVE A *WHAT?*

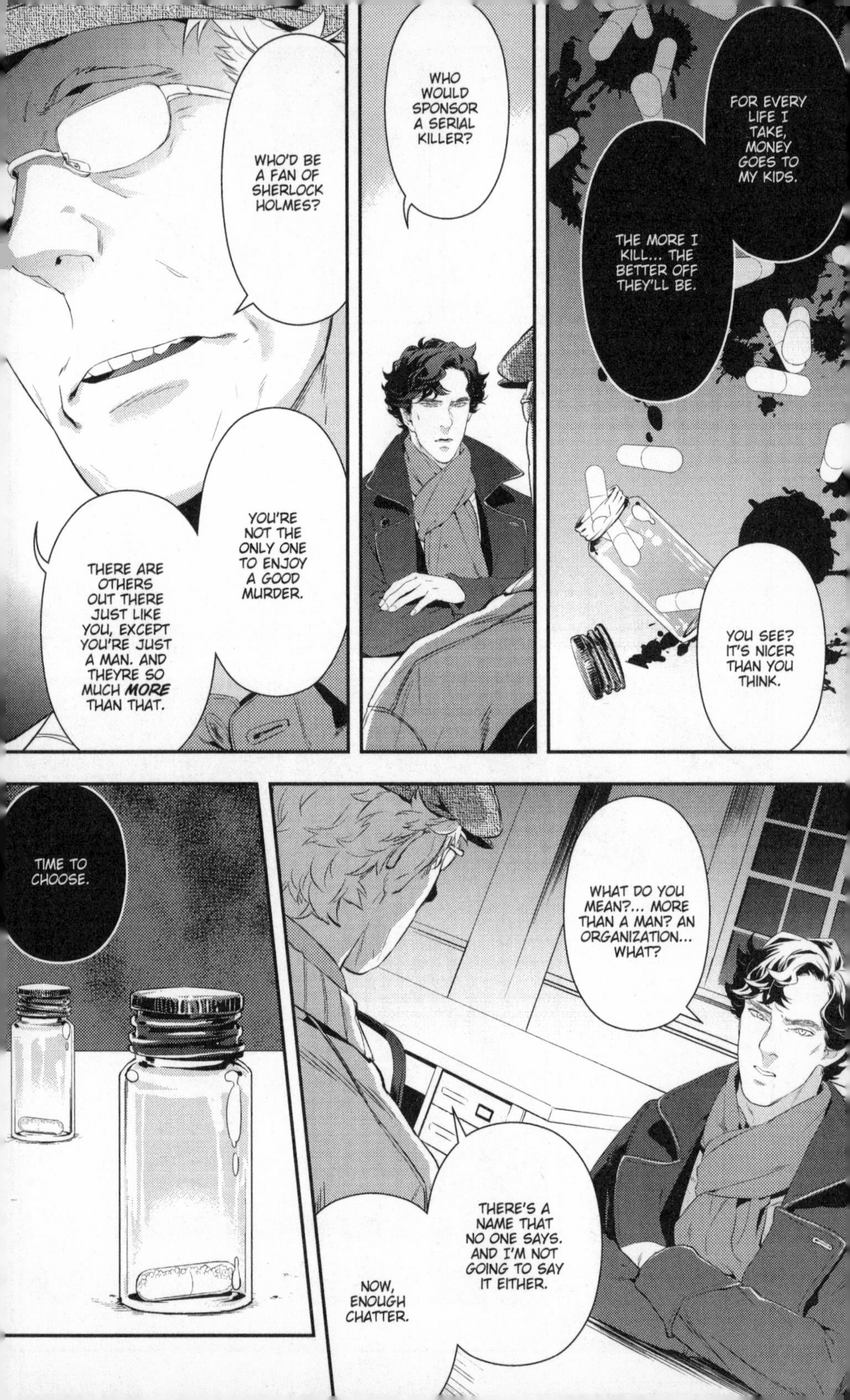
FOR EVERY LIFE I TAKE, MONEY GOES TO MY KIDS.
THE MORE I KILL... THE BETTER OFF THEY'LL BE.
YOU SEE? IT'S NICER THAN YOU THINK.
WHO WOULD SPONSOR A SERIAL KILLER?
WHO'D BE A FAN OF SHERLOCK HOLMES?
YOU'RE NOT THE ONLY ONE TO ENJOY A GOOD MURDER.
THERE ARE OTHERS OUT THERE JUST LIKE YOU, EXCEPT YOU'RE JUST A MAN. AND THEYRE SO MUCH ***MORE*** THAN THAT.
WHAT DO YOU MEAN?... MORE THAN A MAN? AN ORGANIZATION... WHAT?
THERE'S A NAME THAT NO ONE SAYS. AND I'M NOT GOING TO SAY IT EITHER.
NOW, ENOUGH CHATTER.
TIME TO CHOOSE.

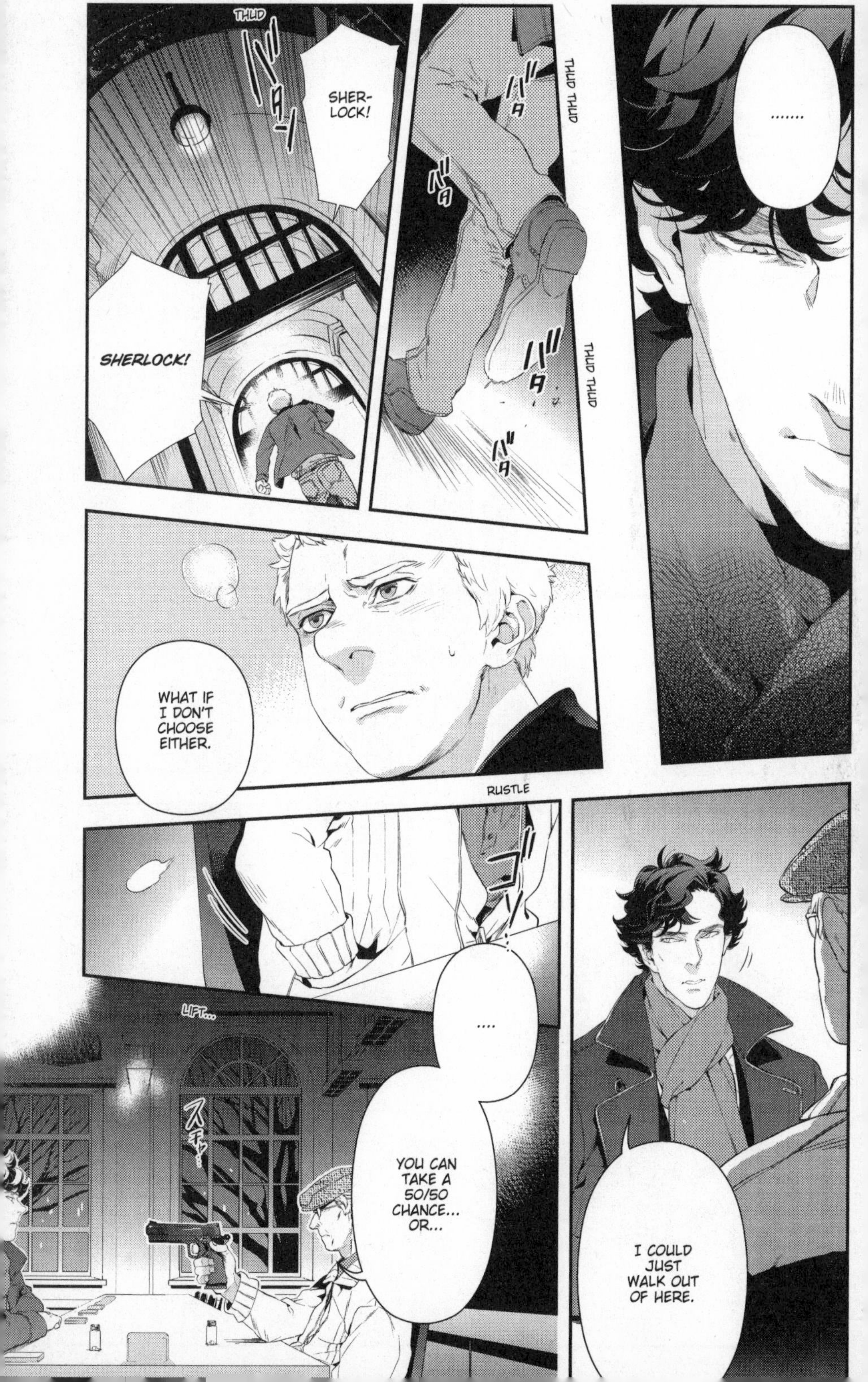
....
THUD THUD
THUD THUD
THUD
SHER-LOCK!
SHERLOCK!
WHAT IF I DON'T CHOOSE EITHER.
I COULD JUST WALK OUT OF HERE.
RUSTLE
....
LIFT...
YOU CAN TAKE A 50/50 CHANCE... OR...

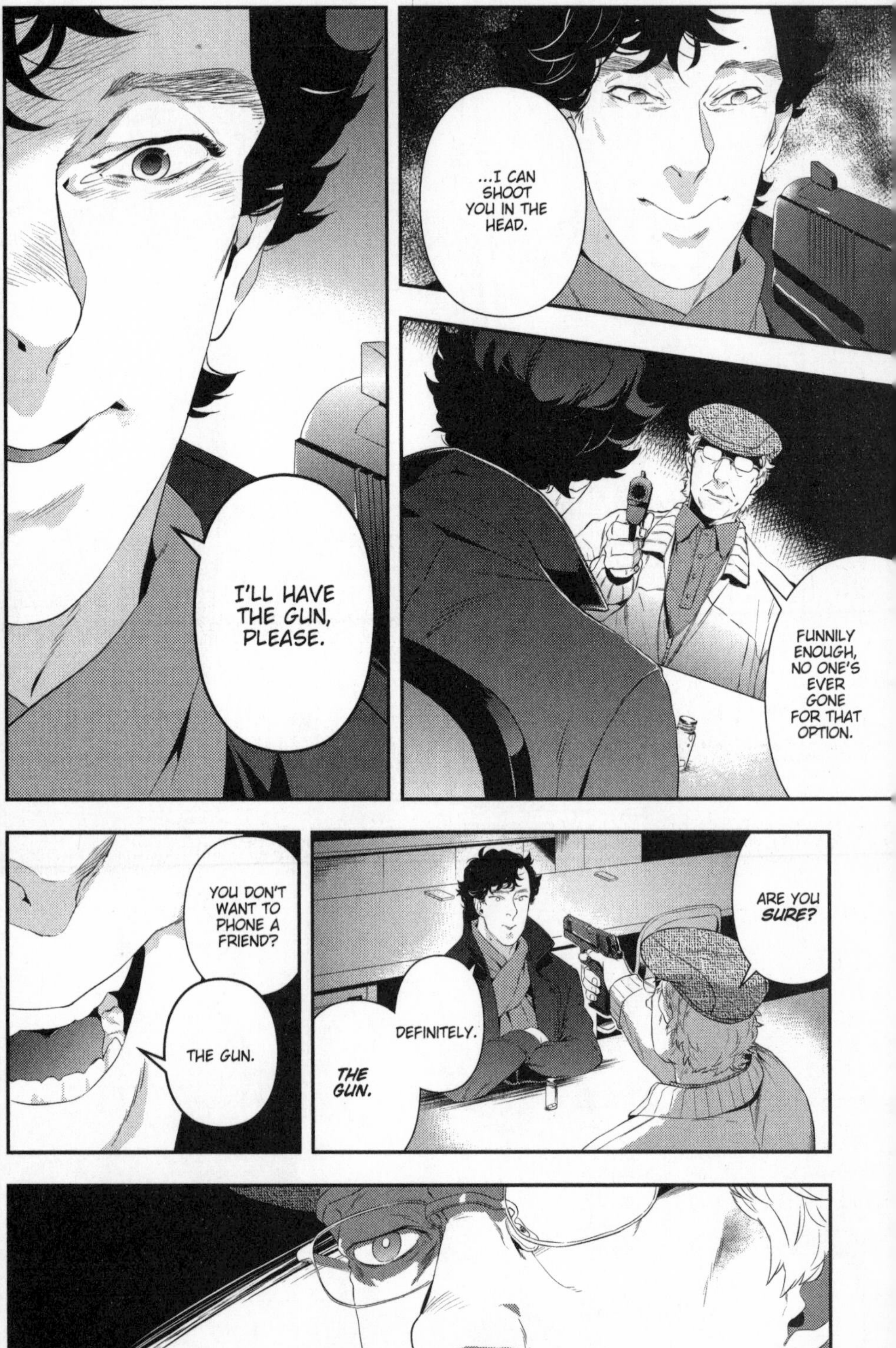
...I CAN SHOOT YOU IN THE HEAD.
FUNNILY ENOUGH, NO ONE'S EVER GONE FOR THAT OPTION.
I'LL HAVE THE GUN, PLEASE.
ARE YOU *SURE?*
DEFINITELY.
THE GUN.
YOU DON'T WANT TO PHONE A FRIEND?
THE GUN.

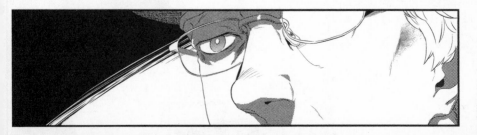

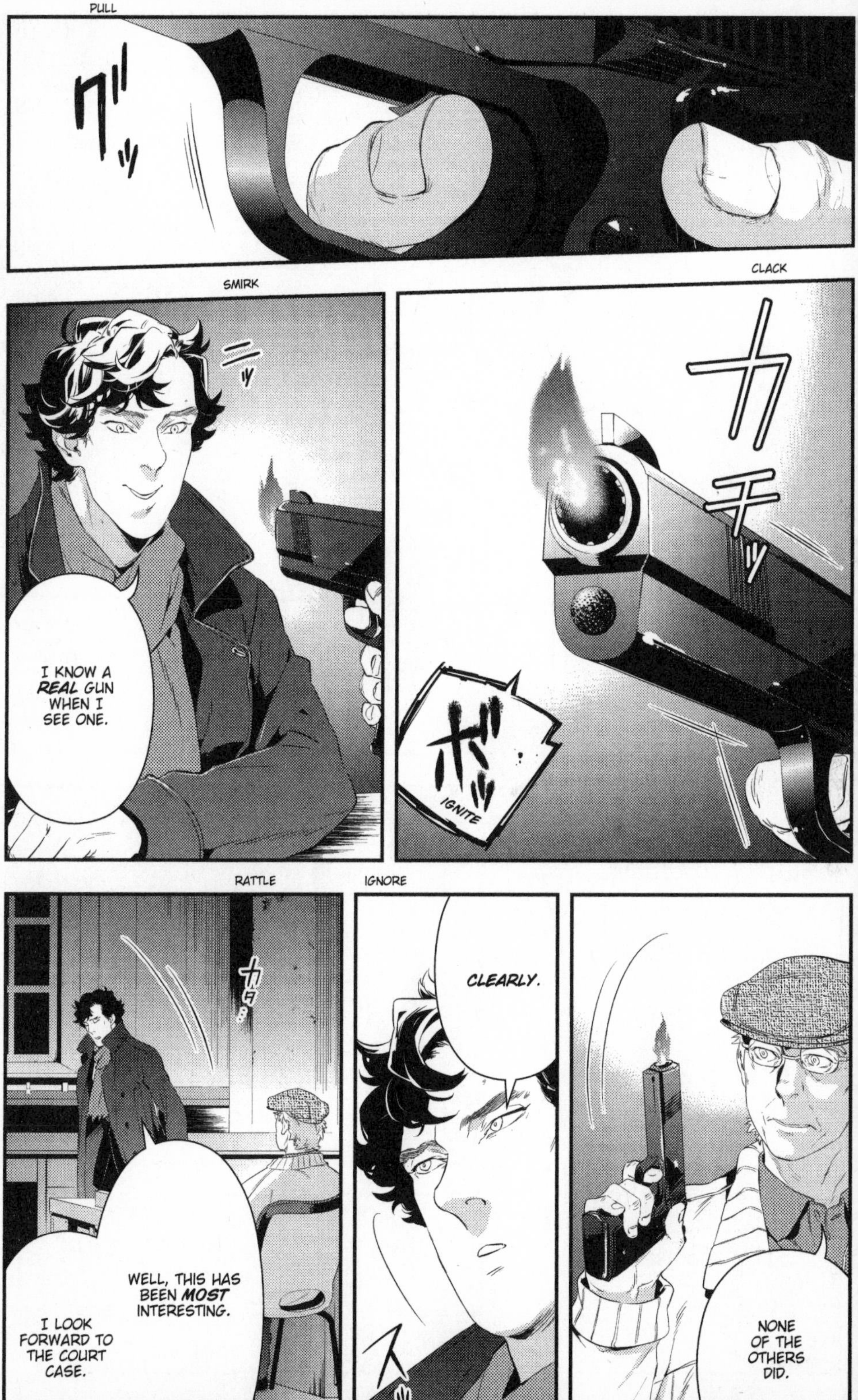
PULL
グッ
CLACK
カチッ
ボッ
IGNITE
SMIRK
ニッ
I KNOW A *REAL* GUN WHEN I SEE ONE.
NONE OF THE OTHERS DID.
IGNORE
CLEARLY.
RATTLE
カタ…
WELL, THIS HAS BEEN *MOST* INTERESTING.
I LOOK FORWARD TO THE COURT CASE.

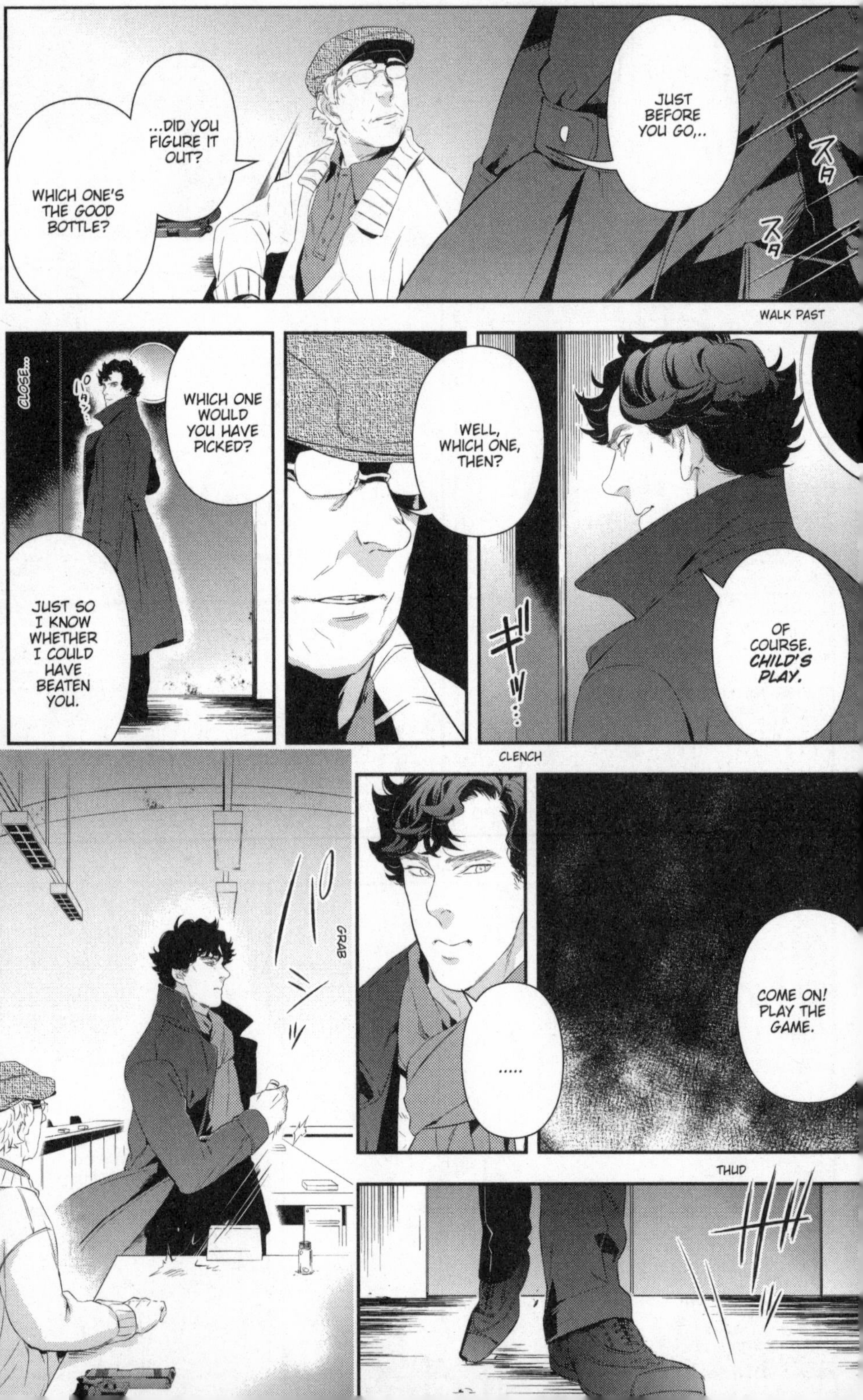
JUST BEFORE YOU GO,...
スタ
スタ
WALK PAST
...DID YOU FIGURE IT OUT?
WHICH ONE'S THE GOOD BOTTLE?
OF COURSE. **CHILD'S PLAY.**
ギリッ...
CLENCH
WELL, WHICH ONE, THEN?
WHICH ONE WOULD YOU HAVE PICKED?
JUST SO I KNOW WHETHER I COULD HAVE BEATEN YOU.
CLOSE...
COME ON! PLAY THE GAME.
.....
THUD
GRAB

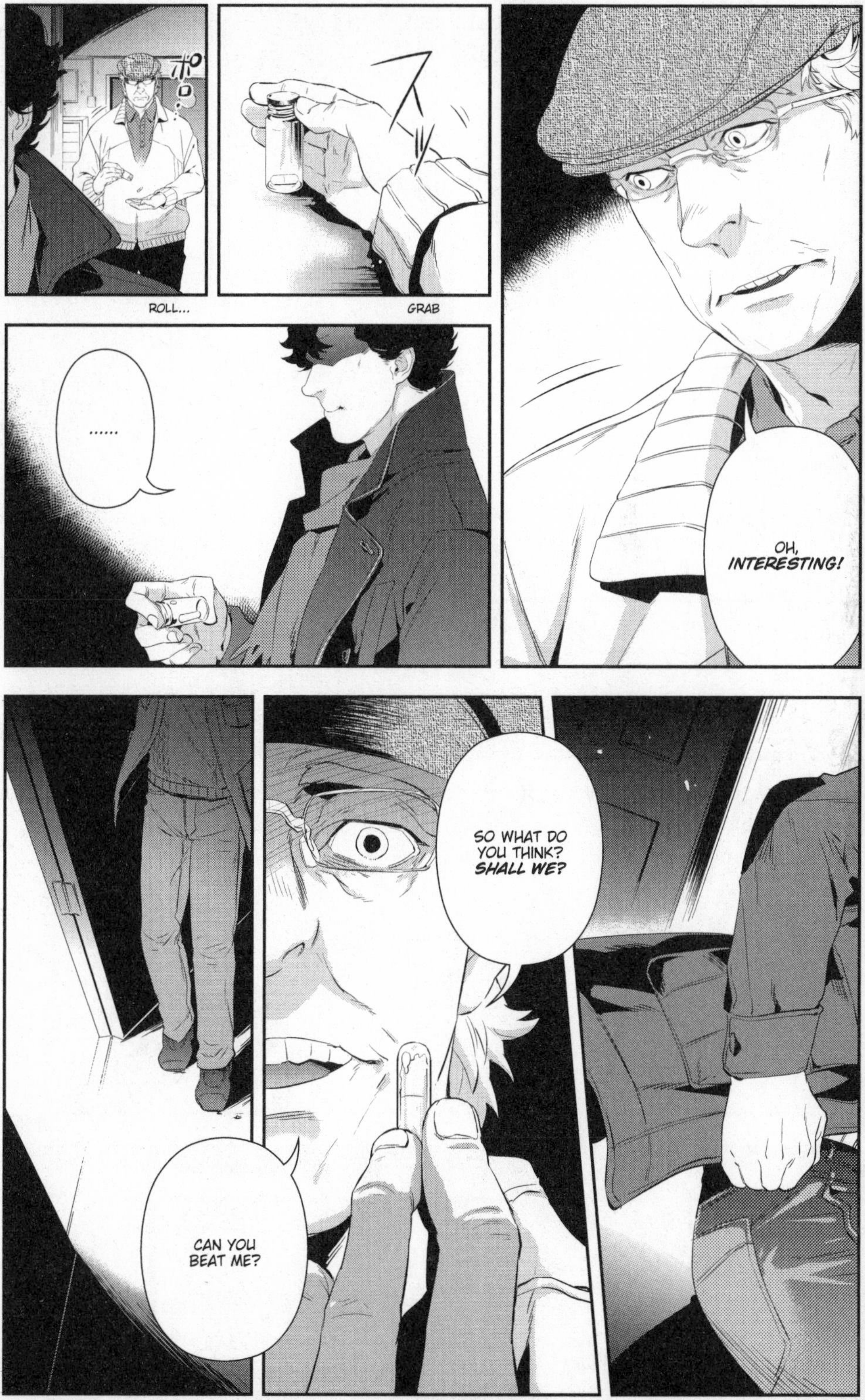
OH, **INTERESTING!**
GRAB
ROLL...
ポロ…
......
SO WHAT DO YOU THINK? **SHALL WE?**
CAN YOU BEAT ME?

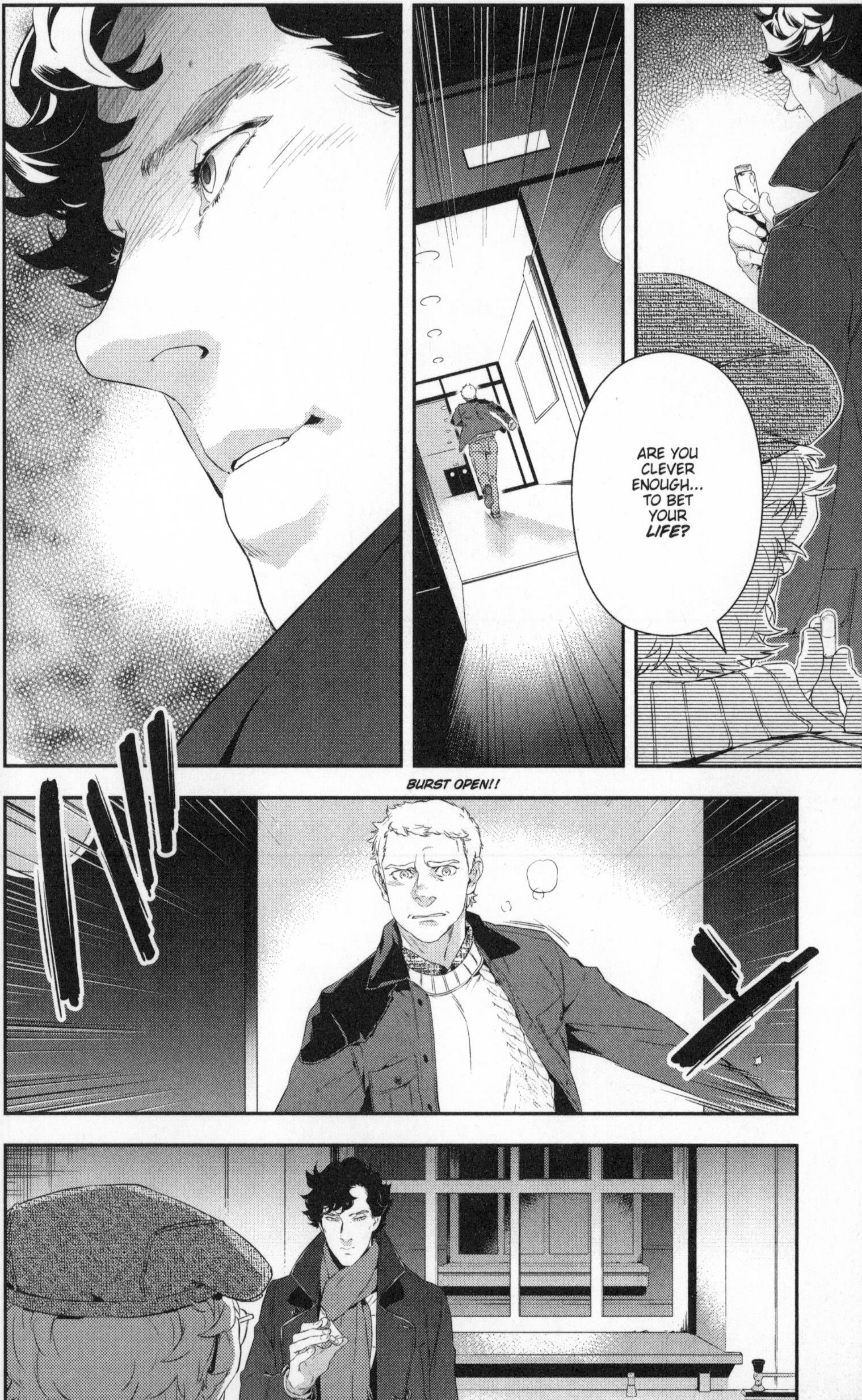
ARE YOU CLEVER ENOUGH... TO BET YOUR LIFE?
BURST OPEN!!

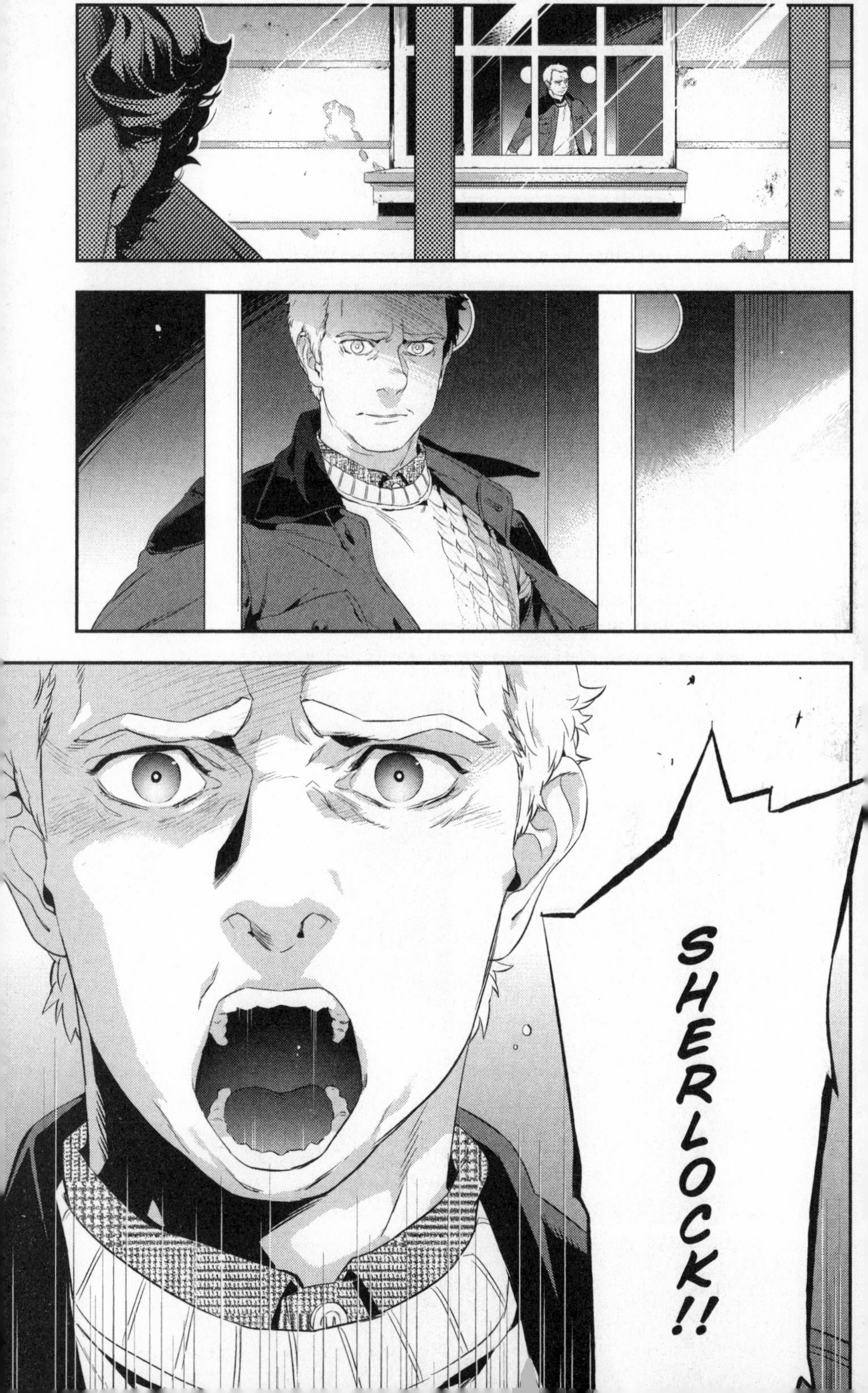
SHERLOCK!!

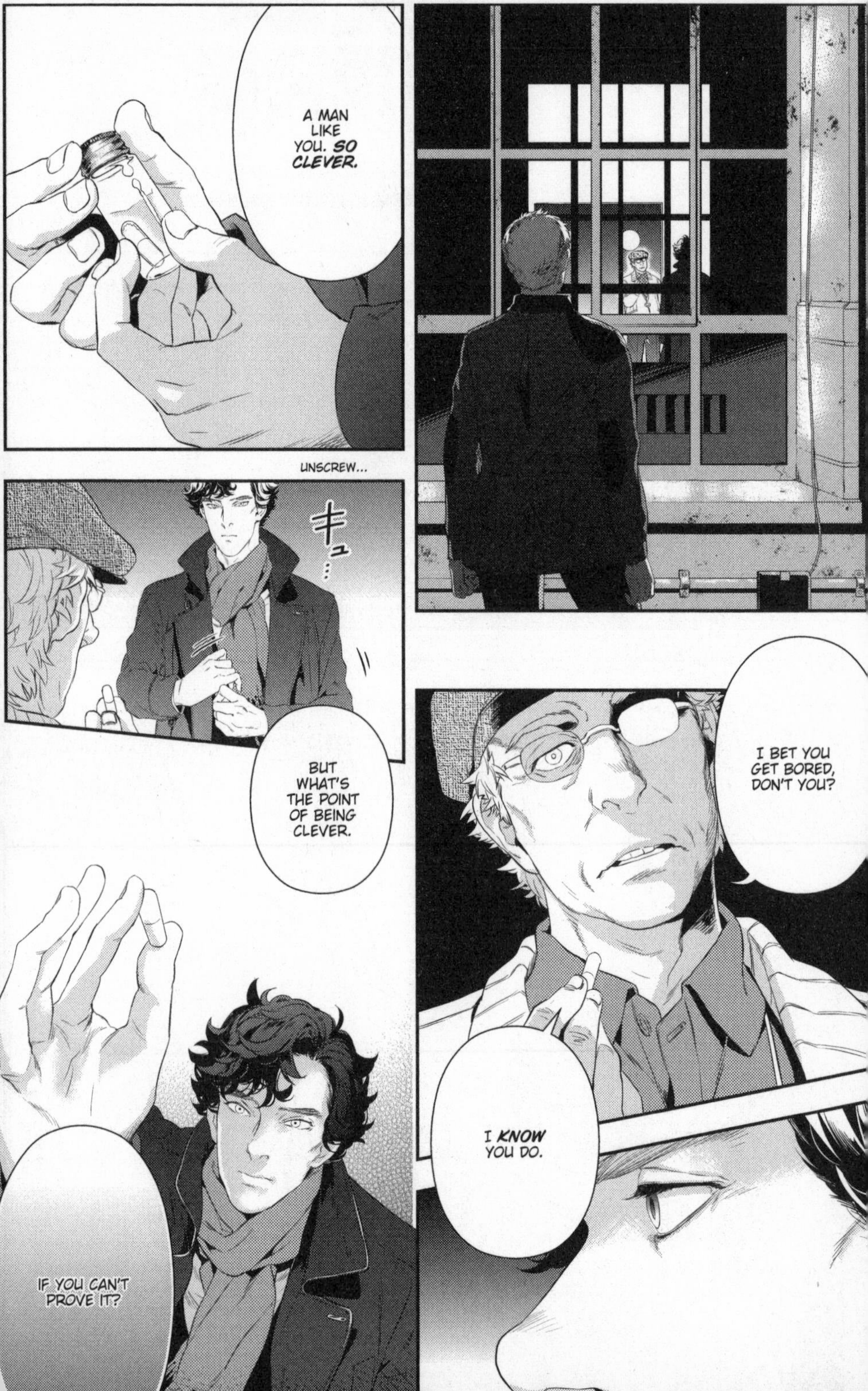
A MAN LIKE YOU. **SO CLEVER.**
UNSCREW...
キュ…
I BET YOU GET BORED, DON'T YOU?
I ***KNOW*** YOU DO.
BUT WHAT'S THE POINT OF BEING CLEVER.
IF YOU CAN'T PROVE IT?

STILL THE ADDICT. BUT THIS...

THIS IS WHAT ...

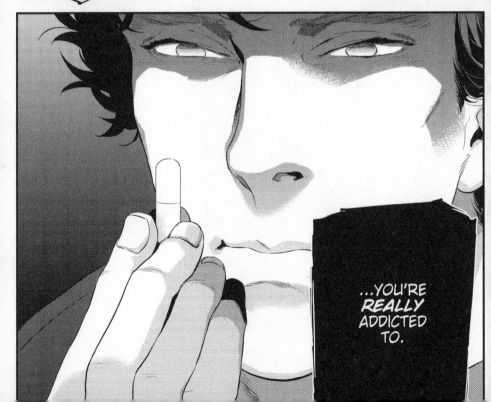

...YOU'RE *REALLY* ADDICTED TO.

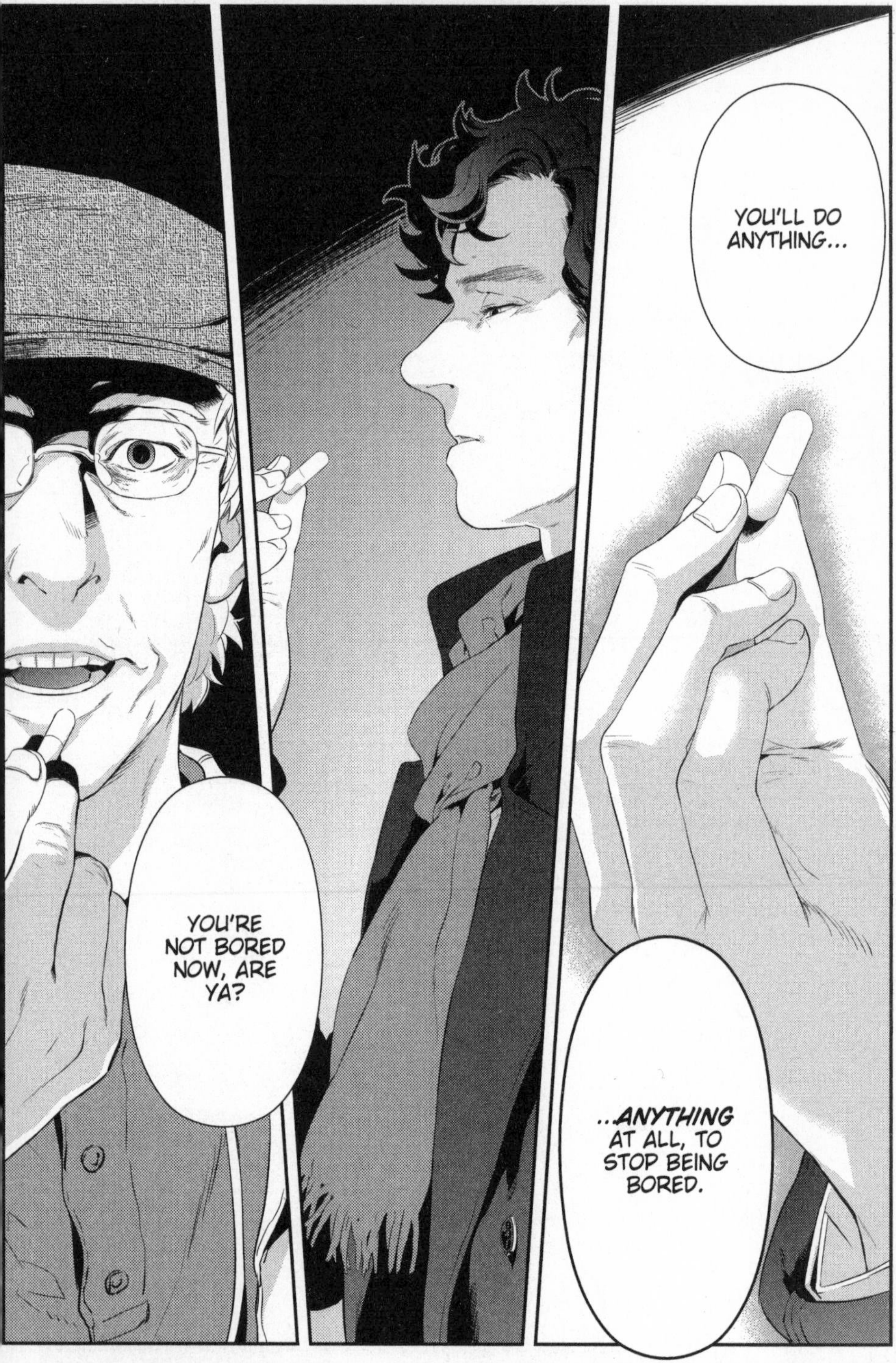
YOU'LL DO ANYTHING...
...*ANYTHING* AT ALL, TO STOP BEING BORED.
YOU'RE NOT BORED NOW, ARE YA?

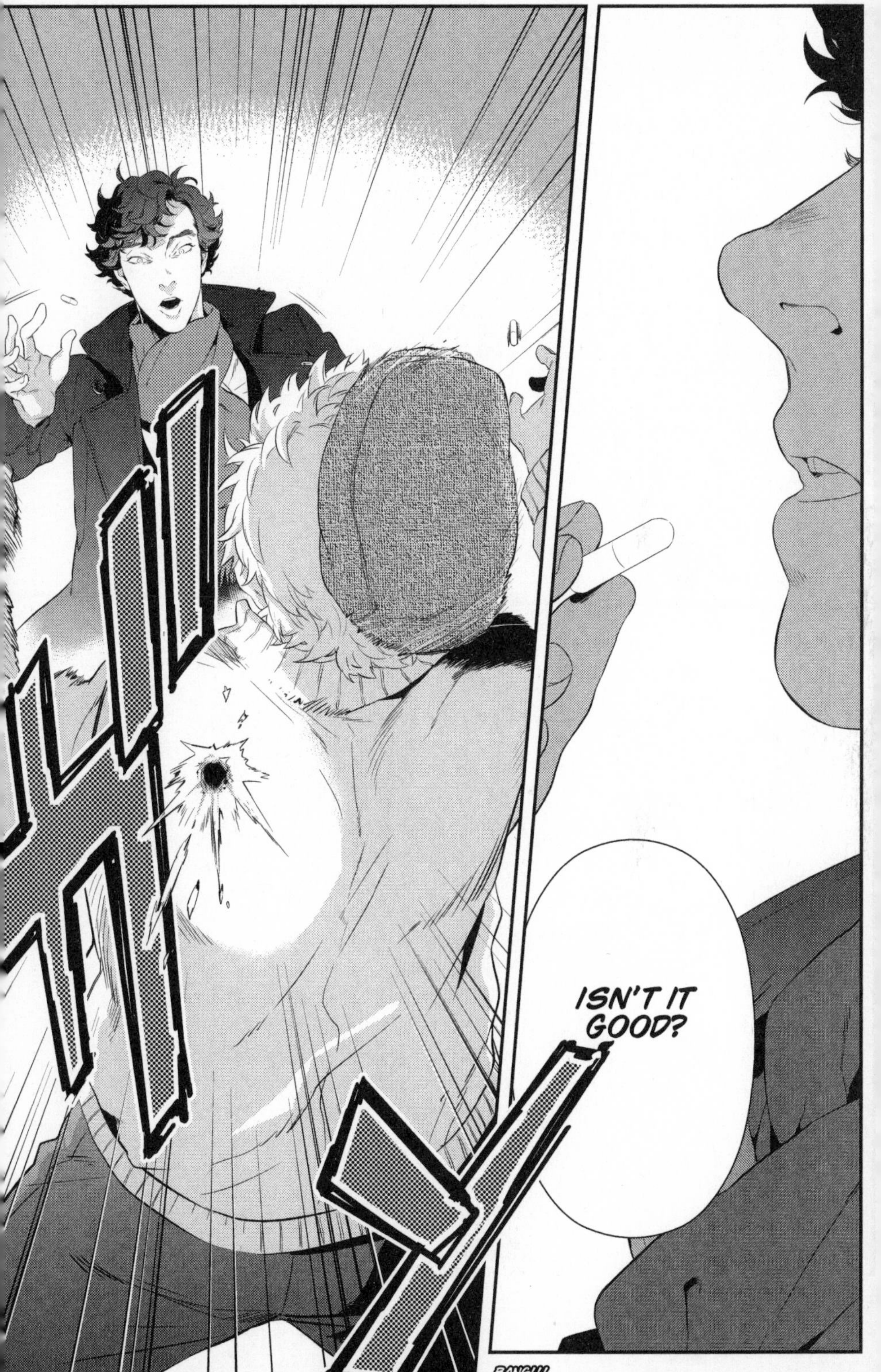
ISN'T IT GOOD?
BANG!!!

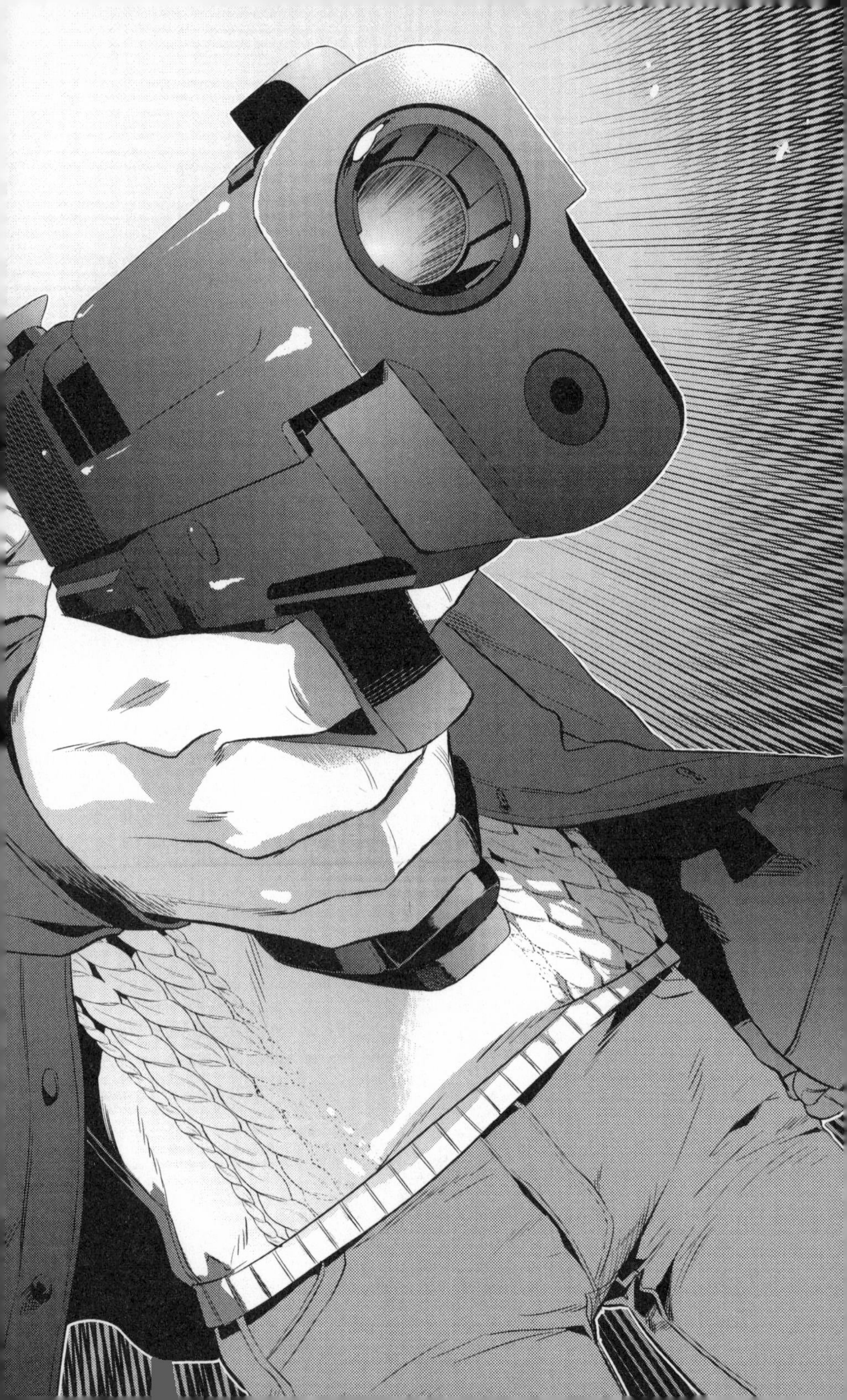

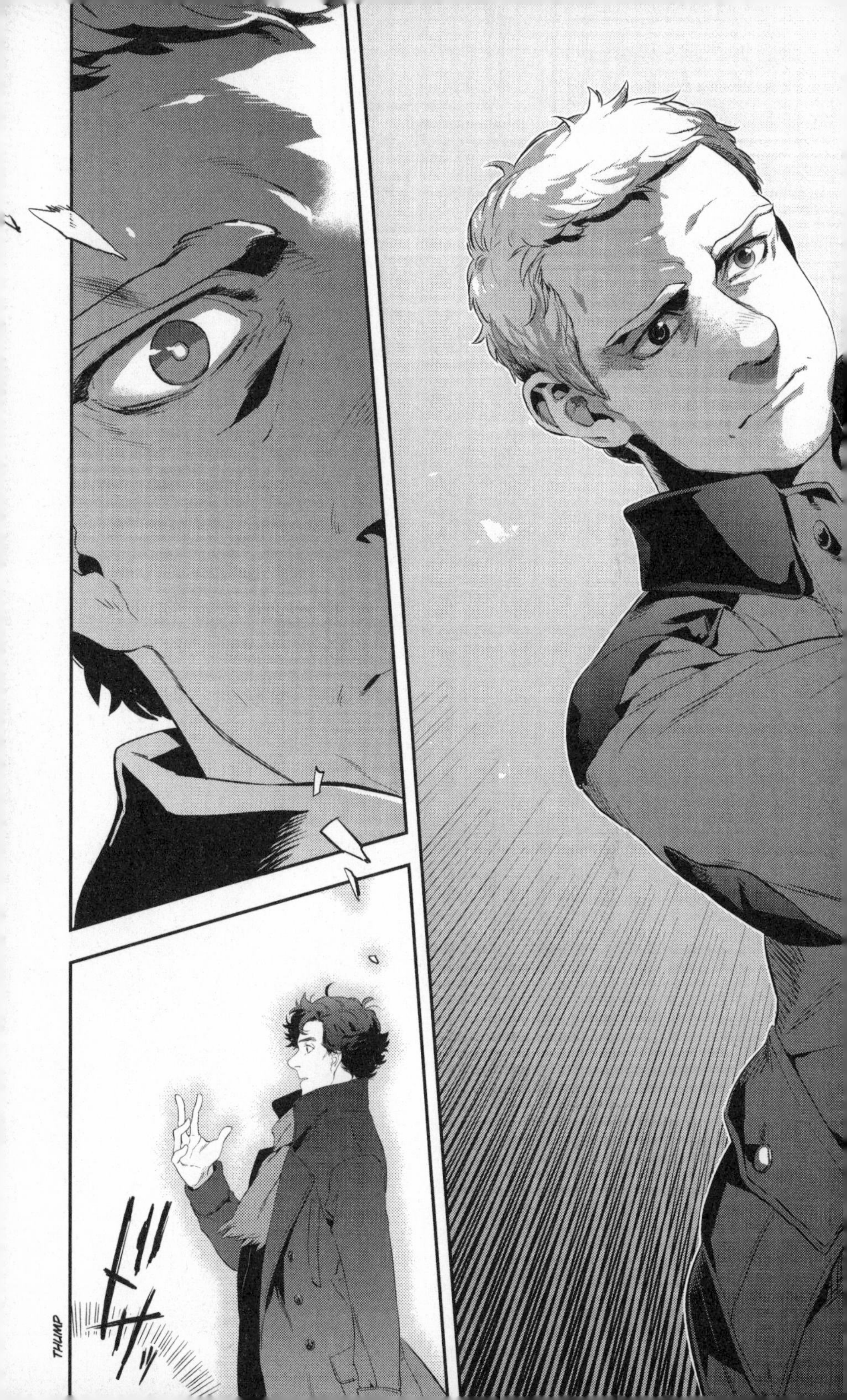
THUMP

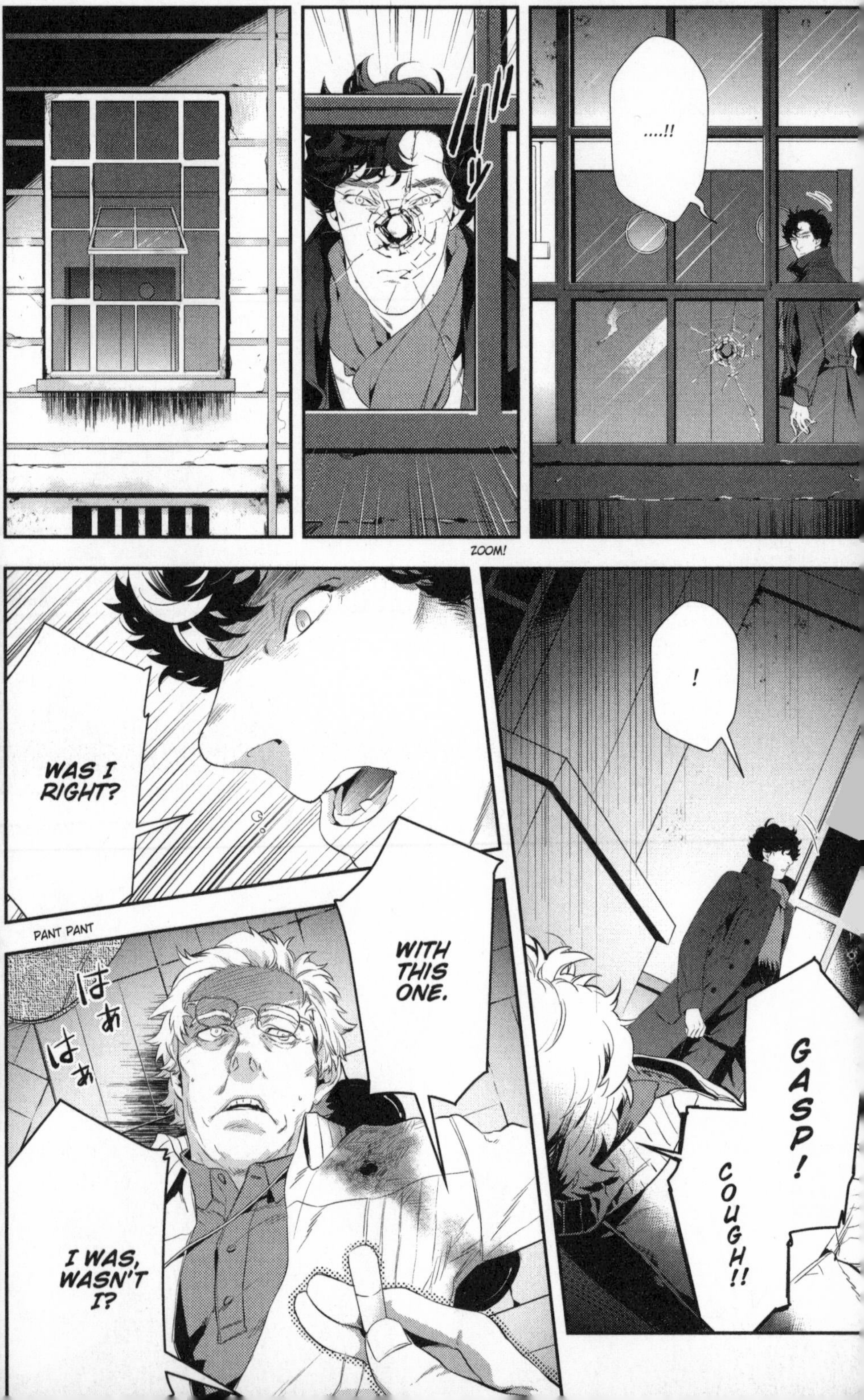
....!!
ZOOM!
!
GASP!
COUGH!!
WAS I RIGHT?
PANT PANT
はぁ はぁ
WITH THIS ONE.
I WAS, WASN'T I?

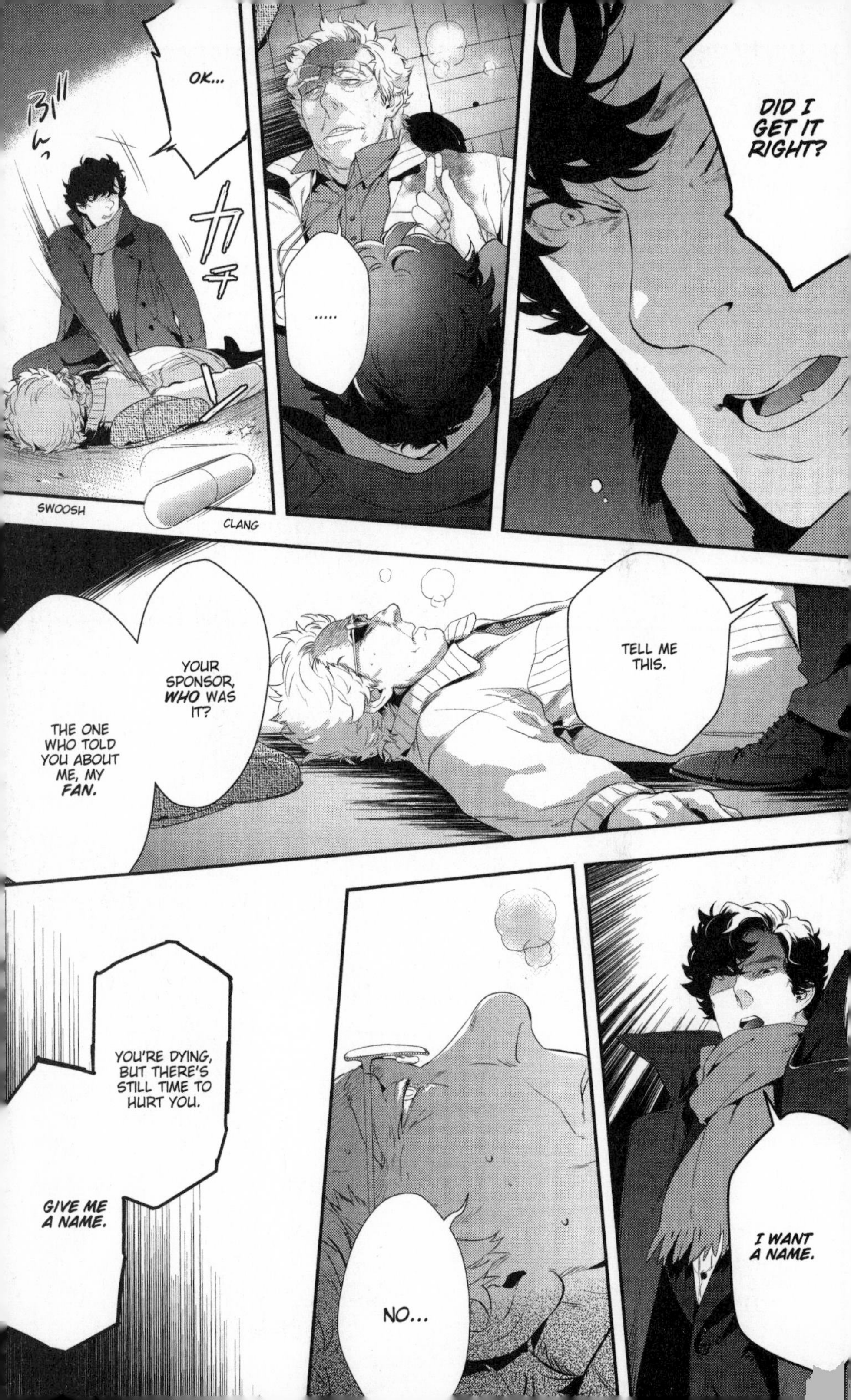
DID I GET IT RIGHT?
.....
CLANG
カチ
OK...
SWOOSH
TELL ME THIS.
YOUR SPONSOR, WHO WAS IT?
THE ONE WHO TOLD YOU ABOUT ME, MY FAN.
I WANT A NAME.
NO...
YOU'RE DYING, BUT THERE'S STILL TIME TO HURT YOU.
GIVE ME A NAME.

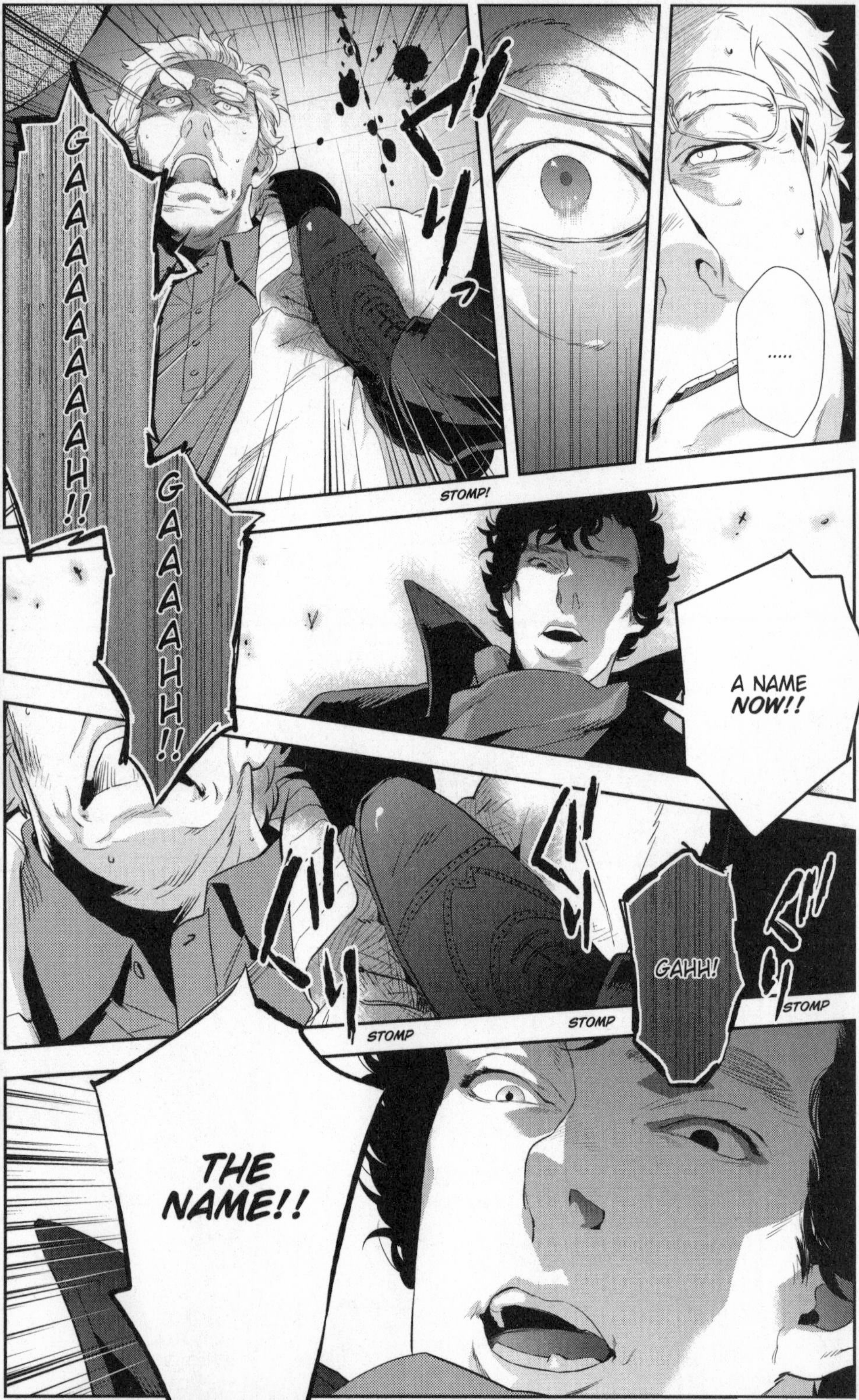
.....
GAAAAAAAAAH!!
STOMP!
A NAME NOW!!
GAAAAHH!!
STOMP
GAHH!
STOMP
STOMP
THE NAME!!

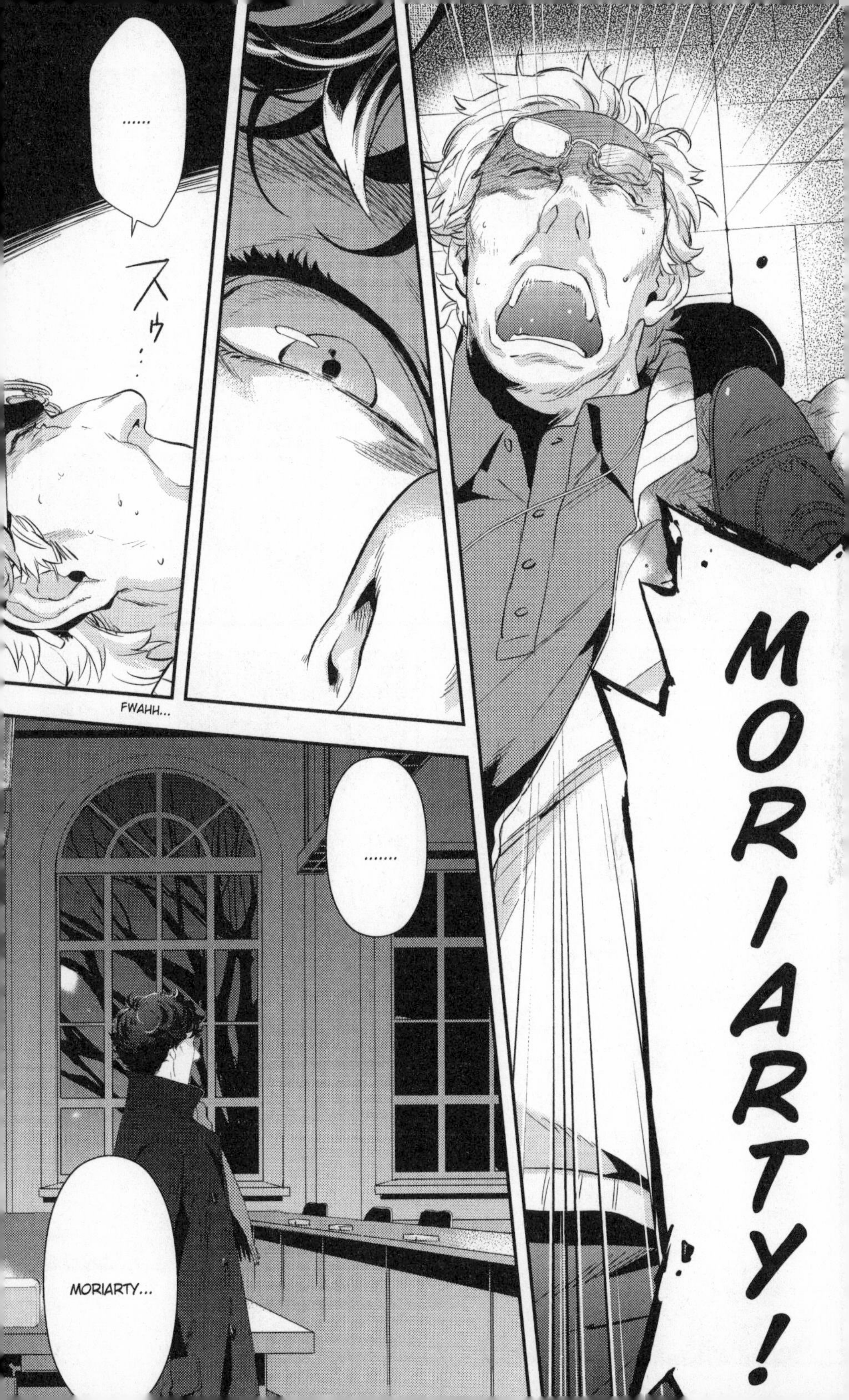

MORIARTY!
......
スゥ…
FWAHH...
......
MORIARTY...

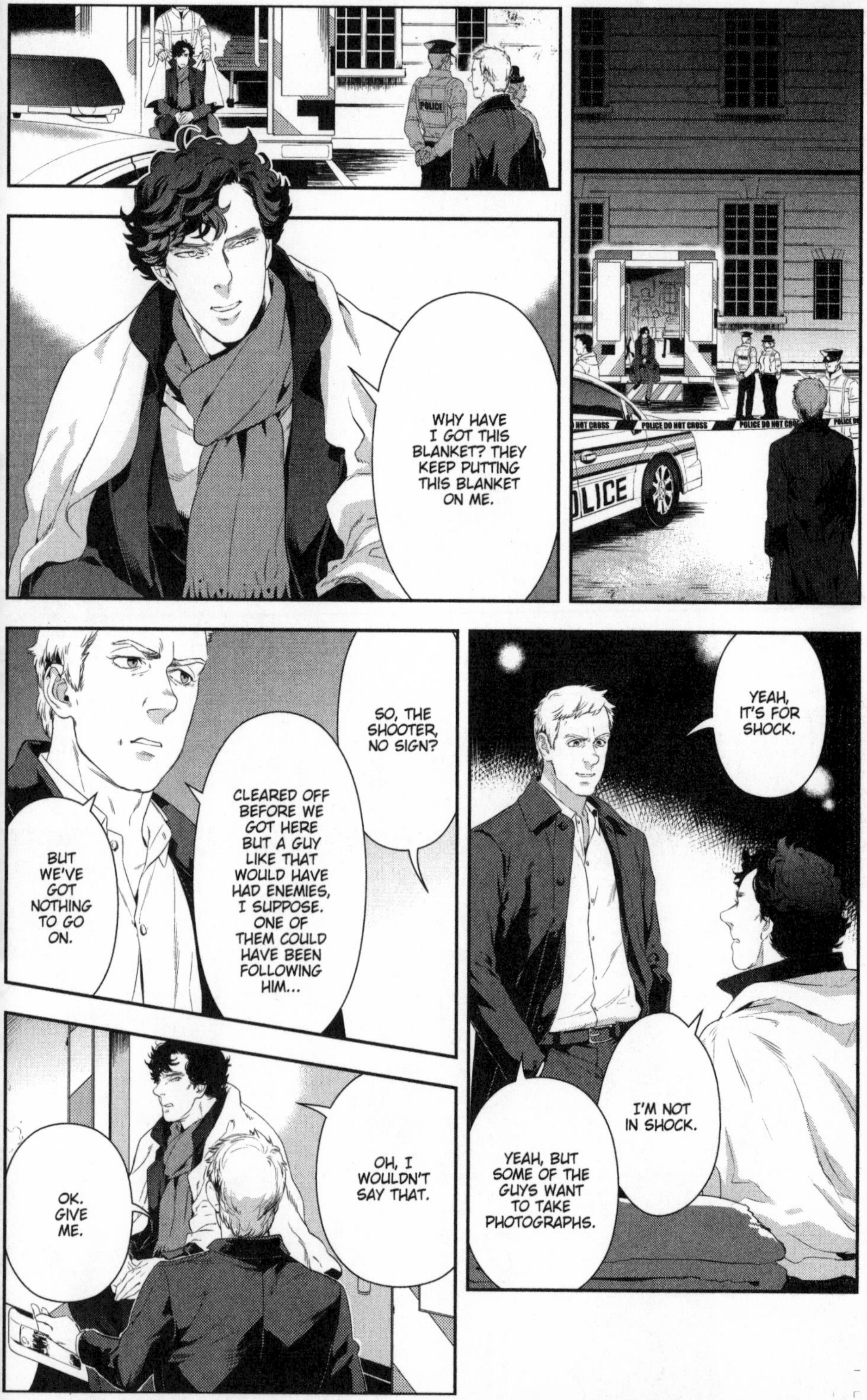
WHY HAVE I GOT THIS BLANKET? THEY KEEP PUTTING THIS BLANKET ON ME.
YEAH, IT'S FOR SHOCK.
I'M NOT IN SHOCK.
YEAH, BUT SOME OF THE GUYS WANT TO TAKE PHOTOGRAPHS.
SO, THE SHOOTER, NO SIGN?
CLEARED OFF BEFORE WE GOT HERE BUT A GUY LIKE THAT WOULD HAVE HAD ENEMIES, I SUPPOSE. ONE OF THEM COULD HAVE BEEN FOLLOWING HIM...
BUT WE'VE GOT NOTHING TO GO ON.
OH, I WOULDN'T SAY THAT.
OK. GIVE ME.

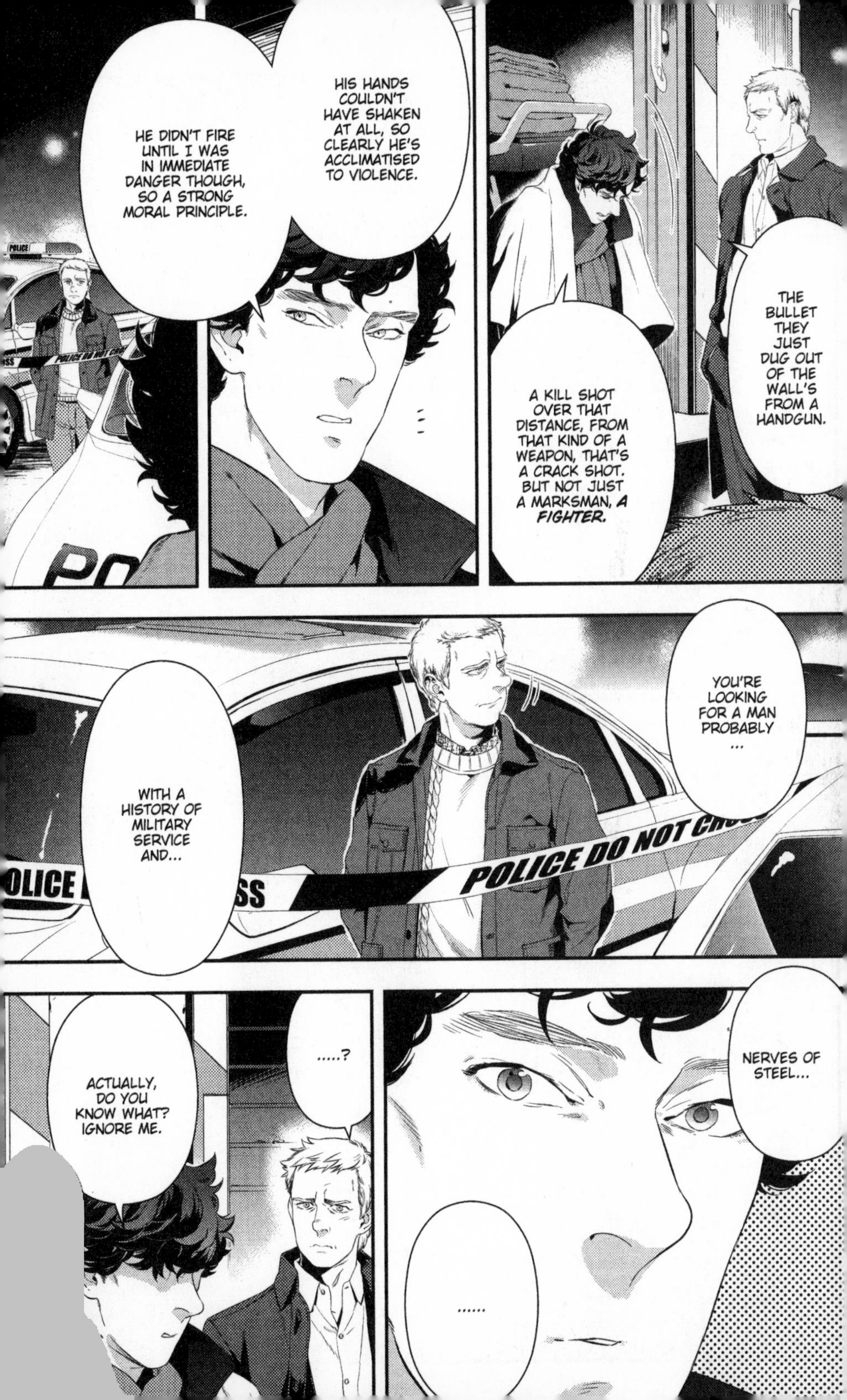
THE BULLET THEY JUST DUG OUT OF THE WALL'S FROM A HANDGUN.
A KILL SHOT OVER THAT DISTANCE, FROM THAT KIND OF A WEAPON, THAT'S A CRACK SHOT. BUT NOT JUST A MARKSMAN, *A FIGHTER.*
HIS HANDS COULDN'T HAVE SHAKEN AT ALL, SO CLEARLY HE'S ACCLIMATISED TO VIOLENCE.
HE DIDN'T FIRE UNTIL I WAS IN IMMEDIATE DANGER THOUGH, SO A STRONG MORAL PRINCIPLE.
YOU'RE LOOKING FOR A MAN PROBABLY ...
WITH A HISTORY OF MILITARY SERVICE AND...
POLICE DO NOT CROSS
NERVES OF STEEL...
......
.....?
ACTUALLY, DO YOU KNOW WHAT? IGNORE ME.

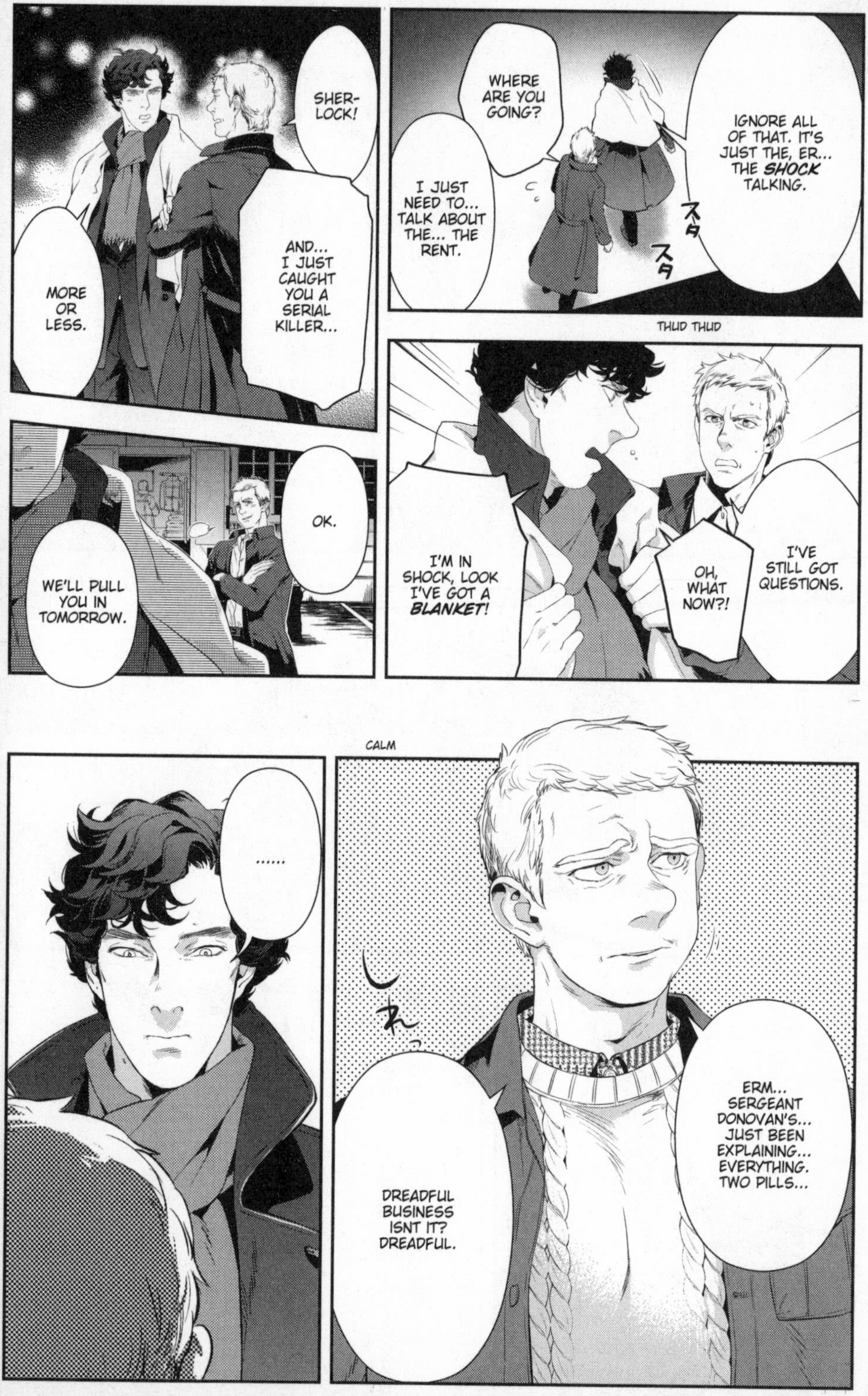
IGNORE ALL OF THAT. IT'S JUST THE, ER... THE SHOCK TALKING.
WHERE ARE YOU GOING?
I JUST NEED TO... TALK ABOUT THE... THE RENT.
スタ
スタ
THUD THUD
SHER-LOCK!
AND... I JUST CAUGHT YOU A SERIAL KILLER...
MORE OR LESS.
I'VE STILL GOT QUESTIONS.
OH, WHAT NOW?!
I'M IN SHOCK, LOOK I'VE GOT A BLANKET!
OK.
WE'LL PULL YOU IN TOMORROW.
CALM
ERM... SERGEANT DONOVAN'S... JUST BEEN EXPLAINING... EVERYTHING. TWO PILLS...
DREADFUL BUSINESS ISNT IT? DREADFUL.
......

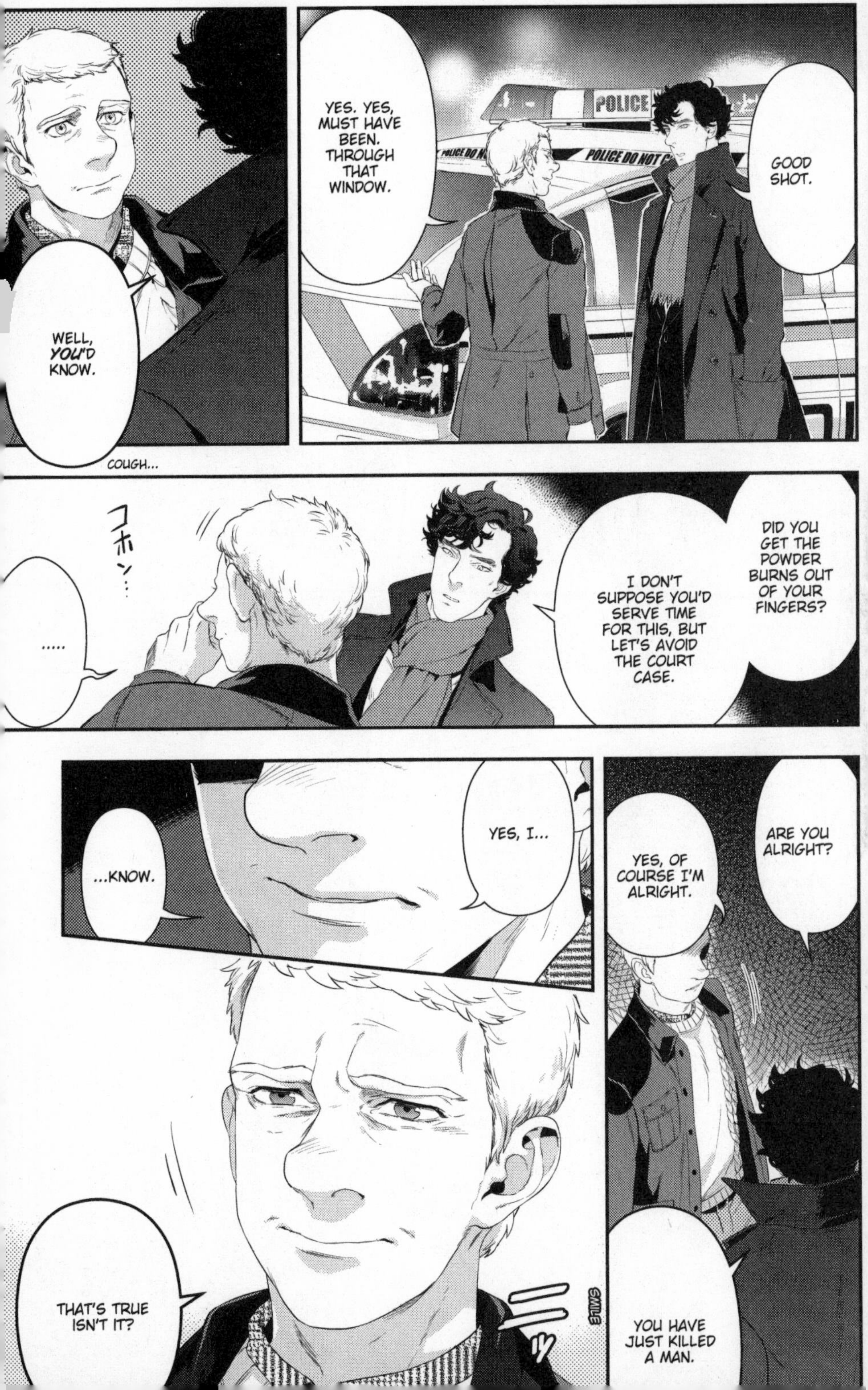
GOOD SHOT.
YES. YES, MUST HAVE BEEN. THROUGH THAT WINDOW.
POLICE
POLICE DO NOT C
WELL, YOU'D KNOW.
COUGH...
DID YOU GET THE POWDER BURNS OUT OF YOUR FINGERS?
I DON'T SUPPOSE YOU'D SERVE TIME FOR THIS, BUT LET'S AVOID THE COURT CASE.
コホン…
.....
ARE YOU ALRIGHT?
YES, OF COURSE I'M ALRIGHT.
YOU HAVE JUST KILLED A MAN.
YES, I...
...KNOW.
SMILE
THAT'S TRUE ISN'T IT?

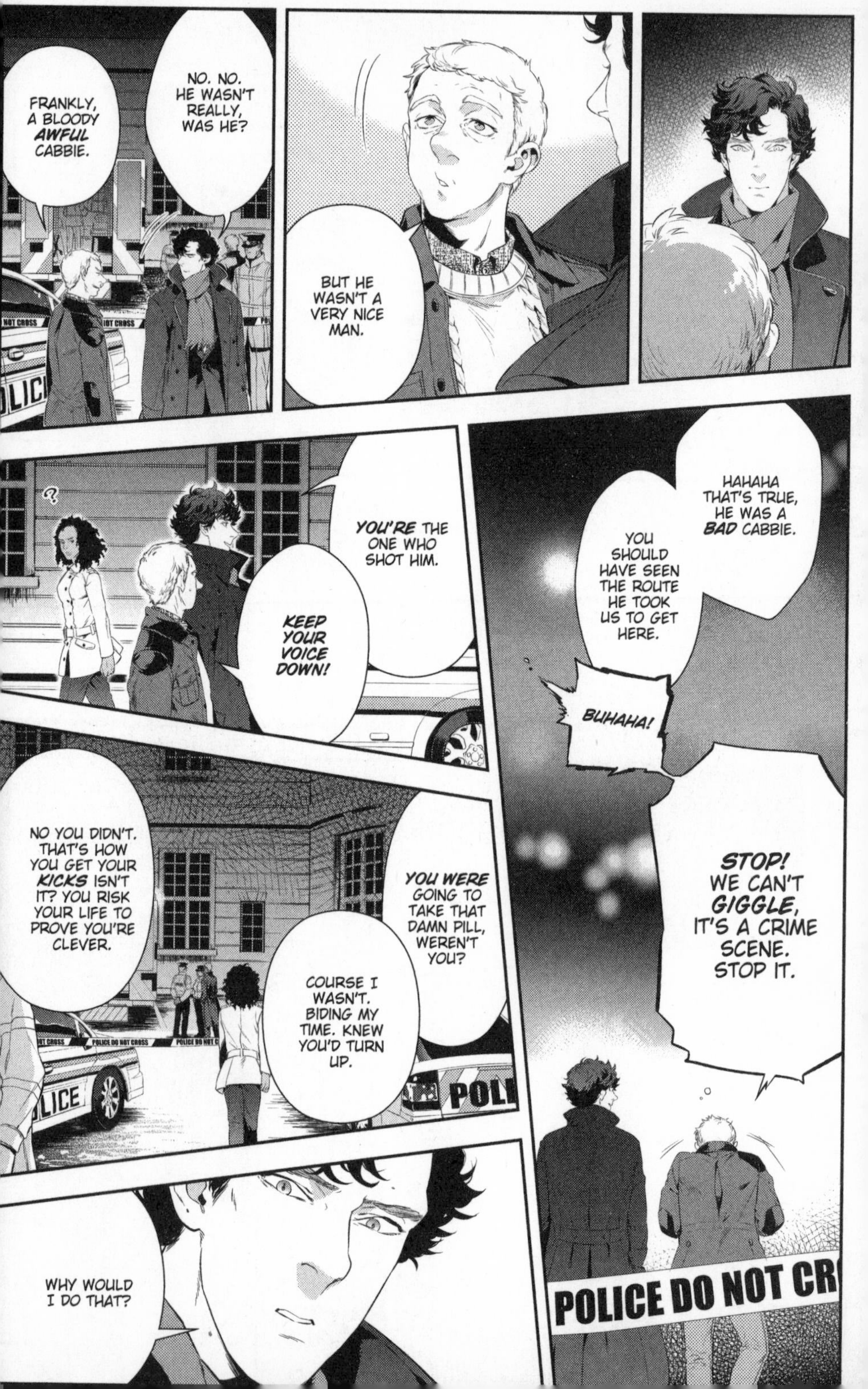
BUT HE WASN'T A VERY NICE MAN.
NO. NO. HE WASN'T REALLY, WAS HE?
FRANKLY, A BLOODY **AWFUL** CABBIE.
HAHAHA THAT'S TRUE, HE WAS A **BAD** CABBIE.
YOU SHOULD HAVE SEEN THE ROUTE HE TOOK US TO GET HERE.
BUHAHA!
STOP! WE CAN'T **GIGGLE**, IT'S A CRIME SCENE. STOP IT.
POLICE DO NOT CR
YOU'RE THE ONE WHO SHOT HIM.
KEEP YOUR VOICE DOWN!
YOU WERE GOING TO TAKE THAT DAMN PILL, WEREN'T YOU?
COURSE I WASN'T. BIDING MY TIME. KNEW YOU'D TURN UP.
NO YOU DIDN'T. THAT'S HOW YOU GET YOUR **KICKS** ISN'T IT? YOU RISK YOUR LIFE TO PROVE YOU'RE CLEVER.
WHY WOULD I DO THAT?

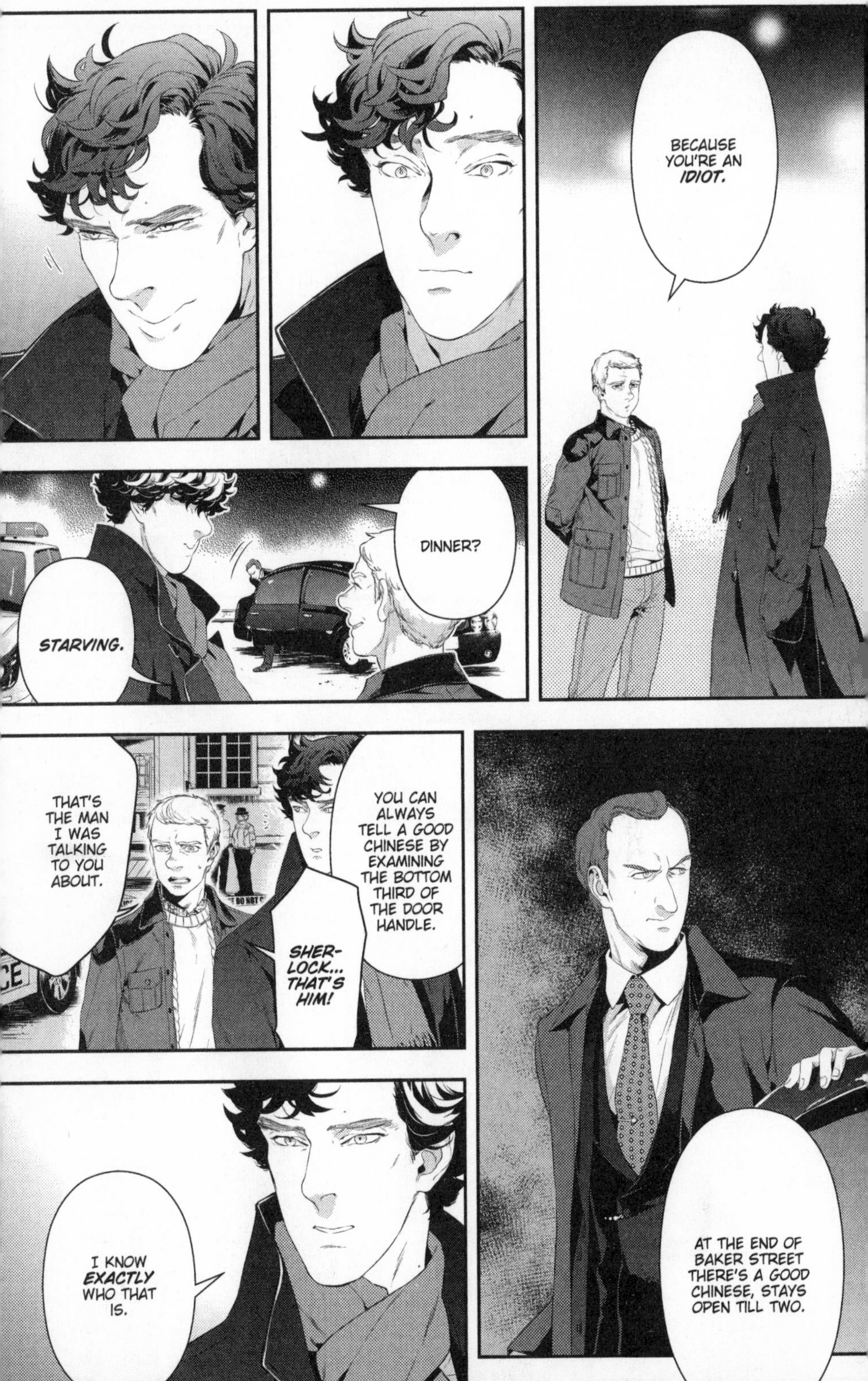
BECAUSE YOU'RE AN *IDIOT.*
DINNER?
STARVING.
AT THE END OF BAKER STREET THERE'S A GOOD CHINESE, STAYS OPEN TILL TWO.
YOU CAN ALWAYS TELL A GOOD CHINESE BY EXAMINING THE BOTTOM THIRD OF THE DOOR HANDLE.
SHER-LOCK... THAT'S HIM!
THAT'S THE MAN I WAS TALKING TO YOU ABOUT.
I KNOW *EXACTLY* WHO THAT IS.

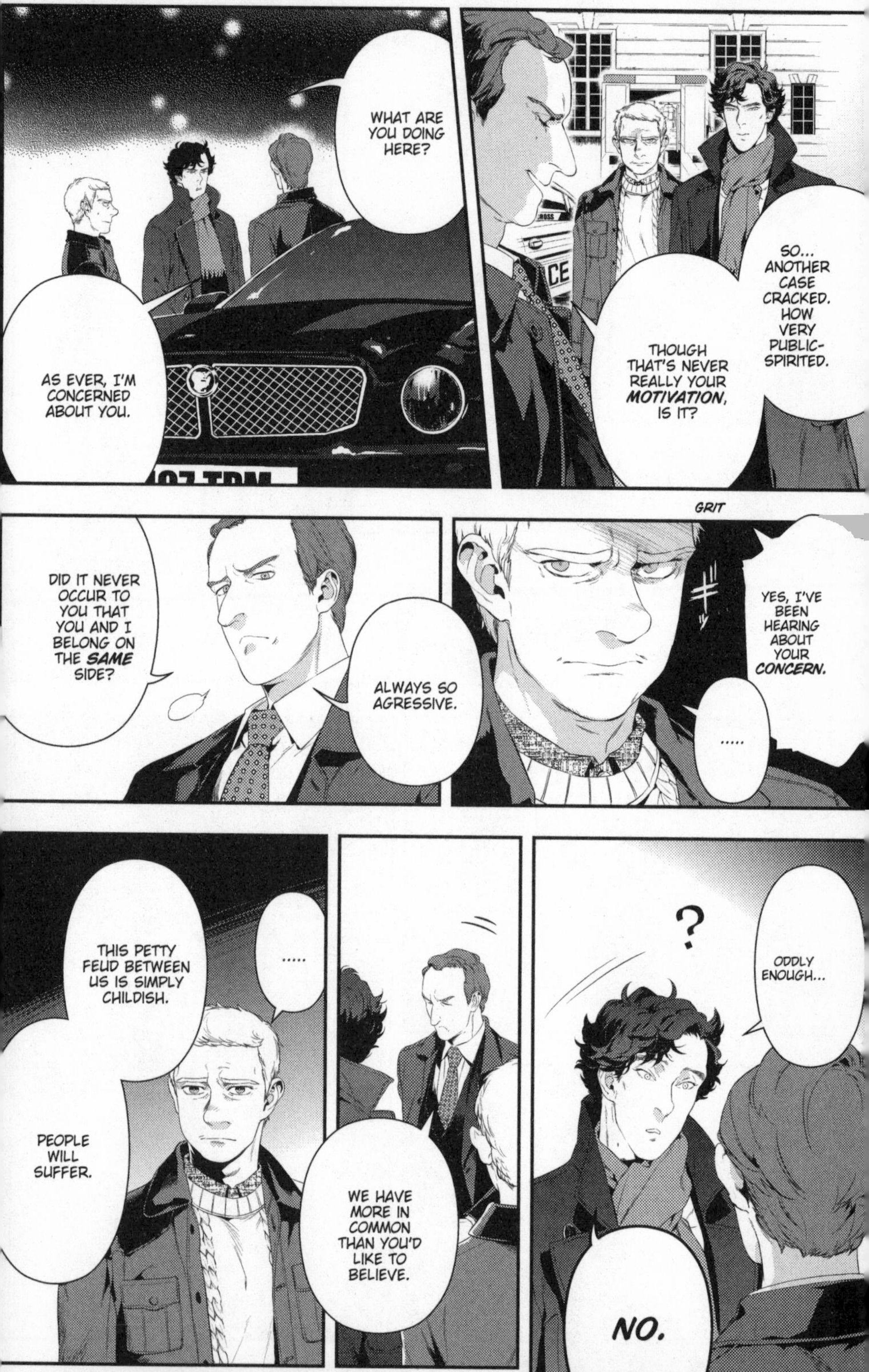
SO... ANOTHER CASE CRACKED. HOW VERY PUBLIC-SPIRITED.
THOUGH THAT'S NEVER REALLY YOUR *MOTIVATION*, IS IT?
WHAT ARE YOU DOING HERE?
AS EVER, I'M CONCERNED ABOUT YOU.
GRIT
YES, I'VE BEEN HEARING ABOUT YOUR *CONCERN*.
.....
ALWAYS SO AGRESSIVE.
DID IT NEVER OCCUR TO YOU THAT YOU AND I BELONG ON THE *SAME* SIDE?
?
ODDLY ENOUGH...
NO.
WE HAVE MORE IN COMMON THAN YOU'D LIKE TO BELIEVE.
.....
THIS PETTY FEUD BETWEEN US IS SIMPLY CHILDISH.
PEOPLE WILL SUFFER.

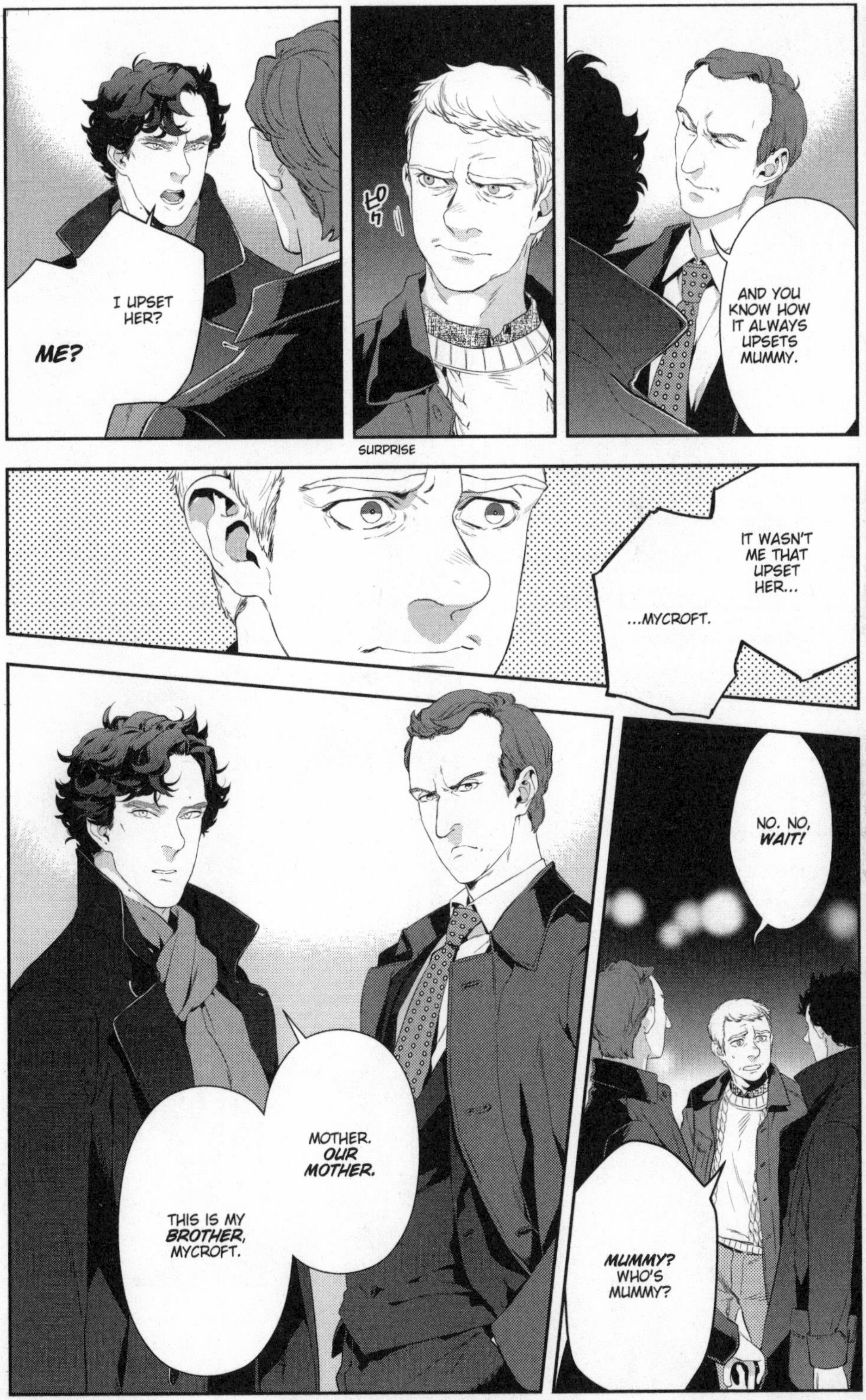
AND YOU KNOW HOW IT ALWAYS UPSETS MUMMY.
SURPRISE
I UPSET HER?
ME?
IT WASN'T ME THAT UPSET HER...
...MYCROFT.
NO. NO, WAIT!
MUMMY? WHO'S MUMMY?
MOTHER. OUR MOTHER.
THIS IS MY BROTHER, MYCROFT.

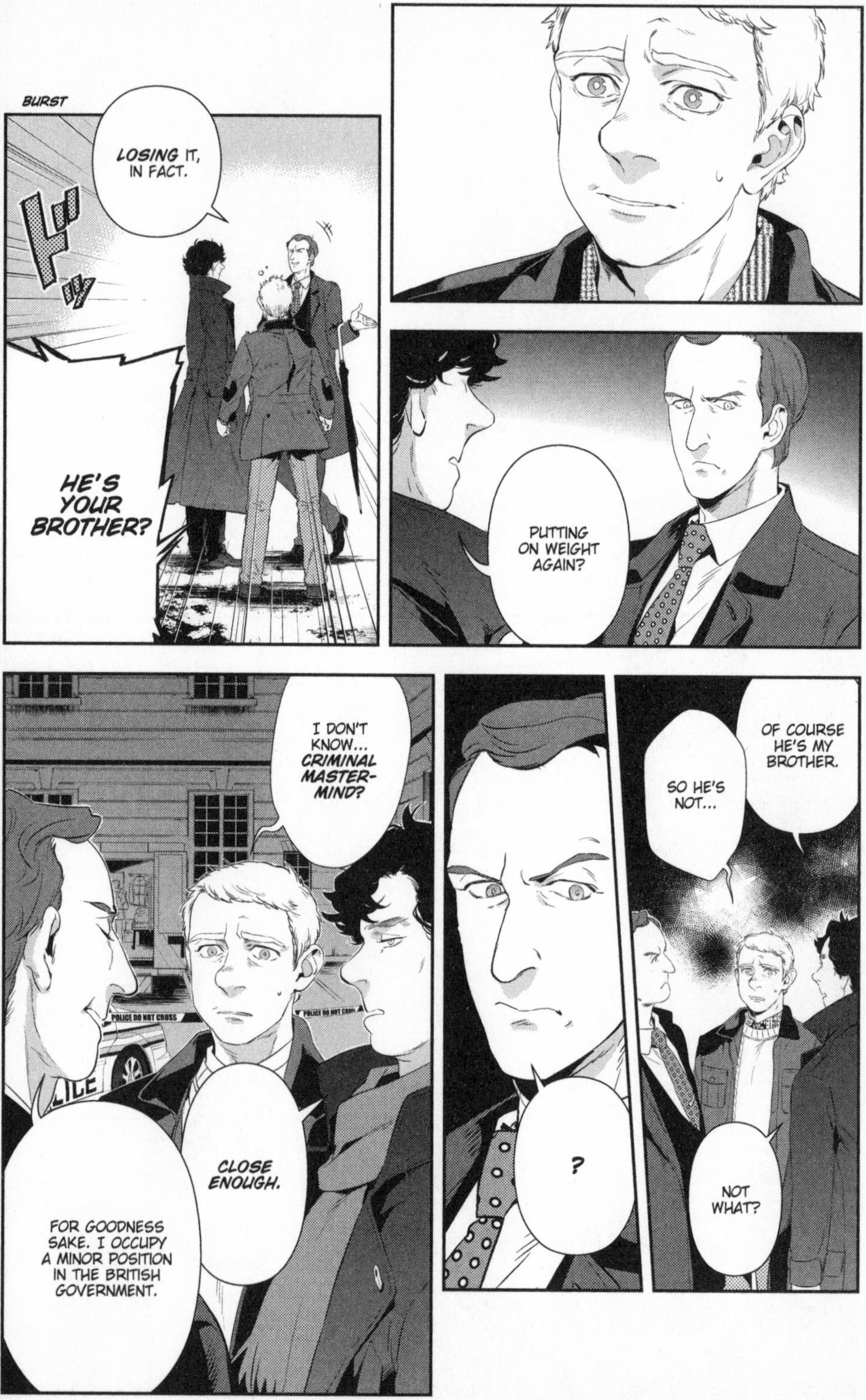
PUTTING ON WEIGHT AGAIN?
BURST
LOSING IT, IN FACT.
HE'S YOUR BROTHER?
OF COURSE HE'S MY BROTHER.
SO HE'S NOT...
NOT WHAT?
?
I DON'T KNOW... CRIMINAL MASTER-MIND?
CLOSE ENOUGH.
FOR GOODNESS SAKE. I OCCUPY A MINOR POSITION IN THE BRITISH GOVERNMENT.
POLICE DO NOT CROSS
POLICE DO NOT CROSS
LICE

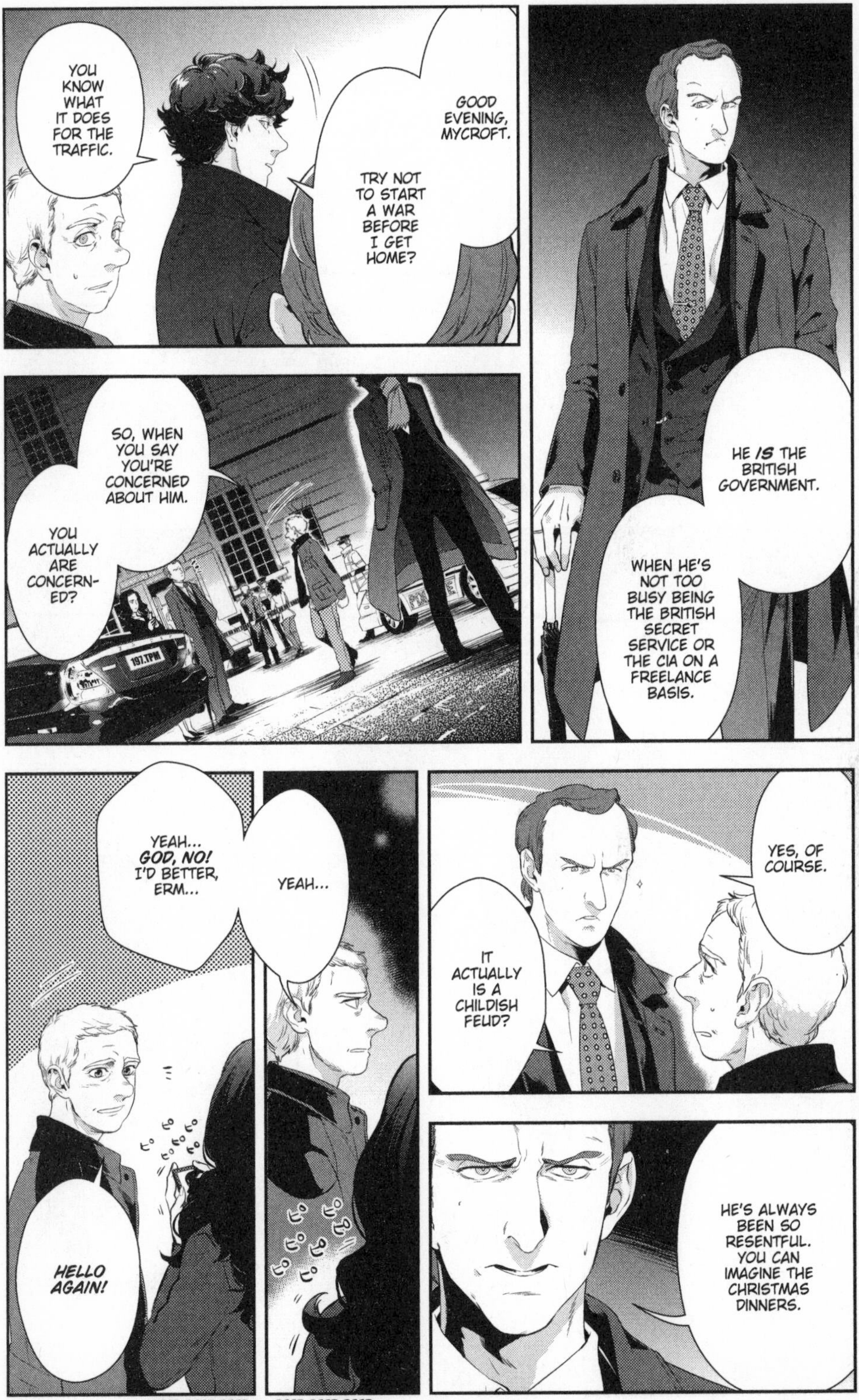
HE *IS* THE BRITISH GOVERNMENT.
WHEN HE'S NOT TOO BUSY BEING THE BRITISH SECRET SERVICE OR THE CIA ON A FREELANCE BASIS.
GOOD EVENING, MYCROFT.
TRY NOT TO START A WAR BEFORE I GET HOME?
YOU KNOW WHAT IT DOES FOR THE TRAFFIC.
SO, WHEN YOU SAY YOU'RE CONCERNED ABOUT HIM.
YOU ACTUALLY ARE CONCERN-ED?
YES, OF COURSE.
IT ACTUALLY IS A CHILDISH FEUD?
HE'S ALWAYS BEEN SO RESENTFUL. YOU CAN IMAGINE THE CHRISTMAS DINNERS.
YEAH...
YEAH... ***GOD, NO!*** I'D BETTER, ERM...
HELLO AGAIN!

BEEP BEEP BEEP BEEP BEEP BEEP

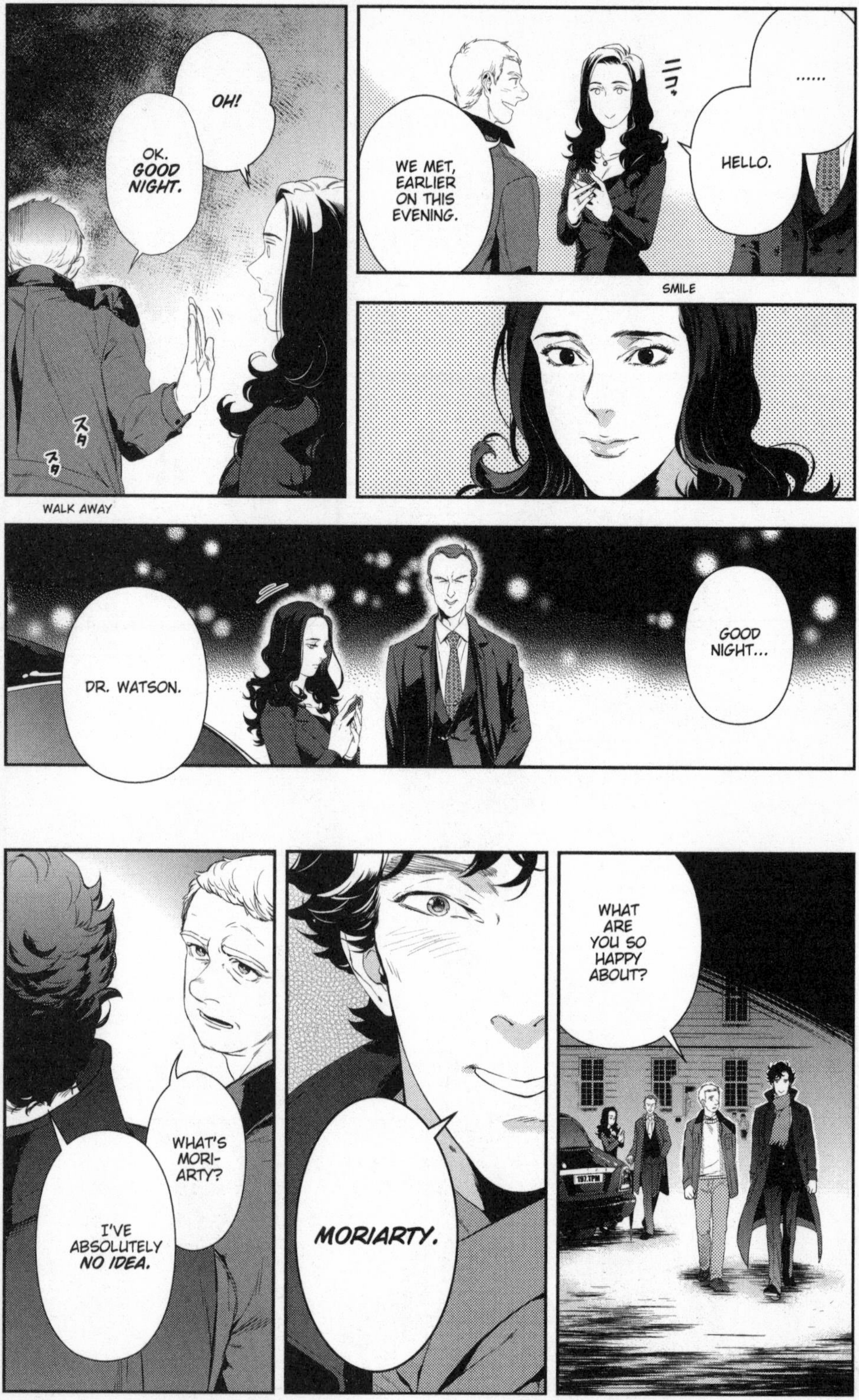
......
HELLO.
ニコッ
WE MET, EARLIER ON THIS EVENING.
SMILE
OH!
OK. GOOD NIGHT.
スタ スタ
WALK AWAY
GOOD NIGHT...
DR. WATSON.
WHAT ARE YOU SO HAPPY ABOUT?
MORIARTY.
WHAT'S MORI-ARTY?
I'VE ABSOLUTELY NO IDEA.

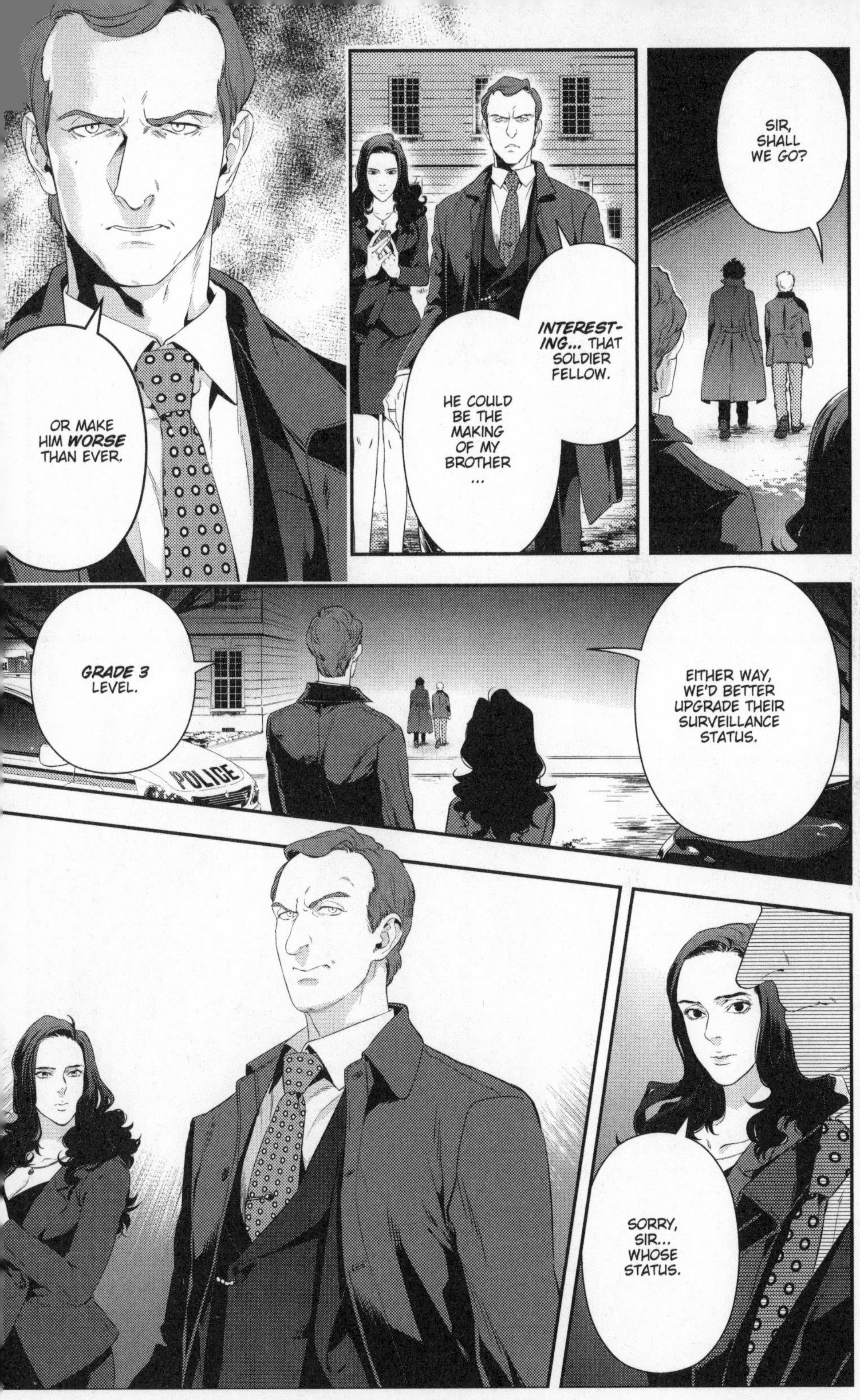
SIR, SHALL WE GO?
INTERESTING... THAT SOLDIER FELLOW.
HE COULD BE THE MAKING OF MY BROTHER ...
OR MAKE HIM WORSE THAN EVER.
EITHER WAY, WE'D BETTER UPGRADE THEIR SURVEILLANCE STATUS.
GRADE 3 LEVEL.
POLICE
SORRY, SIR... WHOSE STATUS.

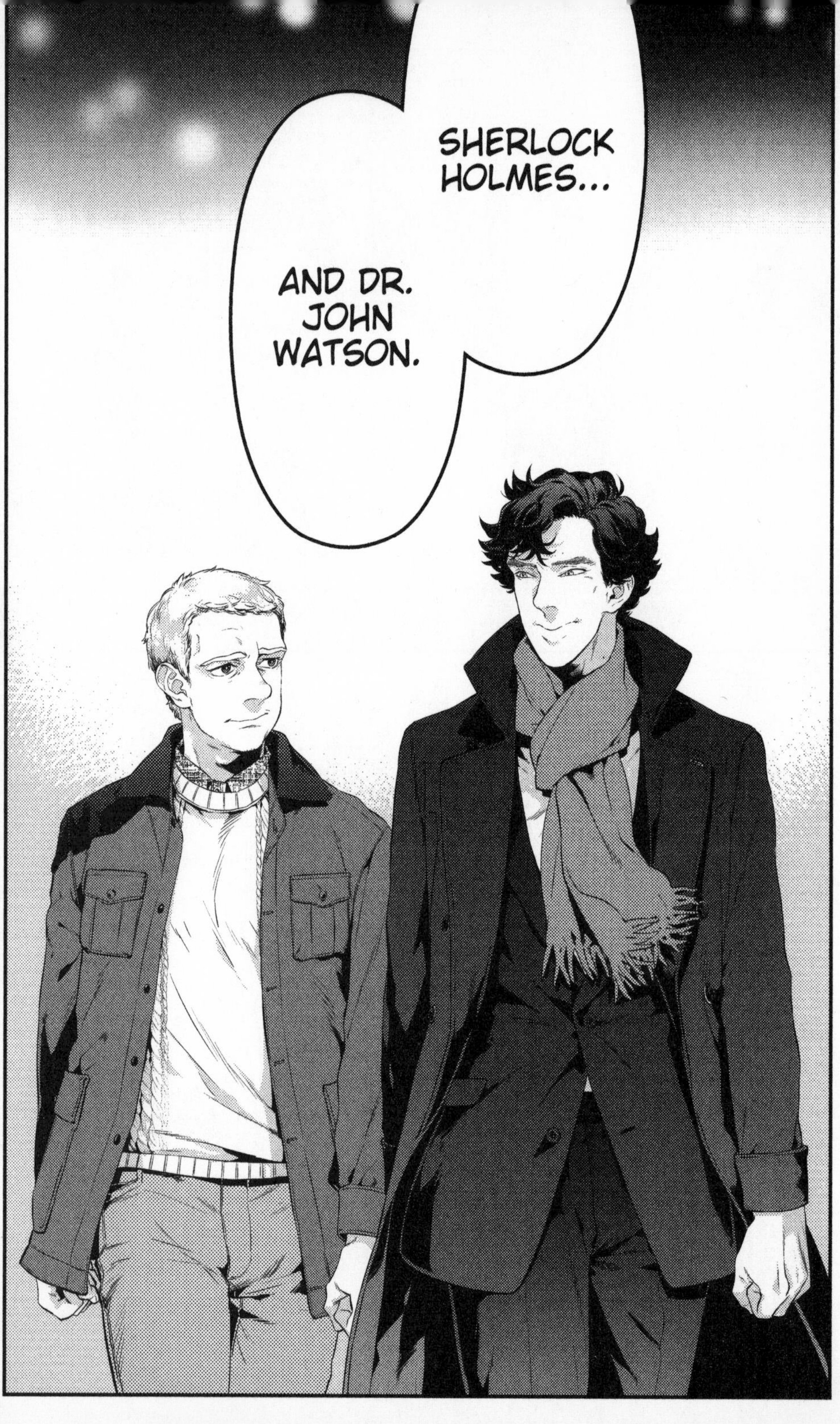
SHERLOCK HOLMES...
AND DR. JOHN WATSON.

SHERLOCK SKETCHES

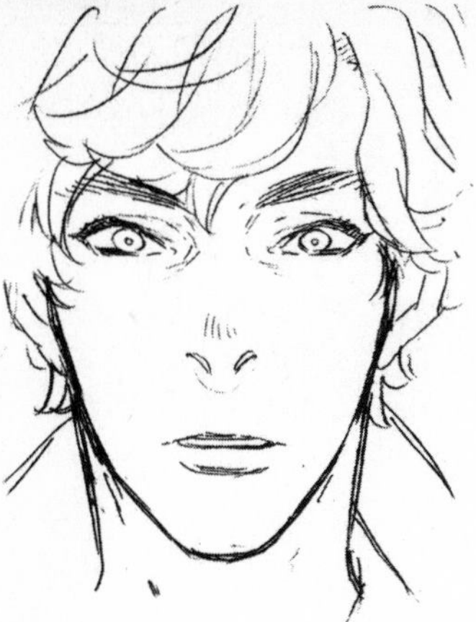

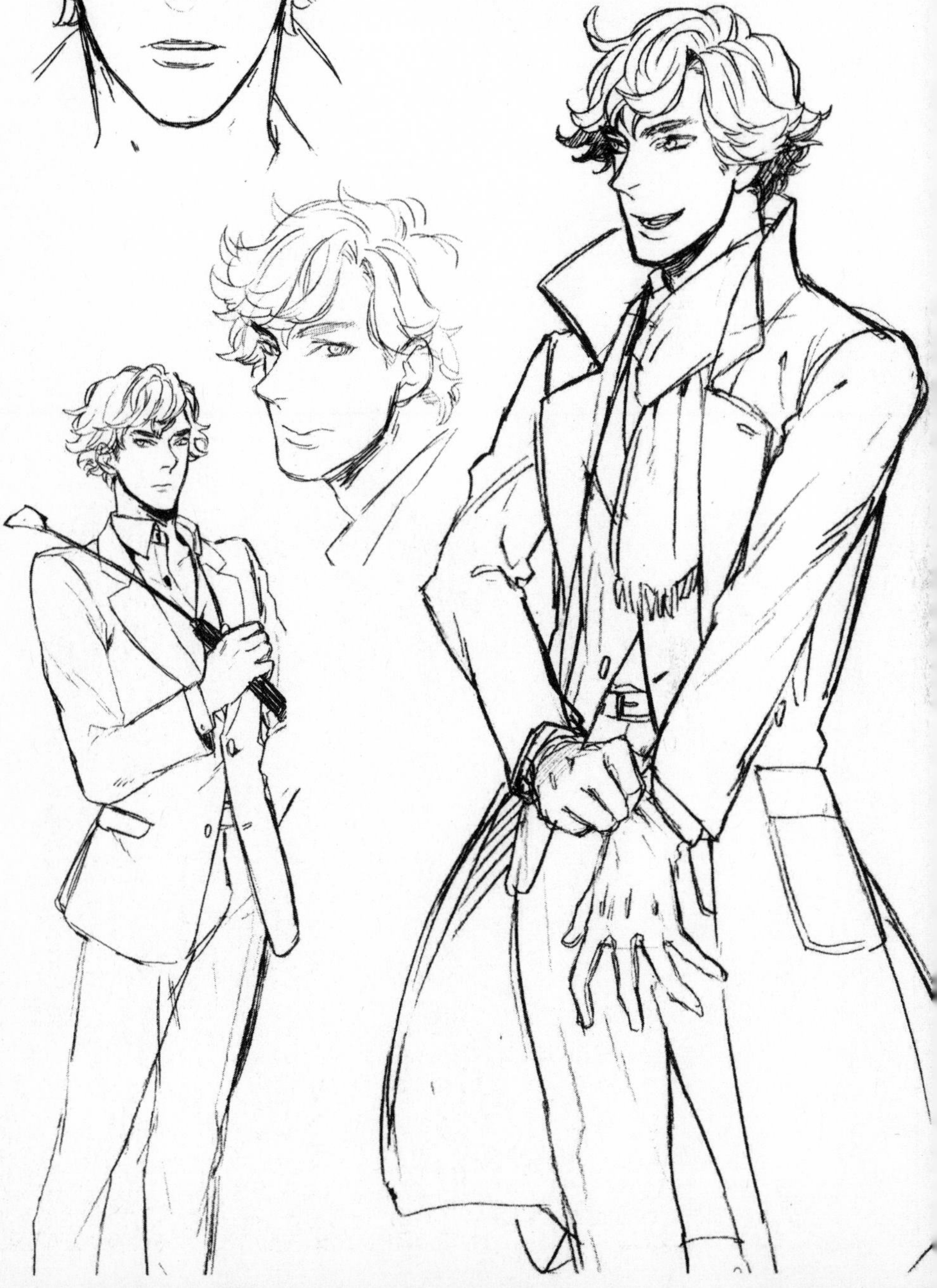

ER GALLERY

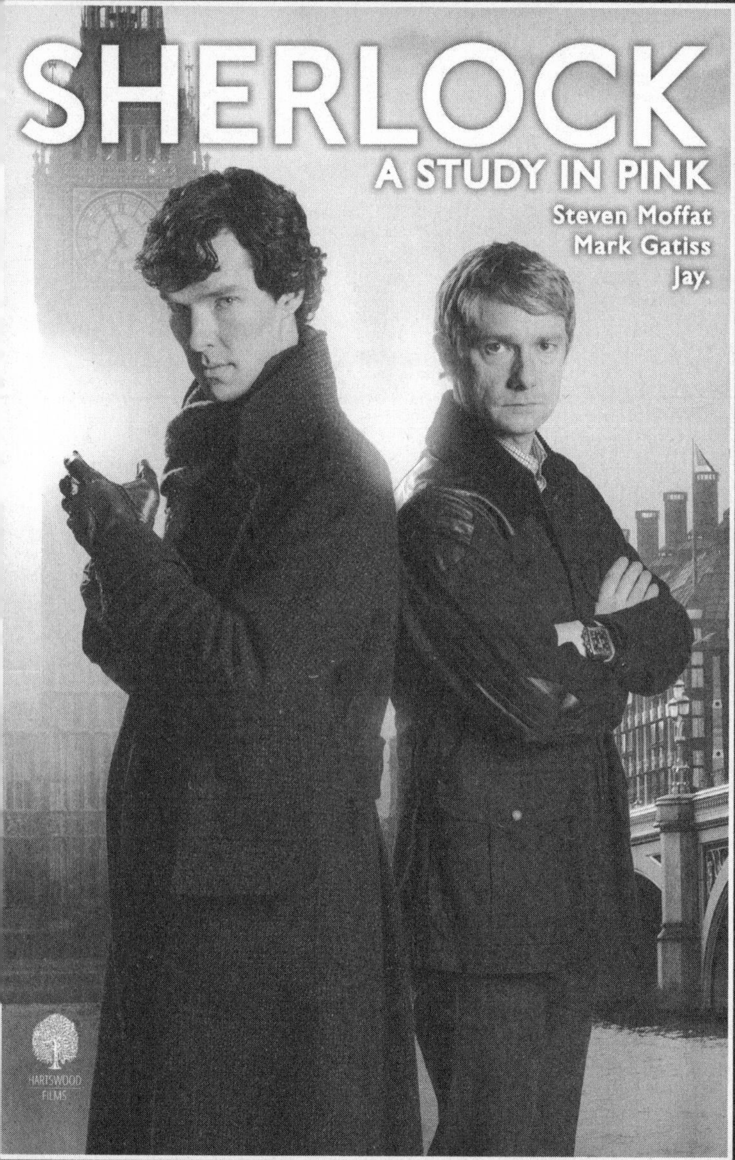
SHERLOCK
A STUDY IN PINK
Steven Moffat
Mark Gatiss
Jay.
HARTSWOOD FILMS

#1 COVER B
PHOTO

SHERLOCK A STUDY IN PINK

VARIANT CO

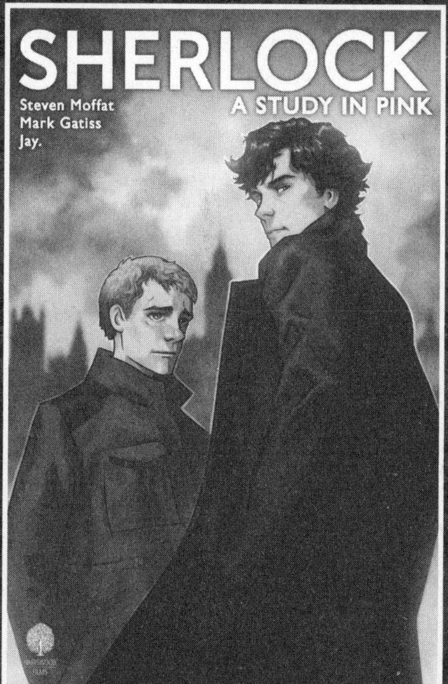
SHERLOCK
Steven Moffat
Mark Gatiss
Jay.
A STUDY IN PINK

#1 COVER C
BY ALEX RONALD

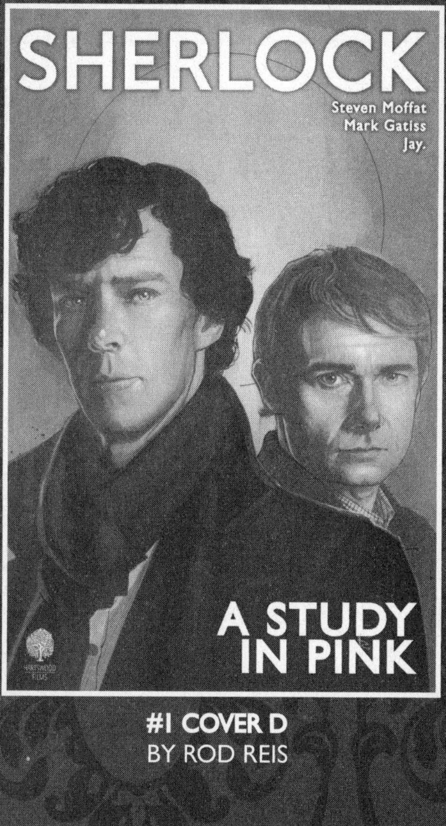
SHERLOCK
Steven Moffat
Mark Gatiss
Jay.
A STUDY IN PINK

#1 COVER D
BY ROD REIS

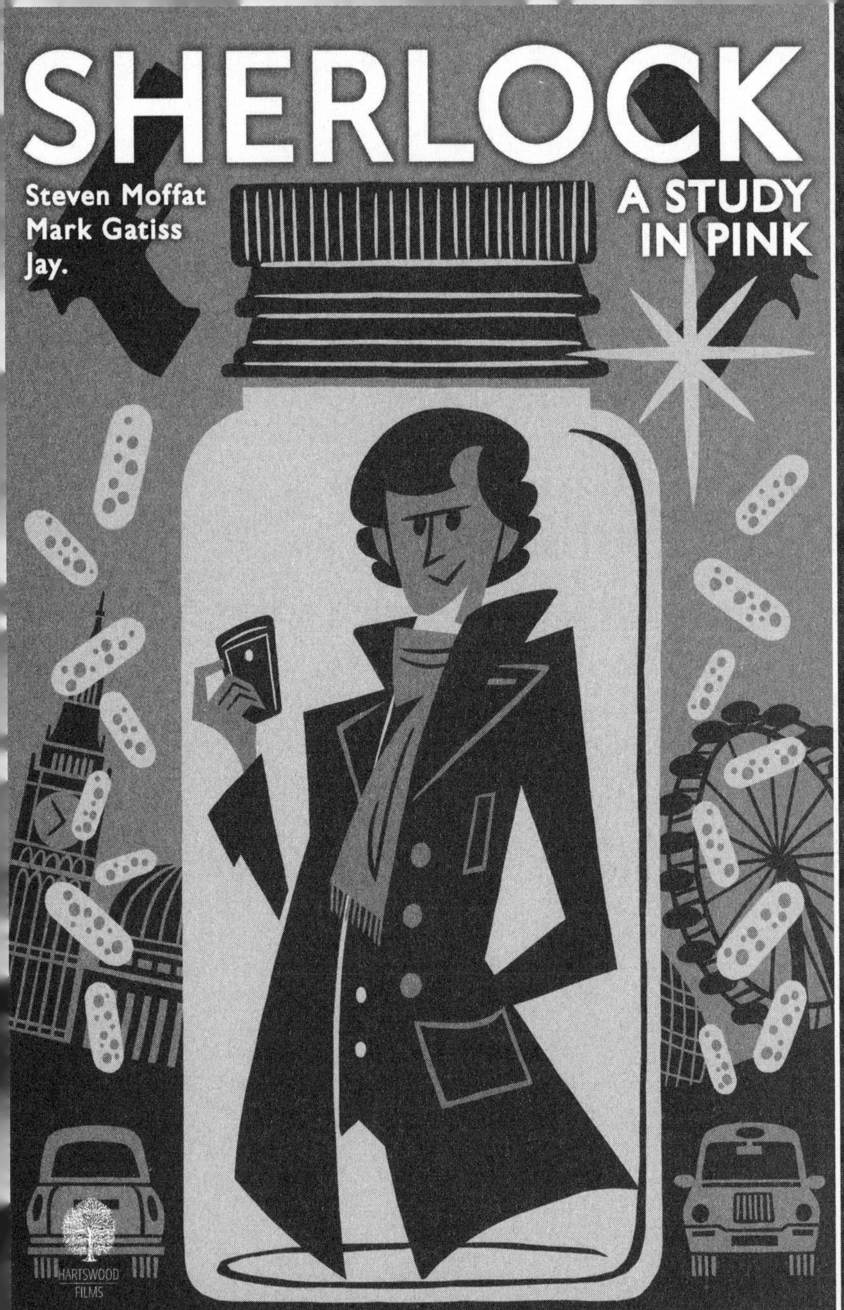
SHERLOCK
Steven Moffat
Mark Gatiss
Jay.
A STUDY
IN PINK
HARTSWOOD
FILMS

SHERLOCK
Steven Moffat
Mark Gatiss
Jay.
A STUDY
IN PINK
GEEKFUEL

#1 EXCLUSIVE GEEKFUEL COVER
BY SIMON MYERS

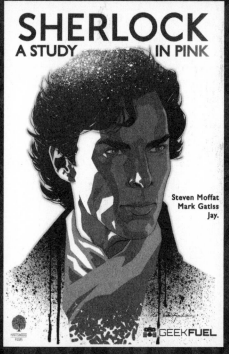

SHERLOCK
A STUDY
IN PINK
Steven Moffat
Mark Gatiss
Jay.
GEEKFUEL

#1 EXCLUSIVE GEEKFUEL COVER
BY ELENA CASAGRANDE

$4.99
JULY 2016
No. 1

SHERLOCK
A STUDY IN PINK

Inspired by John Tyler Christopher

Jay

Steven Moffat
Mark Gatiss
Jay.

FORBIDDEN
PLANET.COM

JETPACK
COMICS
EXCLUSIVE

#1 COVER FORBIDDEN PLANET
BY BLAIR SHEDD WITH JAY.

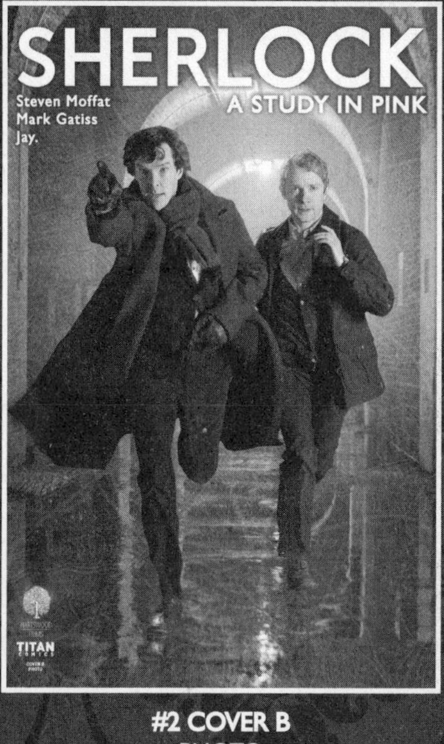
SHERLOCK
Steven Moffat
Mark Gatiss
Jay.
A STUDY IN PINK
TITAN

#2 COVER B
PHOTO

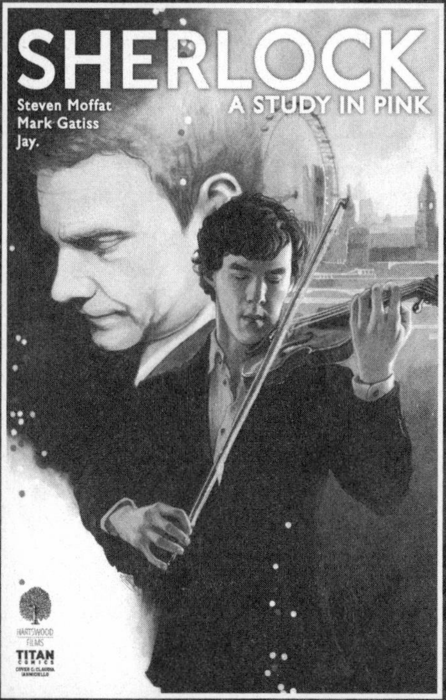
SHERLOCK
Steven Moffat
Mark Gatiss
Jay.
A STUDY IN PINK
TITAN

#2 COVER C
BY CLAUDIA IANNICIELLO

SHERLOCK
A STUDY IN PINK

Steven Moffat
Mark Gatiss
Jay.

HARTSWOOD
FILMS

TITAN
COMICS
COVER D
QUESTION NO. 6

#2 COVER D
BY QUESTION NO 6

SHERLOCK
A STUDY IN PINK

Steven Moffat
Mark Gatiss
Jay.

HARTSWOOD FILMS

TITAN COMICS
EXCLUSIVE COVER
CLAUDIA CARANFA

#2 SAN DIEGO COMICCON EXCLUSIVE COVER
BY CLAUDIA CARANFA

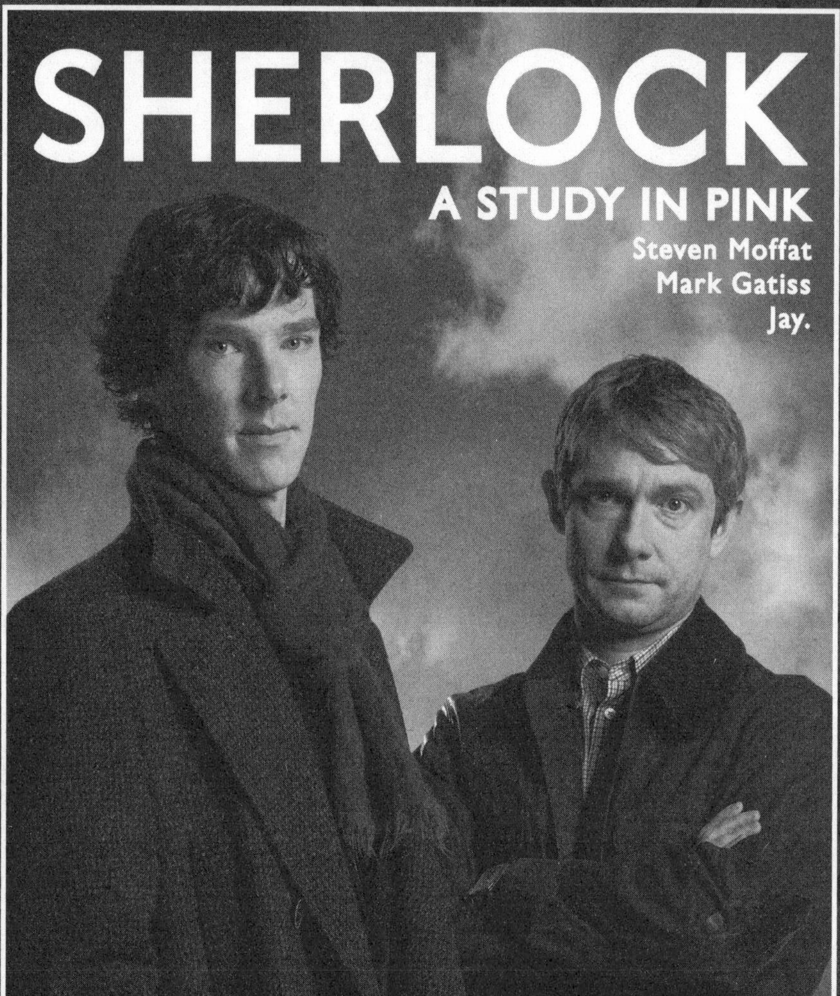
SHERLOCK
A STUDY IN PINK
Steven Moffat
Mark Gatiss
Jay.
HARTSWOOD FILMS
TITAN COMICS
COVER B PHOTO

#3 COVER B
PHOTO

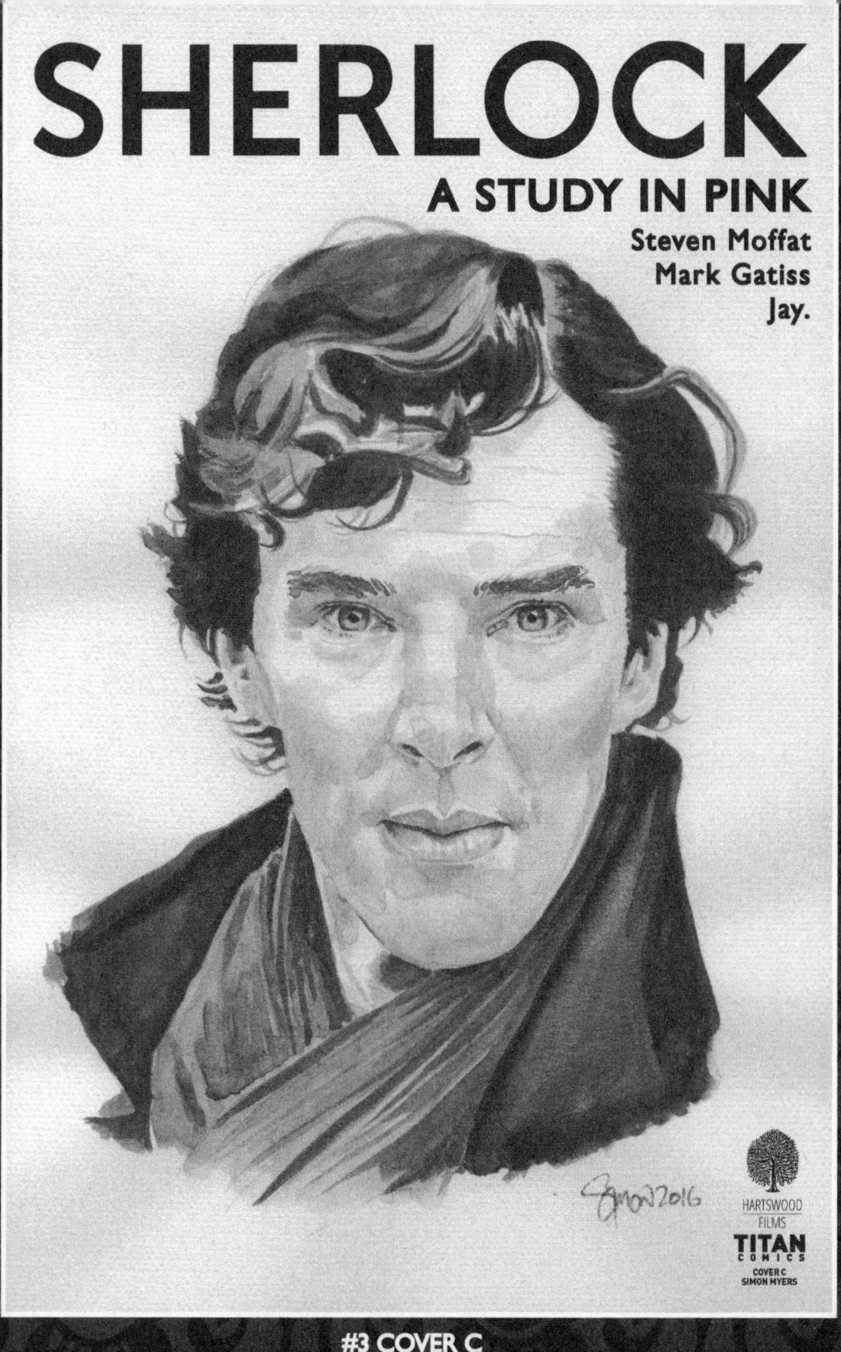
SHERLOCK
A STUDY IN PINK
Steven Moffat
Mark Gatiss
Jay.
HARTSWOOD FILMS
TITAN COMICS
COVER C
SIMON MYERS

#3 COVER C
BY SIMON MYERS

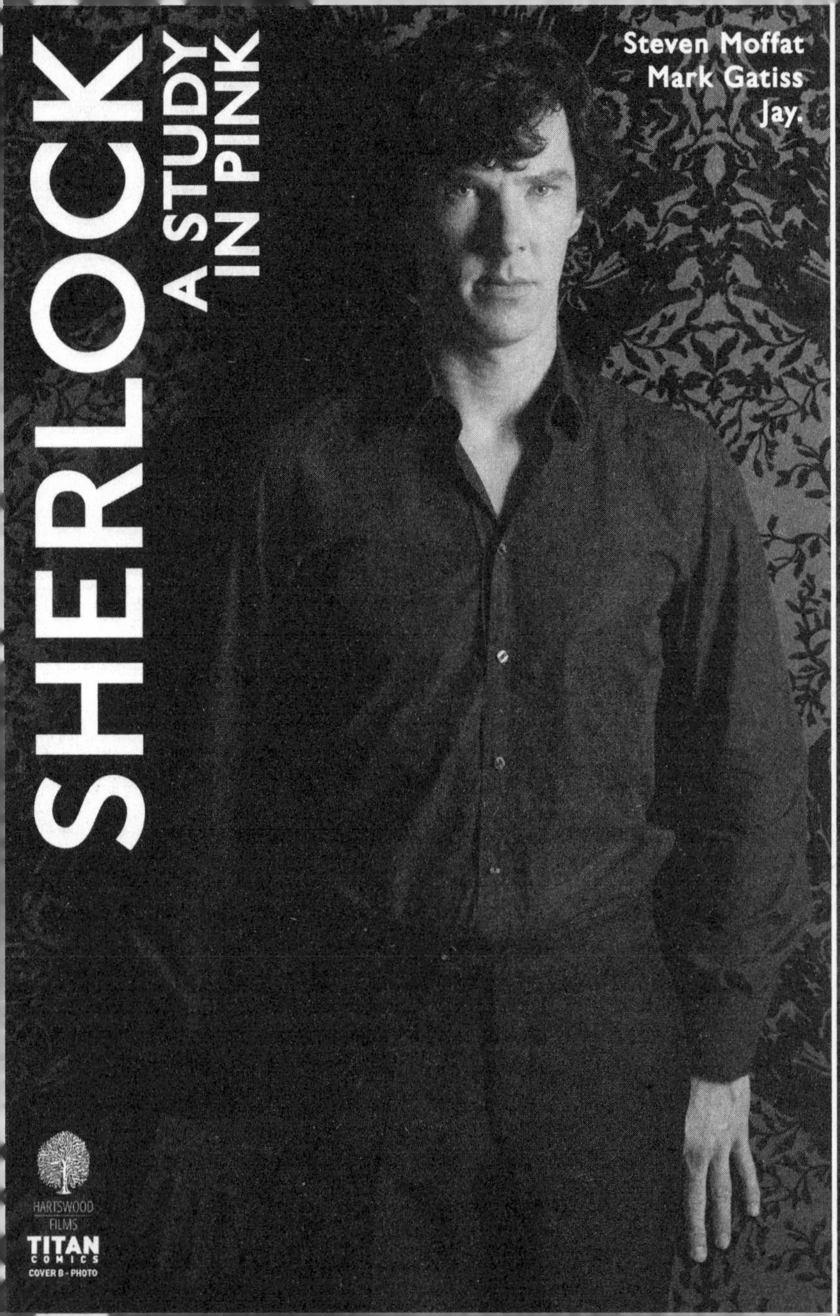
SHERLOCK
A STUDY IN PINK
Steven Moffat
Mark Gatiss
Jay.
HARTSWOOD FILMS
TITAN COMICS
COVER B - PHOTO

SHERLOCK
A STUDY IN PINK

Steven Moffat
Mark Gatiss
Jay.

HARTSWOOD
FILMS

TITAN
COMICS

COVER C
SIMON MYERS

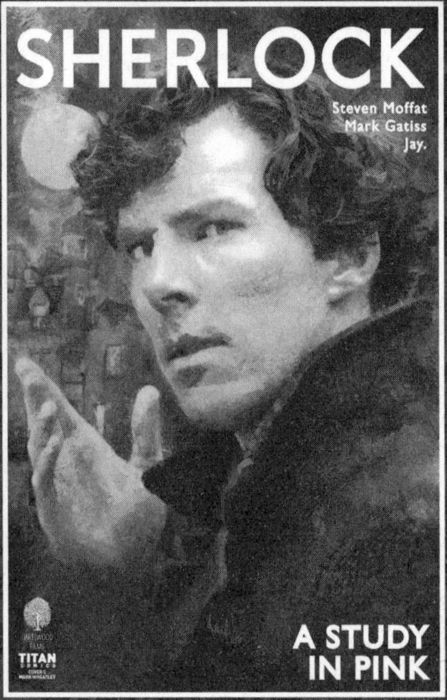
SHERLOCK
Steven Moffat
Mark Gatiss
Jay.
A STUDY IN PINK
TITAN

#5 COVER C
BY MARK WHEATLEY

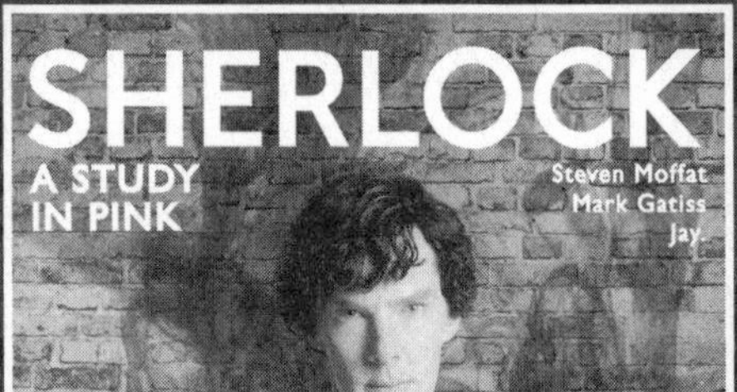
SHERLOCK
A STUDY IN PINK
Steven Moffat
Mark Gatiss
Jay.
TITAN

#5 COVER B
PHOTO

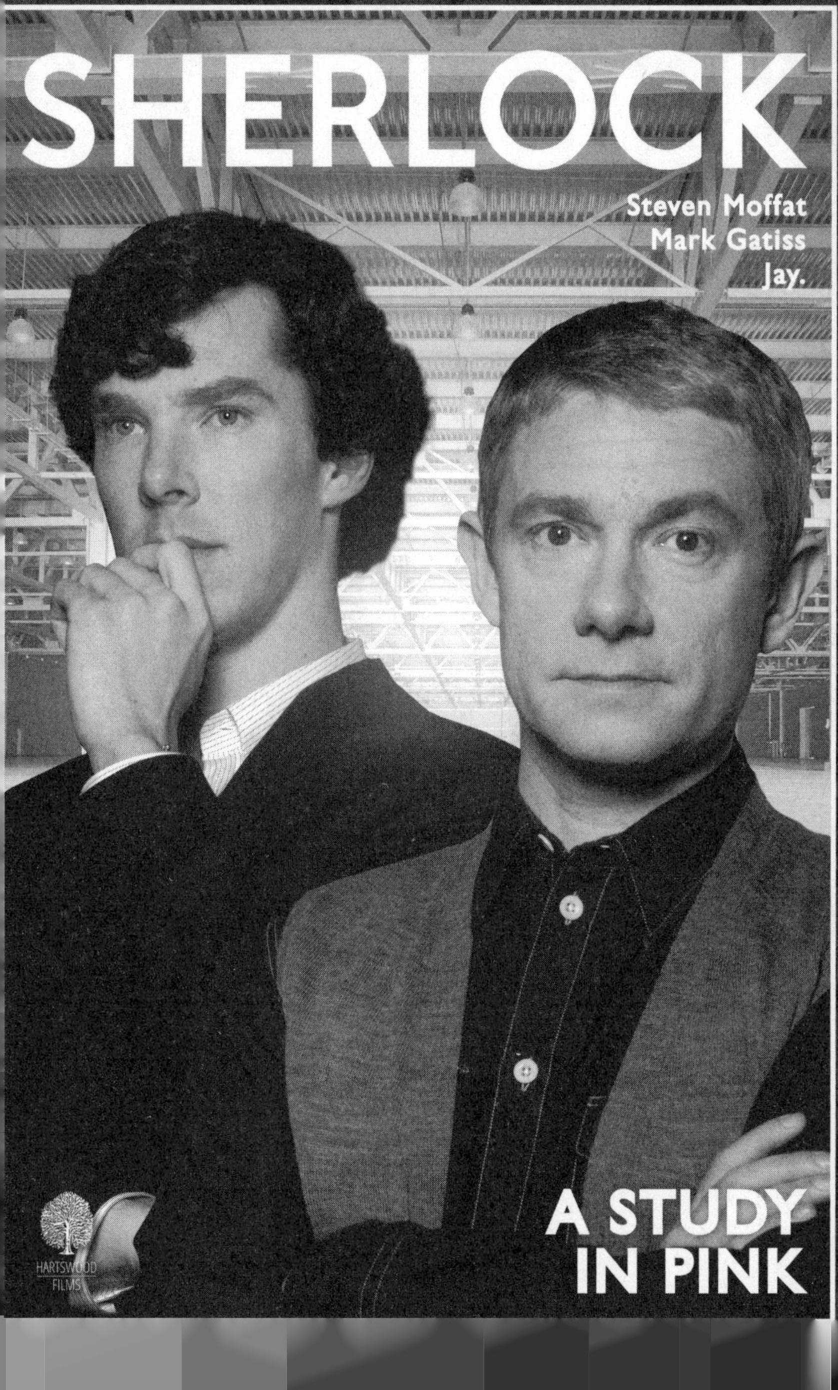
SHERLOCK
Steven Moffat
Mark Gatiss
Jay.
A STUDY
IN PINK
HARTSWOOD
FILMS

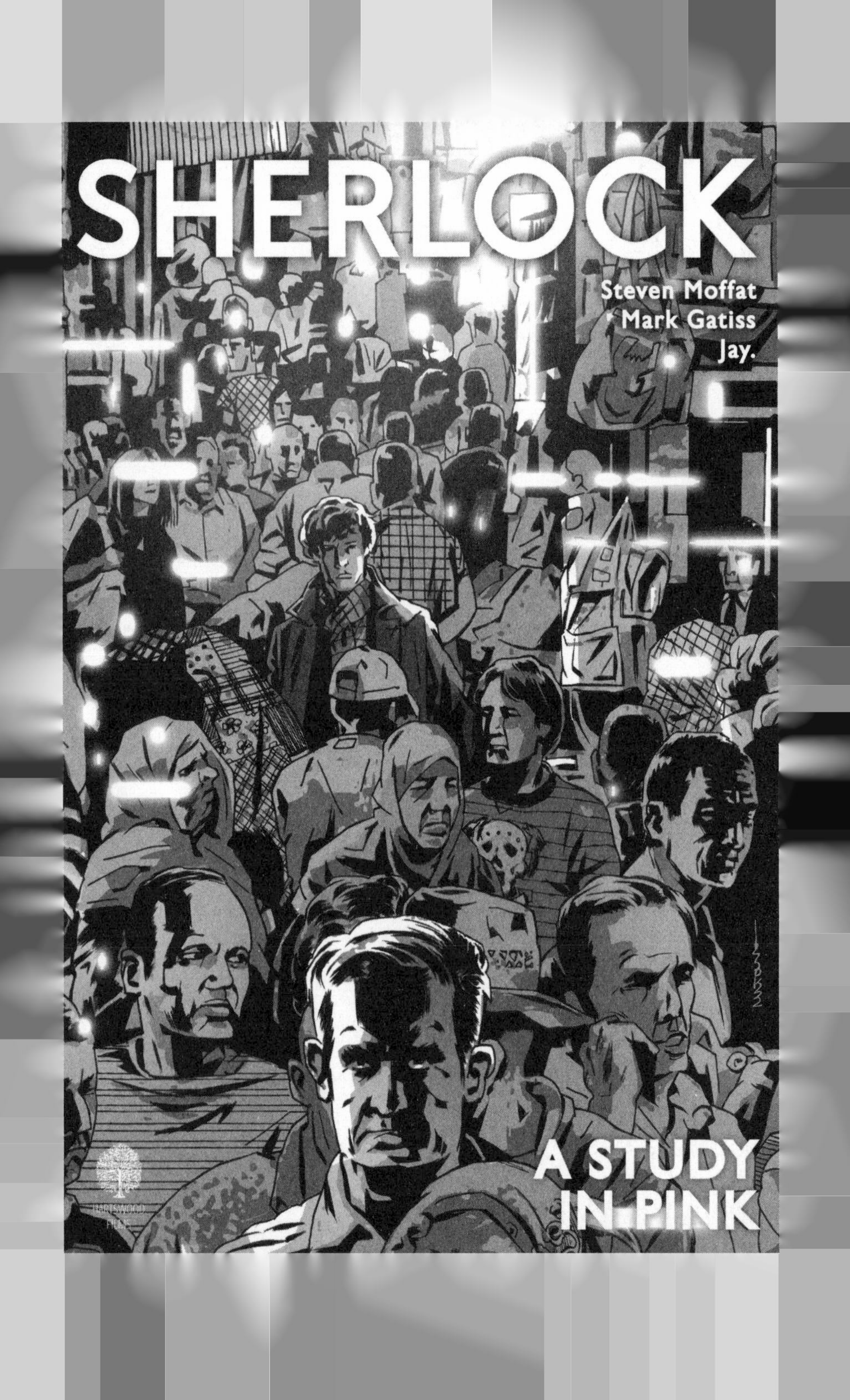
SHERLOCK
Steven Moffat
Mark Gatiss
Jay.
A STUDY IN PINK

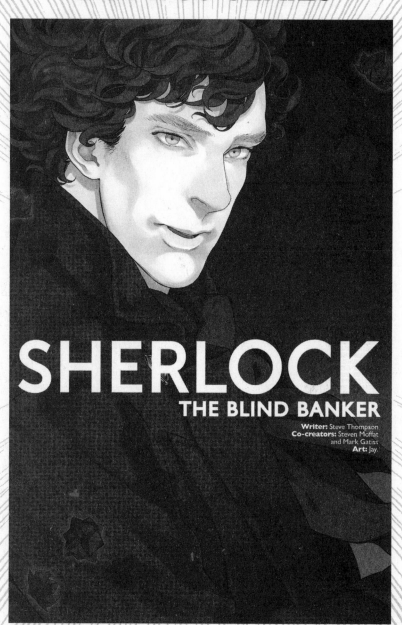

STOP!

This manga is presented in its original right-to-left reading format. This is the back page!

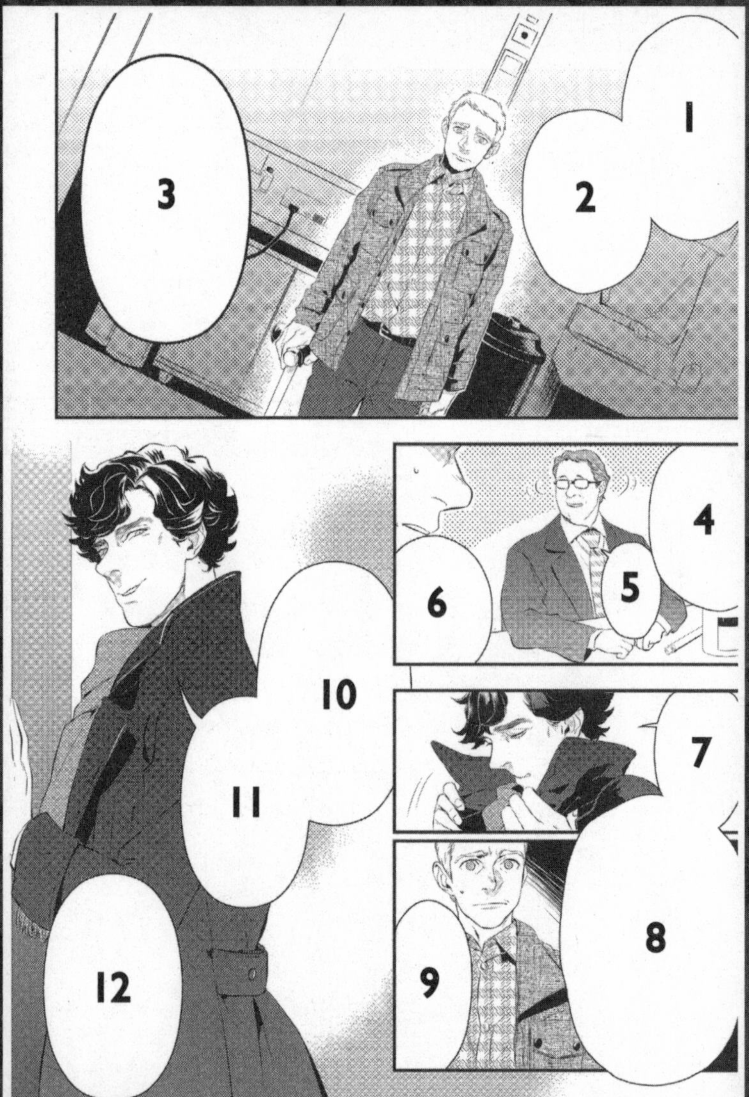
1
2
3
4
5
6
7
8
9
10
11
12

Pages, panels, and speech balloons read from top right to bottom left, as shown above. Sound effects are translated in the gutters between the panels.